Gifts of Clothing in Late Antique Literature

Both clothing and gifts in the ancient world have separately been the subject of much scholarly discussion because they were an integral part of Greek and Roman society and identity, creating and reinforcing the relationships which kept a community together, as well as delineating status and even symbolising society as a whole. They have, however, rarely been studied together despite the prevalence of clothing gifts in many ancient texts. This book addresses a gap in scholarship by focusing on gifts of elite male clothing in late antique literature in order to show that, when they appeared in texts, these items were not only functioning in an historical or 'real-life' sphere but also as a literary space within which authors could discuss ideas of social relationships and authority. This book suggests that authors used items which usually formed part of the costume of authority of the period – the *trabea* of the consul, the *chlamys* of the imperial court and the emperor, and the *pallium* of the Christian bishops – to 'over-write' wearers and donors as confident figures of 'official' authority when this may have been open to doubt.

N.K. Rollason studied at the University of Nottingham for her BA (Hons) in Classical Civilisation and MA in Ancient History. After a period of working in the public sector she completed her PhD in Classics at the University of Nottingham in 2013. Both during and after her doctoral studies she worked as a Teaching Affiliate at the university, in addition to convening a course in Medieval Latin for MA and undergraduate history students at Nottingham Trent University. She is currently an Honorary Research Fellow and a Teaching Associate in Classical Studies at the University of Nottingham.

Gifts of Clothing in Late Antique Literature

N.K. Rollason

LONDON AND NEW YORK

First published 2016
by Routledge
2 Park Square, Milton Park, Abingdon, Oxon OX14 4RN

and by Routledge
711 Third Avenue, New York, NY 10017

Routledge is an imprint of the Taylor & Francis Group, an informa business

© 2016 N.K. Rollason

The right of N.K. Rollason to be identified as author of this work has been asserted by her in accordance with sections 77 and 78 of the Copyright, Designs and Patents Act 1988.

All rights reserved. No part of this book may be reprinted or reproduced or utilised in any form or by any electronic, mechanical, or other means, now known or hereafter invented, including photocopying and recording, or in any information storage or retrieval system, without permission in writing from the publishers.

Trademark notice: Product or corporate names may be trademarks or registered trademarks, and are used only for identification and explanation without intent to infringe.

British Library Cataloguing in Publication Data
A catalogue record for this book is available from the British Library

Library of Congress Cataloging-in-Publication Data
Names: Rollason, N.K.
Title: Gifts of clothing in late antique literature / by N.K. Rollason.
Description: 2016. | Includes bibliographical references and index.
Identifiers: LCCN 2015038143 | ISBN 9781472435736 (hardcover : alkaline paper) | ISBN 9781315584713 (ebook)
Subjects: LCSH: Greece–Social life and customs–Sources. | Rome–Social life and customs–Sources. | Gifts–History–To 1500. | Men's clothing–History–To 1500. | Gifts in literature. | Clothing and dress in literature. | Authority in literature. | Social structure in literature. | Greek literature–History and criticism. | Latin literature–History and criticism.
Classification: LCC DE71 .R595 2016 | DDC 306.4–dc23
LC record available at http://lccn.loc.gov/2015038143

ISBN: 9781472435736 (hbk)
ISBN: 9781315584713 (ebk)

Typeset in Bembo and Times New Roman
by Apex CoVantage, LLC

Contents

List of figures vi
Acknowledgements vii
List of abbreviations viii

Introduction 1

1 Threads of history: Clothing gifts in Greek and Roman society before Late Antiquity 22

2 Weaving a tranquil work of peace? Clothing gifts in late antique diplomacy 55

3 Portable portraits: Consular *trabeae* and figural decorations in Late Antiquity 89

4 Holy habits: Clothing gifts in late antique Christian contexts 129

5 Drawing the threads together: Conclusions 170

Bibliography 179
Index 199

Figures

3.1 The Halberstadt diptych of Flavius Constantius (consul 417) (left panel). Halberstadt, Domschatz, inv. 45 (photograph: Juraj Lipták). 95
3.2 The diptych of Basilius (consul 541) (left panel). Florence, Museo Nazionale del Bargello, inv. 8. 96
4.1 Detail of late antique wall hanging of Elijah and Elisha (fourth century), Egypt; Abegg-Stiftung, CH-3132 Riggisberg, inv. no. 2439 © Abegg-Stiftung, CH-3132 Riggisberg, 2003 (photograph: Christoph von Viràg). 147

Acknowledgements

I would like to take this opportunity to thank Professor Doug Lee and Dr Mark Bradley, who have been supportive, always encouraging, and exceptionally generous with their knowledge, kindness, and time. I would also like to thank Professor Mary Beard for setting me on the right path, in addition to Dr Mary Harlow, Dr Carl Buckland and the anonymous readers for their insightful and helpful comments and corrections. Finally, my thanks also go to my family and friends for their loving support over the last few years.

Abbreviations

Abbreviations of classical authors follow those used in the *OCD*³, abbreviations of later authors not included in the *OCD*³ follow those used in *PLRE*, and abbreviations of journal titles follow those used in *L'Année Philologique*. Note also the following:

AnTard   *Antiquité tardive*
DarSag   Daremberg, C. and E. Saglio (eds) (1873–1919) *Dictionnaire des antiquités grecques et romaines d'après les textes et les monuments* (Paris)
Historia   *Historia: Zeitschrift für Alte Geschichte*
OCD³   Hornblower, S. and A.J.S. Spawforth (eds) (1996) *The Oxford Classical Dictionary* 3rd edition (Oxford)
PLRE   Jones, A.H.M., J.R. Martindale and J. Morris (1971–1980) *The Prosopography of the Later Roman Empire* (Cambridge)
RAC   Klauser, T. (ed. Bd. 10) and Schöllgen, G. (ed. Bd. 20–) (1950–) *Reallexikon für Antike und Christentum: Sachwörterbuch zur Auseinandersetzung des Christentums mit der antiken Welt* (Stuttgart)
RE   Wissowa, G., W. Kroll, *et al* (eds) (1893–) *Paulys Real-Encyclopädie der classischen Altertumswissenschaft* (Berlin)
RM   *Römische Mitteilungen*
TLL   (1900 –) *Thesaurus Linguae Latinae* (Leipzig)

Introduction

As soon as his father Damnazes died, Tzath immediately travelled to the emperor Justin in Byzantium . . . and asked to be proclaimed king of the Lazi and to become a Christian. He was received by the emperor and baptised; having become a Christian, he married a Roman wife named Valeriana, the granddaughter of Oninus the patrician and former *curopalatēs*, and he took her back with him to his own country. He had been appointed and crowned by Justin, the Roman emperor, and had worn a Roman imperial crown and a white *chlamys* of pure silk (χλαμύδα ἄσπρον ὁλοσήρικον). Instead of the purple *tablion* it had the gold imperial *tablion* (ἔχον ἀντὶ πορφυροῦ ταβλίου χρυσοῦν βασιλικὸν ταβλίον); in its middle there was a <small> true purple portrait bust with a likeness of the emperor Justin (ἐν ᾧ ὑπῆρχεν ἐν μέσῳ στηθάριον ἀληθινόν, ἔχοντα τὸν χαρακτῆρα τοῦ αὐτοῦ βασιλέως Ἰουστίνου). He also wore a white tunic, a *paragaudes*, with a purple border, with gold imperial weavings, equally including the likeness of the emperor. (καὶ στιχάριον δὲ ἄσπρον παραγαύδιον, καὶ αὐτὸ ἔχον χρυσᾶ πλουμία βασιλικά, ὡσαύτως ἔχοντα τὸν χαρακτῆρα τοῦ αὐτοῦ βασιλέως)[1]

In 522,[2] Tzath, heir to the kingdom of the Lazi, decided to break with years of tradition and requested that he be appointed king by the Roman emperor rather than by the Persian king. The reasons given by the sixth-century chronicler Malalas are understandable, coming from a writer resident in the Christian Roman empire – Tzath was rejecting 'Persian customs' because he wished to become a Christian, and this could only be achieved through the support of the Christian Roman emperor.[3] Such a request was a major coup for the Roman empire, for the kingdom of the Lazi was an area of strategic importance for both the Persians and the Romans, lying as it did on the eastern shore of the Black Sea. This location meant it was important for the control of routes from the north into Transcaucasia and further south, while the Romans were also concerned about the potential seaborne access to Constantinople it offered to the Persians. It is unsurprising, then, that the Roman emperor Justin I received Tzath willingly, had him baptised, and further cemented these new bonds with the provision of a Roman wife of patrician status. In addition to these actions, however, he also provided Tzath with the set of clothes described above, clothes which were not only closely connected to the imperial court in their form (the *chlamys* was worn by members of the imperial bureaucracy), but also in their decoration, with Justin's own image featuring prominently. In gifting this particular type of clothing, ornamented in such a way, Justin was using Tzath's body to reinforce the clear and unmistakeable message, to Tzath's and his own subjects in the first instance, but also to his Persian rival, that the king of the Lazi was now under Roman protection. Unsurprisingly, as Malalas goes on to explain, when the Persian king Kavadh learnt of Justin's activities, he interpreted them as antagonistic and sent a message to the emperor claiming: '. . . your actions are hostile (τὰ ἐχθρῶν πράττεις)'.

This episode provides a useful entrée to the themes of this study, whose primary purpose is to investigate the significance of gifts of male clothing in a range of contexts in Late Antiquity. It will argue that clothing gifts which appear in the literature of this period were used in the negotiation of social, political, and religious positioning and the transference of authority, and Tzath's garments bring together many of these strands. Like a number of the other gifted items that will be discussed throughout the chapters, his attire is strongly associated with secular authority, although, as will be seen, religious authority could also be examined through gifted clothing. Through its decoration with Justin's image, the clothing transforms Tzath's body into a canvas for propaganda, exemplifying a recurring topic in this work; that this type of gift is almost always operating in the interests of the giver rather than those of the receiver. The decoration also ensures that the relationship between giver and recipient is clearly understood, an important aspect of the gift whose significance runs through these discussions, as it communicates to viewers the source of the wearer's authority, and thus is part of the wearer's ongoing social negotiation. The literary description of the decoration serves to reinforce this bond between giver and receiver; furthermore, because it ensures that the decoration (and its associations) is 'seen' by a wider audience. When there is no such explicit decoration to make the connections clear, however, it will become apparent that the literary representation of the clothing takes on this role instead. The willingness of authors to discuss from whom these items came ensures that the links between the giver and receiver are as strongly understood as if all the items considered in these pages were decorated with their donor's image.

Additional features of Tzath's experience highlight further themes of importance. His status as a foreign visitor gifted with clothing is reflected in other examples of clothing gifts examined and, far from being unique, it will be seen that this late antique practice can ultimately be traced back to hospitality customs in Homeric Greece, which saw clothing a stranger as a vital part of a host's welcome. Furthermore, the changing of Tzath's dress is particularly apt in the context of his marriage and adoption of Christianity, as this was a common metaphor employed by Christian authors and their protagonists to signal the acceptance of a new way of life and the 'putting on' of Christianity. Just like secular garment gifts, in a Christian context this also signified a willingness to participate in and maintain the authority received from the donor of the clothing, and so Tzath's wardrobe change implies that it will not only be a Roman wife, but also an imperial religion that returns with him. Tzath's clothing, as a gift, is moreover imbued with the concepts surrounding gifting such as obligation, protection, and submission. Thus, as with all the sartorial gifts examined in these chapters, Tzath is not only receiving and broadcasting the messages conveyed through dress, he is also enveloped in the associations of gift-giving.

It will be proposed, therefore, that gifts of clothing are never simple. The multi-layered meanings that come from both dress and gifts, and the personal nature of such items, means that they were used by ancient authors in all periods of the Greek and Roman world as important devices through which to discuss social relationships and authority, and the tensions surrounding them. As this implies, the literary existence of clothing gifts in Late Antiquity will be more of a concern here than their historical reality. This in turn accounts for the primary focus of this study on the three garments that appear in late antique texts as gifts more than any other clothing items (the *trabea*, the *chlamys*, and the *pallium*); all are outer pieces of clothing, highly visible, and strongly associated with authority.

I. 1 Fashioning ancient dress

In order to contextualise this work and its central argument that clothing gifts are complex both historically and as narrative devices, a brief discussion of the current scholarship on clothing and gift-giving is included here. It will become apparent that while considerable work has been done separately on the individual topics of gift-giving and clothing in the ancient world, this has focused predominantly on the earlier Roman and Greek periods, with much less attention paid to Late Antiquity or to gift-giving and clothing in combination. An investigation of clothing gifts in late antique literature, therefore, can provide valuable new insights not only for the study of both clothing and gifts, but also for the wider cultural landscape of Late Antiquity.

Although dress research has a long history in classical scholarship, until recently the focus has tended to be on what the garments looked like, to help the modern student visualise the people they study, often including photographs of reconstructed items being worn by models.[4] Such investigations are important, not least because they can provide other dress scholars with the foundations on which to build their own conclusions, while the wearing of reconstructed clothing can reveal problems the original dressers may have encountered, but which are not always obvious from textual or material evidence.[5] The body as shaper and displayer of clothing certainly has a vital place within dress studies, and for the historian of Roman attire who has to rely on written evidence, static art, or archaeological finds to get a sense of the garment they are studying, the body is too often left out of the clothing. Although literature and art can demonstrate how, why, and when certain clothes are worn (and are thus arguably often more useful than looking at the raw garment itself), they do little to communicate the essence of the clothing as a living, human body could.[6] The impact of the play of light on certain fabrics, combined with the movement of

4   Introduction

the wearer, the restriction on those movements that the clothes themselves may have encouraged, the smell of the dyes mingled with the smell of bodies, and the noise and feeling of the fabric when it encountered the body of the wearer are all sensations completely lost to the modern scholar of antiquity, who can experience clothing only through the prism of someone else's words or vision.[7] This is unfortunate for they have an important part to play in 'reading' dress, particularly when it is precisely those qualities, which can make certain gifts of clothing, especially in a Christian context, particularly significant.

Indeed even when a garment survives, such experiences remain elusive, for while the feel of the fabric might be recaptured, often the colours have faded, and the fragility of the material does not allow the clothing to be worn and experienced. When displayed in a museum or collection the clothing becomes even more distant from its relationship to the body, for '[o]nce clothes have become "detached" from their wearers and placed in safe keeping in collections they take on quite different semiotic characteristics . . . . [T]he whole range of human experience attached to the wearing of clothes is inevitably lost on the static dummy placed behind glass'.[8] It becomes easy to treat ancient clothing as sterile pieces of art, rather than objects that were seen and understood every day, and studies that include dye experiments or attempts to wear the reconstructed clothing have an important part to play in recapturing the sensory experience of Roman dress.

Attempts to reconstruct clothing from any period in Roman history are, however, fraught with problems. Although a substantial amount of archaeological textile evidence has survived from many parts of the empire,[9] much of it cannot be securely classified as clothing, and of those pieces that can be definitively labelled as such, only some can be positively identified with the clothing terminology given in literary descriptions. Indeed these descriptions themselves are not always helpful, few give a clear explanation of what the item discussed may have looked like or how it was worn, and any scholar of dress must factor in problems such as localisation, which could lead to the same garment being called by different names.[10]

Although written about women's fashion magazines of the 1950s and 60s, Roland Barthes' *Système de la mode* (written between 1957 and 1963) has implications in particular for these problems because the 'real' Roman garment does not always correspond to the 'written' garment labelled by authors (modern or ancient). His theory that the dress item depicted in a magazine and described in print is actually three different garments – the 'real' or 'technological' garment, the image-, represented-, or 'iconic'-garment, and the written- or 'verbal'-garment – [11] is of particular value for understanding the issues historians of Roman dress face. His observation that, once described, the image-garment becomes the written-garment, has consequences for the study of Roman dress because, as noted above, often the 'real' garment no longer survives or is easily identifiable with written clothing terminology. If it is extant, the piece is often only available to be viewed through photographs of museum pieces, or through Roman art, each of which has their own agenda and 'language',[12] and therefore can never be the 'real' garment. They thus behave in a similar way to the clothes in Barthes' fashion magazines:

> I open a fashion magazine; I see that two different garments are being dealt with. The first is the one presented to me as photographed or drawn – it is image-clothing. The second is the same garment, but described, transformed into language; this dress photographed on the right becomes on the left: *a leather belt, with rose stuck in it, worn above the waist, on a soft shetland dress*; this is a written garment.[13]

As a consequence the 'real' garment that may have once been worn by a Roman becomes over-written, in the same way that the image-garment is in the above. This idea that a written-garment can obscure the original 'real' garment and replace it is an especially valuable concept for the chapter discussions that follow. Barthes' interpretation of the authority of the written word – that it limits freedom, but also a kind of uncertainty – [14] is a particularly important idea for this study as a whole, which proposes that literary clothing gifts allow authors to over-write wearers, donors, and circumstances in order to convey authoritative meanings about uncertain relationships with official power.

Within the context of modern clothing scholarship, however, these problems are to be continually considered by the scholar of Roman dress who must apply terminology only cautiously.[15] Attempts to match a piece of clothing worn by a statue or in a portrait with a clothing term found within ancient literature are not always successful, yet these assertions can then become the defining description of the garment.[16] In this volume, therefore, images, detailed discussions of clothing terminology and ancient clothing artefacts have mostly been avoided except where necessary for the sake of clarity, primarily because they often raise more questions than they answer. Instead the names of the garments discussed have generally been left untranslated, unless for variation, to avoid over-writing these items with the connotations which surround the English terms.[17]

The influence of theories of modern fashion from authors such as Barthes, who saw clothing as a part of the language of signs or semiotics or as a language within society in its own right,[18] has encouraged a change in focus in scholarship on ancient clothing. Moving away from attempts at definition and reconstruction, many recent studies into ancient dress examine instead the ways in which clothing operated and was represented in society and literature, and this work is situated within this line of scholarship.

While initially it may seem that modern fashion theory would have little relevance to Roman dress study, 'fashion', in its guise as a communicative system of dress and 'profoundly cultural phenomenon', can be applied cautiously to the study of Roman clothing.[19] This is because some of the areas of 'fashion' that form the basis of many modern studies also have relevance to Roman dress. These areas include fashion as communication and signifier to show status, gender, sexuality, wealth, political affiliation, and ethnicity; fashion as spectacle and display; fashion as an example of consumption and trade relations within society; and fashion as a 'civilising' force within global and domestic society.[20] Therefore, coupled with the knowledge that, no doubt due to high levels of illiteracy, the Romans were adept at understanding and using visual signs and markers,[21] the influence of sociological research into modern fashion has led to a reassessment of what the study of Roman clothing can achieve.

Investigations into what clothing as a 'cultural symbol' can say about an ancient society are recognising that what people wore mattered in antiquity.[22] Drawing on modern fashion theory, they have shown that clothing was closely associated with identity: by the clothes they dressed in, a person was believed to be demonstrating who they were, and where they fitted into society. The briefest glance at their dress could reveal their age group, ethnic background, gender, wealth, social status, religious affiliation, position in the life cycle, and so on,[23] codifying the individual's place and thus how the viewer should react to and interact with them. It separated those who belonged to the community from those who did not, identifying and elevating the former in the process.[24] Garments can conceal the true nature of both the physical and social body, alienating the body from the self by dressing to a 'socially controlled image'.[25] Although ancient authors like Martial, Juvenal, and later Jerome imply that the discerning viewer can always spot a fake, it is clear that there were those in the Roman period who attempted to commit social (and religious) fraud through their clothing. That this was a worrying scenario is indicated both by the scorn poured on such attempts and by the concentration in ancient literature from the earliest periods to Late Antiquity on departure from dress norms. When ancient writers talk about dress it is often because the wearer is exhibiting deviant behaviour and this behaviour is expressed and identified by their inappropriate clothing;[26] wrongdoers are almost always bad dressers. Thus, dress not only creates social distinctions, but it also maintains them. The norms prescribed by the moralising rhetoric of that society's writers are reinforced and gain assistance from the wearers themselves who dress as they are supposed to.[27] The clothed body was a social body that was expected to wear its inner character on its sleeve, but it could also be a problematic body, for clothing seemed to reveal all to the viewer, while actually contriving a cover up.

This was (and is) due to clothing's intimate and personal relationship to the body: it is in constant contact with it, and can take on the body's smell, essence, and character, but it is also an extension of the body, moulding its shape, changing it into something more (and sometimes something less) than itself. It can therefore subject the body to transformation.[28] However, it is also restrictive, preventing it from moving freely in gesture or gait, from going to the places it wishes, or from being socially mobile: '... the physical body when dressed reflects the "social body" or surrounding societal system ...'.[29] Dress, then, was an important part of the self-regulation, which the Romans exercised on themselves as individual and social bodies to maintain public order.[30] Peer pressure was clearly not always enough, however, as laws were also issued in an attempt to keep people appropriately dressed and in their correct places, preventing them from usurping statuses to which they were not entitled and, particularly in the Later Empire, to limit the influence of 'barbarian' culture in the main urban centres.[31]

Any research into classical dress must, therefore, continue to recognise the importance of putting the body back into clothing, and scholarship on the body in antiquity has an important part to play in ancient dress studies – particularly those publications that feature the body as a cultural symbol.[32] Recent work has shown that the body was something that could be admired, but was often feared. Particularly under the influence of Christianity, it was an object that needed to be controlled and administered,[33] and the conflicting tension between the desire to display and the need to police that display is mirrored in the act of dressing itself, which at once expresses and controls the body. This notion of 'control clothing' is an important undercurrent to the discussions in the following chapters, where gifts of clothing function for their wearers, donors, or authors as attempts to control a particular narrative body of authority.

Much of this important new research has centred on the Republic and Early Empire, where there is generally better documentation of clothing's place within society. In the late antique field, however, clothing does not often benefit from this type of concentrated scholarship, appearing mostly as part of a larger general study on either dress or the Later Empire, which often focuses on a recognition of its important function in late imperial court spectacle.[34] The exception to this is in the area of Christian literature, particularly on the decision made by elite women to turn to an ascetic lifestyle, a transformation frequently depicted and discussed in the works of hagiographers and the church fathers by a change in dress. The contrast of a woman's previous lavish garments with her new sombre attire allowed the authors (and the women themselves) to demonstrate the woman's commitment and adherence to this new lifestyle, while also signifying that they had made the decision to overcome and abandon that particularly sinful and feminine part of their nature which expensive clothing revealed. Her new garments then became a simple yet powerful visualisation of both triumph and punishment, symbolising all that was wrong with general womanhood, but all that was right with that individual female ascetic.

This conflicting dichotomy between praise and condemnation found in Christian literature of the period has fascinated modern scholars, particularly because the women *were* praised lavishly, and the study of female clothing has been the subject of a number of articles and volumes by scholars.[35] The current interest in late antique female attire and earlier male clothing has contributed to a neglect of examining later elite male dress beyond its role in court spectacle and religious transformation or in demonstrating how tastes had changed.[36] There is, therefore, a scholarly lacuna in recent work on male attire, and scope to draw on the research of the last few decades which has shown that clothing was never just a piece of fabric on a body, but a vital part of the way ancient society communicated ideas about itself and the roles individuals played.

I.2 Clothing as a literary device

When clothing appeared in ancient literature, it was not always about social identity, however. Modern scholars have shown that in Late Antiquity, for instance, dress could function as a metaphor for literary composition, much as it had in earlier periods, which reflected the 'brilliant, highly coloured fragments' decorating later elite clothing.[37] In addition, John Scheid and Jasper Svenbro (1996) have shown that in early Greek and Roman writing, weaving and its final products, textiles and clothing, were more than just analogies of the poetic process: they could also represent marriage and, of particular importance to this study, the ideal of a harmonious society. They suggest that in ancient thought, just as fabric is made by weaving together the disparate threads of the masculine warp (ὁ στήμων) and feminine weft (ἡ κρόκη)[38] to make a complete and beautiful product, so a unified society is made by the harmonious interaction of its different elements, be that man and woman, rich and poor, or citizen and non-citizen.

The interweaving of these different social threads to create a complete product furnished Greek and Roman writers with particularly suitable material for discussing the elements that made up society and the relationships that bound it together. After all, '... the Fates symbolise[d] and control[led] all human life through the processes of textile manufacture'.[39] It provided a valuable perspective from which to view and understand social organisation: '... the practice of weaving ... offers a simple model to the mind seeking ideas about the nature of social cohesion ...'.[40] The finished cloth (and, by extension, clothing), as the 'harmonious whole', can be viewed through this idea as a representation of the 'fabric' of society, made up of different and distinct components, but whose members must bind and tie themselves to each other correctly in order to maintain the overall cohesion and thus the continuation of the society in which they live.[41] This is an idea of central importance to this study as a whole, for it provides a framework within which to understand why and how gifts of clothing were employed in literary texts and engages with wider issues in Late Antiquity.

For Scheid and Svenbro this concept is almost always positive, and they do not consider that when the warp and weft combine to create the completed textile, they are of course locked into position. Thus while the social fabric is by implication a fully and harmoniously integrated textile, it is so because of a structure which is rigid and allows little room for individual repositioning, and this was certainly felt by some ancient authors to be restrictive. The early second-century Stoic philosopher Epictetus, whom Scheid and Svenbro do not discuss, is presented in Arrian's *Epicteti dissertationes* as using this metaphor to highlight how fear had suppressed individualism during Nero's principate:

> Florus was deliberating whether he should go down to Nero's spectacles and also perform in them himself... 'If I do not take a part in the tragic acting, I shall have my head struck off'. Go then and take a part, [Agrippinus

replied], but I will not. 'Why?' Because you consider yourself to be only one thread of those which are in the tunic (ὅτι σὺ σεαυτὸν ἡγῇ μίαν τινὰ εἶναι κρόκην τῶν ἐκ τοῦ χιτῶνος). Well then it was fitting for you to take care how you should be like the rest of men, just as the thread has no design to be anything superior to the other threads (ὥσπερ οὐδ' ἡ κρόκη πρὸς τὰς ἄλλας κρόκας θέλει τι ἔχειν ἐξαίρετον). But I wish to be purple (ἐγὼ δὲ πορφύρα εἶναι βούλομαι), that small part which is bright, and makes all the rest appear graceful and beautiful. Why then do you tell me to make myself like the many? And if I do, how shall I still be purple (καὶ πῶς ἔτι πορφύρα ἔσομαι;)? (Arrian, *Epicteti dissertationes*, 1.2.12–18)[42]

The qualities of competition and setting oneself apart, which had been a tenet of elite senatorial masculinity, are here (and elsewhere in the *Epicteti dissertationes*) shown to have continuing importance in the early imperial period, but are felt by Arrian's Epictetus to be increasingly dangerous to put into practice due to the power of the emperors. For Epictetus the 'tunic' is oppressive; made up of homogenous threads, it is locked into a pattern of complicity. He employs the metaphor of clothing and its adornment as a call to the senatorial elite to reassert their importance and authority in the empire, for 'what good does the purple do for the toga? Why, what else than this, that it is conspicuous in the toga as purple, and is displayed also as a fine example to all other things?'[43] For emperors, ancient authors and their audiences, people who make up a community must, just like the threads of a fabric, remain in their place, or they have the potential to threaten the integrity of the whole, although some strands could shine brighter than others. Clothing, therefore, is not only a method of ensuring social stability by displaying and enforcing status or marking out those who represent the established order like the emperor and his officials. It could also be a literary metaphor for what this control achieves: a rigid social structure, flexible only as a whole, secure but also potentially oppressive. As will be seen in many of the following discussions, however, it was exactly this rigidity of structure that made the metaphor so appealing to late antique authors discussing problematic authority; it proposed security by suggesting disparate elements could be locked into a correct and familiar position within the fabric of society.

I.3 The value of clothing in gift-giving practice

Correct interaction and interweaving was, then, one of the ways that the social cloth was kept intact; in this context, community relationships were bound together, literally and metaphorically, and in the ancient world one of the ways that these ties could be established, maintained, and reinforced was through the giving of gifts. Modern anthropological and sociological studies drawing on Marcell Mauss' seminal work *Essai sur le don* (1923–1924) have shown the importance of social reciprocity in pre-modern societies. Although subsequent sociologists, economists, and anthropologists have criticised and modified his findings (particularly with regards to whether gifts really exist at all), Mauss' ideas still provide a useful framework within which to consider such things.[44] This is because they echo thoughts on reciprocity found in the ancient literature,[45] even after the advent of Christian charity, which theoretically (if not in practice) removed the recipient's obligation to return a favour. In every period of Greek and Roman history, gifts were given by all levels of society and appear in various different forms and contexts, from money and carriages to drinking cups and roof tiles, as birthday or religious presents, as a way to help a friend, or as a payment for a service rendered. They could even create ties between people so strong that generations later a mere reminder could prevent a fight between the descendants of the original participants.[46] However, they could also be problematic items, not always given for the explicit benefit of the recipient, sometimes indistinguishable from a bribe,[47] and (as Martial and Juvenal frequently pointed out) possessing the ability to keep people in their (inferior) place. As Mauss' research showed, this was because to give a gift was to create an obligation, a debt that the recipient had to pay with an equal or superior gift in order to maintain his position within the relationship and not lose social standing.[48]

That this also occurred at all levels of Greek and Roman society has long been recognised by classical scholars, and different aspects of reciprocity have been the subject of several monographs, particularly with regard to the Homeric period and Roman patronage.[49] Although these works sometimes include research regarding clothing gifts, it is in discussions of diplomacy that these items become more prominent. However, they rarely are the sole focus; rather, the general trend is to mention them as part of a catalogue of diplomatic presents or as part of a wider survey of a historical period, mainly to demonstrate what items were available for exchange.[50] Closer to the time frame of the material addressed here, in late antique and early Byzantine studies considerations of textile gifts are given more weight, although still mostly within the confines of diplomatic studies. In this context research has focused on the role silk and silk clothing played in maintaining foreign relations during the period through trade and diplomacy.[51] Along with gold and silver (whether in the form of money or crafted items), these examinations have demonstrated that clothing ranked high in the calculus of gift-giving in the late antique and Byzantine periods, and items made from silk were often listed as a luxury item of the greatest expense.[52]

Clothing was certainly an important and expensive gift to give and the semiotics of the garment gifts that will be considered should be set within the context of clothing as an economic asset. Generally woven to shape, the manufacture of garments was labour-intensive, time consuming and costly from sheep to shoulder.[53] The price of clothing varied relative to material, provenance, and colouring, and this will be discussed in more detail at relevant points, but whether of cheaper quality or made of premium resources, it was never something one simply threw away. It was an investment, as the evidence for a number of domestic slave jobs concerned with caring for clothing, the patching in extant ancient clothing, as well as the *collegia* of *centonarii* ('patch-workers/patchwork dealers') attests.[54] Clothing was worn, and when worn out, mended – or turned into other items, such as quilts, caps or garments to be sold on the second-hand market or to the poor.[55] Its value also made it a target for thieves, a gambling stake or meant it could be taken as a guarantor of small or large amounts of money for different status customers.[56] The range in quality of both materials and technical skill displayed in tunics from archaeological sites suggests not only the prevalence of weaving workshops but also that they catered to clientele at all levels of society.[57] Whatever the wearer's means, then, clothing was a portable and highly visible space for displaying relative wealth, as the literature and material evidence from the Greek and Roman periods make clear. In Late Antiquity this could be demonstrated in the elaborately woven and highly colourful *clavi*, *orbiculi* and *tabulae* found on many of the tunics which survive from this period.[58] At the highest end, raw materials, such as certain fibres and dyes, the quantities in which such items were used, and the quality of technical skill added their contribution to this performance of expense;[59] fashioned from silk, dyed purple and interwoven with gold thread and precious gems, some garments could be a dazzling canvass of cost made up of the most expensive goods known to ancient humanity.

Yet it is rare to find evidence which provides a systematic understanding of prices, although the earlier epigraphic evidence of clothing regulations and dedications (such as the mid-fourth-century-BCE catalogues of clothing displayed in the temple treasury of Artemis Brauronia, near Athens) do help to support the indicators of worth found in the literature.[60] This is particularly useful because, when the cost of a garment is specified in texts such as Martial's *Epigrams* for example, it is often due to other authorial concerns which makes it difficult to assess whether this should be taken as reflecting accurate value. For a brief moment in 301 CE, however, things appear to become a little clearer due to the emperor Diocletian's 'Edict on Maximum Prices', which gives us a glimpse (although no more than that) of the prices that could be charged for clothing.[61] Found in over 40 locations, mostly in the eastern provinces, the Edict is of significant value to the understanding of textile production and trade in Late Antiquity because of the detail with which these goods are listed. Indeed, garments and the materials they could be made from form some of the longest sections of this text.[62] The extensive sections (26–28) dealing with linen, for example, are systematic in their treatment, listing the prices by provenance (Scythopolis, Tarsus, Byblus, Laodiceia, Alexandrian Tarsus), grade (first–third quality with levels below of 'inferior quality, but prepared in more places'(26.65)), as well as by the status of those whom it will clothe (e.g. 26.31: '[Price] of coarse linen for the use of common people or slaves').[63] It is clear from this that textile production was regulated and highly organised, unsurprising for such an important commodity in the empire.[64] It is impossible to understand whether these were prices actually charged by the *vestiarii* (clothing merchants) – as maximums, they suggest that there was variation in cost. This is supported by the imperial preface, which implies proximity to resources was an important factor, particularly as the total price charged (whatever that may have been) was to include all associated transport costs.[65] The continuing prevalence of domestic textile manufacturing also may have contributed to the perceived need to set a limit, although from this period it appears that weaving was primarily a professional industry, with clothing produced in large towns 'in a specialised manner'.[66]

What it does provide, however, is comparable data, and this suggests that even the most basic linen garments of the lowest grade would have been an expensive outlay for many of the empire's inhabitants at this time: the maximum price of the cheapest linen tunic is 500 denarii, to be compared with the maximum daily wage of 25 denarii for labourers.[67] Furthermore, certain clothing pieces or the materials they are made from are amongst the most costly items listed in the Edict – raw silk dyed purple (μεταξαβλάττα), for instance, has its maximum at 150,000 denarii (24.1a), while section 29, although incomplete, appears to price clothing based on the amount and quality of its purple borders. This suggests the continued importance that such items had as status symbols in the empire (the maximum price within this section for a linen *mafortium* – perhaps a woman's short cloak – with *clavi* containing one pound of purple is 55,000 denarii (29.44)) and indeed, as will be seen in Chapter 2's case study this continues into the sixth century. In addition, another fragmentary part (section 19) appears to be dedicated to dress items available for soldiers, while from heading 32 onwards in this division items are identified by their country of origin and are also costly. Even those that merely resemble items from other places can still have a high maximum set (19.27 lists a Laodiceian *birrus* as similar to one from the Nervii and is priced at 10,000 denarii – 5,500 denarii more than a Laodiceian *birrus* that was not). These suggest that there were locations famous for the production of certain materials or items of clothing, whose products were identifiable by origin and quality and were highly sought after.[68] That this was the case for certain places such as the linen centres mentioned above, as well those which produced wool or types of purple, is confirmed by the concern to catalogue the material from these areas within the 'first grade' of quality and from their comparative prices.[69] The proximity of these places to resources likely meant that prices for their goods were lower within the vicinity, but the high value of some of these items suggests both that they were highly prized by those who lived at a greater distance, because they were difficult to come by and thus required wealth to obtain, and that garment had value in and of itself within society. The concentration of the Edict on clothing implies its importance in (and externally to) the trade of the empire, while the range of prices and the interest in listing certain grades of clothing quality or material by status of wearer suggests a concern with the semiotics of social hierarchy clothing displayed. The common practice of bequeathing clothing in wills, and the prevalence of fullers and dyers, clothing merchants and 'shops' throughout the empire, even outside of urban spaces, suggests that garments were an investment that was to be cared for carefully and continually.[70] Therefore, when all of the examples in the following chapters are examined, they are being considered against this background; that is, that clothing was valuable in literary texts as a rhetorical device because it was also valuable in society as an economic asset. Because this certainly is the case, it has meant most scholars rarely go beyond discussing this aspect of clothing when it appears as a gift.[71] It will be argued, however, that garments meant more than this when given in ancient society. This work will consider what was symbolic about cloth that may have made it an especially appropriate present in this context. Too often, little attention is paid to why a particular item may have been offered or thought suitable for those special circumstances, and this oversight leaves unacknowledged the conversation being held at a deeper level by both parties through the gifts.

I.4 Research questions and methodology

Both clothing and gifts in the ancient world, therefore, separately have been the subject of much scholarly discussion because they were an integral part of Greek and Roman society and identity, creating and reinforcing the relationships which kept a community together, as well as delineating status and even symbolising society as a whole. They have rarely been studied together, however, despite the appearance of clothing as a gift in many late antique (and earlier) texts and even though they are conceptually related: gifts bind people together to reinforce social bonds, which can be represented by clothing, bound together as it is by the interwoven relationships between the threads.

These chapters, then, seek to address a gap in scholarship, by focusing on gifts of elite male clothing in late antique literature between the late 300s and the sixth century. This is in order to show that when they appeared in texts these items were actually functioning not only (or even primarily) in the historical or 'real-life' sphere, but as a literary space in which authors could discuss ideas of social relationships and authority. It will be argued that this can be discerned not only because the writers use specific pieces of clothing which had special associations with secular and religious authority (the *trabea*, the *chlamys*, and the *pallium*), but because in being made to perform as a gift, these items function as part of a wider debate in Late Antiquity about whence that authority derived. In a period when usurpers were not uncommon, 'barbarians' could be among the most influential men in the empire, lowly soldiers could be emperors, and a once persecuted sect had imperial benefaction, the traditional markers of authority – birth, education, wealth – were no longer the only routes to power.[72] It was, therefore, increasingly problematic to be clear about who should have access to it, and it will be suggested that certain authors used clothing gifts as a way to address these issues.

It will also become apparent that clothing gifts often form part of a text that serves to justify, and reinforce, the authority of the protagonist, who was sometimes additionally the author. This is because these special items of clothing (which transformed the wearer into a symbol of authority) combined the concepts surrounding power and gift-giving to demonstrate both the wearer's own authority, and the derivation of this authority from the donor, who was usually in a superior social or religious position. As a consequence, it will be argued, these items were also useful for negotiating power relationships, not only between the giver and receiver, but also between the participants and the wider community. Furthermore, it will be considered that, by choosing to present these particular garments as gifts, the authors were deliberately covering the recipient of the present in the mantle of orthodox authority, political or religious, particularly when this may have been open to question due to background or religious leanings.[73] This was because all three, the *trabea*, the *pallium*, and the *chlamys*, were symbols of those who held 'official' imperial and religious power. The *trabea* was part of the costume of the new consul, the *chlamys* was worn by the emperor and his court, and the *pallium* came to be associated with bishops and official church authority, and was to be distinguished from the *melōte* worn by monks whose charismatic power derived from their identification with the Biblical prophets.[74] Finally, developing Scheid and Svenbro's ideas, it will be suggested that clothing was a particularly appropriate present, not only because of the messages surrounding identity it could convey. As a finished product that combined different elements it was the perfect representation of what the gift ritual itself was trying to achieve – a harmonious relationship that enabled social cohesion. It was thus a way for late antique authors to conceal disparities between reality and ideal.

This was further strengthened by the context of the presents within the texts, where gifts are often presented or discussed as part of a public spectacle like the inauguration of a new consul or the arrival, conversion, and baptism of a foreign ally, and through the texts themselves, some of which would have been read aloud in church. The public aspect of these documents allowed the clothing gift to be 'viewed' by many more people; the original circumstances and even the reality of the gift no longer matters for it is over-written by the literary reality which, as Barthes contended, becomes the limiting authoritative interpretation. In this setting, then, the question of whether the clothing gifts described in the texts should be taken at face value or were real becomes less important. Some, such as Ausonius' *trabea* and the *chlamys* given to Tzath, almost certainly existed, while others, such as the garment Athanasius gives to Antony, are not so clear-cut. This means that non-literary evidence, such as that from extant textiles, art, and archaeology, has seldom been utilised in the discussions, particularly as they rarely provide information about gift-giving practices. They also come with their own problems, particularly as the material culture that survives is often of unclear origin and more to do with the bias of climate. Except in the case of fourth- to sixth-century diptychs, employed in Chapter 3, and the tapestry of Elijah and Elisha (cover image and Figure 4.1, discussed in Chapter 4), literature therefore forms the body of evidence for this study.

Indeed, it is precisely because it is so difficult to tie the literary representations of clothing gifts to 'reality' that the texts are of such importance. The dubious existence of these presents outside of the literary landscape, in addition to the fact that garments given are always related to special types of authority, rather supports the idea that they are functioning in this context not primarily as descriptions of actual events or even as real clothes. Rather they are working as metaphors negotiating social relationships and the transference and use of authority. It is also of significance that, while it is confined to gender (since these are traditionally masculine garments), this metaphor is not constrained by genre, language, time, or geography. Instead, it appears more or less intact in the religious writings of, for instance, Jerome, Athanasius, Basil, Gregory of Tours, Gregory the Great, and Cyril of Scythopolis, the histories of Priscus, Malalas, and Menander, and the poetry of Ausonius, Claudian, and Sidonius Apollinarius.

Such authors are invaluable because they were often participants in gift exchanges in their general social interactions, and were sometimes even recipients of the clothing gifts about which they write. They therefore demonstrate exactly how utilising the semiotics of both clothing and gifts was integral to furthering their own authorial agendas, as well as the social or religious standing of their protagonist, who could, of course, be themselves. Focusing on elite male clothing, therefore, becomes a more obvious choice: it was strongly associated with authority, there is a range of authors who include these items in their texts, and, because these authors are male, they are writing about practices they know intimately. There is, however, clearly a strong bias in such texts towards how clothing works in cities such as Rome, Constantinople, and Trier, as these are the landscapes the writers operated in, but comparisons with authors who lived a monastic life away from these urban centres of power show that clothing gifts were understood across geographical (and religious) boundaries. This does not just apply to within the confines of the empire either. When investigating gifts of clothing presented to within foreigners, non-Roman works[75] provide invaluable insight not only into how clothing gifts were understood as similar symbols of authority by those on the 'other side' of the frontier, but also how this knowledge was sometimes exploited by them to achieve recognition both within the empire and in their own communities.

This work, therefore, aims to demonstrate that when a gift of clothing is given between two people in the ancient texts it is more than simply an act that cements a relationship. This is not only because these clothes were almost always items that were associated with or clearly marked those in authority. As pieces of cloth, they were also objects made by the correct interweaving of different threads, which could protect and shelter as well as transform and mould a body, making it something more than itself. To give such a present, then, was to hand over the symbolisms associated with gift-giving as well as with clothing, dressing the recipient as a figure of authority while also highlighting to whom he owes this honour. By using a range of authors from the late 300s to the sixth century, writing in various genres and found in locations across the empire (and beyond), this work will suggest that, real or not, these gifts provided a perfect platform to demonstrate how elite Roman men negotiated their relationships with authority. Furthermore, it will argue that such gifts enabled audiences to understand the correct transference of power, and were employed particularly to strengthen claims to authority when the gift recipient's credentials may not have been wholly convincing.

16 *Introduction*

I.5 Chapter outline

Three chapters, therefore, will examine gifts of clothing to show how these items were used to explore tensions and anxieties about secular and Christian authority within late antique social, political, and religious landscapes. It will move from the use of clothing gifts between the empire and its foreign allies to imperial and consular examples, and end with an investigation into their use in religious texts. Each chapter will employ the use of a 'case study' to draw together the threads of the whole. This is also the case for Chapter 1, which lays out the background for this study, examining instances of clothing gifts in earlier periods of Greek and Roman history in order to place the chapters on Late Antiquity in context. It contains important groundwork for the rest of the discussions, as it demonstrates what was available to the authors of Late Antiquity, and what was already in the collective literary consciousness that could be utilised about gifts of clothing. It will, therefore, be seen in later chapters that there are significant parallels between the way in which earlier and late antique writers understood clothing presents. Unsurprisingly, however, there are some developments in late antique usage, and these are foreshadowed in the work of Martial. His uniquely extensive use of clothing gifts in his epigrams, to discuss his role and duties as a *cliens* and patronage in general, make him a valuable case study for this chapter and for the work as a whole. Indeed, the motives and attitudes behind his broadcasting of dress items received (which may or may not be real) echo across the following chapters in surprising contexts.

Moving into Late Antiquity, Chapter 2 takes in a broad range of chronological and geographical sources to present late antique gifts in a diplomatic setting. Here the gifts may be 'real', but their appearance in literary works means that they should not be taken at face value. As the initial sections of the chapter will show they symbolised what the embassy itself was trying to achieve: weaving was a peacetime activity, but these gifts were also now being presented as part of a wider diplomatic 'policy' to justify and secure the empire's continued hegemony and even existence in the world. By including them in their histories, authors were using clothing gifts to reinforce this narrative of power. These circumstances can be seen in the empire's relationship with Sassanid Persia, of which the subject of the case study – the clothing gift presented to Tzath by Justin I – was also part. The investiture itself, and the gift's existence as a real item described within a historical text, has close parallels to Early Republic and imperial investitures of foreign rulers encountered in Chapter 1. That certain clothing gifts strongly associated with Roman authority were given to foreign rulers like Tzath is interesting, and this chapter will consider throughout for whom were these items actually for. It will suggest that these gifts function as a way to place 'barbarian' rulers into the context of familiar power for Roman audiences, while simultaneously working to suggest their submission to the empire. Thus, they should be considered as gifts designed to reinforce the uncertain authority of the empire during this period. Both in the literature and real circumstances of diplomacy, these presents functioned to create a narrative of luxury and superior power, aimed as much at those within the empire as those without.

The use of real clothing gifts in literature to shore up insecure authority will additionally be addressed through the narrower lens of Chapter 3, particularly in the case study. This considers the gift of a *trabea* Ausonius of Bordeaux received from the Emperor Gratian upon the former's promotion to the consulship in 379, but decorated with the image of Constantius II. As will be examined, this decoration was unexpected and Ausonius' few but significant comments in his thanksgiving speech suggest that the surprising ornamentation, the item itself as part of the consul's ceremonial dress, and its function as a gift are all working together. The aim of this collaboration, it will be argued, is to transform Ausonius' body into a canvas to represent Gratian's own authority, a transformation in which Ausonius is happily participating and which he is perpetuating through his speech, which provides his audience with the tools to 'read' the garment correctly. This case study will be set against and draw from a consideration of other examples of figural decoration on contemporary consular clothing, particularly *trabeae* in the consular diptychs and the poems of Sidonius and Claudian. Although these were not always gifts, they serve to show that Ausonius' *trabea* was part of a wider employment of decorated clothing as a space to display and negotiate connections to authority and power.

Displaying and negotiating connections to authority is also at stake in Chapter 4, which brings together several previous themes to show that clothing gifts were employed by Christian authors in much the same way as their secular counterparts. Here gifts of clothing will be seen working not only in the context of charitable donations, but also as a way to own tangible holiness. This was possible through the possession of clothing relics, thought to have imbibed the power of the saint due to beliefs about apparel that went beyond their close proximity to holy bodies. Gifts of clothing taken from saints or given by them were thought to continue to contain their charismatic authority, but because with great power comes great responsibility, these items become sites on which wider anxieties about who should be allowed access to this power come into play. This was because the gift of a cloak item in particular was often felt to mean that the wearer is literally taking on the mantle of his predecessor's charismatic authority. This chapter will also demonstrate that clothing becomes an important part of the debate over charismatic, monastic authority versus institutional religious authority, and that, in order to reconstruct charismatic figures as paradigms of orthodoxy, writers can clothe them in the *pallium* associated with a bishop. One person dressed up in this way was Antony, whose gifted garment and the conflicting narratives told about it by Jerome and the original donor Athanasius are the subject of this chapter's case study. As in the preceding chapters, it will be clear that this gift is designed to reflect on the giver more than on the receiver. Yet it will also be shown that, in this Christian context, gifts of clothing which had connections to religious authority were also functioning to co-opt charismatic figures for other reasons, while having the additional benefit of covering over their problematic status as influential figures who operated outside of the confines of the Church.

These chapters as a whole suggest the larger theme that gifts of clothing are an important and largely overlooked part of the late antique literary landscape, and contends that they were doubly potent because the themes related to clothing such as control, participation, social position, authority and relationships, were also deeply embedded in the practice of gift-giving. Together the chapters work to demonstrate that clothing gifts were not confined to one sphere of late antique literature, but were an important part of the political, social, and religious landscape. In a period where authority came in many guises and it was not always easy to tell who had, or should have, the upper hand (Christian? political? usurper? emperor? monk? bishop?), such items were employed to clarify where power derived from, and who was suitable to wield it. Clothing people like Ausonius, Tzath, and Antony – people, who for various reasons, might otherwise have been slightly dubious holders of official authority in whatever guise that meant – in the 'correct' attire enabled the readers of the empire to 'place' them correctly within the system. Such gifts did more than signify that they were legitimate power players, however. Since the very make up of clothing meant it was a representation of the civic order, these items also transformed their clothing into the perfect canvas for authors to portray the relationship between those who were entrusted with keeping that social fabric intact.

Notes

1 Joh. Mal. 17.9 (413–414) (tr. E. Jeffreys, M. Jeffreys, and R. Scott (hereafter Jeffreys et al.) with Woodfin (2012) 159 and further revisions). Other translations my own except where stated.
2 All dates are CE except where noted.
3 Joh. Mal. 17.9 (412–413). For a fuller discussion of this event, see Chapter 2 case study.
4 E.g. L.M. Wilson (1924) and (1938); Sebesta and Bonfante (1994); Croom (2000). Cf. e.g. Cleland, Davies, and Llewellyn-Jones (hereafter Cleland et al.) (2007) 159–60 s.v. 'Reconstruction of clothing', Harlow (2012b) 1–6, Harlow and Nosch (2014b) 1–33, and Upson-Saia, Daniel-Hughes, and Batten (2014b) 1–18 for overviews of the early scholarship.
5 Cf. Vout (1996) 205–6.
6 L. Taylor (2002) especially 24–63.
7 L. Taylor (2002) 24; cf. Corrigan (2008) 3–7.
8 L. Taylor (2002) 18, 24.
9 See in e.g. Pritchard (2006); Alfaro, Wild, and Costa (eds) (2004); Alfaro and Karali (eds.) (2008); de Moor, Fluck, and Linscheid (eds) (2013); Harlow and Nosch (eds) (2014a).
10 Cf. Harlow (2004a) 45; Rothe (2012a), (2012b), (2013). A modern example of this is the use of 'sweater' (US English) and 'jumper' (UK English) for the same type of garment, and conversely, 'pants' denoting underwear in Britain, but trousers in America.
11 Barthes (1967) 3.
12 Barthes (1967) 4 in reference to 'the Fashion photograph', Chapters 3, 16–19; cf. Vout (1996), especially 206–9.
13 Barthes (1967) 3.
14 Barthes (1967) 13 (cf. Upson-Saia et al (2014b) 13), also of importance: 213–23, 235–9, 277–89 (summary of 'A' and 'B ensembles' of which A is more relevant).

15 Cf. Rothe (2012a), (2012b), (2013).
16 For a discussion of use of visual evidence for textiles, see Lovén (2014).
17 Cf. Rothe (2012a) 140 for issues of terminology such as 'costume' and 'dress'.
18 Cf. Ross (2008) 7.
19 Quotation: Barnard (2007) 4. It could be argued that Romans also had fashion trends in their clothing and accessories (Harlow (2004a) 46–7); Cleland *et al.* (2007) 67 s.v. 'Fashion' (cf. 109 s.v. 'Late Antiquity': costume that was appropriate to the elite in the sixth century CE would have looked 'barbaric and alien' to a first century CE. Roman); Harlow (2012b) 1–6; Harlow and Nosch (2014b) 1–33.
20 E. Wilson (1985) 393–7. Cf. Barthes (1967) 276.
21 Particularly those written into dress: Reinhold (1970) 38 (cf. (1969), (1971)); Harlow (2004a). See also Chapter 1 case study particularly in reference to recognition of dyes.
22 Chausson and Inglebert (2003); Cleland, Harlow, and Llewellyn-Jones (2005); von Rummel (2007); Colburn and Heyn (2008); Edmondson and Keith (2008); Olson (2008); Daniel-Hughes (2011); Harlow (2012a); Rothe (2012a), (2012b) (2013); Upson-Saia, Daniel-Hughes, and Batten(eds) (2014a).
23 These are listed as clothing's mediating functions in Perani and Wolff (1999) 29; cf. Harlow (2004a) 46.
24 Harlow (2004a) 45–6. Cf. Barthes (1967) 283: '... Fashion ... is ... present as a hidden order, a silent terror, for not to respect [this year's Fashion-sanctioned style at a certain event] ... would be to fall into the "fault" of the unfashionable ...'
25 Calefato (2004) 2. For utilization of dress in the 'social control of the body' in more recent history, see Arthur (1999). The mistrust of the female use of cosmetics (κόσμος or *cultus*) by ancient authors because of their abilities to conceal and deceive is comparable (see Olson (2008) Chapter 2) suggesting that clothes can perhaps be viewed as a form of body or material cosmetics. Cf. Barthes (1967) 258–60.
26 Heskel (2001); Dyck (2001); Harlow (2004a) 44, 46.
27 Harlow (2004a) 45; Upson-Saia (2011) 8–9, with reference to gender boundaries.
28 Calefato (2004) 1; cf. Barthes (1967) 236.
29 Damhorst (2005) 2.
30 See, e.g. Cleland *et al.* (2007) 110–11 s.v. 'Laws, Roman'; Edmondson (2008) 21–46.
31 E.g. *lex Oppia* 213 BCE. (Liv. 24.1, 8; Val. Max. 9.1) (see Hurlock (1965)); Tiberius banned silk clothing for men (Tac. *Ann.* 2.33); Claudius insisted a defendant in a citizenship trial changed clothing depending on whether the plaintiffs or defence was speaking, in an attempt to demonstrate his impartiality (Suet. *Claud.* 15); restriction on barbarian clothing in major urban centres: *Cod. Theod.* 14.10.1–4 (382, 397–399) (Arce (2005) 33–45; von Rummel (2007) 156–66)); cf. HA *Alex. Sev.* 27.1–4 (Harlow (2005) 151)); *Dig.* 34.2.23.2 (early third century; see Harlow (2004a) 48).
32 E.g. Brown (1988); Stewart (1997); Wyke (1998); Porter (1999); Fredrick (2002); Cairns (2005); Hopkins and Wyke (2005); Squire (2011).
33 Brown (1988) 31: 'Like society, the body was there to be administered, not changed'.
34 E.g. MacMullen (1990) 78–106; MacCormack (1981); McCormick (1986); Roberts (1989); Delmaire (2003); Parani (2007); von Rummel (2007); Dewar (2008).
35 Clark (1993) especially 105–18; Cloke (1995); Coon (1997) 27–8, 31–2, 36–40, 114–15; Harlow (2004b), (2007); Upson-Saia (2011).
36 Notable exceptions are Coon (1997) 28–51, 52–70; Harlow (2004a) and (2005); von Rummel (2007); and more recently: Daniel-Hughes (2011); Upson-Saia (2011); Upson-Saia, Daniel-Hughes, and Batten (eds) (2014a).
37 Roberts (1989) 111–18, quotation 116. Cf. Faber (2008).
38 Scheid and Svenbro (1996) 13.
39 Cleland, Davies, and Llewelyn-Jones (2007) 128 s.v. 'Mythology'.
40 Scheid and Svenbro (1996) 9, 10.
41 Scheid and Svenbro (1996) 12: 'To weave ... is to interweave what is different, contrary or hostile, in order to produce a unified, harmonious textile ...'. Cf. Claud. *in Ruf.* 2.50–54: 'An empire won and kept at the expense of so much bloodshed, born from the

20 Introduction

toils of countless leaders, knit together through so many years by Roman hands (*quod tantis Romana manus contexuit annis*)'.

42 Tr. G. Long (1980).
43 Τί δ' ὠφελεῖ ἡ πορφύρα τὸ ἱμάτιον; τί γὰρ ἄλλο ἢ διαπρέπει ἐν αὐτῷ ὡς πορφύρα καὶ τοῖς ἄλλοις δὲ καλὸν παράδειγμα ἔκκειται; Arr. *Epict. diss.* 1.2.22–23.
44 Osteen (2002a) 2–3 '. . . *The Gift* bears within it the seeds of virtually every important study of gift-giving that has succeeded it . . . it would be difficult to find a text in the human sciences that has had more impact than Mauss' brief monograph'.
45 Particularly those found in Seneca, *De Beneficiis*, not discussed by Mauss but examined in detail with reference to ancient gift-giving by Peterman (1997); cf. Sadashige (2002); Osteen (2002b). The debate surrounding gifts is wide-ranging and vast, and beyond the scope of this study to discuss in any detail.
46 As Glaucus and Diomedes found in *Il.* 6.219 (see further: Herman (1987) 1–2; Donlan (1989); Harries (1993)).
47 Herman (1987) 73–115; Sadashige (2002) 151, 152, 155, 156, 165.
48 Mauss (1923–24 [2002]).
49 Homeric period: e.g. Donlan (1982); Seaford (1994); von Reden (1995); Gill, Postlethwaite, and Seaford (1998); Finley (1999a), (1999b). Roman patronage: e.g. Saller (1982); Wallace-Hadrill (1989c); Verboven (2002); cf. Herman (1987) (Greek *polis*); Peterman (1997) 4 n.11, 5 n.14.
50 E.g. with reference to diplomacy: Braund (1984); the majority of essays in Shepard and Franklin (1992); Tinnefeld (1993); Wood (2000); Campbell (2001); Gillett (2003); Canepa (2009).
51 E.g. Anna Muthesius' (1992) research on the importance of silk in the context of trade and exchange in the same period (c.700–1200) and (of particular relevance for this work) Antony Cutler's articles ((2001), (2005a) and especially (2005b)) on gifts and gift-exchange between Byzantium and Islam during the ninth to twelfth centuries. Cutler's work has been invaluable, especially in his identification of the significance of clothing – in its highly personal nature – as a gift between Byzantine and Muslim rulers.
52 Muthesius (1992) 237; Cf. Acts 20.33 (discussed by Peterman (1997) 61); Men. *fr.* 25.2.
53 For discussions of textile manufacture see e.g. Wild (1970), (1994) 30–31; Granger-Taylor (1982), (1983); Alfaro, Wild and Costa (eds) (2004); Pritchard (2006); Cleland *et al.* (2007) e.g. 30 s.v. 'Care of clothing', 188 s.v. 'Textile manufacture', 209–10 s.v. 'Weaving;' Alfaro and Karali (eds.) (2008); De Moor, Fluck, and Linscheid (eds) (2013); Harlow and Nosch (eds) (2014a). For an extensive examination of textiles, dyes and manufacture pre-400 BCE, which is nonetheless relevant for later periods see Barber (1991). I am indebted to the anonymous readers of this work for their helpful notes and references concerning this section.
54 Slaves in Livia's household dealing with clothing and textile production: Treggiari (1975) 52–54; evidence of patching on a third of textiles found at the Mons Claudianus rubbish dump in Egypt (Mannering (2000b) 12); Granger-Taylor (1983) 148; Pritchard (2006) 19, 49; Cleland *et al* (2007) 208 s.v. 'Wealth', 31 s.v. 'centonarius' (which includes reference to *Cod. Theod.* 16.10.20.4); Liu (2009).
55 Second-hand market: Petr. *Satyr.* 12–13; Mannering (2000a) 289; Cleland *et al* (2007) 30 s.v. 'Care of clothing', 119–20 s.v. 'Maintenance of clothing;' Bogensperger (2014). Recycled clothing and textile ornaments in archaeological evidence demonstrates 'existence of trade in second-hand clothing, which operated on more than a domestic scale' (Pritchard (2006) 60). Even Livia had slaves to repair clothing (Treggiari (1975) 54).
56 Thieves: Mart. 8.48, 59; Petr. *Satyr.* 12, 30; gambling: Plaut. *Curc.* 355; guarantor: Liu (2009) 72 n.68 for examples from Oxyrhynchus.
57 Pritchard (2006) 61.
58 Pritchard (2006) 70, 72.
59 Granger-Taylor (1983) 138. When the tomb of the Emperor Honorius' wife (d. 400) was opened in 1544 her body was discovered wrapped in a large quantity of golden fabric.

When the decision was taken to melt this down her robes yielded 15–20kg of pure gold (Gleba (2008) 62 n.3).
60 Cleland (2005).
61 Text and Translation: Graser (1940) 305–422.
62 Which makes it all the more surprising that all reference to clothing has been omitted from reproductions of the text in some modern sourcebooks such as Lewis and Reinhold (1990); Rees (2004).
63 Jones (1960 [1974]) 352–3; Pritchard (2006) 27.
64 Pritchard (2006) 28
65 Preface (Graser (1940) 314–16).
66 Jones (1960 [1974]) 352; Pritchard (2006) 28, 61 (quotation 28).
67 Linen tunic: 26.77; labourer's wage: 7.1a. In contrast, certain textile and clothing workers were some of the better-paid wage earners – particularly those who worked with premium materials like silk and superior quality wools, dyed purple, or who had superior technical skills, such as the ability to work in gold brocade (see e.g. 7.42 and a number of workers in sections 20–22). Cf. *Cod. Just.* 8.13.127 where the *metaxarii* (silk merchants, or possibly makers) are listed with the *argentarii* (silversmiths and bankers) as wealthy people in Constantinople who are able to buy court sinecures (Jones (1960) [1974]) 362).
68 Rothe (2012a) 143.
69 Wool: section 25; purple: section 24. Jones (1960 [1974]) 354–5; Pritchard (2006) 27, 61; Rothe (2012a) 143. Not all clothing that was valued because of its 'brand recognition', as it were, was necessarily produced in the region it was named after, however, as the above example of the *birrus* similar to that from the Nervii but which was instead 'Laodiceian' shows. There appears to have been a common trend in the clothing of the ancient world (as in modern times) for imitating more expensive fabrics and, in particular, dyes by the use of similar, but less expensive, materials. Thus, perhaps, like the 'Fair Isle' style of decoration on knitted clothing that has been fashionable in recent years, the regional identifier of some ancient garments indicated a certain look, style or technique or colour of pattern, rather than its actual production location, while still indicating its initial origins (in this case one of the Shetland islands). Cf. Barthes (1967) 238: '. . . certain species of clothing function as old signifieds "fossilized" into signifiers (*sport shirt, Richelieu shoes*) . . .'.
70 Jones (1960 [1974]) 363 with n.14, 561; Bradley (2002); Pritchard (2006) 61.
71 A notable exception is Cutler in his (2005b) article. Serfass (2014) discusses the *pallium* in Gregory the Great's letters within the context of gift-giving to a certain extent, but considers it with regard to ideas surrounding gift-giving practice and does not consider the nature of dress as special in and of itself.
72 Cf. Harlow (2004a) 44 on the 'blurring of the physical and social frontiers and boundaries' in Late Antiquity and its relationship to Roman male identity.
73 Orthodoxy is primarily used to suggest ideas of 'institutional' or 'official' authority in this study, although its religious connotations are also relevant.
74 I have deliberately refrained from describing these items in more detail for the reasons stated in the first part of this Introduction relating to terminology. Apart from the *trabea* and *chlamys*, which are bound up in ideas of authority and will be examined in the relevant chapters, the look of the garment is not as important as the knowledge that items are associated with the certain roles and that, crucially, they are the outermost garment in an outfit. See following chapters for relevant discussions.
75 E.g. the history attributed to a seventh-century Armenian bishop named Sebeos (see Thomson and Howard-Johnston (1999) xxxii–xxxviii for problems in the identification of the author) and those included by M.H. Dodgeon and S.N.C. Lieu (1994) and Geoffrey Greatrex and S.N.C. Lieu (2002).

1 Threads of history

Clothing gifts in Greek and Roman society before Late Antiquity

As discussed in the Introduction, clothing has been recognised in modern scholarship as an important indicator of cultural and social identity. It distinguished and separated humanity from animals, and in its manufacture indicated both skilled labour and trade. Furthermore, when combined with its employment as a status symbol which implied social organisation, these factors meant clothing was a potent emblem of civilisation and cohesion. Gift-giving also performed functions that had much in common with the social role of clothing: reciprocity in pre-modern societies allowed for trading and the establishment and maintenance of one's place within the social structure, and it was of vital importance to the smooth running of society. That the ability to give a gift can signify so much makes it less surprising that clothing has long been part of the narrative of Greek and Roman cultural history. By examining a range of texts from the Homeric period to the Early Roman Empire, this chapter will investigate the presence of garments as gifts in various periods before Late Antiquity (Homeric, Classical, Hellenistic, and Early, Republican, and Imperial Rome).[1] The texts considered here are not exhaustive, and by necessity they are only brief glimpses into garment gift-giving practices in the literature of this period. Yet, in discussing the purpose and the wider cultural implications of such items as literary devices in the texts from these earlier times, the chapter functions as a foundation for the discussions that follow. When clothing gifts are encountered in the later chapters, it will be clear that the late antique authors who employ them in order to discuss ideas surrounding authority are often drawing on concepts and practices that had a long tradition within Greek and Roman culture, which saw gifts of clothing employed as spaces to explore female agency, social relationships and imperial behaviour. However, while there is a clear link to earlier practice, these later writers did not simply copy previous usage. Instead, they adapted clothing gifts to suit their own contemporary concerns, in order to examine and negotiate the changing relationships and dynamics of authority between themselves, their foreign neighbours, their emperor, and their religious leaders in a period of anxiety. The initial stages of this development can be seen in the Early Empire in the epigrams of Martial, and his work thus forms the case study of this chapter. Building on this foundation, the following chapters will explore how these gifts took on new meanings in their late antique context, enabling writers to reinforce and explore the positions of those who had been handed religious or political authority. That they could do so was due to the cultural consciousness of familiar clothing gift metaphors found within the literature of the earlier periods this chapter examines.

1.1 The Homeric period

Gift-giving in the Homeric world needs little introduction. Since Moses Finley's seminal discussions much scholarship has been dedicated to investigations into reciprocity, exchange, and the importance of gifts in establishing and maintaining relationships between Homeric heroes.[2] However, although more recently a few scholars have started to explore some of the symbolic functions of clothing gifts in this context, this subject has received little attention previously despite clothing's repeated appearance within Homeric exchange.[3] Indeed, the repetition of this ritual in both the *Iliad* and the *Odyssey* demonstrates that it had meaning as a poetic device within the Homeric world. This value may have arisen from its reflection of a respected social practice. While discussion of the historicity or otherwise of the *Iliad* and the *Odyssey* lies outside the remit of this chapter, the poems are taken here as a reflection of recognisable social practices between elite members of the Greek world before the eighth century, which were likely still happening when the poems were performed.[4] That there is no need for an explanation accompanying the gifting of clothing within these poems, however, suggests this type of exchange was familiar to the audience within a literary context if not also in real life, regardless of whether or not there was an Achilles or Odysseus accepting clothing in the period before the eighth century. This is of importance because it shows that the late antique clothing gifts encountered in the following chapters can trace their literary (and social) roots back to the earliest phase of the classical world. Furthermore, the enduring influence of Homer in ancient literature and education meant that late antique authors were well versed in these poems, which provided a store of imagery they could and did adapt to their contemporary needs.[5] The gifting of clothing in the Homeric world still resonated for later writers and their audiences therefore, and the use these items were put to in the literature of the later period shows both a continuity with and transformation of ideas that had a long tradition.

In the Homeric poems, clothing functions within the context of the more positive aspects of gift-giving (such as hospitality and *xenia*, prevalent in the *Odyssey*), but it also has a place within exchanges that are potentially hostile and thus negative (such as between enemies in the *Iliad*). As a rule, gifts of clothing are not as ubiquitous in the *Iliad* as they are in the *Odyssey*, most likely because the figures of the *Iliad* appear less frequently in the hospitable situations that made the practice of *xenia* appropriate. Yet when these items do appear in the *Iliad*, their occurrences are to be found within the context of more momentous events.[6] The appearance of clothing as part of the ransom Priam offers Achilles in book 24, for example, and its position at the head of the list of items exchanged, makes it central to an episode of heavy symbolic and emotional significance within the poem:[7]

> He spoke, and lifted back the fair covering of his clothes-chest
> and from inside took out twelve *pepla* surpassingly lovely
> and twelve *chlaīnai* to be worn single, as many blankets,
> as many great white *pharea*, also the same number of *chitōnes*.
> (Iliad 24.228–231)[8]

These items are followed by a list of other objects, including ten talents of gold, two tripods, four cauldrons, and a goblet. However, the fact that the greater part of the gift is comprised by clothing pieces, and that these are mentioned first, allows the poet to emphasise their economic, cultural, and symbolic value within both the ransom and the ritual of exchange as a whole. The presence of *pepla, chlaīnai, chitons,* and *pharea* among the gifts that Priam had been divinely ordered to choose from the treasure stores of Troy, highlights that clothing could be precious and was certainly a gift worth giving. Yet such garments may not have been significant within this episode just for their economic value. John Scheid and Jesper Svenbro's suggestions discussed in the Introduction can be applied here, for the garments can also be seen to represent the brief harmony between the opposed figures of Priam and Achilles, which enabled the return of Hector's body. The successful exchange of gifts between Achilles and Priam reinforces the symbolism of unity the garments, as complete textiles woven from disparate elements, embody. The clothes signify the context and desires of both participants: like the warp and the weft, Achilles and Priam bond together peacefully, at least for a short time. As will be seen in Chapter 2, over a thousand years later such concepts are still to be found in the garment gifts of late antique foreign diplomacy.

That gifts of clothing are employed by the poet in this way is further suggested by their absence from another significant gift-giving scene within the *Iliad*: they are not included among the gifts with which Agamemnon attempts to win Achilles over in 9.121–157. Through the omission of items that represent interwoven harmony, this episode may be a deliberate strategy on the part of the poet to foreshadow that these gifts will be unsuccessful in repairing the relationship between Achilles and Agamemnon.[9] Perhaps it might even be that including such pieces would be inappropriate for this poetic situation: even when they are eventually accepted, in 19.147–148, these presents will not create the unity, however brief, which clothing gifts symbolise. Such items, therefore, have no place in a relationship that will always be discordant and incomplete.

The lack of clothing gifts in the *Iliad* reflects its wider context of dissonant relationships as well; there is little scope in a war for the practice of *xenia*, guest or ritualised friendship, in which such items appear to have played an important role.[10] Enacted by a host when a stranger or visitor came to their home, a change of clothing, and the provision of food, shelter, and the means of returning home was the right of every caller. The practice can be seen at work in the

Odyssey, and it is the prevalence of clothing gifts in this poem particularly that has led modern scholars to the conclusion that such items were a normative part of what was expected of a host.[11] For this discussion, however, the reality of such situations is of less importance than the symbolism. Within the context of the metaphorical protection a host was expected to extend to a guest, the provision of clothing (a separate category to guest-gifts) in combination with food and a roof over their head is unsurprising. It was a particularly apt gift when it is considered that clothing could also double as a literal shelter for the wearer, an idea that is developed later by Plato and discussed further below. Thus, both in 'real life' and in literature, clothing theoretically allowed the receiver to take some of this protection away with him.

However far from civilisation he wanders, Odysseus often carries away clothing gifts provided by his hosts. Their significance as a narrative device has been identified in modern scholarship, particularly with regards to the theme of disguise and the poem's broader programme of an exploration of cultural identity.[12] In several episodes Odysseus receives clothing which 'makes' him, disguising his true identity and transforming him into the person the garment donor wishes him to be, a theme which will be returned to in the final sections of Chapter 4 in a late antique Christian context. Odysseus is clothed by the donor in their ideas and expectations about him and his relationship with regard to them; he is at various times husband, immortal, beggar, guest, and Odysseus himself.[13] Whether he will ultimately conform to these identities or not creates tension within the narrative, and clothing's ability to disguise and conceal a person's true character is the metaphor through which these conflicts are played out.

The clothing has further symbolism for this theme of identity through its material make-up. In ancient thought the completed fabric is commonly associated with its material origin and method of manufacture, reminding the viewer of the process and beginnings of its transformation. Because wool is closely related to and connects the wearer with its agricultural origins, it symbolises the taming of the landscape, through the process of transforming raw wool into useable thread.[14] This is further enhanced when it is considered that clothing was woven to shape in antiquity – when made into a garment, the natural product is trained into a more human form. Therefore, when Odysseus is clothed he is moulded and tamed into a representation of civilisation as perceived by the donor, and returned to human status, for dress was a signal of the divide between man and animals, and the civilised world from the surrounding, natural, and wild environment.[15] The naked and brine-covered Odysseus who first horrifies Nausicaa and her companions by the river is likened to a wild animal, a mountain-bred lion (λέων ὀρεσίτροφος); his lack of clothing transforms him back to the appearance of an animalistic state.[16] However Odysseus' speech soon convinces Nausicaa that he is a man ('Why do you flee from the sight of a man?' (πόσε φεύγετε φῶτα ἰδοῦσαι)),[17] while his request for clothing helps to demonstrate his innate humanity and desire to be returned to civilisation. Indeed the (human-shaped) gifts she gives transform the terrifyingly inhuman Odysseus to such an extent that Nausicaa can even think of him in one of the roles which defined men in ancient thought: 'That is the kind of man whom I could call a husband, if he would live here' (αἲ γὰρ ἐμοὶ τοιόσδε πόσις κεκλημένος εἴη ἐνθάδε ναιετάων . . .).[18] Thus, his return to humanity is complete.

Odysseus' receipt of garments often occurs in the *Odyssey* within the context of hospitality, and because of this the provision of clothing in the poem signifies the integration of the receiver into the household, and by extension the society of which it was part. In 7.313, the poet highlights through clothing gifts that Odysseus will be fully integrated into Phaeacian society by King Alcinous, as the resulting invitation to become his son-in-law and Odysseus' ability to drink with the Phaeacian men peacefully attests. Later, clad in the attire given to him by Queen Arete in 8.438–447, he is both enveloped in the symbolism of harmonious integration represented by the garments and dressed correctly for the role. In the *Odyssey* gifts of clothing also become signifiers of the changing relationships between the characters, and Odysseus moves between social levels with the help of the different gifted outfits in which he is clothed.[19] The garments require Odysseus' talents as a master of deceit to negotiate correctly his new statuses and the change of relationships, without revealing his true character. The issues of the potential deceitfulness of clothing and (when given as a gift) its ability to reflect the expectations of the giver rather than the wearer continue to be part of the problematic nature of the giving of clothing into Late Antiquity. Within the *Odyssey*, however, these items are part of the overarching theme of recognition and deceit in the poem. Additionally, their ability to mould Odysseus into the appropriate role for the context also reflects the poetic process and form a fitting metaphor for the work of a rhapsode who was literally a 'song-stitcher'.[20] The skill of the author in moulding his protagonist with gifts of clothing to his own agenda is not lost in Late Antiquity, and becomes an important part of the Christian narrative of those who held religious authority.

1.2 Classical Greece

As noted above, one of presents Odysseus receives is from Queen Arete, and within the *Odyssey* women are the primary givers of clothing gifts to the wanderer, often made by their own hands. As Melissa Mueller has observed, 'When a guest is ready to depart, the standard protocol in the *Odyssey* is for female hosts to offer gifts that represent their own role within the domestic sphere', and within the Homeric epic these items are valuable, not just for their monetary worth but for their narrative meaning.[21] They were also items by which a woman's fame could be spread, but without competing with that of her husband; indeed they were rather enhancing this by weaving, displaying, and then appropriately distributing his wealth through their own skill. Yet, the seeming ignorance of men about this sphere in the ancient Greek world, and the example of Penelope, also meant that expertise in the craft of weaving implied undesirable wifely abilities, like duplicity.[22] Exploiting social concerns and the influence of Homeric epic, textiles and clothing become spaces during the Classical period in particular where male anxieties about female agency come to be expressed.[23]

Receiving clothing could be a deadly pastime in tragedy: Hercules is the receiver of a poisoned cloak from Deianeira, which leads to his death, while Agamemnon's murder by Clytemnestra is foreshadowed by the red cloth laid out for him upon his homecoming and facilitated by a garment with holes for neither head nor arms.[24] As gifts from women to men, they fall outside of the main focus of this study, yet the use by male writers of clothing as weapons demonstrates how presentations of garments could be deployed as devices within a variety of genres and contexts. Deborah Lyons' thorough exploration of these 'dangerous gifts' from women to men during these periods has highlighted that their use centres around the issue of women's social and economic role, which finds its definition in marriage; and it is within this context that anxieties about women and exchange are expressed.[25] As daughters who then become wives, these 'figure[s function] as a kind of double agent, part of two families, that of her birth and the one she enters by marriage. In this way, she is part of each but belongs fully to neither'.[26] The ambiguity of this figure and the uncertain loyalty she may have brought with her, were not eased by the act of marriage itself, which at least in Classical Athens was often to an older man not of her own choosing. The idea that '[a]t best she is kind of metic, a resident alien, in the *oikos*; at worst, like Pandora, a sort of robot programmed to create havoc',[27] coupled with a woman's economic power through and control over the craft of weaving, meant that textiles and clothing provided a perfect canvass for male anxiety over female agency and usurpation of male authority.

In addition, murder by clothing is also peculiarly suitable in these narratives because it is used by women such as Deianeira, Clytemnestra, and Medea, who had been, or felt they could be, stripped of the shelter of their husband's home upon the arrival of a potential replacement figure. During this period the idea of the function of clothing as protection is given explicit expression in philosophical thought. Plato saw the resultant product of weaving as something that aimed to protect against suffering. It was a defence against the heat and cold of the external world, and could work like the roof of a house, the ultimate shelter – and from the more general cloth, he makes the short step to clothing's ability to function in the same way.[28] Xenophon expresses similar ideas: the walls and roof of the house of Antisthenes are compared to very warm tunics and thick mantles.[29] These ideas continue into the Roman period, where the toga had similar connotations. Its etymological association with *tegere* (to cover) allowed it to be understood as a synonym for a roof, while it was believed that the toga could potentially shield the wearer from harmful external influences.[30] The women of Classical tragedies, however, provided clothing which instead strips their husbands or rivals of life; the inherent symbolism of clothing as bodily protection is therefore as violently upturned as society's gender roles within these plays.

Furthermore, the problematic nature of these gifts may reflect a wider change in 'real' cultural and political tastes regarding the nature of individual gift exchange from the Homeric period. It has been noted by modern scholars that personal gift-giving among the upper echelons of Athenian society in the democratic *polis* does not appear to have been common in the Classical period.[31] The problematic nature of gifts in general and their close and often indistinguishable relationship to bribery came into sharper focus in the literature of Archaic and Classical periods of Athenian history, where the desire to curb individual power in favour of the good of the community began to be explored.[32] The close bond that garments in particular could create between the donor and recipient, and the highly personal nature of clothing, may suggest reasons for this apparent decline. Unlike many other gifts, the very act of wearing the garment brings the item into immediate contact with the receiver's body, transforming and surrounding the latter with the donor's benevolence. In effect, the wearer is enveloped by the gift, absorbed into and surrounded by it and all it stands for; he is physically marked as connected to the donor. Furthermore, as an often-expensive gift, the item of clothing can increase the individual's personal wealth.

It is this sense of individuality that makes a gift of clothing unsuitable within democratic Athenian literature, for it has the potential to put the individual above his peers and aligns him with another single person, rather than the community. Clothing can only be worn by one individual at a time and thus by its very nature could not benefit the community as a whole. During this period, individual gifts became easy to (mis)construe as bribes and had no place in the democratic ideal; indeed private gift-giving between those who were part of the public institutions of Athens even appears to have been prohibited.[33] Set against this context it is easy to see how the personal gifts of clothing had no positive place within the writings of Classical Athens; they are designed to connect the wearer closely with the giver only, increase personal rather than collective wealth, and above all can make the wearer stand out from the crowd. Thus their use as weapons of murder within the literature of this period may not only be connected with males anxieties about feminine spheres of influence, but may have suggested the negative connotations, taken to the extreme, of accepting individual clothing gifts within the 'real' male political domain.[34]

The performance contexts within religious festivals of these plays could also point towards destructive garment gifts as a platform for addressing apprehensions about the relationship the *polis* had to its divine protector. Gifts to the *polis* as a whole were welcome, as they could not enhance the reputation of one person above the rest. While they elicited a negative and suspicious response when given to an individual, they played an important role in attempting to maintain a beneficial relationship for the collective *polis* with its gods. Indeed garments and textiles, almost always made by the women of the *polis*, formed part of the gifts given to the gods, and dedicating wool and vestments, as well as clothing the statues, was an important method of maintaining harmony between the divinity and the *polis*.[35] These items often appear in the literature to have been created in response to a situation that appeared to endanger the city; the gifting of a textile that symbolised cohesion and integration was a particularly suitable way to express the hopes and desires of the *polis*.[36] In both society and literature during this period, clothing gifts were one of the locations upon which social anxieties could be expressed.

Away from Athens, presents of garments appear to have maintained their Homeric place in the relationships between the elite members of other Greek city-states during this period. Although the nature of the evidence is problematic, it appears that these items had symbolical value in these places precisely because of the personal and distinguishing qualities that had sat uneasily with democratic society. Furthermore, the evidence from all the periods covered in this chapter suggests that clothing gifts had worth within the literature of monarchical and oligarchic societies of the ancient world in particular precisely because of these attributes. It is interesting to see that Plutarch thought that in Spartan society, which was hierarchical and ruled by kings, there was a place for clothing gifts given specifically to differentiate (and restrict access to) a particular group of the elite. He writes that Agesilaus II (444–360 BCE) gave a cloak (χλαῖνα) to those he made members of the Spartan *gerousia* 'in order to honour and exalt the dignity of their office' (ἐκ δὲ τούτων τιμᾶν δοκῶν καὶ μεγαλύνειν τὸ ἀξίωμα τῆς ἐκείνων ἀρχῆς), thus visibly marking out their special status within society.[37] That such clothing was considered to enhance the prestige of both the wearer and the donor is suggested by Plutarch's comment that Agesilaus 'was, unawares, increasing his own influence and adding to the power of the king a greatness which was conceded out of good-will towards him' (ἐλάνθανεν αὔξων τὴν ἑαυτοῦ δύναμιν καὶ τῇ βασιλείᾳ προστιθέμενος μέγεθος ἐκ τῆς πρὸς αὐτὸν εὐνοίας συγχωρούμενον) because he had given a gift that was valuable as both an economic and a social asset. It is not clear, however, whether this was actually practised in Sparta, or was suggested by Plutarch's own contemporary context. Whether 'real' or not, however, Plutarch's inclusion of this tale suggests that it continued to have culturally recognisable features for his own audience, which evoked ideas about the delegation of authority, political relationships, and reciprocity. These characteristics, which may have resonated with the Roman customs of Plutarch's time, had parallels with Persian[38] and later Hellenistic practices (which were also monarchical or oligarchic societies), where it had developed into a system enabling the recognition of those few members of society who derived their authority from a central figure of power.

1.3 The Hellenistic period

Many of these Hellenistic and Roman customs derived from practices that appear to have been introduced by Alexander and are detailed in the sources for the period.[39] While the majority of these are from the later Roman period, their use of authors contemporary to Alexander and the commonality of many narrative events of his life enables some understanding of both the social practice and literary use of clothing gifts within this earlier period. It is of particular interest, therefore, that the more 'positive' attitudes to clothing gifts encountered in Homeric epics make a return appearance in the sources. The individuality of clothing, outlined above, is once again significant here, for during this period the desire to advertise one's standing in relation to the small group of the ruling elite seems to have become a consistent avenue to power for others outside the royal house. Clothing, particularly those items dyed purple, seems to have distinguished the officials and court of Alexander and his Hellenistic successors to such an extent that later Latin authors used *purpurati* to refer to them. This blurring of social reality and literary shorthand enabled audiences to understand quickly the status of those discussed in the sources, for this rare and extremely expensive shade of purple is restricted only to this set of people in the literature, just as it seems to have been in that period.[40] Furthermore, many of these items are presented as gifts from Alexander in the sources; Alexander is said to have appropriated purple garments from various Ionian cities, particularly Chios, especially for the purpose of dressing his friends in garments dyed with this particular colour.[41] In the so-called 'vulgate' tradition of the histories of Alexander, these items are among other practices which signify Alexander's descent into barbarian luxury due to his adoption of Archaemenid court customs; distributing such gifts helped to spread this corrupting influence further through the Macedonian ranks.[42]

Yet, as A.B. Bosworth has highlighted, the purple garments were also a way for Alexander to keep 'Persians and Macedonians distinct and the Macedonians ... in a privileged position'.[43] The personal and portable nature of clothing enabled these gifts to emphasise the special relationship the wearer had with their royal donor and also highlighted their association with his new style of authority and their own participation within it. Distinctive clothing allowed the wearer the ability to advertise his connection with Alexander in a way that other gift items (such as money, drinking vessels, etc.) were not able to do in such a public fashion; these garments were not just for private occasions, and in being written about, they would be 'viewed' by more than just the chosen few. Because only certain people received such items, these clothing gifts functioned in social and literary reality to both allow and restrict access to certain levels of society. They were given to visibly mark out and separate from others a special minority thought worthy to wear such important clothing, fitting into wider practices that increasingly restricted access to Alexander, while also echoing later uses of clothing gifts. Thus, these items became social and literary markers of those close to Alexander through a double origin – as a gift from Alexander and an item strongly connected with the Persian expedition on which they had accompanied him – and this is signified in the histories through *purpurati*.

However it was not just Alexander's companions who were felt to be worthy of distinguished clothing. The practice of investing vassal kings such as Abdalonymus in Sidon with royal insignia (including purple garments), which also has equivalences in the Roman period and continues to be important in Late Antiquity, was either initiated by Alexander or copied by him from the Persian kings.[44] Such procedures demonstrate that gifts of clothing could be understood well enough across cultural boundaries to ensure that a visual connection to Macedonia or the Hellenistic kingdoms was also beneficial and recognisable to those outside its boundaries. Associating themselves with a greater power theoretically gave these vassal kings (and their people) a measure of protection from hostile neighbours through the threat of external support, and the individual nature of clothing symbolised the personal element of the relationship between the two rulers. It was through this particular king alone that the relationship had been established, it was through him that it would be maintained; furthermore, he had the clothes to prove this.

Yet for Alexander's historians this episode, which saw Abdalonymus given clothing gifts as part of his investiture as a new ruler, became something more. The transformation of a distant heir to the throne of Sidon from scraping out a living tending garden-plots dressed in a cheap rag, to royal robes and the title of king and friend (φίλος 'philos') of Alexander, was clearly an attractive story, and Curtius Rufus, Diodorus Siculus, and Plutarch make the most of it. In Curtius Rufus' version the gift of lavish royal robes is the contrast between the new king's current lifestyle with his prospective one; indeed, like the baptised discussed in Chapter 4, he must wash away the dirt of his previous existence before assuming the clothes of his new life.[45] Furthermore, Alexander's good judgment and largess can be shown through his acceptance and reward of the humble character brought before him as king. Finally Alexander's willingness to ignore the opinion of the richest of Sidon regarding Abdalonymus contrasts with the weakness of the previous ruler of the city. He had surrendered the town on this account, despite his own support of Darius, and he had been deposed by Alexander as a result.[46] Perhaps based on a common interpretation, for Diodorus Siculus and Plutarch the transformative power of clothing allowed for a brief philosophical digression. It became an opportunity to moralise that 'thus does shifting Fortune create kings, change their raiment, and quickly and easily alter the status of men who expect nothing of the sort, and do not even hope for it', and, for Plutarch in particular, it suited an overall desire to show Alexander as a philosopher in practice.[47] For the historians of Alexander, then, this investiture at Sidon presents an opening to depict something more than simply the elevation of a new king: the donation of garments, and their ability to transform a body, becomes instead an occasion to discuss the nature of fortune and further their characterisations of Alexander. The purple clothing gifts, while honouring the recipient, thus reflect more brilliantly on the donor, and this is a narrative device that would have been recognisable in Late Antiquity.

Clothing gifts could also be used as a narrative device by Alexander himself within the histories; Arrian's Alexander, for example, utilises this tool during the mutiny at Opis in 324 BCE. Here, Alexander needs only to employ the memory of the garment gifts, rather than the clothes themselves, to remind the mutinying Macedonians of their duty to himself as the son of Philip and persuade his audience to a certain course of action. Echoing Homeric usage of clothing as a civilising and humanising force in the *Odyssey*, he recalls the gifts of cloaks Philip gave to his people, which transformed them from helpless sheepskin-wearing farmers, barely distinguishable from the sheep they herded, into a civilised and city dwelling people who were no longer threatened by their neighbours.[48] Alexander's appeal to the deeds done by both himself and his father was successful, but it can also be seen that the messages contained within gift-giving and clothing were controlled and adapted to suit the specific needs of ancient authors and their protagonists. Here Arrian's Alexander combines the symbolism of clothing as a civilising force, with the obligations that become attached to the receiver in the practice of gift-giving, for '[Philip] gave you cloaks to wear instead of sheepskins (χλαμύδας μὲν ὑμῖν ἀντὶ τῶν διφθερῶν φορεῖν ἔδωκεν) . . . He made you city-dwellers and civilised you with good laws and customs (πόλεών τε οἰκήτορας ἀπέφηνε καὶ νόμοις καὶ ἔθεσι χρηστοῖς ἐκόσμησεν). . .'. He does this in order to highlight that the Macedonians owe a debt of gratitude by proxy to the son of the man who effectively brought them into the human race with (among other things) his gifts of cloaks.[49] Clothing, therefore, functions in this speech to explore the relationship between civilised man and untamed nature and the bond between the people and their ruler, as well as their status vis-à-vis their enemies and neighbours.

For Alexander and his authors, then, gifts of clothing had special historical and social applications that could then be utilised to illustrate further messages about the king in the literature surrounding him. This could also apply to those who succeeded him. Plutarch, for example, includes the story that in 321 BCE Alexander's secretary, Eumenes of Cardia, gave clothing to his Macedonian bodyguard, who had volunteered to protect him when letters had been scattered in the camp offering a hundred talents and honours to any who would kill him. These garments marked them above others within the army and were items particularly associated with the honour a king bestowed on his friends (τιμὰς ἠγάπων παρ' αὐτοῦ λαμβάνοντες ἃς οἱ φίλοι παρὰ τῶν βασιλέων). These were purple caps and military cloaks (ἐξῆν γὰρ Εὐμενεῖ καὶ καυσίας ἁλουργεῖς καὶ χλαμύδας διανέμειν), 'a gift of royalty among Macedonians' (ἥτις ἦν δωρεὰ βασιλικωτάτη παρὰ Μακεδόσι).[50] As with those who received purple garments from Alexander, both the colour and the clothing items visually designated the receiver as part of a specific, honoured group of authority figures within Macedonian society, Alexander's *philoi*, who had also received special garments. Although valuable in economic terms, their cultural significance was worth more, and bound the wearers to the donor with ties of gratitude and pride. The inclusion of these details by Plutarch, furthermore, suggests that this would have been recognised by his own audience, for whom purple was also a luxury good with connotations of royalty, primarily due to its use in the Hellenistic period.

These gifts are functioning within the text (and perhaps the historical reality) not only to demonstrate the benefits received by those who remained loyal. In fact, the context implies that Eumenes had deliberately chosen to bestow this particular gift at this time because its strong associations with the Macedonian royal house served to bolster his own position and authority among his troops.

In presenting such items, which were 'a gift of royalty among Macedonians', while at war with other members of Alexander's court, Eumenes can clearly be seen to be associating himself with the legitimate Macedonian rulers through this practice, participating in their authority, although not in order to take the throne himself. Plutarch's claim that he was 'allowed to distribute' (ἐξῆν γὰρ Εὐμενεῖ . . . διανέμειν) these garments suggests rather that clothing gifts are being used to demonstrate he is acting on behalf of Alexander's son and legitimate successor. He has therefore been empowered to distribute a gift normally bestowed by the king, and it can be seen that the original associations inherent in these very specific gifts of clothing were being manipulated to imply that those troops who are under Eumenes' command, and in particular those who have been given the garments, are the only ones fighting for Alexander's legacy. This episode may be a literary construct of Plutarch's rather than a reality of the time, but it is no less potent for that. In a period where it was unclear who was the heir to Alexander's authority, Eumenes' clothing gifts function as compelling visual rhetoric for either his audience or Plutarch's. As will be seen in the following chapters, this is strikingly echoed in late antique practice when the heirs to political and religious power were not always immediately obvious during a similar period of deep uncertainty.

1.4 The Roman Republic and the transition to empire

Indeed, it appears that clothing gifts were particularly useful literary devices for authors narrating times of insecurity, even if they were living in a relatively peaceful era themselves, and it is likely that this is because they reflected recognisable historical social practices. In the literary accounts of the Second Punic War given by Livy (who lived through the anxious period of the Later Republic and wrote under Augustus), there appears to be a concern with gifts of clothing given to foreign, specifically African, potentates.[51] As a crucial time in Rome's history it is perhaps significant that clothing is employed as the present of choice in literature and historical reality to establish, remind, and maintain these allegiances, particularly as they are given exclusively to those rulers who are close to Carthage and therefore of vital strategic importance. Livy reports that in 210 BCE envoys to King Syphax of Numidia were given a *toga et tunica purpurea* to present to the king, as a reward for his successes over the Carthaginians, with instructions to then continue on and give a *toga praetexta* to each of the other African rulers friendly to Rome, including Cleopatra and Ptolemy in Egypt.[52] Unfortunately, Syphax's clothing gift did not produce a lasting effect: by 201 BCE he had died a prisoner in Italy, having gone over to Carthage and expelled Masinissa, King of the Massylii from his kingdom. Once won over to the side of the Romans, Masinissa himself received part of Syphax's kingdoms after the latter's death as part of a peace treaty, and during 200 BCE he also received lavish clothing – *toga purpurea et palmata tunica . . . toga praetexta* – together with a request for his cavalry.[53] The Roman presents were visually related to the insignia of curule magistracies and Roman kingship;[54] therefore it implies that receivers such as Syphax and Masinissa would be recognised outside of the borders of the Republic (and so by the Carthaginians they came into contact with) as having a connection with Roman power through their clothing.

Yet it was also important for the audience (both Livy's and those of the earlier period he describes), for it dressed these external rulers up in familiar visual markers of authority, allowing both their status and their position as those who were to aid the Romans to be easily understandable. Just as Odysseus at the beginning of the chapter was transformed by the clothes which his host was obliged to provide and became the person and the status such items represent, so the receivers of the Roman clothing became associated in the literature with the authority these garments symbolised. Furthermore, it presented the Romans as creating a buffer of friendly rulers around Carthage, using specifically Roman clothing to project visually how far from Rome (and how close to Carthage) their power could extend. In a period of uncertainty, this suggested a reassuring continuance of Roman influence and domination in both the literature and historical reality, and it was a device that was employed to full effect during Late Antiquity.

A later period of uncertainty for the Republic appears to have prompted another desire to gift a garment, although the chronological distance and nature of the source for this event makes its historicity uncertain. Yet for Phlegon of Tralles, a freedman of Hadrian living in the comparatively stable early second century CE, and his audience, a veneer of believability is important within his *Book of Marvels* for '[i]n paradoxography [recordings of unusual phenomena] the incredible has to be true, or at least believable as truth, otherwise there is no point'.[55] Thus, it is interesting that he includes a tale from the fraught period of the Gracchi that is concerned with gifts of clothing. In 125 BCE, a consultation of the Sibylline oracle required the Romans to produce decorated garments (ὑφάσματα ποικίλα) for the goddess Persephone in order to avert civil war; as with many of the examples discussed in this chapter, dissension had to be countered with what was whole and complete.[56] The finished textile served as an important figurative binding of the incongruent elements within Roman society; in Rome, as in the Classical *polis*, gifts of garments adorned the statues of the gods, and they were often woven in order to satisfy the demands of an oracle to prevent disaster.[57] Indeed, it is seen by Scheid and Svenbro as a significant factor in the appeasement of the gods, ensuring the reestablishment of social unity. Thus, it seems that a symbolic 'political . . . garment' was present within Roman discourse, early and late, which had an important and continuing rhetorical function to describe and negotiate the bonds between a city, its people, and its gods.[58] Furthermore, this episode reflects Phlegon's work as a whole, which, with its tales of ghosts, vampire brides, and births of androgynous children (the latter of which prompted the above consultation of the oracle), appears as an attempt to catalogue and thus bring under control that which was out of place in the fabric of society. A gift of clothing that may have had historical importance in the Republic, then, becomes in the hands of the author of the Early Empire a metaphor for his own literary intent.

Gifts of clothing were also put to use by Republic authors themselves to discuss uncertainty. During this period and the Early Empire, such items can be found working to debate and explain types of relationships in literary deliberations on patrons and clients.[59] Cicero, for example, in *Laelius de amicitia*, has Gaius Laelius (cos. 140 BCE) recall that Cato used to make the connection between textile terminology and the ideal patron–client relationship, while addressing the desirability of an amicable end to the association over a violent one:[60]

> Therefore the ties of such friendships should be sundered by a gradual relaxation of intimacy, and, as I have heard that Cato used to say, 'They should be unravelled rather than ripped apart (*dissuendae magis quam discindendae*)', unless there has been some outbreak of utterly unbearable wrongdoing ... (*Laelius de amicitia*, 21 [76])

That Cato uses this metaphor lends it a certain amount of *gravitas* in the context, and this is enhanced by Laelius' own qualities of knowledge and wisdom. Furthermore, it may be a way for Cicero to draw attention to his other work written in a similar style and around the same time, the *Cato Maior*, through the reference to Cato.[61] Most importantly for this discussion, however, is that Laelius' (and Cicero's) willingness to employ a weaving metaphor implies that some members of Roman society saw how apt this literary device was for describing the patron–client relationship.[62] It may be that the phonetic similarity between *amicitia*, 'friendship' and *amicus*, 'friend', with *amicire* 'to clothe', and *amictus* '(manner of) dress, clothing', suggested this concept, although they are not etymologically linked. However, the idea that clothing and textiles symbolise the interweaving of different elements to produce a harmonious society also seems to be at play here, as the image suggests the unbinding of an intertwined patron and client, a relationship that was of great importance to the continued *concordia* and social cohesion of Roman society.

Patron–client clothing gifts were not always positive experiences in the literature of the Republic. Writing during the transition from Republic to empire, Horace provides evidence that garments could also be used in poetry as part of a negative gift exchange, where one party explicitly seeks to damage the fortune and reputation of the other:[63] 'If he wished to harm someone, Eutrapelus gave him precious clothes (*Eutrapelus cuicumque nocere volebat/vestimenta dabat pretiosa*)'.[64] Eutrapelus gives gifts of expensive clothing in order to financially ruin his enemies; they struggle to maintain the lifestyle expectations their new clothes have created for them. Because clothes were transformative visual markers of status, particularly economic status in antiquity, these fine tunics may have altered their wearer into a rich man, but unfortunately this change is only dress deep. The happy man puts on new plans because of his beautiful clothes (*beatus enim iam/cum pulchris tunicis sumet nova consilia*),[65] acts in a way expected from dressing in such a manner (sleeping late, getting into debt by spending his money on prostitutes) and is promptly ruined by his costume, ending as a gladiator or driving a grocer's cart for hire; his new clothing has over-written his reality. For Horace, literary clothing gifts suggested comedic situations, but it can also be seen that they provided a space on which to discuss anxieties about access to, and the correct display and use of, *luxuria* and wealth in the culture of the Late Republic. They were additionally ways to voice concerns surrounding visualising and appropriating identity and new statuses, and the dependent and sometimes detrimental relationship between a client and his patron.

1.5 The Early Empire: Case study – Martial

The development of these ideas of clothing within the practice of gift exchange continued into and beyond the Early Empire and during this period literary clothing gifts worked in contexts both familiar and different to those discussed in the previous sections. The patron–client relationship appears to have continued functioning in a similar way to that of the Roman Republic, centred on the elite, although the emperor and those close to him increasingly became the focus of patronage, with the emperor portraying himself as a universal patron. One of the ways authors and the emperor could present him in this role was during the Saturnalia, a holiday which included the giving of gifts by patrons to their clients.[66] The continuing importance of clothing within this relationship can be seen in Suetonius' catalogue of presents Augustus gave out during this festival, where clothing is listed first. That this item was costly is inferred by its heading an inventory made up of valuable objects like gold, ancient coinage, and silver.[67] However, like Priam's ransom and Plato's cloth, the clothing may have also served to symbolise the protection and shelter Augustus' principate was to provide for the citizens of Rome, as well as the peace and harmony he had finally brought after the civil wars of the Late Republic.

Clothing gifts continue to make an appearance within the context of this relationship during the early Imperial period although, as in the Republic, it is not always the positive aspects which are on show. In his writings, particularly the *De Beneficiis*, Seneca sees clothing as a defective gift, because it is quickly used up.[68] The role of clothing as a visual memory aid here works with the idea that garments are 'soon worn out' (*brevis deterat*) to discuss the concerns felt by patrons that their generosity does not live long enough in the minds of their clients.[69] As will be seen in the case study below, this statement is reminiscent of Martial's portrayal of clothing gifts, for it perhaps implies that giving a durable object prevents a client from returning too frequently to be a drain on the patron's resources.

Seneca's comment suggests the possibility of a shift in the way gifts of clothing are presented in literature and thought of in society during the Early Empire, and this is borne out in more detail by Martial. Particularly within the context of the patron–client relationship, clothing gifts become more associated with the discussion of problematic elements in social relationships, and not just within times of uncertainty. This is undoubtedly the case within the specific context of Martial's poems, as such gifts no longer enhance the prestige of the wearer, as they did in earlier Greek contexts, but instead are used by the poet to show his degradation.[70] He inverts the expectations that had accompanied giving particular types of garment in these earlier periods to demonstrate the distance between these notions and 'reality'.[71] The nature of these poems as satire on early imperial society implies that, although exaggerated, many of the practices he addresses were familiar and common to his audience. As a result, when one of the main informants about the relationship between patrons and clients in the Early Empire appears to be preoccupied with gift-giving in general (or more usually, the disappointed hopes of gift-receiving), it should be seen as a comment on a significant social act.[72]

The hopes and frustrations of the shabby poet-client persona of Martial's epigrams,[73] therefore, obligingly allow for an insight into what donations a client may appropriately have expected from his patron(s). As noted in the Introduction, scholars have long understood that gift-giving was integral to the establishment and maintenance of friendships between Roman patrons and clients — those loaded words which are inadequate for translating the complexities involved in *amicitia*, *patronus*, and *cliens*.[74] In the following section, *cliens* has been translated mainly as 'client' and occasionally as 'protégé', *patronus* as 'patron', and *amicus* and *amicitia* as 'friend' and 'friendship' respectively. 'Client' has been favoured above 'protégé' as it appears more suited to Martial's situation as he describes it. His demands for gifts place him in an inferior position by implication, although the reality may have been that his patrons were on a similar social level to him. It should be noted, however, that Martial never uses *patronus* or *cliens* to refer to his own self or those he looks to for reward. It is likely he found *cliens* degrading when applied to himself and so he uses the language of *amicitia*, along with, for example, *rex* or *sodales* in varying degrees of sarcasm or sobriety, to describe this relationship.[75] It should also be made clear that women could be patrons as well; Martial claims that he himself had one called Marcella, who provided him with a villa in Bilbilis.[76] As gifts of clothing come almost from exclusively male patrons, however, it will be this relationship that will be explored.[77]

While gifts of money are naturally his primary concern — they are arguably the most useful and certainly the most common donation in his corpus outside the *Xenia* and *Apophoreta* — property, roof tiles, and a carriage also make an appearance.[78] Yet it is gifts of clothing that appear in over five per cent of the epigrams, and this is without including the 29 poems about garment presents in the *Apophoreta*.[79] Indeed, it is because Martial's corpus provides one of the greatest bodies of evidence for the function of clothing gifts in literature that the detailed analysis of his work that follows is justified. His poems demonstrate a mid-point between the literary uses of this practice in the periods already discussed, and those in Late Antiquity, which will be the focus of subsequent chapters. While the evidence he provides demonstrates a continuity with previous customs, it also shows that clothing gifts could be subverted and used for the wearer's own gains, and that they were, furthermore, canvasses for commenting on the problematic nature of the relationship between giver and receiver. This anticipates the discussion of clothing gifts found in late antique literature and, as will be examined in later chapters, these items become sites of debate about relationships between the empire and its foreign neighbours, as well as between those who live within its boundaries. His poems, therefore, utilise garment giving in both traditional and unexpected ways, and bring together many of the ideas surrounding clothing and gifts that have been and will be examined in these pages.

It has been seen previously that clothing was a valuable asset, in both economic and social terms.[80] Martial claims some items were worth thousands of sesterces, although typically these belong to other people,[81] and this continues to hold true in the late antique period – an important factor behind its presentation to foreign dignitaries in the diplomatic contexts discussed in Chapter 2. Even if poetic exaggeration is allowed, it is still clear that some garments were costly during the period Martial in which was living, and this aspect has been the main focus of modern scholars when discussing clothing gifts in his work.[82] However, simply seeing such items in terms of increasing personal wealth undervalues the symbolic and social currency clothing has; and it is by examining garments in this context that the suitability of such pieces as gifts and as literary devices becomes fully apparent.

For Rome's status-conscious society (as in all periods of history) clothing functioned as a visual reference for the onlooker to assess the wearer's self and personal worth, their social and economic value, their gender and position in the life cycle, their political power and occupation, and even their religious affiliations. In Martial's work, the ostentatious figures who scuttle through the epigrams often draw attention to their *gausapinae* and *lacernae* to emphasise not only their wealth, but their moral and social status.[83] Similar to the imperial *chlamys*, consular *trabea*, and bishop's *pallium*, which will be discussed in subsequent chapters, as outer layers these garments (and their colours) were, of course, highly visible and therefore were a particularly appropriate and, moreover, rapid way of demonstrating a person's wealth. Martial's frequent references to the colours of clothes shows that certain hues could increase the value of an item considerably[84] or that some colours were considered cheap and common (such as blues and greens because they were easy to manufacture).[85] His observations imply that some Romans were able (or at least pretended they were able) to differentiate the gradations of shades of, for example, purple, distinguishing a Tyrian cloak from one dyed with *coccinus*.[86] The implication was that, for the discerning viewer, the quality of a garment could serve as an index of the wearer's personal wealth.

In addition, in society and literature colours could communicate the wearer's moral or even political agenda:[87]

> That lover of sad *lacernae*, who goes about in Baetic [wool] or ash grey, thinks those who wear red unmanly, and calls amethyst-hued clothes for women; though he praises and wears natural things and always values sombre colours, his morals are green. (1.96.4–9)[88]

Dark colours were used to show *gravitas*, the steady, sober character important for the senatorial elite.[89] It helped to justify their predominance in society, as it showed that they could use their position and power responsibly and wisely and did not waste their wealth on frivolities like brightly coloured cloth, a contrast to Late Antiquity where the clothing of officials was often highly decorative. In the Early Empire, greens and yellows, because they were thought of as feminine colours, when worn by a man implied that he had the 'feminine' traits of immorality, lustfulness, and irrationality (hence 'his morals are green'). This was not only by association, but because a man was suspect who deliberately sought to cover his masculinity by dressing in feminine colours.[90]

Differing fabrics could also underline the wearer's wealth and morality; silk was more costly than wool because rarer, and was therefore the most coveted of textile fibres in antiquity, a taste which continued into the Later Empire.[91] Thus, when seen by an onlooker it could quickly establish its owner as wealthy; the key was moderation, however; too much silk implied a lustful, 'soft' nature, and was associated with the decadent East.[92] Martial may be parodying these status symbols; but, nonetheless, as in the Hellenistic and earlier Roman periods, it appears that certain, well-made items may have been associated with a particular class and so would have been a visual marker of status, and this is borne out in the epigrams that mock those who unsuccessfully try to usurp them. The *lacerna*, for example, seems to be particularly associated with the *equites* in his epigrams.[93] They certainly appear on the shoulders or in the presence of the *equites* more than any other garment (except perhaps the toga) in Martial's work, while the quality of the garment often reveals the origins of the owner – too fine a *lacerna* gave the wearer away as not being a 'true' *eques*. The branded slave, in 2.29, who regardless of his ability to meet the property qualification tries to cover his past with beauty patches and lavish clothes, and the freedman in his *lacerna*, in 5.8, who is ejected from the equestrian seats at the theatre, both learn to their humiliation – and the poet-persona's delight – that in the literary world clothing conceals only the body not the background of a man, a sentiment echoed in later Christian literature.[94] It can be seen, then, that clothing could work as currency in establishing the moral and social position of its wearers within society, and served to broadcast their wealth to observers, and this was exploited by ancient writers. Cloth was always valuable within society as a whole, not only because of its material worth, but because of its cultural importance as an indicator of status.[95] To give such a gift, therefore, was to dress up and transform the recipient with complex markers of social identity, and in the later period this was developed by authors to examine ideas of authority.

Receiving an expensive item of clothing in a patron–client situation was a particular distinction, then, because it could over-write the wearer's normal status by enhancing their prestige, which was of vital importance in Roman society.[96] In fact this may have been a means for some clients to access luxury goods (and the social capital that went with such items) otherwise unavailable to them. In the satirical literature, this is not necessarily positive, however: the provision of luxury clothing seems to be the beginning of a slippery slope for the client whose dress creates in the viewer expectations he cannot meet. One of Martial's epigrams states that some pawned their jewellery to keep up appearances,[97] and this echoes the predicament in which Horace placed the recipient of Eutrapelus' clothing gifts, discussed above. In order to maintain a lifestyle that is beyond his own means, the client then must look again to his patron to supply it for him, and this establishes the latter as the one to whom the client must turn for such goods. However, to give in to this demand frequently would be expensive for the patron, and so he does not offer this service to all and sundry or every time. In his reticent behaviour, the patron is thus controlling distribution,[98] and as such is a performing a type of social control. The patron retains his clients, keeping them in an inferior position as they rely on their patron to provide them with luxuries they cannot afford, but which are important to their public appearance and status, while the prospect that he may acquiesce to this desire for special goods creates expectations in the client and leads to repeated demands. As will be seen in Chapter 2, this type of control continues to be used in Late Antiquity on an international scale, in the empire's dealings with foreign allies and enemies, and it is a narrative exploited by the writers of the period. Whereas these items were employed by authors during this later period to cover up the disparity between the perception, based on historical tradition, of a strong empire and the actuality of its lessened military capabilities, for Martial, clothing gifts were instead a way to broadcast the tensions dependence on patrons created for clients.

Martial's frequent petitions, despite his almost universal disappointment in achieving his requests, are more readily understandable when placed into this context of control, for given how unsuccessful Martial is in his poems, his repeated demands otherwise seem surprising. Out of over 30 poems containing references to clothing, he records only three instances of his demands for garments being satisfied, at 8.28, 10.73, and 12.36, yet he continues to solicit his patrons only to be disappointed in his hopes. So why does the poet-persona persist in asking for such gifts? On the strength of other poems in Martial's corpus, garments appear to have been a fairly common present, and they were certainly part of the Saturnalia, the festival which, as has been noted above, seems to have been associated with patronage and the exchange of gifts.[99] In the *Apophoreta*, Martial dedicates 30 poems to clothing items that could be given as presents; and other evidence from outside the epigrams shows that this gift was not particular to Martial's poems. As part of this festival (and the patron–client relationship as a whole), therefore, clothing appears as a customary, and sometimes expensive, gift,[100] which would justify his recurring expectations. Thus, Martial's repetitious requests deliberately play on the fact that such items were relatively commonplace presents to emphasise his lack of receipt, and emphasising this serves to highlight the disparity between the ideal and the 'reality' of patronage.

The suggestion that clothing was a fairly typical gift to give to a client probably meant that these items were not always expensive luxury goods otherwise unavailable to the client. This did not mean lower-value garment gifts were unappreciated by their recipients, however. In addition to food and shelter, clothing was deemed one of life's necessities, and both Martial and Juvenal view garments, and particularly the toga, as part of their lists of essentials for civilised living.[101] One of the reasons for this was that on a practical level the toga was vital for enabling male citizens to participate in Roman public life. Yet it also symbolised their civilisation and inclusion within the community, while simultaneously dividing them from those who were *peregrini*, *barbari*, and *alieni* – natural inhabitants of the untamed lands beyond the empire's influence.[102] The client was expected to dress in a toga when he called on his patron. Indeed, the garment was such an integral part of a client's identity that the word is used in both Martial and Juvenal as a substitute term to represent the *cliens* and his duties, although most often with a negative connotation through the use of the diminutive *togula*, as Michelle George has shown.[103] However, although longer-lasting than that other necessity, food, clothing did eventually wear out with repeated use, even after patching, and Martial's implications about his heavy duties suggests there was an occasional need to replace such items, which Seneca's comments discussed earlier also reinforce. While important, it therefore could have been a significant demand on income for some, and so it is understandable that a client would look to his patron to supply this garment, which was integral to a client's ability to be a client. The high repetition of appeals for Martial's patrons to supply him with such objects (which are often included alongside petitions for food in his epigrams), implies that the poet at least felt that this should be so. Here again clothing is being used to set up a contrast between the ideal and 'real' patron–client relationship, and although he does not make this explicit, his belief that part of a patron's duty was to provide his client with clothing, echoes the expectations a guest would have had of his Homeric host.[104]

However, while Martial may presume this, his indignant tone and his failure to receive clothing gifts in the majority of his poems also hints at real-world practice, where more often than not the client was expected to buy his own toga out of his *sportula*, the dole given out by patrons.[105] This differs from the view of Koen Verboven who claims that the toga was the standard gift of patrons to their clients.[106] While this is an attractive argument in light of the current discussion (as it would establish the relationship by binding the recipient through gift-giving), there seems little evidence of this practice in the sources. Rather, these leave it unclear as to how often a patron provided a toga to his client: both Martial and Juvenal list the garment as one of life's necessities that has to be bought with the *sportula*,[107] and therefore imply instead that this was the usual means of acquiring one. A good toga could be an expensive garment to buy and maintain for some clients: Martial claims a new one could cost the same as a slave, and indeed it appears that some could only pay for the item in instalments (*pro togula debes*).[108] Moreover, depending on how demanding his duties were (very, according to Martial and Juvenal)[109] it would have worn out over time. It may have been a considerable purchase for some clients, therefore, and even if there were people, such as clothing merchants or, more likely, relatives, servants, or slaves, who could sell, make, or repair clothes, this would still incur an expense for the owner.[110]

Martial's demands should be seen as part of the wider narrative surrounding clothing gifts, yet to provide a client with an expensive item of clothing would have demonstrated a patron's unusual generosity (as well as giving his client the benefit of an unlooked for increase in the latter's spending money).[111] Because of its associations with patronage, however, to give a toga in particular connected the patron with the qualities that underpinned *amicitia*: *liberalitas*, *gratia*, *fides*, and *amor* or *benevolentia*.[112] Yet to give any clothing item meant the patron could expect to be viewed as a *homo liberalis* who was primarily concerned with demonstrating his generosity, in order to enhance his social status – 'noblesse oblige'–[113] and Martial's poet-persona takes advantage of this reflection on reputation to ask for new clothing. In 6.82, for example, he laments that, in order to save the reputation of his patron, Rufus, Martial has had to explain away his *mala lacerna* by slighting his own poetic abilities (*sum malus poeta*), a drastic action which can only be repaid by new good *lacernae* (*Hoc ne saepius accidat poetae, /mittas, Rufe, mihi bonas lacernas*). By relieving a client of the expense of buying clothing, the patron could expect a gift appropriate to that individual's means in return, due to the reciprocal nature of gift-giving.[114] The obligations of the client are thus doubly reinforced, for he had to reciprocate his patron's *beneficia*, not only because it was expected of him as part of his duties, but also because of the conventions surrounding gift-exchange.[115] To provide a client with a toga (or any other clothing for that matter) thus demonstrates a patron's generosity and, reminiscent of Hellenistic practice, binds the receiver to the donor through this generosity and the expectation of reciprocation, while the manufacture of clothing makes the garment gift a potent symbol of these ties in both society and literature. As will be seen in subsequent chapters, these are concepts that also lie beneath late antique discussions of imperial patrons such as the Emperor Gratian and the wealthy laity who supported the Church.

Furthermore, in the expected scheme of this relationship, gift-giving would form an important part of this type of poetry because it specifically set up the premise for the poem; the epigram exists because the patron has been generous, and this is his reward (see further below). In giving such a gift the patron could therefore anticipate having his own wealth and generous behaviour reflected back at him, particularly as clients were apparently often all too willing to publicise that their clothing had been a present from someone else. In fact, it appears that this may have been expected of a client as part of his repayment for his patron's benevolence. For example, although ridiculing Mancinus for boring him with tales of the gifts he receives in 4.61, Martial himself dedicates epigrams to patrons in order not only to show sufficient gratitude, but also to broadcast his patron's kindness.[116] As will be explored further below, the successful clothing gift enables Martial to behave as the perfect client in and through his work.

Acknowledging that the garment was bought by someone else minimises the client's connection with the garment,[117] and it will be seen in the case study of Chapter 3 that this is also exploited in Late Antiquity. The wealth and prestige inherent in wearing, for example, a luxurious *lacerna*, are transferred instead to the patron; the client is not the affluent one, but rather it is the patron whose wealth and reputation is enhanced.[118] Just like donations of money or property, an expensive present of clothing demonstrates that he can afford to give something of value away. He thus appears as a man of means, and in Late Antiquity this use of clothing as an indicator of hidden resources, continues to be employed in a diplomatic context to both enhance the empire's prestige and subtly to threaten its foreign neighbours. Therefore, publicising the origins of the garment serves the patron's social needs as well as, and perhaps more than, those of the client, while the latter conforms to the conventions of his role – promulgating his patron's reputation as among the great and good. The garments and Martial's poems function together to achieve the same ends, and, as will be seen in Chapters 3 and 4, this practice is reflected in a different context in late antique literature.

Furthermore, although it may seem unlikely that to the uninformed observer it was clear when the wearer was dressed in someone else's wealth, Martial alleges that he could detect when a garment was a gift.[119] This may be because such items were almost always outer layers. Like the garments that appear most often in late antique literature, the majority of the items listed as clothing for men in Martial's epigrams, and all of those catalogued in the *Apophoreta*, are outer garments (e.g. the toga, *lacerna*, *laena*).[120] This may be significant, especially when it is observed that the clothing for women in the *Apophoreta* are exclusively undergarments.[121] The implication is that men, unlike women who were never clients, needed gifts that would be visible in order to broadcast their status as presents bought with another's wealth.[122] Outer layers would be the items most noticeable, and so would obviously display this more prominently than undergarments. It may have been an effective method for emphasising the ties between a particular patron and his client to the detriment of another patron. It appears that clients could have more than one patron.[123] Yet, while gifts of food and property could flaunt the latter's wealth while reinforcing his bond to the client, food was consumed far more quickly than clothing wore out and property was not portable in the way that clothing was, so would of course not be constantly visible when the client made his appearance. Clothing, therefore, could act as a reminder of a particular patron's bond with his client,[124] but at the same time was also working to reflect the donor's wealth back at him. If the garments were obviously bought by someone else, furthermore, it would enhance the wearer with the donor's own reputation, while also serving to cover the ties the client may have had with another patron. Therefore, it may be that gifts of *lacernae* and *togae* for example, were given as a deliberate attempt to exhibit the bond between a client and a particular patron in social reality and that this could be appropriated by writers.

By bonding two parties together, Martial's clothing gifts are functioning in his poems in a similar symbolic way to those gifts examined in the previous sections, where it was suggested that the finished textile product could be symptomatic of the harmonious interweaving of disparate elements. Within this context, gifts of clothing, as completed, unified wholes, can be viewed as representing the ideal form of the patron–client relationship within Martial's epigrams, as well as in Cicero's text, so that when Martial receives a present of clothing, it can be seen as a particularly potent way of signifying that a patron understands the importance of, and is living up to, this ideal. The tangible evidence he receives in the form of a garment and the symbolic nature of cloth confirms that his patron understands and accepts their relationship. Martial then must become the perfect client in his poems, as the weaving together of these two participants is important to the smooth running of Roman society.

These poems thanking the donor are suitably grateful and, as a client was expected to do, Martial performs positive services in return for the gift. He immortalises their act of generosity,[125] and publicises their status as true *homines liberales* through his poetry. He does this by showing them as patrons of talented individuals, emphasising that these notables were cultivated, and reinforces their claims to literary awareness and intelligence through obscure, tongue-in-cheek descriptions of the whiteness of his toga,[126] an act echoed in Ausonius' thanksgiving speech discussed in Chapter 3. In doing so Martial is acting as a client should, for, in an unequal exchange relationship, the inferior party is expected to praise and honour his superior.[127] This Martial does, and not merely through transient vocal support in the forum or courts, but by emphasising their reputation and generosity in epigrams about clothing gifts which will be read by contemporaries and future generations.[128] Through the successful act of giving and receiving clothing, therefore, Martial shows that the interwoven relationship represented in the cloth is strengthened. In these poems, Martial weaves together the threads of his patron's appropriate behaviour and his own services, the perishable cloth and his immortal poems, to produce epigrams that reflect this instance of a successful and harmonious relationship.

Because his poetic talent, of course, also serves to enhance Martial's own status above those of their other clients,[129] it seems that the poet-persona Martial believes one toga is not necessarily equal to immortal fame, however. The contrast consequently leaves the patron in his debt, simultaneously implying that he should not be viewed as the lesser party and this allows him to feel well within his rights to hint at the need for a new *lacerna*.[130] Martial thus appears to use gifts of clothing as a device to discuss the wider issues of his relationship with this patron, or rather the imbalance of poetic patronage, where wealthy individuals pay material goods for immaterial fame. These tensions come to the fore in the epigrams where Martial's pleas for clothing go unanswered, because his relationships are unsuccessful and unfinished. These form the majority of the epigrams dealing with clothing gifts and contain loud criticism of the parsimony of patrons, particularly of those whom 'Martial' believes are wealthy enough to regard such an appeal as trivial.[131] Within these poems, as complete textiles that bind together differing threads, the gifts of clothing work as a reminder of the perfect patron–client relationship and allow him to play with the expectations surrounding the correct behaviour of both parties. The patron's refusal to acquiesce to Martial's demands for garments in these contexts becomes not only a refusal to satisfy the poet's needs, but stands for a rejection of the entire relationship. Thus Martial's client cannot interweave and become bound to his patron in the right way to produce the accordant relationship symbolised by the non-existent cloth.[132] To refuse to give can be 'interpreted as a relapse into hostility' or at the very least ingratitude.[133]

As a result, instead of acting as the perfect client of epigrams 8.28, 10.73, and 12.36, Martial inverts this role. As opposed to spreading their good reputation, he emphasises their hypocrisy and miserliness, portraying them as concerned with keeping as much wealth for themselves as possible, rather than distributing gifts to those who need it; his patron's behaviour encourages this licence. Such people are the opposite of liberal men, afraid to cheat the moths of a couple of rags from their clothes-presses shining with cloaks, as they gaze indolently at their freezing friend, as Naevolus does in 2.46.[134] Some of these unforthcoming patrons are shown to be preoccupied with their own clothing, or other trivial matters, therefore implying that they are more concerned with the superficial material world than with trying to educate themselves. This concern with external appearances, especially when it related to clothing, was perceived as the domain of women,[135] and so a patron who has hundreds of outfits was more female than male. By association, such men were unfit for the superior position within society; they undermined their own standing by forfeiting their *virtus* and therefore instead of immortalising their fame to enhance their reputation, he immortalises their bad qualities. In this way Martial both uses clothing to highlight his patron's hypocrisy, and through its representation as the model patron–client relationship, employs gifts of clothing to emphasise the contrast between the ideal and 'reality' of the human connections in the poems. While Martial appears to delight in emphasising this discrepancy through gifts of clothing, it will be seen that the authors of Late Antiquity employ them instead as a device to cover disparities with a blanket of unity.

In Martial's epigrams, therefore, gifts of garments function as a means of negotiating and discussing the relationship between a patron and his client; he anticipates later usage while being part of a long literary tradition that uses clothing gifts as a literary device. Within the poems, these bequests demonstrated not the client's concerns, but rather the patron's desire to publicise their wealth, morality, and status to their peers. They also stemmed not just from an altruistic concern to shelter and protect or provide something useful, but rather from a desire to enhance their own prestige by broadcasting such a wish, and these implications will be revisited in an imperial and consular context. Furthermore, in a comparable manner to the diplomatic context explored in the following chapter, the very nature of cloth as a harmonious interweaving of disparate elements made the gift of clothing a potent and appropriate endowment for a client to receive. The cloth within these poems, then, becomes a representation of the ideal patron–client relationship. By placing clothing within the framework of a patron's refusal to bestow such a gift, Martial contrasts the 'ideal' with the 'reality' of the patron–client relationship as he experiences it, and this allows the poet-persona the licence to disregard his duties as a client.

In Late Antiquity, clothing gifts continue to be spaces upon which authors negotiate the tension between these different perceptions, particularly in the context of authority. Martial uses this literary device to highlight the disparity between 'reality' and 'paradigm' in order to loudly explore, consider, and criticise his social environment. As will be seen, however, the uncertainties that surround late antique authors led to attempts to employ it instead to quietly patch over any inconsistencies between these two viewpoints.

1.6 The transition to Late Antiquity

In the centuries after Martial, clothing gifts continued to be used as rhetorical devices in literature in ways similar to those examined previously, including his own – particularly in the fourth century where the epigrammist was read widely.[136] However, while clothing may have continued to have a place within the gift-giving practices of the elite (particularly in a Christian context), in the later literature the emperor, as the ultimate patron, became particularly associated with this gift.[137] In the *Historia Augusta*, for example, the reader encounters a number of instances where the emperor is shown to be a provider of clothing, and garment gifts form part of one of the three main contexts, identified by Mary Harlow, in which dress appears in this text.[138] Echoing Augustus' dispensation of clothing at the Saturnalia, emperors such as, Hadrian, Caracalla, and Aurelian distribute largess to their subjects or household, provide clothing to their troops, or donate money to them (and the treasury) obtained through the sale of a previous 'bad' emperor's inappropriate clothing.[139] The author of the *Historia Augusta* uses clothing gifts here as a device to demonstrate that these emperors have some of the qualities usually associated with 'good' emperors like Augustus: they use the money and influence of the imperial office correctly in order to look after their subjects and the military, and are thus capable of wielding power effectively.

This is further emphasised by the author of the *Historia Augusta* in the contrast they provide to their 'bad' predecessors, who instead divert imperial resources for the selfish purpose of dressing themselves decadently and inappropriately. The 'good' emperors also became a source of clothing for officials, as the Hellenistic rulers had before, providing the appropriate costume for those entering office or to increase their wealth as befitting one of their newly appointed status, while at the same time tying those officials to that particular emperor's authority.[140] Although the later *Lives* may be fictitious, it will be seen throughout Chapters 2 and 3 that these examples reflect real fourth-century imperial practice, and were thus a literary device that held meaning for their audience. Gifts of clothing in the *Historia Augusta* (including those cited above) are also used to denote, and consequently legitimate, the appropriate or 'true' successor to imperial power, for many of the 'good' emperors receive garment gifts from their predecessors, marking them out for future authority.[141]

Emperors also continue to be the focus of foreign gift-giving practice, both externally to the world of the *Historia Augusta* (Constantine, for example, receives decorated clothing from foreign nations)[142] and within its narrative. For the author of the *Historia Augusta*, clothing gifts are particularly useful in this context to show the problematic nature of foreign allies. In the example provided by *Aurelian* 29, there is an implication that they should be treated with suspicion, for even the best imperial agents could not find the special dye that coloured the garment gift from the Persian king. Contempt for this untrustworthiness is demonstrated further in *Hadrian* 17.12, a particularly interesting instance of the symbolic importance and use of presents of garments by both emperors and authors. In this episode, the author has Hadrian employ the expensive gold-woven clothing gifts sent by Pharasmanes II to dress 300 criminals in the arena, in order to display his anger at the Iberian king's earlier refusal to pay homage to him, in 129, and his allowance of access to the Caspian Gates through his kingdom by the Alani, threatening Cappadocia in 135.[143] It is a powerful symbol that Pharasmanes' attempt to appease the emperor with lavish gifts after his actions left him diplomatically isolated[144] were seen as fit only to clothe the condemned; not only does it imply that Pharasmanes' help is suitable only for criminals, but it also brings with it death, a sentiment echoed in some of the Christian texts of Chapter 4.

Due to the problematic nature of the source, it is difficult to ascertain whether these instances of gift-giving are factual episodes within the imperial reigns; yet this is less of an issue within the premise of this study. Even if fictitious, they remain of value because they can be seen as reflecting the use of dress as a literary tool in the period in which it was written (that is, the late fourth century),[145] and this is a principal which is carried forward into the remaining chapters. While, particularly in Chapters 2 and 3, social reality certainly informs many of the examples examined in the subsequent pages and gives them meaning, in a similar way to the episodes discussed within this chapter, the historical reality of whether these gifts were physically given is of less importance than how they are then utilised within the texts. As will be seen in the following discussions, in the historical reality of Late Antiquity, for example, the emperor certainly becomes the focus of almost all elite gifts of clothing, both within the empire and without, and this is a practice which the *Historia Augusta* then plays with and reflects to further its own narrative intentions.

1.7 Conclusions

Yet, the ways in which such clothing gifts are employed within this text, as a means to discuss and debate the relationship of the elite to their emperor, and the empire to the rest of the world, have strong foundations and connections with the previous periods discussed in this chapter, and this is a thread which runs throughout the following. Thus, the use to which presentations of garments are put in the Homeric epics – for recognising relationships and obligations or to mark certain members of society in Classical and Hellenistic Greece and Early and Imperial Rome – provide late antique authors with a pre-existing cultural consciousness in which to discuss connections in a changing empire.

Furthermore, the employment of these items as spaces to explore anxieties about female agency or relationships between an *polis* and its divine protector, or a *cliens* and *patronus* in previous periods, also have their parallels in the later Roman Empire (albeit observed through a late antique perspective).

Moreover, as will be seen, the advent of Christianity and Christian notions of giving, do little to change the framework of how clothing gifts were viewed.[146] Rather, the function of these items appears to be employed within contexts that would be recognisable to a certain extent even in Homeric times, enabling new encounters to be viewed within a framework of long-established traditions. What does change in this period is the renewed connection between gifts of clothing and their importance in defining the transference of authority, which had been seen in the monarchical and oligarchic societies of earlier times. In late antique literature, this becomes the dominant function of clothing gifts and it develops as a way to attempt to settle the questions, or cover over the problems, which had appeared due to the changes in the way authority was conceived after the third century. How, when, and why this narrative device was applied by late antique authors will be the focus of the remaining chapters, which begin with a consideration of clothing gifts within the context of late antique diplomacy.

Notes

1 Although separating the history of Ancient Greece and Rome into neatly defined periods is not without problems, the chapter has been divided in this way to enable a clearer survey of the examples presented.
2 Finley (1999a), (1999b). For a bibliography of works on reciprocity and exchange in Ancient Greece see, for example, Gernet (1981); Donlan (1982); Seaford (1994); von Reden (1995); Gill, Postlethwaite, and Seaford (1998).
3 Particularly in the *Odyssey*. See e.g. Block (1985); Murnaghan (1987) 91ff.; von Reden (1995) 31ff; Lyons (2003). See also Hands (1968).
4 Cf. Donlan (1998) 52ff.
5 See Cameron (2004) 345–6.
6 '. . . Many of the dramatic encounters between individual heroes [in the Homeric poems] occur in the context of gift transactions' (Donlan (1998) 51).
7 For a discussion of the Achilles–Priam scene in relation to reciprocity (but not clothing) see, for example Zanker (1998); Postlethwaite (1998).
8 Ἡ καὶ φωριαμῶν ἐπιθήματα κάλ' ἀνέῳγεν· ἔνθεν δώδεκα μὲν περικαλλέας ἔξελε πέπλους, δώδεκα δ' ἁπλοΐδας χλαίνας, τόσσους δὲ τάπητας, τόσσα δὲ φάρεα λευκά, τόσους δ' ἐπὶ τοῖσι χιτῶνας. Tr. R. Lattimore.
9 Cf. von Reden (1995) 21ff.; Postlethwaite (1998).
10 See e.g. Herman (1987) for a study of *xenia*.
11 Block (1985) 3: 'A host honours his guest, and establishes his own rank, with textile gifts and with the offer of baths and new clothing'; Murnaghan (1987) 91.
12 Cf. e.g. Block (1985); Murnaghan (1987) 91ff.; von Reden (1995) 27ff.; Morrell (1997) 142–145; Yamagata (2005). This section draws on some of their arguments.
13 Block (1985). Husband: 6.244; immortal: 5.167, 264, 372ff., 7.259f., 265; beggar: 13.399–400 (for a Christian parallel where Christ is dressed as a beggar, see Sulp. Sev. *V. Mart.* 3.3–4, discussed further in Chapter 4); guest: 8.392ff. (cf. 13.367–69); Odysseus himself: 16.173f. (where Telemachus mistakes Odysseus for a god), 19.215ff., 24.276ff. Cf. 6.239–245; 8.438–447; 13.367–69; 14.340ff., 508–522; 15.125ff.

14 Scheid and Svenbro (1996) 1, n.1; Perani and Wolff (1999) 41; cf. Cleland et al. (2007) 69–70 s.v. 'Fibres'. Cf. Barthes (1967) 278.
15 von Reden (1998) 59; Perani and Wolff (1999) 1, 9. Cf. Arr. *Anab.* 8–9, where Alexander claims that the gifts of cloaks from Philip to the previously sheepskin clad Macedonians civilises them, see below. For modern parallels where Western clothing was part of a broader programme of 'civilisation' during 'colonialism', see Ross (2008), while Chapter 2 in this volume provides further ancient examples.
16 *Od.* 6.127–138. Cf. Mueller (2010) 4.
17 *Od.* 6.199.
18 *Od.* 6.244–245.
19 Block (1985) 4; Morrell (1997) 143. The changing appearance of Odysseus before Telemachus (16.173–215) demonstrates Odysseus' negotiation of his changing situation and status through clothing.
20 My thanks to Professor Alan Sommerstein for bringing this to my attention.
21 This is also true in works influenced by Homeric epic: in a scene reminiscent of Helen's gifting of a glittering robe to Telemachus in the *Odyssey* (*Od.* 15.104–108, 123–130), in the *Aeneid*, Andromache presents to Ascanius 'clothing patterned with gold weft and a Phygrian [decorated] *chlamys*, burdening with woven gifts' (*fert picturatas auri subtemine vestes/et Phrygiam Ascanio chlamydem . . ./textilibusque onerat donis*) to remind him of 'her who made them with her own hands' (*. . . manuum tibi quae monumenta mearum* (Virg. *Aen.* 3.482–488)). See Mueller (2010) with bibliography. I follow some of her arguments here. Quotation p.6. See also Cleland *et al* (2007) 89 s.v. 'Helen'.
22 Mueller (2010) 2–3, 4.
23 Due to the nature of the extant sources, Classical Athens will feature prominently in the discussion of literary clothing gifts in this period, as it is difficult to reclaim parallel practices from other city-states. This is also the case for the Archaic period (however, see Morris (1986)).
24 Hercules: Soph. *Trachiniai* (cf. Apollod. *Bibl.* 2.7.7; Ov. *Met.* 9.126–272; *Her.* 9.159–164; Sen. *Herc. Oet.* 527ff.); Agamemnon: Aesch. *Agamemnon* (see Lyons (2003) 115–24 with bibliography). Glauce also receives killer clothing gifts from Medea: Eur. *Med.* 1167ff. (cf. Apollod. *Bibl.* 1.9.28). See also Rabinowitz (1993) 143–5; Roth (1993) (general gifts); Wohl (1998) 23–9; Lee (2004). It continued to be a deadly pastime in Late Antiquity, see Chapter 4.
25 Lyons (2003).
26 Lyons (2003) 125.
27 Lyons (2003) 126.
28 Pl. *Plt.* 279c–e (cf. Artem. 4.30; Hierocles *Philogelos* 14; Isid. *Etym.* 19.24.17) cited and discussed by Scheid and Svenbro (1996) 25; Blondell (2005).
29 Xen. *Symp.* 4.38 (Mueller (2010) 18 n.14).
30 Lewis and Short s.v. *toga*, especially I.B; Perani and Wolff (1999) 25–6; George (2008) 102; Rothe (2012a) 155–7. Within the context of patronage, it demonstrated and reinforced the patron's role as the protector of his client, a role that was legitimated and enforced by a moral code defending clients from abuse at the hands of their patrons (Cf. Dion. Hal. *Ant. Rom.* 2.9–11; Saller (1983) 256; Brunt (1988) 409ff. for a discussion of the legal rights of the client). For Martial's use of clothing to discuss the relationship between patrons and clients see case study below.
31 Seaford (1998) 7; von Reden (1998) 260.
32 Herman (1987) 73–115, (1998) 211; Seaford (1998) 10–11. Cf. Squire (2011) 125 in reference to the lack of statues commemorating living individuals in Athenian society during this time.
33 Herman (1987) 73–115; von Reden (1998) 260.
34 It could also suggest the duplicity of male 'others': the Persian king, Kambyses, gives the Ethiopians purple garments. However, the Ethiopian king understands this clothing not as items of luxury, but rather as indicators of the Persian king's deceitfulness, as the

50 *Threads of history*

dye conceals their true character (Hdt. 3.22, discussed by Braund (1998) 168–169). This also demonstrates the problematic nature of clothing gifts as concealers of bodies and status, especially as the Ethiopian king is shown to be wise in his distrust of Kambyses' intentions. Weaving itself was used as a metaphor for Greek politics through the complex associations surrounding Athena – her 'sphere of influence included, through war and weaving, the defining activities of *metis* . . . for both men and women . . . Athena was a particularly political deity'. (Cleland *et al.* (2007) 13 s.v. 'Athena').

35 Cleland (2005); Cleland *et al.* (2007) 3 s.v. 'agrēnon', 12 s.v. 'Artemis', 23 s.v. 'Brauron, catalogues of Artemis Brauronia', 46 s.v. 'Dedications'; von Reden (1998) 260 (for gift exchange in general functioning in this way). On women and the production of ceremonial textiles in pre-Roman Italy see e.g. Meyers (2013) *passim*. For a reversal of this type of clothing gift cf. Thuc. 2.13.5; Plut. *Vit. Per.* 31 for the story that the gold on the statue of Athena Parthenos (which included the folds of her robe) could be removed and turned into 40 talents to finance the city when the necessity arose (in Squire (2011) 166).

36 For a detailed discussion of the significance of such garment gifts in Greek religious rites, see Scheid and Svenbro (1996) Chapter 1, section 1 and Chapter 2, section 1 (cf. Bundrick (2008) for scenes of textile production on Athenian vases expressing the harmony of *oikos* and *polis* through the dual metaphor of weaving and marriage).

37 Plut. *Ages.* 4.3–4.

38 Hdt. 3.20.1, 3.22 (Kambyses' present to the king of the Ethiopians); Xen. *Cyr.* 8.2.7–8, 3.1–5 (Cyrus distributes ceremonial robes to his friends and allies), both in Reinhold (1970) 18–19.

39 For Alexander the Great see e.g. Hammond (1981); Bosworth (1988); P. Green (1991); Stoneman (2004); Heckel and Tritle (2009), esp. Weber's chapter (pp.83–98).

40 Alexander: Curt. 3.6.4, 3.12.7; Quint. *Inst.* 8.5.24; Vitr. *De arch.* 2 Praef. 1; Hellenistic kings: Cic. *Tusc.* 1.43.102; Val. Max. 6.2; Liv. 30.42.6, 31.35.1, 33.8.8, 37.23.7, 37.59.5, 42.51.2, 44.26.8, 45.32.4 (references from Reinhold (1970) 30, 31–2, 34).

41 He also took large amounts of such clothing from the treasuries and storehouses of the Persian king: Ath. 12.539f.–540a; Curt. 5.2.18–19 (Reinhold (1970) 30).

42 E.g. Dio. Sic. 17.77.5–6.

43 Bosworth (1980) 5. Cf. Collins (2012) 387 n.99. Unlike the examples of Late Antiquity explored in Chapters 2–4 (and others examined in this chapter), it appears that it was the expensive colour of the garments, rather than special clothes themselves, which distinguished those associated with Alexander and his expedition.

44 Curt. 4.1.15–26; Plut. *De Alex. fort.* 2.8.1 (*Mor.* 340D); Diod. Sic. 17.47 (Reinhold (1970) 30). See below and Chapter 2 generally for late antique practices.

45 '*Habitus*', inquit, '*hic vestis, quem cernis in meis manibus cum isto squalore permutandus tibi est. Ablue corpus inluvie tetrisque sordibus squalidum . . .*' Curt. 4.1.22.

46 Curt. 4.1.15–16, 24–26.

47 οὕτως αἱ τύχαι ποιοῦσι βασιλεῖς, μεταμφιάζουσι, μεταγράφουσι ταχύ, ῥᾳδίως, μὴ προσδεχομένους μηδ' ἐλπίζοντας. Plut. *De Alex. fort.* 2.8.1 (*Mor.* 340D); Diod. Sic. 17.47: '. . . an instructive example to those who do not know the incredible changes which Fortune can effect' (. . . παράδειγμα τοῖς ἀγνοοῦσι τὴν τῆς τύχης παράδοξον μεταβολήν). Bosworth (1980) 4.

48 Arr. *Anab.* 7.9 For a comprehensive analysis of this passage and its cultural context, see Nagle (1996).

49 It is noteworthy that despite possessing flocks the Macedonians are 'without resources' until Philip provides them with the correct clothes, implying that appropriate garments are the base from which the process of civilisation is begun.

50 Plutarch, *Eumenes*, 8.6–7. For a discussion of this passage and the significance of the *kausiai* and *chlamys* for distinguishing status among the Macedonians, see Fredricksmeyer (1994) 141–2; Hammond (2000) 149.

51 I have deliberately chosen not to discuss the restrictions the *lex Oppia* placed upon clothing during this period (Liv. 34.1–8). Although it does highlight the economic value of clothing and the part it plays in displaying status, its concern is with female clothing, and is thus outside of the focus of this discussion.
52 Liv. 27.4–10. Cf. Tact. *Ann.* 4.26 where a later Ptolemy is given clothing in 24 for remaining loyal during the war in North Africa (with Beard (2007) 274, who suggests that this episode is presented as a contrast with Tiberius' refusal to give triumphal insignia to Publius Cornelius Dolabella, the general who had actually won the war – another example of a clothing gift functioning as a narrative device).
53 Liv. 31.11 (cf. Briscoe (1973) 84–5); peace treaty: 30.45.12. (cf. 10.30 soldiers receive clothing as part of the spoils from the battle of Sentium; 43.5 clothing as appeasement to the Gaul princes during the Third Macedonian War; see Chapter 2 for similar practices in Late Antiquity).
54 Salomonson (1955) 106 n.55; Briscoe (1973) 85; Braund (1984) 27ff., 79; Marotta (1999); Nechaeva (2014) 174–5. See also Beard (2007) 274–5 for a discussion of these diplomatic 'presentation sets' and the problems of identifying such items with the costume worn by generals during a triumph.
55 Morgan (1999) 303. For this work see the translation of Hansen (1996); Ziegler (1949) 1137–66.
56 Phlegon of Tralles, (B) 30–70; Scheid and Svenbro (1996) 35–8.
57 See Scheid and Svenbro (1996) Chapter 1, section 2 and Chapter 2, section 2 for a detailed discussion.
58 Scheid and Svenbro (1996) 40.
59 The difficulty of translating *patronus* and *cliens* in a way that sufficiently conveys their meaning is much-discussed (cf. White (1978) 79–80; Wallace-Hadrill (1989a) 5; Saller (1989) 54, 57; Howell (2009) 94–5).
60 For this work see e.g. Grayling (2013) 42–60 with bibliography.
61 For the similarities between these two works see Coleman-Norton (1948), although he does not discuss this metaphor.
62 Lewis and Short s.v. *dissuo*; s.v. *discindo* for the latter's use with clothing terminology. Cf. Arr. *Epict. diss.* 1.2.12–18, 22–23 discussed in the Introduction.
63 Verboven (2002) 80. For a discussion of Horace and his relationship to the 'gift economy of patronage', see Bowditch (2001).
64 Hor. *Epist.* 1.18.31–36.
65 Hor. *Epist.* 1.18.33.
66 Saller (1982) 123; Verboven (2002) 83, n.85 'the *Saturnalia* were most of all associated with patronage;' Rimell (2008) 142: 'The Saturnalia . . . is a politically loaded occasion, prime time for imperial image-making and propaganda . . .'
67 Suet. *Aug.* 75: *Saturnalibus, et si quando alias libuisset, modo munera diuidebat, uestem et aurum et argentum, modo nummos omnis notae, etiam ueteres regios ac peregrinos . . .*; Mohler (1928) 250.
68 Sen. *Ben.* 1.12.1–3.
69 For clothing as a visual memory aid in Late Antiquity see Krawiec (2014).
70 George (2008).
71 E.g. 6.82, 12.36. Cf. 8.3 for Martial's assertion that his poems discuss 'real' life.
72 Saller (1983) 246; Verboven (2002) 71–2, however, warns that Martial's evidence may reflect his favourite literary themes as opposed to social reality.
73 Livingstone and Nisbet (2010) 109 for the different Martials in his epigrams.
74 White (1978) 86, 88; Saller (1982) 1, 123; (1983) 247; Marshall (1987) 1, 2; Wallace-Hadrill (1989a) 3, 5; Sullivan (1991) 13, 122; Leary (1996) 4; cf. Damon (1997) 159–60, 165; George (2008) 97.
75 White (1978) 79–80; Wallace-Hadrill (1989a) 5; Saller (1982) 127; (1983) 256; (1989) 54, 57; George (2008) 97.

76 Mart. 12.31.
77 Another female patron appears in 4.61, but this reinforces the idea that it was inappropriate, or emasculating for a woman to provide clothing to her client.
78 Property: 11.18; roof tiles: 7.36; carriage: 12.24; clothing: e.g. 8.24. Saller (1982) 123; (1983) 253; Cloud (1989) 210 n.1 gifts in kind occupy more epigrams than the dole; Sullivan (1991) 117; unless otherwise stated, citations of Martial's poems follow the Loeb (1994) numbering scheme.
79 Cloud (1989) 210 n.1: 'Togas are obsessional with the epigrammist . . .'.
80 Saller (1983) 252; Sullivan (1991) 117; cf. Plin. *Ep.* 2.20.10–11; Suet. *Aug.* 75 (with Mohler (1928) 250).
81 Mart. 4.61 (where the gift is from a woman); 8.10; Verboven (2002) 80 who claims Martial 'deliberately exaggerates the value of the cloak to underline the absurdity of the (no doubt fictitious) case'. This may be correct in this instance, but it is not inconceivable that some items of clothing were worth thousands, particularly if made and coloured with costly and rare materials – see Introduction.
82 Saller (1983) 252; Sullivan (1991) 117. Of course some scholars fail to include clothing at all (e.g. White (1978) 90–92 who omits clothing completely from his list of gifts to clients).
83 What exactly the *gausapinae* and *lacernae* were is uncertain. The *lacerna* is relevant here as an outer garment sported by both the wealthy and poor, as is the fact that it was the material or dye which determined its value. It appears in Martial's work more than any other type of attire. The *gausapina* was perhaps a cloak made of felt or perhaps a heavy woollen weave (cf. Lewis and Short, s.v. *gausapina*, although, as noted in the Introduction, clothing terminology is notoriously difficult to translate correctly). Mart. 1.96; 4.61; 6.59; cf. Howell (2009) 73–7; Livingstone and Nisbet (2010) 107 for discussion of the literary characters who populate Martial's poems. For the 'world' of Martial's epigrams in general, see Fitzgerald (2007).
84 See, for example, the contrasting colours and owners of the same item in 1.92 and 4.61. In addition, see Mart. 14.131 '*lacernae coccineae*', which in the alternating scheme of the *Apophoreta* is costly by its position. For scarlet being the expensive part rather than the *lacerna* itself see Mart. 2.16.2; Plin. *NH.* 37.204 (Leary (1996) 195).
85 Leary (1996) 196. For the importance of colour in the Roman world, in terms not only of economic, but also of literary and social value, see Bradley (2009).
86 *Pace* James (1996) 46. Cf. Pliny's descriptions of differing purples *HN.* 9.71–72; Wilson (1938) plate 1. Overdyeing or weaving with two or more shades to create a third colour was often used to create the look of more expensive dyes and to imitate 'true' purple in particular (Pritchard (2006) 32).
87 Cf. the symbolism of white, red, and black in African textile culture (Perani and Wolff (1999) 28).
88 *Amator ille tristium lacernarum / et baeticatus atque leucophaeatus, / qui coccinatos non putat uiros esse / amethystinasque mulierum uocat uestes, / natiua laudet, habeat et licet semper / fuscos colores, galbinos habet mores.*
89 Leary (1996) 194. In Late Antiquity sombre, mourning colours like browns and blacks were associated particularly with displaying upright Christian morals, and especially asceticism; see Harlow (2007).
90 Shackleton Bailey (1993) 109 n.111 (cf. Mart. 2.39); Leary (1996) 204; cf. Hopman (2003); Olson (2008): 'Women's colours', pp. 11–14.
91 Wilson (1938) 5; Wild (1970) 10.
92 It was commonly the attire of 'bad' emperors – both Caligula (Suet. *Calig.* 52) and Elagabalus (HA. *Elag.* 26) wore such garments (the latter was supposedly the first to be clothed all in silk) – and under Tiberius it was banned for men (Tac. *Ann.* 2.33). For the importance of wearing suitable attire as an emperor or member of the imperial family, see Hales (2005).

93 This may be why Cicero, attempting to shock his audience, claims Antony wears one in *Phil.* 2.76–77.
94 For freedmen (who are often guilty of status fraud in literature), see e.g. Petersen (2006), Mouritsen (2011).
95 Perani and Wolff (1999) 31, 34.
96 Saller (1982) 126; Sullivan (1991) 122 for the importance of reputation in Roman society.
97 See e.g. 2.57, where the subject of the poem is not to be outdone by 'the number-one man of cloaks' (*alpha paenulatorum*), despite having to pawn a ring to buy his dinner.
98 Cf. Wallace-Hadrill (1989b) 72–3, for patronage as a method of social control via a manipulation of scarce resources, and Perani and Wolff (1999) 32, 81 for wealth and prestige being formed from an ability to control allocation in African textile culture.
99 Saller (1982) 123 for Martial listing more 'ordinary' gifts than someone like Pliny would describe; Verboven (2002) 83 n.85. For a discussion of the Saturnalia in Martial's poems, see Leary (1996); Rimell (2008) 140–80.
100 Mohler (1928) 252–3 for a discussion of clothing as evidence of the fullness of Martial's list of presents. He also cites as external evidence for giving clothes as *xenia*: Hom. *Od.* 8.392ff., 15.125f., 24.276f.; Verg. *Aen.* 3.482ff.; Diod. Sic. 13.83 (253 n.36), and Suet. *Aug.* 75 (250).
101 Mart. 7.92, 10.15 (14); Juv. 1.117–122. Garnsey and Woolf (1989) 153, 154 list clothing along with food and shelter as necessaries to 'sustain life'.
102 The clothing of a client, therefore, echoes the transformation of Odysseus by his hosts' gifts and also Philip's clothing gifts to the Macedonians, both discussed above. For the toga, see Vout (1996), Stone (2001).
103 E.g. Mart. 1.108; 9.100; 14.125; Juv. 9.27–31. Leary (1996) 205; George (2008).
104 E.g. Mart. 8.92; 10.15 (14).
105 Cf. Mart. 3.30, 36; 4.26; Juv. 1.119–120; George (2008) 101, 102, 109 n.10.
106 Verboven (2002) 112.
107 Mart. 7.92, 10.15 (14); Juv. 1.117–119. Cf. Howell (2009) 97–8 for a brief discussion of the *sportula*.
108 Slave: 2.44.1–44 (cited in Cleland *et al.* (2007) 205 s.v. 'Value'.); instalments: 7.10.11.
109 E.g. Mart. 3.36; 9.100; Juv. 9.27–31.
110 cf. Wilson (1938) 27–8; Bradley (2002); cf. *P.Mich.* 15.752 (Alexandria, late second century); *PSI* 4.341 (Philadelphia, 256 BCE); *PSI* 6.599 (Philadelphia, undated) (in Rowlandson (1998) 145 no. 109, 265–6 no. 201a and b)). Clothing could also be recycled (see further Chapter 4).
111 Sullivan (1991) 122.
112 Verboven (2002) 35ff.
113 Saller (1982) 126; Marshall (1987) 32; Verboven (2002) 100–101.
114 Sen. *Ben.* 2.34.5–2.35.1, 5.2.5; Mart. 5.18.7 *imitantur hamos dona*; Marshall (1987) 2–3; Peterman (1997) 54; Verboven (2002) 37; Rimell (2008) 149.
115 Sen. *Ben.* 2.34.5–2.35.1; Mauss (1923–24 [2002]) 64; Marshall (1987) 10; Sullivan (1991) 13; Braund (1998) 162. See Chapters 2 and 3 for this working in late antique diplomatic and political contexts.
116 E.g. 9.49. Cf. 8.28 and 10.73.
117 Cf. Saller (1982) 127 for the idea of a client publicising his inferiority without there being any problem for him; Marshall (1987) 2.
118 Cf. Verboven (2002) 101 for the idea that a patron's generosity was directed not only towards the recipient, but also towards himself and wider society.
119 Cf. 2.58; 7.10 although these may imply rather that the wearer still had to pay for the item. It seems clothing could be paid for in instalments, which also reinforces the idea that some clothing could be expensive – or at least too expensive for the buyer's budget. Cf. 8.10.

54 Threads of history

120 *togae* (e.g. 2.85; 10.15 (14); 13.48), *lacernae, laena* (12.36; 13.48), *alicula* (12.81) (Mohler (1928) 252–253); Mart. 14. 124–133, 135 (137)-138 (136), 140 (139), 142–143, 145, 153.
121 Mart. 14.66 (*mamillare*), 134 (*fascia pectoralis*), 149 (*amictorium*), 151 (*zona*). Gifts of clothing for women do not appear in the rest of the epigrams, apart from in a small number of cases (i.e. at 2.39 where brightly coloured garments are given to a notorious adulteress and at 10.29 where Sextus has made a present of a *synthesis* to his mistress). As the focus of this work is on male clothing, however, these will not be discussed here. See Mohler (1928) 255–6; Leary (1996) 5 for an examination of the gifts for women in the *Apophoreta*; cf. Cleland *et al.* (2007) 39–40 (esp. 40) s.v. 'Construction of clothing'.
122 Sullivan (1991) 124 '. . . possessions and extravagance needed to be conspicuous to serve their purpose in a status-conscious society, and Martial is fully aware of this . . .'.
123 Martial himself lists, according to White (1975) 265, 'at least threescore persons who might be patrons, and many friends besides'. Cf. Howell (2009) 99.
124 Cf. Mart. 9.49 *Partheniana fuit quondam, memorabile vatis/munus.* . . .
125 Cf. Plin. *Ep.* 3.21 referring to Martial's poem about him (10.20) after the latter's death: *Tametsi, quid homini potest dari maius quam gloria et laus et aeternitas? At non erunt aeterna, quae scripsit; non erunt fortasse, ille tamen scripsit, tamquam essent futura* (cited by Howell (2009) 27–8).
126 E.g. 8.28: *Dic, toga, facundi gratum mihi munus amici, / . . . /Apula Ledaei tibi floruit herba Phalanthi, /qua saturat Calabris culta Galaesus aquis?*; Verboven (2002) 100.
127 Peterman (1997) 72.
128 Cf. Saller (1983) 252; Sullivan (1991) 117, 118 for Martial's unique status as a client due to his poetic talent; Damon (1997) 165.
129 Saller (1983) 256; Howell (2009) 94, 98–9.
130 Mart. 9.49; Saller (1982) 124 n.29; Sullivan (1991) 14, 122.
131 These poems are 2.43, 46, 85; 6.11, 59, 82; 7.10, 86 (where Martial himself refuses, and so does not get an invitation to dinner); 7.92; 10.15 (14), 29; 12.81.
132 The use of clothing gifts to highlight a failure to live up to expectations continues to be used by late antique authors, although in a different way; see Chapter 4.
133 Herman (1987) 80 with reference to the Greek *polis*. Sen. *Ben.* 5.13.2. Cf. Mauss (1950 [2002]) 17.
134 *Florida per uarios ut pingitur Hybla colores, // sic tua subpositis conlucent prela lacernis, // Tu spectas hiemem succincti lentus amici/pro scelus! et lateris frigora trita tui. /Quantum erat, infelix, pannis fraudare duobus – /quid renuis? – non te, Naeuole, sed tineas?.*
135 Olson (2007). See also Berg (2002).
136 Amm. Marc. 28.4.14; Harlow (2005) 152.
137 Delbrueck (1929) 72–3; Granger-Taylor (1983) 140.
138 Harlow (2005) 144, and especially 149–50, whose arguments these paragraphs follow.
139 Distributors of largess: *Aurel.* 48.5, 50.3; *M. Ant.* 9.7–8 (cf. *Opel. Macr.* 5.3)); providing clothing to their troops: *Hadr.* 17.2; *Aurel.* 46.6; donating money through sale of imperial clothing: *Pert.* 7.11, 8.2–4 (cf. *Alex. Sev.* 40.1). Cf. Anastasius I who sold the emperor Zeno's wardrobe to pay for his Isaurian wars (John of Antioch, 214b.4 (Cutler (2001) 263 n.88)).
140 *Alex. Sev.* 42.2; *Claud.* 14.5, 8, 10 (although these were to be returned); *Aurel.* 12.2; 13.3.
141 e.g. *Claud.* 14.5, 8, 10; 17.6–7; *Aurel.* 12.2, 13.3. See further, Chapter 3.
142 Euseb. *V. Const.* 4.7.2.
143 *Hadr.* 13.9; Bosworth (1993) 230–31, 250.
144 Bosworth (1993) 231.
145 Harlow (2005) 144.
146 Cf. Peterman (1997).

2 Weaving a tranquil work of peace? Clothing gifts in late antique diplomacy

We have seen that in earlier periods the manufacturing process of cloth could symbolise the desired outcome of a gift-bearing embassy – a united and harmonious alliance between differing peoples – for the combinations of different threads resulted in a completed, unified whole. Weaving and ambassadorial duty had already been associated as early as Aristophanes, who, in the *Lysistrata*, had the titular character propose that one way to solve the Peloponnesian War was to do '[a]s we do with our thread: when it is tangled, we take it and raise it with our spindles here and there. In the same way we would dissolve this war ... untangling the thread by means of ambassadors sent here and there'.[1] Weaving appears to have also been understood within this framework in Late Antiquity, and this metaphor continued to be applied in diplomatic contexts, for a certain Maximianus who was an envoy between the eastern and western halves of the empire, explicitly connects the duties of an ambassador with the task of weaving:

> Sent to the lands of the dawn on the duty of an envoy,
> To weave for the sake of all a tranquil work of peace (*tranquillum cunctis nectere pacis opus*),
> While I strove to bring together covenants of the twofold realm
> I met with impious wars of my own heart.
> (Maximianus, *Elegia*, 5.1–4)[2]

This poem, possibly from the early sixth century, suggests that, as an envoy, Maximianus saw his duty as a weaving together of disparate elements to maintain the unity of an empire made up of different parts in this later period. This was reflected in the ritual at the court of Constantinople where envoys from the court of the western empire were expected to change into the clothes of their Constantinopolitan counterparts when they attended the consistory. Through these clothes, the western official became visually indistinguishable from their eastern opposites and thus emphasised, but also created, the idea of the unity between the two halves of an empire whose government supposedly worked as a coherent whole.[3] War was untangled by ambassadors of peace,[4] and cloth and clothing can be seen to be particularly appropriate gifts within a diplomatic context, therefore, for they represent what the envoys were attempting to achieve.

As in the earlier periods of Greek and Roman history examined in the previous chapter, then, late antique authors could draw on a the tradition of gifts of literary clothing that was supplemented by the reality of these types of gifts forming an important part of the diplomatic exchanges between the empire and foreign peoples.[5] Clothing was one of a number of items, including money and metalware, that were given over the years to external forces and functioned as part of the wider framework of diplomatic gift-giving in the empire's relations with its neighbours. It was not the most frequent diplomatic weapon of choice; coinage held the prime position in the diplomatic gift hierarchy, as did various items made of gold and silver. Yet clothing followed close behind, due to its potential costliness, as examples of silken garments encrusted with precious gems or robes of gold suggest.[6] Indeed, 'silken clothes' are listed by the sixth century historian Menander Protector as one of the three best presents to give in a diplomatic context, because of the status it shared with gold and silver as a 'valuable commodit[y]'.[7] The practice of giving clothing to foreign potentates had occurred from the Republic onwards, but appears with more regularity in the sources for the later period studied in this chapter.[8] Presents of garments, therefore, were part of a long culture of gift exchange that was central to the methods employed by the Romans (and others) in order to develop and maintain diplomatic relations.

These relations were of vital importance to the expansion and maintenance of the empire in all periods, and a variety of gifts were given by both sides, although, in the main, the general meanings of these other items do not appear to be markedly complex.[9] This does not seem to apply to the gifts of garments given to foreign rulers, however, particularly when the intricate semiotics certain items of clothing held for those within the borders of the empire are considered. This was especially the case for vestments which would have had special meaning for a Roman audience primarily connected to authority, some of which have been seen in an earlier context in the previous chapter. While it will be argued that a knowledge of Roman clothing culture was not always necessary to appreciate the significance of the gift, the suitability of presenting these garments as part of diplomacy appears to be problematic, because in order to communicate such meanings effectively there has to be a basic understanding of the semiotics of clothing and its decoration. The importance of presenting items specifically tied to Roman authority is suggestive, then, and necessitates a consideration of at whom were these gifts actually aimed. Drawing on examples discussed previously in Chapter 1, and using literature describing late antique diplomatic episodes,[10] this chapter will consider the implications of experiencing these real gifts in literary texts. It will suggest that by describing in detail the clothing given to foreign rulers, particularly those who were friendly to the empire, authors were over-writing the unknown, giving their audiences the important opportunity to 'see' and understand these leaders within familiar roles of authority. The garments themselves were also a way of visualising allies, particularly those of border kingdoms like Lazica and

Armenia, as rulers who had a personal relationship with the late antique empire and a high status externally to it, while simultaneously indicating that this ruler had submitted to the power of empire. The messages of authority, submission, and protection expected from both sides are woven together most distinctly in the clothing gift given by Justin I to Tzath, the King of the Lazi, and it serves as the 'case study' for this chapter. It will be seen, then, that both in literature and reality presentations of garments signified the empire's continued dominance, authority, prestige, and resources during a period when this was becoming increasingly difficult to demonstrate in an unequivocal manner.

This chapter, therefore, serves to show that the many messages which could be read into clothing made it a particularly suitable gift to give as part of a diplomatic exchange, even across often very different cultural lines, and that it had a vital role in displaying and negotiating authority for those on both sides of the empire's borders. It also functions as a background against which the next two chapters should be considered, due to its broad chronological focus (from early fourth to seventh centuries) and its link to the more 'traditional' uses of garment presents discussed in the previous chapter. Such 'real' instances of gift giving provided one contemporary framework for authors and their Roman audiences to understand and utilise the messages of clothing pre-existing in the cultural consciousness,[11] enabling these items to perform as meaningful narrative devices in the range of late antique texts and genres considered in subsequent chapters.

2.1 Woven works of peace

The peaceful symbolism of harmoniously bound textiles seen at the start of the chapter has a long history in classical literature, where the juxtaposition of the manufacturing process of weaving with war for contrast reaches back to Homer; when war was finished, the peaceful activity of weaving could take place uninterrupted within the home.[12] These connotations continued in Late Antiquity: as will be discussed further in Chapter 3, Ausonius, for example, understood Gratian's gift of a consular *trabea* was a symbol of peace to be set against the background of the emperor's military campaign.[13] While in this later period, it was the imperial ateliers who were responsible for providing the *comes sacrarum largitionum* with the precious garments which were to be given to foreign recipients, clothing manufacture was traditionally rooted within the domestic sphere.[14] Such a gift could perhaps continue to take advantage of these domestic and weaving connections, which had strong overtones of peace. For woven items to work as this type of symbol, they needed to be interpreted in this way by both sides, of course, but as an activity universal to most cultures, and often the prerogative of the women, weaving may have been understood in a similar way by those Rome dealt with as having strong non-violent domestic associations. This could still apply even when such items were presented within the palace of the emperor or seat of the foreign ruler, for, whatever other associations such places held, they were viewed as his symbolic home by both his subjects and those outside his power. In his famous account of the embassy to

Attila in 449, the peaceful scene as Priscus presents his gifts to one of Attila's wives appears to show that the Huns understood the language of the activity in this domestic context, for Hereka is surrounded in her home by servants weaving clothes.[15] Indeed, the implication is that Attila, at least, comprehends it well enough to employ it for his own purposes, and furthermore knows that the message it conveys will be 'read' correctly. Giving a gift within this setting of domesticity demonstrates that both Attila and the Roman Empire (as represented by Priscus) understand that these are peaceful negotiations designed to cement a relationship.[16] Furthermore, it suggests that Attila is not preparing himself for immediate warfare – weaving could only be accomplished by those uninvolved in warfare when stable circumstances allowed for an uninterrupted period of security.

In permitting an ambassador to witness such a scene of domesticity, however, Attila is also potentially using the symbolic act of weaving as a subtle form of intimidation. The ambassadors were only allowed to go where he wished them to, and this may imply some careful stage management on the ruler's part in order to convey an atmosphere of confidence. Due to its connotations discussed above, Hereka's setting among her weaving servants functions to demonstrate Attila's perfect security in his position and power to the people it was most important to display this to – the representatives of the empire. It shows Attila to have no fear of an imminent attack from internal enemies, and as supremely unconcerned about the might of the Roman army. Even before the clothes themselves were encountered and understood, therefore, the manufacture of clothing items provided an initial point for comprehending the symbolism of diplomatic clothing.[17] This suggests that the Roman practice of giving clothing was not to present an item whose significance could only be understood on one side. The universal custom of weaving and its intimate relationship with a domestic setting and the feminine (and thus the traditionally non-warrior) side of a culture[18] meant that clothing could be seen by both parties as a gift which signified peace and the desired outcome of the embassy itself. Thus, it was functioning with (and within) the performance of gift-giving to strengthen the symbolism of the act of diplomacy itself. Even if the significance of the clothes themselves as *insignia* of Roman officials (discussed further below) was incomprehensible, recognising weaving as a peacetime activity enabled the presentation of clothing to serve as an emblematic and suitable act. For a Roman audience, still educated in the works of Homer, these connotations would have been all the more apparent. Scenes of weaving (as well as the woven gifts themselves) within late antique descriptions of diplomatic situations thus allowed authors to say something further about the intentions of both sides.

2.2 Clothed intimidation

As a diplomatic gift given in settings associated with the home and primarily during peace negotiations, clothing – the product of weaving – strengthened the intentions and authority of the envoys in texts and historical reality. Those envoys could also understand their ambassadorial duties and goals through these metaphors. Furthermore, by extension garment gifts served to fortify the aims of the emperor the embassy represented. This was also the case for the high value of the clothing given to foreign neighbours, for its costliness conveyed meanings for the relationship between the two powers.[19] As one of the premier diplomatic gifts, it is no surprise to see expensive silk garments included in the items Priscus and his group brought with them for the embassy to Attila. This example in particular has led to the suggestion that this material, especially in the form of vestments, made up part of the typical gifts Roman ambassadors carried with them.[20] If this is the case, then clothing may have been a common diplomatic present. Themistius, for instance, commenting on the peace settlement between the Roman empire and Athanaric in 369 states that it ended the despatch of 'ships freighted with clothing', which, along with gold coin and talents of silver, had previously formed the yearly subsidy to the Goths.[21] In this instance, giving gifts of clothing had clearly been an important element in the regular practice in diplomacy with the Goths since Constantine's agreement with them in 332.

Yet, specific references to clothing are often lacking; when an exchange or presentation of gifts is mentioned by the source, particularly from Late Antiquity, the reference made is usually along the lines of '[unspecified] gifts (δῶρα) were given'.[22] These gifts may have included clothing, of course, and there is evidence to suggest that this should be understood in some contexts even when clothing is not specifically mentioned. In the later sixth century, the Avars seem to have received annual gifts of apparel: Menander Protector documents almost 20 years of gift-giving to them, ending in 579/80.[23] While clothing is not mentioned in every passage referring to this tribute, he comments that the original items were received by the Avars ἕκαστον ἔτος ('every year').[24] Thus the silk garments, which are positively identified by Menander as being part of the first and last subsidy, must have remained a staple part of the unspecified δῶρα σύνηθες in the intervening years.[25]

From this it appears that clothing was a regular gift in the Later Empire's diplomatic relations with at least some of its foreign neighbours, but that does not mean that all unspecified δῶρα definitely included clothing. While the theory, held by many scholars, that this practice was so normal it was unremarkable may be supported by the silence of ancient authors regarding garment gifts, that clothing is mentioned *at some point* during these descriptions appears rather to imply the opposite. As argued throughout, garments had other meanings that made them remarkable, but on a primary level the particular notice taken of clothing gifts by late antique authors was down to their value. Like gold during this period, it is plausible that clothing is mentioned to highlight the costliness of the gift as a whole, suggested by the fact that these garments are often called 'magnificent' or 'wondrous',[26] and the material they are made from is often documented only if it is valuable (which accounts for the prevalence of references to silk clothing). As noted above, this value, signified by the rarity of the material and the beauty of the gift, will have enabled the recipient to understand that they were being given an item of considerable worth, and that this was a reflection of their relationship with the empire. Thus the comparative rarity with which they are mentioned by the sources during this period suggests instead that these gifts were special, not presented to every foreign ruler or people at all times, and worth mentioning on the rare occasions they were distributed precisely because of their exclusivity.

This exclusivity was not necessarily employed only as a positive reflection of the foreign recipient, however, but may have been a way for the emperor and empire to 'save face' when negotiating from a position of weakness or with an enemy (a context relevant to the examples above). This is because these valuable items hinted at vast resources, as well as the careful control of luxury goods, which could only be acquired through satisfactory relations with the empire. For most of the time, only a few privileged members of a foreign ruler's subjects had the opportunity to be impressed by the grandeur of the empire's power through visiting places like Rome or Constantinople. It was in the best interests of the empire and its writers, therefore, to build upon and further emphasise its glory and prestige. This suggested a continuing dominance on a wider scale, even after a defeat, for exposing foreign neighbours within their own territory to imperial treasures via diplomatic gifts enhanced the empire's authority by bringing the power of the empire to them.[27] By presenting such people with exquisitely made items which sometimes included expensive garments made of silk, gold, and precious gems – often from other lands beyond the empire's borders – the ambassadors were working to create a narrative of power. Thus, they indicated the continuing stature of the empire, even if current circumstances placed it in a less dominating position in reality, deploying these luxury items as a method of subtle intimidation.

Moreover, because this was a device which was all the more potent when the empire was in a place of power, it was in turn embraced by authors (occasionally, like Priscus, envoys themselves), in order to cast the empire as the superior in the relationship; Menander, for example, has an Avar envoy claim that the Romans used gifts to entice their enemies, only to then utterly destroy them.[28] In both literature and reality, this therefore enabled the empire to be presented in a position of authority for negotiating terms favourable to itself.[29] For many of its neighbours particularly in the west, silk, an extremely rare and expensive commodity from the east, would have been difficult to come by without purchasing it through trade with the empire itself.[30] Giving such gifts, therefore, demonstrated the emperor's beneficence to foreign and domestic audiences (the latter of which would 'see' this through texts), and suggested that it was in the external power's best interests to remain on good terms. Otherwise, they would be excluded from accessing those luxuries that could only be obtained through the empire. Particularly in Late Antiquity, by gifting clothes to foreign rulers the empire was perhaps engaging in a method of control, distributing scarce resources to a small minority, whose possession of rarities could increase their prestige within their region and reinforce the position and authority of the ruler as the focal point of relationship with Rome.[31] Through this control, the empire's own superiority and authoritative position within the relationship was therefore justified by authors and ambassadors alike. This was likewise the case for its hegemony within the world at large during this period, for it demonstrated an ability to acquire resources beyond the means and imagination of those outside the empire, as well as many within it.[32]

In the reality of diplomacy, then, clothing was being used as a form of control beyond its borders – the empire maintained its relations with foreign powers through the lure of valuable commodities, the potential of trade, and, depending on the emperor, the promise of costly goods each year. Acting like Martial's patrons, encountered in Chapter 1, this helped to keep foreign neighbours in an inferior position, as they had to rely on it to provide them with the possessions they desired.[33] And by relating the situation, authors reinforced the empire's position of authority through literature. This was further enhanced by gifts of expensive items, because they suggested that the empire not only had vast wealth and resources, but had them in such abundance that they could freely give them away. Presenting such items, then, could have been viewed both at home and abroad as a subtle threatening reminder to neighbours. Priscus, for example, includes the detail that a potentially problematic situation during this diplomatic mission to Attila was smoothed over through the gifting of expensive silk garments to members of Attila's elite, Edeco and Orestes.[34] The fact that items of this kind could be gifted to Huns of a lesser status than Attila's, suggests that they were not intended as part of a present to Attila himself or were perhaps part of a cache carried to be distributed as circumstances dictated on this visit. That the empire could provide valuable items like silk garments with apparent ease implied a wealth of resources at its disposal; a store of movable assets which could be converted to money and, further down the line, to troops.[35] The empire and its writers were therefore showing that it could give away economic assets like silk for purely political and diplomatic ends.[36] By displaying the empire's riches, envoys were participating in an attempt to justify and maintain its authority and dominance in the world through a display of wealth and beauty meant to overawe the 'uncultured barbarians' into submission.[37] This was a outlook shared by authors, who supported and reinforced this impression by describing these events and labelling luxury objects, especially the clothing, as 'wondrous' and 'marvellous'.

Reinforcing this superior position was of increasing importance in the Later Empire. In the Republic and Early Empire, Roman diplomacy had commonly been conducted from a position of strength, but this changed to a general strategy of defensive diplomacy in Late Antiquity, enabling the empire to survive and restore itself rather than expand.[38] Thus, while late antique diplomacy continued to implement the general practice of the earlier period, which combined peaceful negotiations with the threat of military force, it had become increasingly clear to many – inside the empire and without – that this threat was much diminished.[39] This is a simplification of the complex diplomatic changes that took place over many centuries, of course. However, a general outline serves the purpose here to show that, although the display of valuable commodities was supposed to place the empire's neighbours in an inferior position, this increasingly became a symbolic rather than a factual situation. It could also be inferred that by exposing external powers to such commodities as luxurious clothing on the one hand, yet controlling access on the other, the empire's wealth became a more desirable, and, it appeared, an increasingly achievable target. Thus diplomatic gifts such as clothing, which were meant to display the vast resources of the empire as a show of subtle threat, could instead become an incentive to push further towards Constantinople where much of that wealth was stored.[40]

Indeed, in the Later Empire it appears that controlling such resources did increase demand from the exterior, and as the gifts exacted in the later sixth century by the Avars (discussed above) implies, this could take an aggressive form to which some emperors, realising the weakened nature of the empire, were prepared to acquiesce.[41] The Avars, who were a regular threat to the empire at the height of their power, are seen to be claiming their tribute (including clothing) from Justinian with increasing violence over the years as they came to realise their strengthened position relative to the empire.[42] In the reality of these circumstances, gifts of garments could work as a recognition of the necessity to pay off potential enemies, while at the same time controlling the amount of distributable funds.[43] Thus, when part of the wealth they received was in the form of valuable clothing, it reduced the amount of hard currency that needed to be given to the aggressors (which of course then had the potential to be divided among their subjects).[44] Giving clothing was a more subtle method of bribery than money, therefore, and it enabled writers favourable to imperial policy, along with the emperor himself, to deflect accusations that the latter was undermining his authority by buying off foreign enemies.[45] For Menander, the decision to give the gifts allows him to demonstrate Justinian's shrewdness and wisdom, through the presentation of the Avars as those who will protect the empire only upon receipt of these items.[46] That this is a completely opposite view to the sixth century poet and historian Agathias, who sees this policy as the feebleness of old age, demonstrates that authors used the historical reality of these items to further their own narrative concerns.[47] In both the reality and literature of this period, therefore, diplomatic clothing gifts had the potential to cover over and also expose weaknesses in the empire's relations with its foreign neighbours. There seems to have been a greater concern with enacting the former, however, and in doing so they helped strengthen the impression of imperial authority with the suggestion of access to and a controlled distribution of surplus precious resources and all that implied. Furthermore, by giving currency wrapped in the form of finery, the emperor was not crudely buying off enemies; instead, such actions were over-written in the empire as a worthy attempt to spread Roman culture and reinforce its superiority over inferior 'barbarians'.

2.3 Recognisable robes, recognisable roles

While the notion of 'Romanisation' and the irresistibility of the empire has been called into question by recent scholarship, it cannot be doubted that the Romans felt that their culture was superior to others they encountered.[48] Moreover, it was felt that its dissemination through the provinces and foreign neighbours was important to diplomatic relations. Throughout Roman history, this spread of influence was partly achieved through the repeated embassies between the empire and its foreign neighbours by, among other things,[49] the clothes they wore and gave. Furthermore, in the transmission of Roman culture through clothing, envoys had an important part to play. During embassies, foreign powers would have come into contact with members of the aristocracy acting as ambassadors, whose dress and appearance would have been working with the gifts they bought to show the empire's access to luxury resources. Even as independent canvasses, the wealth, beauty, and resources of the empire could be dramatically showcased by ambassadorial clothing, brought within foreign territories on the bodies of envoys.[50]

However, these clothes would also function as subtle educators on dress codes of the empire through which status and hierarchy was established and maintained. That this was expected by a Roman audience at least is clear in Claudian's depiction of Rufinus in the *In Rufinum*.[51] Dressed in the outfit of a Gothic warrior during his embassy to that tribe in the 390s, Rufinus has such an impact because Claudian is here subverting the conventions of the duty of an envoy as an instructor through Rufinus' behaviour. Instead of educating the 'barbarians' about Roman dress and the method of recognising a consul, it is Rome who is taking instruction in barbarian ways, for '[o]ne who drives a consul's chariot and enjoys a consul's powers has no shame to adopt the manners and dress of barbarians . . .'[52] Although, as part of a wider invective, the poetic depiction of this event is unlikely to be factual,[53] it nonetheless demonstrates Roman attitudes about the expected dress and behaviour of their envoys. Clearly, ambassadors were expected to be attired in a manner appropriate for reflecting the glory and prestige of the emperor and empire they were there to represent,[54] and Claudius' decision to dress Rufinus up as a Goth is all the more shocking because he is a consular envoy. The image of a consul draped with 'tawny skins of beasts about his breast' (*fulvas in pectora pelles* (79)) is deliberately jarring; his consular clothing would have consisted of the most expensive dyes and materials, but it was also a way to recognise the holder of the highest office of the Roman empire, outside that of the emperor. Dressing appropriately would have ensured he appeared as the visualisation of Roman resources and authority, and his costume is therefore particularly ill-suited. Expected to educate and overawe their foreign neighbours in the power of the empire, an envoy clothed instead in the garb of the tribe they were visiting suggested quite the reverse: that they came as a suppliant, willing to be amalgamated with the barbarians.[55] In the Later Empire, legislation appears forbidding the wearing of clothing such as *tzangae*, *bracchae*, and *indumenta pellium* within the walls of Constantinople and its environs, and such clothing restrictions imply that the empire was anxious to retain its role as influencer and educator within the relationship between foreign neighbours and itself.[56] That it was important to maintain this superior position in reality is reflected in the poetic world of Claudian. For its survival, the image of degradation was to be avoided at all costs in both in literature and real life,[57] and is used here as part of the poem's overall objective of destroying Rufinus' character.

Through envoys from both sides, however, Rome's foreign neighbours usually had the potential to become familiar with the dress of the Roman aristocracy and those in high office and become acclimatised to these aspects of its culture.[58] This meant that when garments that had specific associations with the imperial bureaucracy were given to foreign allies, there was a strong possibility that they would have recognised them as symbols of power and high status within the empire. If they did not, the Roman envoys would have been on hand to provide the correct interpretation, enabling the foreign allies to understand themselves as literally taking on the mantle of authority which these items signified. It has been seen already that earlier texts suggest gifts of special clothing were given to foreign allies in the Republic, particularly during the Second Punic War – interestingly, another period of defensive uncertainty for the Romans – and that this continued into the Early Empire. The *toga praetexta*, *tunica purpurea*, and *sagula* of these periods evoked the high offices of civil administration or the military role of the curule magistrate, were comparable to those items worn by a consul, and had some connotations of Roman kingship. By gifting these types of associative clothes, the empire thus signified that the foreign king was a trusted and valued ally on a par with the elite members of Roman society, worthy to wear the clothes of Roman authority which in turn reinforced his own.[59] Yet this was not merely (or perhaps even primarily) aimed at a foreign audience. The description of such gifts within the literature of the earlier periods allowed domestic 'viewers' to understand the status and importance of these foreign rulers within a familiar visual language of authority.

This practice continued into Late Antiquity and was clearly understood to work in a similar way in both the literature of the period and in real diplomatic exchanges.[60] Malalas, in describing the reasons why the queen of the Sabir Huns switched her allegiance in 528 from Persia to the empire, suggests that it was partly due to the gifting of special clothing:

> Having been won over by the emperor Justinian with many gifts of royal [or imperial] raiment (καὶ προτραπεῖσα ὑπὸ τοῦ βασιλέως Ἰουστινιανοῦ ξενίοις πολλοῖς βασιλικῆς φορεσίας) and a variety of silver vessels and not a little money, [the queen of the Sabir Huns] took captive two other Hunnish kings whom Kavad, the king of the Persians, had persuaded into alliance with him against the Romans. (18.13 (430–431))[61]

The Sabir Huns resided north of the Caucasus Mountains, and were thus poised to sweep down on the lands of either the Persian or Roman empires through Transcaucasia. However, they could also act as a buffer or threat to prevent other northern tribes from entering either empires. Their alliance therefore not only gave the Romans an advantage over the Persians, but also allowed them some measure of power over who controlled the lands north of the Caucasus Mountains, important to the safety of both empires. Her decision was a valuable one for the empire, therefore, and Roman approval and recognition of her status as royalty was signified through the gifting of imperial clothing. Furthermore, that she decides to aid the empire only after she receives the diplomatic donations is clear from Malalas' passage, and is of particular interest. This demonstrates the significance of gifts, including clothing, in creating and maintaining the relationships between the empire and its foreign neighbours. While all the Roman presents listed here were expensive, the gift of clothing could be seen as the most important element in persuading the queen to switch her allegiance; by giving her clothing that was 'royal' or 'imperial', there is an acknowledgement of her status as a ruler.

This is also the case in Malalas' text – being named 'royal/imperial', these particular clothes dress a foreign ruler in terms which make her authority and position of power recognisable and familiar to a domestic audience. Her position of authority is clearly demonstrated and reinforced both within the Sabir Huns and in relation to the empire, in the text and in the historical situation. Furthermore, her actions upon switching allegiance then become easier to understand, for she is now visually part of the empire, and thus she behaves as expected in its defence whilst reciprocating the gift.[62] By using her position to protect the empire, she acts in a similar way to those who would have received items of military apparel in the Republic, implying to Malalas' readers that she understands the expectations of both her clothing and relative status. This protection worked both ways, however: the inherent symbolism of shelter and binding which was held within clothing[63] meant that there was an implication that the recipient could also expect to receive support from his (or her) imperial donor due to the bond which the clothing gift had created and symbolised. When dressed in the clothing of its officials, the foreign ruler was thus not only cloaked in the prestige of the empire; these garments demonstrated to his subjects and any potential internal or external aggressors that he personally had the backing of the empire.[64] It is likely that this would have been understood to an even greater extent by a Roman audience 'seeing' his investiture through an author's description.

2.4 Protective and subordinating clothing

This protective, reciprocal relationship became symbolic of a personal relationship between the king and the centre of Roman authority, particularly when garments, as opposed to textiles, were given to foreign potentates: clothing by its nature and function is a personal present. On a monetary level, a single gift of clothing was a boost only to the wealth of the receiver, because, unless the garment was cut up (and so instantly devalued), it could be possessed and worn by just one person at a time. Thus, it was unlike the gifting of coin which could be easily divided and distributed to many. Therefore, by providing items which would bolster the individual assets and prestige of the foreign potentate alone of his people, the empire and the author who recorded this act were demonstrating that that particular ruler was highly valued and was to be rewarded for his close and mutually profitable relationship with the empire. As the receiver of the diplomatic garment, the foreign king himself was to be the central focus through whom the personal relationship with the empire could be maintained.[65] Moreover, this was intensified when the emperor took over the role of the senate and Roman people in interacting with foreign powers, and so dealt with such kings himself.[66] Therefore, when Roman clothing was bestowed on a 'friendly king'[67] upon ratification of his accession during the Republic and Early Empire, this was not just a valuable present. It signified, in both literature and historical reality, the approval from the centre of that particular king's suitability to rule, demonstrated his connections with the empire, and it signalled that he was someone they could do business with. Above all, it indicated that he and his lands were under imperial protection and influence.[68]

While clothing may have protected the foreign king and reinforced his authority, the very act of accepting – and more importantly wearing – clothing given by the empire, implied that the receiver submitted to the empire's superiority in power. This is particularly the case in the literary-historical examples from the Republic and Early Empire, where clothing was given as part of the *appellatio* of a foreign king, the formal recognition of the ruler as *rex sociusque et amicus*.[69] Under these circumstances the king had often been chosen by the senate or emperor to rule; here the foreign ruler was a vassal in truth, although there were gradations of this.[70] This appears to have continued to a certain extent in Late Antiquity. In accepting and wearing such clothing the king could have been seen, by both the empire and his subjects, as acknowledging the empire's superiority and allowing the latter to extend its influence even beyond its borders.[71] The foreign ruler became visually a subject of the empire, who owed his wealth and position to the Romans. This was because, as has been noted above, such gifts often echoed the dress of the highest offices in Rome and, later on, in Constantinople, and literary descriptions of his clothing allowed wider audience participation in 'seeing' this acceptance.

Thus, giving these items of clothing connected the foreign king to the power of the empire (its magistracies), but were a double-edged sword – honouring the ruler on the one hand, while on the other suggesting his subordination and integration through these symbols into the Roman world.[72] That some rulers understood this in the late antique period is suggested by Priscus' silence regarding the receipt by Attila of clothing gifts during the former's ambassadorial visit. While it has been seen above that some of his elite had no objections to being gifted expensive silk garments – such items were desirable and were probably seen as a way to mark distinction both among the Huns and to those within the empire – at no point in Priscus' account does he mention the gifting of clothes to Attila.[73] Instead Priscus employs a description of the ruler's own clothing to imply that this would be unsuitable for him, for Attila is as 'homespun' as the best Roman rulers, clothed in plain dress, 'which differed not at all from that of the rest'.[74] This literary depiction enables a Roman audience to conceptualise the foreign 'barbarian' within a familiar (positive) framework. Presenting the foreign Huns, and particularly Attila, in a way that would have been familiar to a

Roman audience, and in settings that would have comprehensible associations, loses none of the impact potentially gained from presenting them as wholly 'barbaric'. Indeed, the portrayal of Attila as a 'civilised barbarian', through a strategic use of clothing, by either Priscus in a literary world or Attila in the real one, is instead designed to underline that Attila is unusual, and to emphasise the danger he posed. His elite may have been happy to be seen in clothing that related them visually to the emperor's officials in Constantinople, and to be wrapped in its wealth, but this was not the case for Attila. The ostentatious clothes often given in diplomatic situations would have been considered an unsuitable gift for this particular ruler, and as the gifting of appropriate presents was an essential component of imperial diplomacy,[75] this would have reflected badly on the empire's conception of itself as a civilised power. However, the lack of garment gifts to him also suggested something further about the nature of Attila's relationship to the empire. Priscus clearly understood that Attila had higher aims than to be seen as a vassal of the empire,[76] and he appears to suggest this through the depiction and omission of clothing gifts which, in literature and reality, would have ordinarily reinforced the authority of the empire and placed the foreign king in an inferior position.

In Late Antiquity it was important to maintain this impression of superiority even outside the empire's borders, and particular clothing gifts, through their associations with the military officials of the empire and the empire as a whole, signified an imperial ability and desire to protect and shelter the ruler who received them. It was therefore all the more potent when such symbols were not just omitted, as in the case of Attila above, but removed through the stripping of a foreign ruler's clothing, perhaps given as part of the original investiture. It would signify the ability of imperial authority to obliterate the independence of a territory at any time, creating the impression that it was at the Roman emperor's discretion or whim whether a region would be annexed or a made a kingdom.[77] In the Later Empire, this impression was violently expressed by the *cubicularius* and exarch Narses sending the blood-stained clothes of Totila, king of the Goths, to Constantinople. As a symbolic denuding of power, such an act signified Totila's complete destruction in the both reality of the event and in Malalas' retelling, although this could also be articulated by the slightly tamer stripping of Gelimer during Belisarius' triumph in 534.[78] Through this forcible disrobing (which, of course, is the antithesis of the gift-giving practices discussed in these chapters), the foreign ruler was symbolically transformed back into a naked *barbarus*, again becoming an 'other' placed outside the Roman οἰκουμένη. They were thus shown to be an inferior enemy whose eventual submission to the superior civilising and military forces of the Roman world was inevitable,[79] and literary accounts of these actions preserved and reinforced these ideas. To the audience of the texts describing these events, just as much to those who would have been present, this act clearly signified a leader unworthy to wear the mantle of authority they had claimed for themselves.

For those considered deserving of such vestments, however, the clothes were a sign of the favourable relationship the ruler enjoyed with the empire, and that it would be dangerous (although never impossible) for other powers to attempt their removal.[80] This is reflected in Agathangelos' narrative of the relations between the empire and Trdat (Tiridates the Great), an Armenian king of the early fourth century whose father was captured and then killed during a Persian invasion.[81] Trdat himself escaped and was taken to Constantine I where the emperor '... greatly honoured Trdat and bestowed handsome gifts on him. He crowned his head with a diadem and decorated him with the purple and imperial insignia. And he entrusted to him a great army for his support, and sent him to his own land of Armenia ... [where the Persian king had recently] imposed his own name'.[82] By investing Trdat with royal clothing, the Roman emperor was sending a clear signal – backed up by an army – of his support for the Armenian and his claim to royal authority. Depicted by Agathangelos, it appears that the gift of clothing provided Constantine with an excuse to exert his own influence over Armenia by restoring Trdat to the Armenian throne with Roman support. As clothes were often given by the empire as an acknowledgement of a new foreign king's ascension to the throne, this investiture would have suggested Trdat's new status, while implying both his expectation of protection from and vassalship to the Roman Empire.

A similar instance also occurred in the mid-fourth century during the reigns of Trdat's and Constantine's sons, Khosrov and Constantius II, and the letter sent by the Armenians along with Constantius' reply is apparently preserved by the fourth century Armenian historian, Moses Khorenatsʻi, in his *History of the Armenians*.[83] In this Archbishop Vrtʻanēs, the bishops 'and all the princes of Greater Armenia' appealed to Constantius on the basis of their mutual Christianity and 'the sworn covenant of your father Constantine with our King Trdat' to send an army to aid their bid to make Khosrov king. This Constantius agrees to, sending 'purple robes, and a crown' in addition to military aid. Phrases in both the letter from the Armenians – 'we desire that you rule over an ever-greater empire' – and in Constantius' reply – 'I have sent an army ... in order that, having established good order, you may serve us loyally' – make it clear that the Armenian request for help will place them as vassals to the Roman emperor. They may have their own king, but in the text his power is visualised through Roman attire, suggesting that using clothing to signify authority was understood across cultural and geographical borders.

Indeed, Procopius employs presentations of garments in an analogous way to the examples from the Armenian histories of Agathangelos and Moses Khorenatsʻi. Using similar phrases in his account of the request for authority symbols made by the Moors to the general Belisarius, the petitioners call themselves 'slaves of the emperor (δοῦλοί τε βασιλέως ἔφασκον εἶναι) and promise to fight with him', as part of their request for the 'symbols of office (τά τε ξύμβολα ... τῆς ἀρχῆς)'.[84] These tokens included clothing – '... a kind of white *tribōn* gathered by a golden brooch on the right shoulder in the form of a Thessalian *chlamys*, and a white *chiton* with embroidery ...'.[85] As in the examples encountered already, this suggests that there was an understanding that providing gifts of clothing signifying authority would be reciprocated through

Weaving a tranquil work of peace? Clothing gifts in late antique diplomacy 69

military aid to the empire. To Procopius, as to the earlier Armenian historians, garment gifts appear as an important part of the supplicant's relationship to the donor and their understanding and visualisation of authority and support; indeed, in this case the tokens had already been given by the Vandals in an attempt to secure the assistance of the Moors against the empire.

In a similar way, the clothes also visualised the extension of Roman influence outside its own borders, particularly as he equates the cloak they are given with a *chlamys*. This significant garment will be discussed in more detail in the case study, but in referring to the item that marked out the emperor, the magistrates, and the elite of the empire, Procopius was ensuring that his audience understood the symbols of power requested by the Moors in the language and image of Roman authority.[86] In likening it to a *chlamys*, there is a suggestion that the apparel given has to be equated with another garment his audience would understand, perhaps because it was called another name by the Moors in the reality of this situation. Yet it also places the Moors' request within a familiar framework of authority through a garment that was one of the symbols of Roman bureaucracy. Thus, as in previous examples, it would be clear to Procopius' audience what was expected of these potential allies. However, that the cloak was only similar to a *chlamys*, and furthermore appears to be a *tribōn* (often a worn-out cloak in classical literature),[87] also suggests an added layer of nuance in Procopius' depiction of these negotiations: the absence of a 'true' *chlamys* in their clothing gift introduces the implication that the Moors are play-acting at authority. Furthermore, the low-quality material from which the item seems to have been made portends not only shabby behaviour on their part, but also intimates that Procopius sees them as possessing low status among the foreign societies with which the empire interacted.[88] Their subsequent actions may have then been unsurprising to Procopius' audience. Despite the declaration that 'it was a law among the Moors that no one should be a ruler over them, even if he was hostile to the Romans, until the emperor of the Romans should give him the tokens of the office', and their own claims that the Vandals did not have the authority to bestow these gifts (ἅπερ ἤδη πρὸς Βανδίλων λαβόντες οὐκ ᾤοντο ἐν βεβαίῳ τὴν ἀρχὴν ἔχειν), the clothing did not secure the support of the Moors for either side. In Procopius' text their request for an imitation, poor quality *chlamys* portends the insincere and valueless service they offer in exchange.

Priscus' use of clothing gifts also touches on ideas of subservience and the relationship between a foreign ruler and the empire. But, in contrast to the examples above, it is the empire that now seems to appear as a suppliant. Upon releasing a number of Roman prisoners, Attila gifted the ambassadors who had come to request this action with 'the skins of wild animals, with which the Scythian kings adorn themselves'.[89] Like those of Constantine and Constantius II above, his present appears very generous in a context which already demonstrates his superiority – the Roman prisoners had been captured by Attila, but they owed their freedom and their lives to him as well. To give such a gift, then, further reinforces this position in Priscus' narrative, for by placing these

70 *Weaving a tranquil work of peace? Clothing gifts in late antique diplomacy*

ambassadors under the mantle of Attila's protection, he is also using garments to suggest they are in a similar position to the prisoners. As has been seen in previous examples, the putting on of clothing in this type of power exchange situation can imply the submission of the wearer to the donor. This may have been a real diplomatic situation engineered by Attila, but as a literary description of the event clothing and clothing gifts are also functioning as devices within Priscus' text. They presented Attila as acting in a familiar mould of authority to his Roman audience who could in turn understand that it said something about Attila's character and intentions. Although those who were clothed by him were ambassadors rather than foreign kings, Attila's conduct echoes the empire's own policy of clothing those, such as the borderland kings discussed above, who needed resources and help, and thus had the potential to imply that Attila operated on a similar level to the Roman emperor. Giving garments which have a specific, recognisable identity connected to Attila, then, is suggestive of the capitulation of the empire to the ruler. Furthermore, it parallels the imperial use of clothing as intimidation and an extension of power, demonstrating his encroachment into Roman territory by sending the ambassadors back into the empire dressed up as 'Scythians'.

While Procopius chooses to employ the concepts used by writers in the Early Empire regarding the ratification of foreign kings to suggest Roman superiority through gifts of clothing, it is interesting to note that for Priscus these items could also be used to express concerns over what happened when such concepts were deployed by the 'other side'. In the Armenian histories of Agathangelos and Moses Khorenats'i, the empire continued to be shown as capable of spreading its power and influence through diplomatic gifts, but Priscus' later portrayal of Attila suggests an anxiety within the empire over the problems that could arise when those influenced used the language for their own ends.[90] This may be due to differing perceptions of the empire's status and security in relation to its neighbours, but it is of note that, when compared to the Armenian histories of Agathangelos and Moses Khorenats'i, gifts of clothing do have some corresponding functions and meanings in texts culturally (and chronologically) removed from each other.[91] The authors above portray garment gifts as the visual representations of the language of submission to and friendship with the Roman Empire, using attire to demonstrate the relationship of the recipient to the empire. This suggests that clothing gifts could have similar intimations across literary and geographical borders on certain levels; an important indicator of not only an exchange and understanding of ideas, but also the possibility of shared cultural concepts of clothing that the empire had with its diplomatic connections.

2.5 Clothing gifts and Sassanid Persia

For these authors, then, it seems that some aspects of garment gifting clearly had common meanings beyond the connection of weaving peace (discussed at the beginning of this chapter); even some of the more nuanced implications which seem to apply to Roman sartorial presents had the potential to be understood on the eastern borders of the empire. This was especially true of Sassanid Persia. As presented by the writers of the period, there were certainly similarities in the way gifts of diplomatic clothing were used by the Roman and Sassanid empire during Late Antiquity (especially with regard to their neighbouring kingdoms such as Lazica and Armenia). However, the different diplomatic relationship that existed between Persia and the Roman Empire themselves means that many of the observations made previously in this chapter did not apply in quite the same way in this context.[92] The main reason for this is that Roman relations with Persia represented a 'special case', where, unlike many of its other neighbours, the Romans came to concede that Persia had a culture of comparable sophistication. In addition, as the pressure felt from external forces acted upon both empires there seems to have been a mutual desire to develop and maintain equality (ἰσοτιμία) between two 'civilised' empires in an attempt to protect their own resources.[93] As a result, there was a development of contact and relations over a long period, which enabled an exchange and sharing of a cultural language and ideas that appears to have been on a much larger scale than Roman dealings with other peoples.[94] Clothing certainly played a part in this: Matthew Canepa has argued that the red boots that were worn by the Roman emperor were of Persian origin and were a result of repeated dealings between the two powers; they thus show Persian influence in the empire.[95] While this may be too strong an assertion, since red shoes were worn by senators in the earlier empire, this does not necessarily preclude Persian influence; it could suggest instead a melding of the two cultures – a symbolic incorporation of the function of the senators into the person of the emperor, combined with the increasing influence of Persia on Roman ceremony in the Later Empire. More convincingly, Canepa has shown that architectural ornamentation was influenced by clothing in both empires and this may have been a result not just of cloth that had come to the empires through trade, but also of garments that had come into the court via diplomatic exchange.[96] While it was clearly not acceptable for evidence of 'barbarian' influence to be witnessed in places like Constantinople, the heart of the empire,[97] the same rules did not apply to Persia, because it was a special case with an equally sophisticated culture. The idea of one-way education and attempt at influence through Roman culture, which always had an eye on the possibility of annexation, and which formed the background of much diplomatic traffic between the empire and its other neighbours, was not as strong. Instead of prohibitions, the absorption and adoption of garments, shoes and clothing ornamentation, exposure to which came from envoys and their gifts as well as via trade, was rather a way for the Roman emperor to display his equality with (or superiority to) the Persian king. Thus diplomatic exchange between Persia and the Roman empire developed along the lines of endeavours to outdisplay the wealth and resources at each of the rulers' disposals,[98] a situation in which contemporary authors also had a part to play.

In both historical reality and literary narratives, this could be expressed in both subtle ways and through the more obvious show of arms. The frequent references to border lands like Armenia and Lazica in the sources with regard to clothing gifts show that these types of regions were areas in which the Roman and Sassanid empires negotiated their positions in the world in relation to one another. Clothing the kings of borderlands was part of a broader framework of diplomacy where these regions could become sites of competition between Persia and Constantinople during the later period in both reality and text. Garments became one of the media through which attempts were made by both empires to undercut their rival's authority, and so it is no surprise to find examples of diplomatic clothing gifts being used by authors to demonstrate this situation. In the *History of the Armenians* by the fourth century Armenian writer Faustus Buzandatsʻi, for example, the author relates that after being put to flight by Constantius II, the Persian ruler sued for peace and was requested to return the Armenian king Tiran, who had been taken prisoner.[99] Although in the weaker position, the Persian king used clothing as a subtle demonstration of the resources still at his disposal, for he robed Tiran 'in the finest array' before sending him back to Armenia. Although Tiran could no longer rule Armenia – his blindness disqualified him–[100] the Persian king used a gift of clothing to ensure it was understood to whom the Armenian king owed both his imprisonment and his restoration of freedom. While the text exposes this as a fiction, for it is the 'Greek king' who requested his safe return as one of the conditions of peace,[101] the clothing functions within the narrative to remind the audience not to underestimate Persian power.

This shared appreciation of some of the language of clothing between the empire and Persia is further elucidated in later the same text. Constantius, obviously thinking along similar lines and perhaps as a response, 'robed and adorned the wives of the Persian king with great honour, and returned … them … to the land of Persia [safely]'.[102] He reinforced his position of authority and superiority by dressing these important women, and then sending them right into the heart of the Persian empire in Roman clothing. In the narrative of the *History*, the author shows that both rulers, could and did employ the gifting of garments to articulate many of the specific messages which it would have otherwise been inappropriate to vocalise within a diplomatic context. By giving clothing, the emperor and the Persian king were displaying the wealth of their respective realms, which then worked as a subtle threat, hinting at convertible resources. This in turn suggested the inevitability of the victory of a superior culture, while conversely implying the benefits of trade between the empire and Persia. Furthermore, the element of protection is also present, for the clothes signify that the wearers are now safeguarded by the ruler. Finally, the context functions to present the garments within a narrative of submission, both of the prisoners to their captors, and of the Persian king to the Roman emperor. For a historian narrating Roman–Persian relations and, it seems, the rulers of the two empires themselves, the attire of these types of prisoners not only served as spaces of competition, therefore, but also enabled the two to negotiate their relationship with one another. As seen above, and in more detail within the case study below, both the Sassanids and the Romans used the bodies of rulers like Trdat, Tiran and Tzath (as well as the Persian king's wives) to stake their claim to power.

Border kings were dressed by the Persian and Roman emperors in ways that deliberately challenged the other side,[103] but gifts within direct diplomatic exchanges between the Persians and the Romans also became spaces with which they could negotiate and try to display their own superiority in both the sources and reality. In light of this, it appears significant that the sources suggest that clothing seems not to have been a given to the Persian king as part of 'regular' diplomatic gift exchanges by the Romans, even though it formed an important part of this practice in dealings with other foreign neighbours. Indeed, it appears that the only instances of clothing given to a Persian king are from the later end of the period considered here and occur under exceptional circumstances: Tiberius II Constantius (r. 578–582) sends many wonderful garments to a pretender to the Persian throne claiming to be the son of Khusro I, and the Roman emperor Maurice (Tiberius' son-in-law, r. 582–602) restores the Persian ruler, Khusro II, to his throne via an army and appropriate attire in 591.[104] As gifts that echo, surely deliberately, the Roman and Persian investiture of Armenian and other rulers, they are not therefore functioning within the 'normal' diplomatic gift exchange between Roman and Persia and are discussed further below. This is similarly the case with the abortive attempt to give clothing to the Persian king by Eustathius, a sophist.[105] He was so persuasive during a dinner with the ruler that the latter almost swapped clothes with him to take up the life of a philosopher, but was dissuaded at the last minute by the Magian priests. Despite the fact that Eustathius was there as part of an embassy, there is no indication from Eunapius' narrative that this would have been seen as a formal gifting of clothing such as those encountered previously in this chapter; it was an impromptu gift, that was, moreover, not in the end given.[106]

The rarity and unusual circumstances of these examples, along with the general silence of the sources on this matter, seem to suggest, therefore, that clothing was not an item normally given to the Persian ruler by a Roman embassy.[107] Because the Roman and Persian empires appear to have shared an understanding of the value of clothing as a symbol of status, this seems contrary to what one would expect and is a circumstance that appears to have been glossed over in modern scholarship.[108] While, of course, the other societies discussed throughout this chapter clearly shared some of ideas that gave clothing the cultural value it held in the Roman empire, Persia mirrored Roman practice by delineating its hierarchy using a complex and subtle language of clothing to a seemingly much higher degree than these other cultures.[109] Furthermore, it appears that both Persia and the Roman empire had a shared understanding of the function of clothing as a gift within diplomatic exchanges.[110] The examples already discussed of the Persian king employing clothing to reward, maintain, or establish external relationships and undercut Roman authority in the borderlands, are at once familiar and strikingly similar to those described in the Roman literature. As Persia understood the complex grammar of clothing as much as the Romans did, it would be natural, to assume that clothing would be an appropriate gift for Persia to receive from the Romans under 'normal' diplomatic practice.

However, the reason for the absence of clothing becomes clearer when the material such gifts would have been made out of during this period is taken into consideration. To demonstrate the wealth and resources the Roman Empire had at its disposal, silk garments (along with other luxury items and coinage) tended to be employed in diplomatic contexts in a bid to awe those outside the empire into friendly relations. It has been discussed near the beginning of the chapter that silk emphasised the benefits that friendship with the empire could bring and also demonstrated the exotic resources to which it had access. However, in respect to Persia, such tactics could not be employed through silk clothing, because, until Justinian managed to establish a silk industry within the empire in the mid sixth century, access to this luxury good had to come through Persia, placing them in a position of superiority in this context.[111] Thus, on a practical level, to present the Persian king with garments made of silk would render such an act of diplomacy redundant, because it was merely adding to their own abundant stores. The importance of valuing and recording diplomatic goods received is clear from the text of the *De ceremoniis*, and shows that there was anxiety on the Roman side to respond appropriately when the time came by matching the value of gifts received with an equal or superior present.[112] Therefore, presenting a silk garment to the Persians not only would have resulted in the Roman empire giving away a valued asset, but also may have been seen as a calculated insult in the presentation of an inferior gift. As a result, metalware appears to have been the diplomatic gift of choice when dealing with the Persians, as this was an unequivocal way in which the empire could display its own wealth, resources, and superior power.[113]

On the Persian side, however, silk clothing was a frequent diplomatic gift to the Roman emperor. Gifts of silk functioned for the Persians much as precious metalware did for the Romans, as well as echoing the Romans' own use of silk clothing in their dealings with other foreign rulers. It was an extremely generous present, because of the value of silk within the Roman empire and the high demand for it: the empire's inhabitants 'made more use of it than any other people'.[114] Yet a gift of this material, whether in clothing form or not, could have also been seen as a deliberate challenge to the Roman emperor's authority, in subtly reminding him who controlled access to the silk trade. An episode related by Menander appears to demonstrate how jealously the Persian monopoly on silk was guarded: when a Turkish embassy to the Persian king Khusro sought permission to sell silk 'to the Medes', he purchased it all before burning it in their presence, then had most of the next embassy poisoned.[115] That Roman emperors resented Persian control of this commodity is shown in their repeated attempts to acquire silk via other peoples, such as the Ethiopians and Turks.[116] Therefore, silk clothing could have been used by the Persians, particularly before the Roman silk industry was established in the mid-sixth century, as part of the wider game of one-upmanship that seems to have been a feature of Roman–Persian diplomatic relations in both texts and reality. Indeed, the concern to present the Persian king as a 'tributary' in Pacatus' panegyric to Theodosius I, partly because he has given a gift of silk to the emperor, can be seen as a way to over-write their inadequacy in this situation – claiming back the superior position in which silk had placed the Persian king and re-establishing the emperor's authority as a result.[117] It demonstrates that the Romans understood these gifts as a challenging display of power and rivalry by the Persian king and this is reflected and (deflected) by the empire's authors.

Yet, challenge was only one aspect of a relationship where rivalry was often counterbalanced with a surface display of a feeling of equality on both sides that could not be achieved with their other neighbours. This has been noted in the language used by the two emperors when referring to each other within diplomatic correspondence: while Lazican Tzath may be the Roman emperor's 'son', and therefore his inferior, the Persian king was his 'brother' and apparent equal in the diplomatic rhetoric, even if this was not believed by either ruler.[118] Persian clothing gifts also appear to have reflected this desire to demonstrate a close relationship – some were even known to have come from the king's personal wardrobe.[119] The Roman emperor was therefore presented with a gift that was extremely personal to the Persian king; it had been worn and touched by him and so, if worn by the Roman emperor it provided a physical connection between the two rulers who rarely, if ever, met. Yet, this could also be another way for the Persian king to show his supremacy and authority over the Roman emperor. That this was problematic for Roman writers may be behind the dismissal by the *Historia Augusta* of a story in which the Persian king gave to Aurelian his own short purple wool *pallium* of such divinely brilliant hue other purple garments looked ash-coloured in comparison.[120] While the failure of three emperors to find its miraculous dye is used to demonstrate the untrustworthy nature of the Persian king and prove the tale false, the desire to disprove this story also stems from the importance of rejecting the image of a Roman emperor clothed like a vassal by another ruler. Although the instances when the Persian king gave the Roman emperor gifts of clothing do not occur within the context of providing him his throne, the principles of protection and submission, and perhaps even ratification to rule, were still there, and as a consequence so was the implication of where each stood in the relationship. By presenting a gift of clothing, and particularly by donating an item from the Persian king's personal collection, the Roman emperor was therefore symbolically wrapped up in the protection of the Persian king. That the former could be viewed as an inferior in this relationship would have been unacceptable to Roman writers, particularly if they wished to present a favourable account of the wearer as the *Historia Augusta* does with Aurelian. It was therefore important to over-write the potential image of vulnerability created by these circumstances in ancient literature, counteracting the difficulty through other narrative strategies.

That the Romans evidently felt clothing gifts symbolised submission is clear in the two circumstances when they themselves garbed a Persian ruler. As noted above, after the Roman emperor Maurice (r. 582–602) restored the Persian king Khusro II to his throne in 591, he provided him with suitably regal clothes. Analogous to previous examples discussed, these were symbols of Khusro's obligation (and thus inferior position) to the Roman emperor as well as of the Roman emperor's authority over him;[121] the connection between clothing, protection, and submission encountered throughout this chapter are also present here. Indeed, as Khusro had come as a suppliant to the empire, and was thus dependent on its help in restoring him to the throne, the gifting of clothing by Maurice reflects the Republican practice of presenting robes as part of the ratification of a foreign king, as well as echoing the later investitures of borderland rulers. Thus Maurice's action symbolically locates Khusro in the role of the allied king and son, and also implies that Persia is a vassal to the empire. This was potent rhetoric in Roman–Persian relations, and it helps explain why Khusro could then seize on Maurice's murder in 602 as an excuse to attack the empire – the traditional expectation of reciprocity in the form of military service for Maurice's gift provided a justification for Khusro to invade the empire to an extent no other Persian king ever did.[122]

2.6 Case study – clothing fit for a king: Tzath of the Lazi

This was not the first time that the gifting of clothing could be seen as an act of war, or could provide the excuse for one between these empires, however. The investiture of Tzath, King of the Lazi, by Justin I (presented in the opening quotation of the Introduction) was also part of this long historical and literary tradition of hostility and negotiation; and it is against this background that the following case study should be considered. Described by John Malalas, this is an event in which can be read many of the ideas this chapter has suggested about the significance of diplomatic clothing, both within reality and literature.

Tzath was a Persian ally who had switched sides in 522, only a few years earlier than the queen of the Sabir Huns. His decision to come over to the Romans, prompted by his desire to convert to Christianity, was a major coup for the Roman empire. The Lazican kingdom, which corresponded roughly with the ancient territory of Colchis on the eastern shore of the Black Sea, had grown to become a region of great strategic importance in the fifth and sixth centuries for both the Roman and Persian empires.[123] This was because control of this kingdom entailed control of the whole Black Sea region for the former, and was a means to expansion and possible access to Constantinople itself for the latter, while its position made it vital to both empires in guarding the routes from the north into Transcaucasia.[124] Therefore, the allegiance of the Lazican kingdom was a matter of some weight to both the Persian and Roman rulers, and Tzath's transferral of loyalty from Persia to the Roman empire gave the Romans a valuable ally.[125]

Recognising and maintaining Tzath as king of the Lazi was of great importance, therefore, and one of the ways this was signified both in historical reality and literature was through the gifting of special clothing. As in the case of the queen of the Sabir Huns, he was presented with an entire outfit by Justin I, which can be read as marking his royalty and his new loyalty:[126]

> He was received by the emperor, baptised, and, having become a Christian, married a Roman wife named Valeriana ... and he took her back with him to his own country. He had been appointed and crowned by Justin, the

Roman emperor, and had worn a Roman imperial crown and a white *chlamys* (χλαμύς) of pure silk. Instead of the purple *tablion* it had the gold imperial *tablion*; in its middle there was a <small> true purple portrait bust with a likeness of the Emperor Justin. He also wore a white tunic, a *paragaudes*, with a purple border, with gold imperial weavings, equally including the likeness of the emperor. (Malalas 17.9 (412–413))[127]

In the context of these discussions, the outfit is notable for its combination of the *chlamys* with a special decoration, which incorporated both an imperial portrait and replaced the usual purple *tablion* with a gold one. Reminiscent of the robes of the curule magistracies in the Republic and Early Empire discussed in Chapter 1, Tzath's clothes had specific and obvious connections to the Roman empire and its bureaucracy, for in Late Antiquity the gift of the *chlamys* was employed in the same way as the clothing presents of the earlier periods. An outer (and therefore highly visible) cape-like garment, it was worn by the emperor, those at the court of Constantinople and imperial magistrates, and it appears to have behaved in Late Antiquity like the toga in symbolising Roman authority and status.[128] For Malalas' audience, as well as those at the investiture itself, the *chlamys*, then, would have marked Tzath as part of the Constantinopolitan society, and displayed connection to the emperor (even without the portrait decoration), just as other garments had in earlier periods.[129]

The *chlamys* would have also suggested to an audience within the empire that his role was to protect and serve it as one of its officials. Although the *chlamys* did not perhaps have such obvious military associations in this period, it retained an impression of this connection – the bureaucrats who wore this item thought of their service to the empire in military terms, and the *chlamys* had also been the cloak of choice for generals in earlier times.[130] The combination of these symbols within the gifts of clothing given to friendly kings was a way, therefore, both to acknowledge and to demarcate the authority of the receiver to a Roman audience. Yet it also signified that he was a valued ally, equating him with officials who had a responsibility to protect the Roman state in civil, and, more importantly, military matters.[131] Like other clothing gifts encountered in this chapter, this item served to demonstrate in literature and reality the significant role that rulers like Tzath had in helping to protect the empire and reinforced their authority in various ways. That the positions of these rulers remained secure and visible was of importance because of the locations of their realms as borderlands or due to their relationships with, or easier access to, the enemies of the empire. It is significant that the special types of clothing, which were both obviously Roman and particularly tied to authority, were mainly gifted to the rulers of these areas during Late Antiquity. Echoing earlier practice, it signals the continued role the borderlands played as buffer states for the Romans, protecting certain parts of the empire from external aggressors.[132] This was underlined for Roman audiences by their writers, who reflected imperial practice (and earlier historians) by dressing up foreign rulers in the clothing of familiar, understandable authority.

If they were decorated as Tzath's was, with a gold *tablion* rather than the usual purple one, however, these gifts took on a deeper significance. A *chlamys* with a purple *tablion* would have marked Tzath as part of the Constantinople elite, and displayed his close relationship to the emperor. The gold *tablion*, however, was designed to set him apart from it; due to its usual appearance on the imperial *chlamys* or those who had been specially granted it because of imperial service, the decoration demonstrated to Malalas' audience and those present at the investiture both Tzath's role and that he was a member of royalty.[133] His garments, along with their decoration, made it easy for an audience within the empire to understand Tzath's status outside its borders, but they were also vital in displaying respect for Tzath's position with regard to the empire. In addition, they clearly mark what that position was, and this is reflected in the other clothing gifts to neighbour rulers detailed throughout the chapter. Thus, these clothes were also a tacit acknowledgement of the important position the king (or queen) of a border land personally held in protecting the part of the empire to which his lands were adjacent, while also indicating that it was the foreign king himself, and only him, who was to be the central focus through whom the relationship with the empire could be maintained.[134] This was suggested through clothing, which by its nature and function is a personal present due to its intimate contact with and covering of the body.

The individual and personal nature of the clothing gift would have been all the more potent when the garment contained imperial portraiture on it as Tzath's did, for it sent out a clear signal as to who was now supporting the king.[135] Although one imagines that, as will be seen for Ausonius in Chapter 3, Tzath had little choice in the decoration of his new clothes, his decision to wear a *chlamys* adorned so obviously with Justin's image signifies his willingness to be subservient and show allegiance to the emperor. It also demonstrated to observers of event both at the time and through Malalas' text as to where the king's loyalties lay.[136] Yet it additionally invoked the protection that was felt to be contained within an imperial image and other clothing decorations (examined more fully in the next chapter). Just like imperial statues which were considered to have the same status in law as the emperor himself and could provide protection to those who were in their presence,[137] in Late Antiquity wearing items adorned with imperial effigies created a strong, protective, and personal bond between the wearer and the emperor, through which status and power were secured by visual association with the source. Furthermore, they adorned some of the empire's highest officials, dressing Tzath in the clothing of recognisable authority.[138] Being wrapped up in the imperial image reinforced the wearer's connection with the power of the emperor and his officials. It emphasised and increased the authority of the former by reminding the viewers that they acted in the emperor's name and were protected by their relationship to him.[139] This would have been all the more potent if this decoration was adorning the *chlamys* of a ruler whose authority was traditionally derived from the empire's bitter rival, Persia, and this applied whether it was 'seen' through a text or in real life.

For Malalas, then, the gifted clothing was also functioning with the ceremony of baptism, literally and figuratively to mark Tzath as belonging to the empire, as his conversion to Christianity meant a loyalty to the Roman Christian empire and his submission and vassalship to the Christian emperor.[140] Although wearing such items may have been viewed by those within the empire, as well as by some of the ruler's subjects, as a mark of subordination, in some circumstances submission may have been a deliberate choice on the ruler's part. While the imperial images might indicate a limitation on his sovereignty, his own shoes signified that he retained some measure of autonomy.[141] Although garnering the protection of a superior power, this residual independence may have been signified through clothing. Malalas appears to suggest that this could be the case, for Tzath manages to keep his red shoes 'which he brought with him from his own country, [and] bore pearls in Persian fashion' (τὰ γὰρ ζταγγία, ἃ ἐφόρει, ἣν ἀγαγὼν ἀπὸ τῆς ἰδίας αὐτοῦ χώρας, ἔχοντα μαργαρίτας Περσικῷ σχήματι).[142] By choosing to highlight their provenance, Malalas uses Tzath's foreign shoes as a visual reminder of his previous allegiance to the Persians. Furthermore, they allow him to suggest, drawn from historic experience, that Roman influence over Armenia was not necessarily permanent because Tzath keeps items that do not belong in his new Roman setting.[143] In the real circumstances and in Malalas' description, therefore, Tzath's footwear becomes a way to demonstrate that he has retained some measure of independence despite his assenting to be under Roman protection.

Tzath's new clothes, investiture, and conversion combined to signify a break from the past, where the Persians had traditionally appointed and crowned the ruler of the Lazi. The clothes then played an important part in visualising Tzath's transformation with regards to the empire, as well as demarcating his continued status externally to it. For those who were able to 'see' his attire, either through Malalas' description or during the investiture itself, his *chlamys*, with its royal gold *tablion* and imperial portraiture, translated the Lazican potentate through Roman clothing language to show him as both ruler and servant. Moreover, in gifting this particular type of clothing, ornamented in such a way, Justin was using Tzath's body to reinforce the clear and unmistakeable message that the king of the Lazi was now figuratively and literally under the mantle of the Roman empire. The imperial portrait on the clothing went further than this, however, for it placed a Roman emperor squarely in a traditionally Persian space. That this was a deliberately provocative move, and should be seen as such, is suggested by other examples in the chapter, and is underscored here by Malalas. He notes that the Persians called Justin's actions 'hostile' and that the result of this investiture was enmity between the Persians and the Romans.[144] Five years later, this animosity came to fruition, and Lazica was attacked by the Persians. The symbolism of protection and connection, submission and vassalship that this chapter has suggested should be read into diplomatic clothing gifts was not forgotten by the Romans, however – the new Roman emperor, Justinian I, sent Tzath an army enabling Lazica to successfully hold off its one-time kingmaker.

2.7 Conclusions

Clothing was therefore an important medium in its dealings with foreign rulers – one through which 'a tranquil work of peace' could be weaved. It was, of course, not the only gift worth giving, and the presentation of garments to foreign rulers should be seen as working alongside other items, such as gold coin or precious metalware, and of course the envoys themselves, to produce an image of imperial power and the empire itself that was beautiful, threatening, and enticing. However, the multi-layered symbolism inherent in clothing is not found in the other diplomatic gifts; although they have their own messages, these are usually straightforward and easy to read. Instead, clothing was a particularly suitable gift to give as part of diplomatic exchange, not only because of its value, but because its manufacture suggested the harmonious relationship which the envoys and their gifts were trying to achieve.

Yet not only did clothing contribute to peace as an important diplomatic gift, but in its other roles as a mantle of protection, submission, power, and authority it allowed the empire and its authors to present an expensive and beautiful gift that was infused with layers of subtlety. It was certainly a gift of Roman influence, but one which could be interpreted and used according to the author's (and perhaps even the recipient's) own understanding of diplomacy, authority, and Roman relationships with the outside world. For those within the empire, therefore, diplomatic clothing gifts were highly polyvalent elements of material culture that could carry different and often contrary meanings with the result that they could be interpreted in a number of ways.[145] Yet because they were 'seen' through the literature of historians such as Priscus, Malalas, and Menander Protector, they were also literary devices that functioned within the wider framework of diplomatic narrative, in order to create and then reinforce the impression of the empire's superior position of authority with regard to its foreign neighbours. During a period when the empire's limited military capabilities resulted in diplomacy assuming a more prominent role and importance in its interactions with its foreign neighbours,[146] clothing gifts played a vital role in the empire's continued survival. Presents of garments, both 'real' and textual, re-dressed the need to rely on external allies for protection instead as the expansion of imperial authority into areas beyond the empire's borders.[147] Those who received the clothing gifts were therefore no longer 'other' to the empire, but fashioned anew into familiar knowable figures of authority through specific garments. Rooted in the reality of diplomatic gift-giving practices, authors exploited these items to create a fiction of superior power both within the empire and without, in an attempt to eliminate uncertainty through an authoritative, written interpretation. It was a contrivance that, as the next chapter will examine, was also harnessed by their contemporaries to express authority, this time within the domestic political sphere.

Notes

1 Ὥσπερ κλωστῆρ', ὅταν ἡμῖν ᾖ τεταραγμένος, ὧδε λαβοῦσαι/ ὑπενεγκοῦσαι τοῖσιν ἀτράκτοις τὸ μὲν ἐνταυθοῖ, τὸ δ' ἐκεῖσε,/ οὕτως καὶ τὸν πόλεμον τοῦτον διαλύσομεν, ἤν τις ἐάσῃ,/ διενεγκοῦσαι διὰ πρεσβειῶν τὸ μὲν ἐνταυθοῖ, τὸ δ' ἐκεῖσε – Ar. *Lys.* 565–570 (cited by Scheid and Svenbro (1996) 15).

2 Ed. E. Baehrens (Leipzig 1879) – quoted and translated in Gillet (2003) 27. Although *nectere* usually has the translation 'to bind', it can also be used in the sense 'to weave'

(Lewis and Short s.v. *necto* I.A) and I follow Gillet's decision to translate *nectere* as such, as this makes sense with *opus*. Maximianus' decision to choose *nectere* in this context over the more common terms for weaving (e.g. *texere* or *contexere*), may also be to signify the binding together through obligation, one possible meaning, particularly in legal texts (*Dig.* 49.14.22.1 (Lewis and Short (1940) s.v. *necto*)).

3 *De cer.* 1.87 (p.394 2.14–15); Gillett (2003) 7, 223–4, 258.
4 Scheid and Svenbro (1996) 15.
5 Cf. Gillett (2003) 8, 28 for definition of the phrase 'foreign relations' and a discussion of problems of labelling such peoples 'foreign' with regard to the post-Roman west. These comments are valid, but the use of 'foreign' to denote those people external to the boundaries of the empire will be retained throughout this chapter for convenience. In addition, cf. Braund (1984) 6. I follow some of his observations. For a concise overview of the interactions between the Later Empire and 'barbarians', see Lee (2013) II.6: 110–33.
6 Cf. Prisc. *fr.* 11.2.34–35; Men. *fr.* 5.2.4; Joh. Mal. 17.9 (412–413) (discussed further below and in this chapter's case study), 18.45 (450) (this last example is within the empire: Justinian bestows his own jewel-encrusted toga on the Antiochenes in 528). Muthesius (1992) 237 for silk's place in gift hierarchy; cf. Cutler (2001) 272. Although they may refer primarily to later practice (c. 700–1200), it will be seen throughout the chapter that this can also be applied to Late Antiquity. For clothing gifts and eastern diplomacy see Nechaeva (2014), who examines them for their symbolic significance as items of insignia denoting a 'diplomatic hierarchy', rather than within a rhetorical framework.
7 Men. *fr.* 25.2.65–66 – 'for gold, silver and silken clothes are valuable commodities' (καλὸν γὰρ ὑπάρχειν κτῆμα καὶ χρυσὸν καὶ ἄργυρον καὶ μὲν οὖν ἐσθῆτα σηρικήν). That this was the case for foreign peoples as well as the Romans is implied by the fact that this is said by the envoy of the Avars (see further below).
8 Which may be due, of course, to the nature of the sources and diplomatic interactions during this period.
9 For the importance of gift exchange to diplomatic relations and its aims: Millar (1982) 21–2; Braund (1984) 5–6, 81; Gillett (2003) 1–3, 4–5, 256–8; Canepa (2009) 30, 154; cf. Veyne (1990) 102–3.
10 For a discussion of texts relating to diplomatic episodes, see Blockley (1981) 1–94, (1983) vii–x, (1985) 1–30; Gillett (2003) 29–34; Nechaeva (2014).
11 Some of whom may have taken part in diplomatic exchanges, see Nechaeva (2014) 25–6, 117–40, 160–61 for the social status of diplomats.
12 Hom. *Il.* 6.490–492; Scheid and Svenbro (1996) 17 n.38. Cf. Cicero's *cedant arma togae* where in peacetime arms are replaced by the (woven) toga (*Phil.* 2.20).
13 Auson. *Grat. act.* 11; Wood (2000) 309.
14 Nechaeva (2014) 30–31; for domestic manufacture of woven products in Late Antiquity, see Introduction and Chapter 3.
15 Prisc. *fr.* 11.2.547–563. This scene also implies that Attila has wealth and access to luxury resources, for it is 'fine linen' (ὀθόνη) upon which they are working coloured weavings. Attila's homecoming, in which he is greeted by girls passing under cloths, should perhaps also be understood within the framework of weaving symbolising peace and concord; his return completes this community, and is symbolised in the finished fabric under which the girls walk to greet him (Prisc. *fr.* 11.2.373–378).
16 Thus it reflects the practice of *xenia* in the Homeric poems and later society (see Chapter 1), although in a diplomatic context it is also the guest who is also expected to provide gifts.
17 The connection between weaving and taming the uncivilised, noted with regard to Odysseus, may also be at play here on the Roman side – on clothing's place in disseminating Roman culture, see below.
18 See e.g. Pantelia (1993); Trinkl (2014) (although see also Thompson (1982) for male weavers in Classical Athens).
19 For the attractive but not entirely convincing argument that the different types of clothing sets given to eastern foreign powers during this period demonstrates their place in a

'diplomatic system', see Nechaeva (2014), who also provides a comprehensive overview of clothing gifts given to these powers in Late Antiquity.
20 E.g. by Peter Heather (2006) 314.
21 Them. *Or.* 10. 135a-b. Heather and Matthews (1991) 43 translate ἐσθῆτος as 'fabric', but 'clothing' is more typical (see Liddell and Scott s.v. ἐσθής). For gifts to the Goths see Nechaeva (2014) 190–91.
22 E.g. Eunap. *fr.* 19 – βασιλικοῖς δώροις; Olymp. *fr.* 19 – ὅπως τε πάλιν βασιλικοῖς δώροις διαπραΰνεται καὶ ἡσυχάζει; Prisc. *fr.* 11.2.39 – δώροις ἐτίμων; Men. *fr.* 5.1.15 – δώροις ἐς τὰ μάλιστα τιμιωτάτοις.
23 Men. *fr.* 5.1–2, 4; 8 (although Justin I refuses their demand); 25.2. On gifts to the Avars, including clothing see Nechaeva (2014) 180–84.
24 Men. *fr.* 25.2.64.
25 Unspecified δῶρα σύνηθες: Men. *fr.* 5.4.27; 8.2.
26 E.g. Joh. Eph. *HE* 4.49–42, 6.23, 29 (Nechaeva (2014) 172, 177, 187–8).
27 Although this could, of course, be interpreted conversely.
28 Men. *fr.* 25.2.66–71.
29 Heather and Matthews (1991) 23–4 in reference to gifts in general.
30 E.g. Prisc. *fr.* 11.2.34–35 – σηρικοῖς ἐσθήμασι καὶ λίθοις Ἰνδικοῖς; Muthesius (1992) 237–9, 248; Canepa (2009) 164. Cf. Prisc. *fr.* 11.2.308–311, where the embassy presents dried fruit to a wife of Bleda, a gift valued by the 'barbarians . . . because they are not native in their own country' (cited in a different context by Nechaeva (2014) 184). Granger-Taylor (1983) 138, 140, 144 posits that there was a widespread and well-established silk weaving industry in the Mediterranean before the introduction of sericulture in the sixth century. This seems to be based on the idea that sources suggest silk had become an 'everyday luxury'; but while there was apparently a high demand for silk in the empire (see below), this should rather be understood as part of the traditional exaggerations of *luxuria* voiced by ancient writers. Nevertheless, it is possible that silks and silk clothing were obtainable for societies particularly west and north of the empire through trade (or raiding). This would be an expensive outlay, however, so it is likely that a gift would still be preferable and valuable.
31 Cf. Perani and Wolff (1999) 32, 81 for wealth and prestige being formed from an ability to control resource allocation in African textile culture.
32 Heather and Matthews (1991) 23; cf. Haldon (1992) 282, for the increasing need for the empire's authors, particularly after the sixth century, to justify to themselves and their foreign enemies 'the continued existence of a state and a city constantly threatened or actually besieged'.
33 Cf. Procop. *Vand.* 2.6 – the Vandals love of luxurious items, including silk garments. Although this may be viewed as part of a rhetoric of corruption and is thus an exaggerated picture, it suggests that something had changed among the Vandals as part of their contact with the empire, and that luxury goods were considered an important feature of that change (which of course then had the potential to be exploited). Cf. Wallace-Hadrill (1989b) 72–3 for patronage within Roman society itself in the Early Empire as a method of social control via a manipulation of scarce resources.
34 *Fr.* 11.2.24–35. Cf. Nechaeva (2014) 184–6. This perhaps implies that clothing, as one of the best gifts, was particularly useful in the most difficult situations, as its high worth (as well as its more subtle connotations) indicated that the recipient was valued (even respected?) by the empire.
35 Conversion of movable assets to cash for military purposes: Haldon (1992) 283, quoting the author Syrianus, who complains in his military compendium that the greater part of the empire's revenues went into maintaining the armies (*Peri Strategikes*, 2.4, although recent scholarship has suggested this text may belong to the middle Byzantine period, rather than to its more traditional dating of the sixth century; see Rance (2007)). Threatening clothing was also used in the Persian empire: the hunter motif on silk garments was a subtle intimidation to rivals (Canepa (2009) 156).
36 Muthesius (1992) 238–9.

37 This was the basic goal of diplomacy and could be achieved in various ways, of which clothing was one part: cf. Cormack (1992) 221–2, 236 – the gift of an artwork was an attempt to flatter enemies into respect by a suggestion of higher and common culture, 227; Gillett (2003) 76; Canepa (2009) 154. Cf. Veyne (1990) 102.
38 Kazhdan (1992) 10; Haldon (1992) 281–2; Campbell (2001) 19; Gillett (2003) 3, 18.
39 Haldon (1992) 282, 284, 286; Gillett (2003) 3.
40 Cf. Maximus of Turin *Serm.* 18.3, who accuses the Huns of acquiring their jewelled gold necklaces and silken garments through pillaging Roman provinces (von Rummel (2007) 117). Although he does not apply it to a diplomatic context, see also Cutler (2001) 278: 'Like goods in trade, gifts functioned as incentives to further consumption . . .'.
41 Cf. Malch. *fr.* 1, which criticises the emperor Leo for showing Amorkesos, an Arab leader, too much of the empire's wealth; Zos. 5.41 – the ransom demand to stop Alaricus besieging Rome in 408 included 3000 silk robes (in Nechaeva (2014) 190–91). A similar instance occurred in the earlier empire, although in the context of criticising provincial recruitment rather than imperial decisions to buy off enemies. The pirate Gannascus of the Canninefates was recruited by Rome to the armies, but he later deserted and used his acquired knowledge to target wealthy areas of the Gallic coast. This demonstrates a Roman fear of the use knowledge learnt by outsiders could be put to (Tac. *Ann.* 2.11.18 cited by Allen (2006) 237).
42 Men. *fr.* 5.1–2, 4; 8 (refused by Justin I); 25.2. Blockley (1985) 18: the repeated embassies between Avars and Romans appear in Menander as 'little more than a series of demands and threats which were met with rebuffs and counter-threats'. Cf. Theoph. Sim. 45.10–13 (Cutler (2001) 249); Joh. Eph. *HE* 6.24, 31 (Nechaeva (2014) 182–3, 244 Appendix 1.2).
43 Men. *fr.* 5.1. Cf. Heather and Matthews (1991) 23–4.
44 Though coin still formed a substantial part of the gifts; Men. *fr.* 5.1–2, 25.2.65. In the Byzantine period silk and gold were interchangeable, with silk garments often used to make up for a shortage of coin in imperial payments and vice versa (Cutler (2001) 261–3).
45 For the relationship between diplomatic gifts and bribes: Braund (1984) 59, 64, 81; Cormack (1992) 219, 228; Gillett (2003) 14; Cutler (2001) 256, (2005a) 11–12 (who discusses in particular the desire in Roman sources to imply these bribes or tributes were free-will offerings, as shown by the language used); Nechaeva (2014) 51–3 with references. Cf. the story of Gregory the Great who accepted the gifts given to him by John of Justiniana as alms, in a bid to deflect potential claims that such items were a bribe to secure John's receipt of the *pallium* which marked him as a bishop (Greg. M. *Ep.* 5.16 in Wood (2000) 305; cf. Serfass (2014) 92). On this item see Chapter 4.
46 Men. *fr.* 5.1.10–26. Cf. Pacatus, *Pan. Lat.* 2 (12) 22.4–5 (Greatrex and Lieu (2002) 16–17), discussed below. For further discussion of clothing gifts implying protection, see below.
47 Agathias, *Histories*, 5.14.1. Menander also comments on Justinian's elderly nature, but his bodily weakness and impending death are instead useful excuses for the imperial inability to crush and utterly destroy the Avars: Men. *fr.* 5.1.17–26.
48 Webster (2001) 209–10. Webster's article provides a summary and criticism of 'Romanisation' and suggests 'creolisation' as a better alternative (cf. Rothe (2012a), (2012b)). However, 'Romanisation', where a two-way exchange was lacking between the participants (Webster (2001) 210), may have validity in this context, because under the circumstances of its dissemination through gifts of clothing from the emperor to foreign rulers, the influence of the empire is in a way forced upon the receiver as they must accept the gift or risk offence. Consequently, there is less opportunity for the foreign recipient to find their own way of 'becoming Roman'. However, this does not mean the empire's attempts to influence through culture could not be rejected, after the fact or used by the foreign ruler him (or her)self for their own benefit. Cf. Allen (2006) 21 n.67, 69, 153, 156, 161, see also 161 n.47, 165. For the influence of Roman clothing on self-representation in the provinces see Rothe (2012a), (2012b) (2013); for a modern comparison of Indian society, see Tarlo (1996). In general I have tried to avoid this loaded term.

49 Cf. Allen (2006) 161. Frequent embassies: Chrysos (1992) 31–2; Gillett (2003) 2, 34, 74. Other contexts for influencing non-Romans could be when they acted as auxiliaries, brides, refugees, prisoners of war (Allen (2006) 21), or hostages: Men. *fr.* 15.1 (Avars, sixth century); Dexippus F7 (Vandals, mid-third century); Amm. Marc. 16.12.25 (Alamannic hostage, fourth century); Braund (1984) 21 (early practice); Allen (2006) 153ff., 156 n.26; Nechaeva (2014) 51–3. Trade was of course another sphere of influence.

50 Cf. Gillet (2003) 76, who discusses how the ceremony surrounding the reception of envoys within Constantinople worked in this way; cf. Nechaeva (2014) 34–44.

51 Claud. *In Rufinum*, 2.75–86. For a discussion of this depiction with particular reference to clothing's place within it, see von Rummel (2007) 143–8. Ancient literature has many examples voicing disapproval of figures of authority dressing in attire which had 'foreign' associations, e.g. Cassius Dio's explanation of how Caracalla acquired his name from his foreign cloak (79.3.3); Elagabalus' Persian tunic studded with gems – *usus et de gemmis Persica* (HA *Elag.* 23.3, cf. von Rummel (2007) 118–19).

52 *nec pudet Ausonios currus et iura regentem / sumere deformes ritus vestemque Getarum* ... (2.82–83). Cf. Cameron (1968b) 393 who queries the translation of *currus et iura regentem* as referring to the consulship and prefers them as symbols of the office of praetorian prefect.

53 On the historicity of the episode see Cameron (1968b) 392–3; (1970) 66f.; Wolfram (1987) 140f.; Chrysos (1992) 30. On the villainous role of Rufinus in Claudian's poetry see Ware (2012) *passim*.

54 Gillett (2003) 1, 4, although not referring to this poem.

55 See further below, for similar issues when Attila sends Roman ambassadors home in 'Scythian' clothing (Prisc. *fr.* 15.4.13–15),

56 *Cod. Theod.* 14.10.2 (Rome, 7 April 397; 6 June 399); 14.10.3 (Brescia, 6 June 399); 14.10.4 (Ravenna, 12 December 416), see von Rummel (2007) 156–66. The poem and this legislation also suggests a mistrust of 'barbarians' within the centres of imperial power. On *bracchae* see Rothe (2012a) 152–4.

57 Haldon (1992) 284–5, 289. This is also why there is a difficulty of understanding from the literature when Rome paid a tribute or a subsidy to a foreign power, because it was the prerogative of the authors to hide any perceived shame or weakness that might tarnish the glorious image of Rome (Kazhdan (1992) 13).

58 Chrysos (1992) 34–35; Canepa (2009), especially 30.

59 Braund (1984) 27–9, 79. See also Nechaeva (2014) 174.

60 The 'ships freighted with clothing' given to the Goths in return for military service (discussed above), while unlikely to have been garments specifically associated with authority, work in a similar way to those given during the Republic and Early Empire as they are a gift partly in return for military service (Them. *Or.* 10.135a-b).

61 Tr. Jeffreys *et al.*(1986) Cf. Canepa (2009) 27 n.112; Nechaeva (2014) 186 (who names the queen Boa, widow of Blach).

62 Cf. The Avars who urge Justinian to give them (among other things) gifts which included clothing so that he can benefit from their protection (Men. *fr.* 5.1.12–15) and defeated various enemies of the Romans (including, incidentally, the Sabirs) upon their receipt (Men. *fr.* 5.2.10–14), see above.

63 Perani and Wolff (1999) 25–6; see also Chapter 1.

64 Cf. Agathangelos, *History of Armenia*, 1.18–37, 46–47, 123; 3.4–5 (in Dodgeon and Lieu (1994) 313, 321).

65 Heather and Matthews (1991) 23–4, for gifts in general functioning in this way.

66 Millar (1982) 23: the circumstances of Valentinian's I death illustrates the personal character of diplomacy; Braund (1984) 153 'The Roman half of the relationship was thereby personalised', 155; Gillett (2003) 19; Nechaeva (2014) 23–4 for Late Antiquity.

67 For the term 'friendly king' as more appropriate than 'client king', and the former's meaning, see Braund (1984).

68 Cf. Liv. 27.4; *Chron. pasch.* p.532 1–3 (in Dodgeon and Lieu (1994) 155); Agathangelos, *History of Armenia*, 1.46–47 (in Dodgeon and Lieu (1994) 313); Procop. *Vand.* 1.25; Braund (1984) 24–9, 55, 85; Pitts (1989) 54; Canepa (2009) 204 (with particular

reference to investiture of foreign kings within Roman and Persian societies). See also the discussions of the queen of the Sabir Huns, above, and case study below.
69 Braund (1984) 23–5.
70 Even if *appellatio* was conferred upon the direct request of the king, the ruler was still effectively chosen by the senate or emperor, as the recognition inferred their support of his claim: Braund (1984) 24, 27f.; Canepa (2009) 32; Nechaeva (2014) 25.
71 Pitts (1989) 45. Cf.Veyne (1990) 103: the acceptance of gifts from foreign neighbours (in the Hellenistic periods) 'signifies a promise of obedience'. Cf. Antiochus IV Epiphanes (175–164 BCE) (Liv. 41.20; Polyb. 30.25.3) which shows that Roman attire could be viewed adversely. Apart from this instance it is not always clear when and where a king would wear his Roman sponsored garments, but this is important because it has implications on the impact such clothes would make on the king's subjects. It could be that he wore them as part of the celebration of his accession and on further diplomatic occasions.
72 Braund (1984) 28, 29; Canepa (2009) 205; Nechaeva (2014) 175.
73 Any gifts the ruler receives are unspecified (cf. Heather (2006) 313–14).
74 'Except that it was clean [!]' (λιτὴ δὲ αὐτῷ καὶ ἡ ἐσθὴς, ἐτύγχανεν οὖσα μηδὲν τῶν ἄλλων πλὴν τοῦ καθαρὰ εἶναι διαφυλάττουσα) – Prisc.*fr.* 13.61–63. Cf. Heather (2006) Chapter 7 'Attila the Hun' for a discussion of Attila; von Rummel (2007) 117, 119.
75 Cf. *De cer.* 1.89, see further below.
76 Prisc.*fr.* 11.2.590–595, 631–636. Cf. Nechaeva (2014) 103, 163 who notes that Attila demanded that visiting envoys from the empire should be of the highest ranks, i.e. those which were usually reserved for Persia.
77 Braund (1984) 84; Allen (2006) 144; cf. the Inca practice that rewarded individuals with cloth or clothing, or stripped them when they were disgraced (Ross (2008) 13).
78 Totila: Joh. Mal. 18. 116 (486); Gelimer: Procop. *Vand.* 2.9.4–13 (Canepa (2009) 170–71). The Persian king also treated his subjects and enemies in this way (Faustus Buzandats'i, *History of the Armenians*, 3.21 (Dodgeon and Lieu (1994) 308); see Canepa (2009) 170–71, 186), and the Romans had themselves suffered a similar fate in 312 BCE at the hands of the Samnites who had defeated them (Liv. 9.5.13; cf. 9.15.8, 13–14 cited by Allen (2006) 98).
79 Allen (2006) 29.
80 Braund (1984) 55, 66–7, 85, 116; Heather and Matthews (1991) 23–4; Canepa (2009) 33.
81 Agathangelos, *History of the Armenians* 1.46; 123 (Dodgeon and Lieu (1994) 313). On this work, with text and translation, see Thomson (1976). For the *insignia* of the Armenian rulers, see Nechaeva (2014) 220–25.
82 Agathangelos, *History of the Armenians* 1.46 (Dodgeon and Lieu (1994) 313).
83 Moses Khorenats'i, *History of the Armenians* 3.5 (Dodgeon and Lieu (1994) 321).
84 Procop. *Vand.* 3.25. For a discussion of these gifts, see Nechaeva (2014) 225–31.
85 . . . καὶ τριβώνιόν τι λευκὸν, ἐς χρυσῆν περόνην κατὰ τὸν δεξιὸν ὦμον ἐν χλαμύδος σχήματι Θετταλῆς ξυνιὸν, χιτῶν τε λευκὸς, ποικίλματα ἔχων . . .
86 For this item see e.g. Delbrueck (1929) 38–40 and case study below with references.
87 For this item within this passage see Nechaeva (2014) 228. For the *tribōn* in general see Urbano (2014).
88 Nechaeva (2014) 228, although she sees this low-status as more 'official', rather than being Procopius' own opinion based on their fickle actions in this particular situation.
89 Prisc.*fr.* 15.4.13–15 – δωρησάμενος δὲ καὶ . . . θηρίων δοράς, αἷς οἱ βασίλειοι κοσμοῦνται Σκύθαι . . . (where 'Σκύθαι' are likely to be Priscus' classicising term for the Huns). Cf. von Rummel (2007) 119: 'Wertvolle Felle (nicht die pejorativen Waldmauslumpen) scheinen jedenfalls eine prominente Rolle gespielt zu haben, da Attila den Gesandten aus Konstantinopel neben Pferden Pelze schenkt . . .'. See also discussion above regarding Claud. *In Ruf.*, 2.75–86.
90 Cf. Gelimer's appropriation of *the* imperial colour, purple, for his cloak in order to show himself as a ruler to the inhabitants of the empire (ἐσθῆτά πού τινα ἐπὶ τῶν ὤμων ἀμπεχόμενος πορφυρᾶν) (Procop. *Vand.* 2.9.10).

91 For a further example, see discussion of Faustus Buzandats'i, *History of the Armenians*, 3.21 below.
92 Gifts of clothing between the empire and Persia: Pacatus, *Pan. Lat.* 2 (12) 22.4–5 (embassy of 394) (Greatrex and Lieu (2002) 16–17); Sebeos, *The Armenian History*, 12 (80); HA *Aurel.* 28.4–5 (although within the narrative the author claims that the story is untrue; the *Historia Augusta* is a notoriously problematic source even without such authorial comments) (Dodgeon and Lieu (1994) 97–98); Canepa (2009) 31, 154; Nechaeva (2014) 195–8.
93 Blockley (1985) 16–17.
94 Blockley (1985) 16–17; Lee (1991) 374; Cormack (1992) 230; Kazhdan (1992) 14; Whitby (2008) 125, 137; Canepa (2009) 21, 22, 31.
95 Pritchard (2006) 60: contact with Sassanids led to changes from the fifth century in cut and tailoring of garments as evidenced from archaeological finds from Egypt, including an increasing trend in stitching clothing together from separate pieces of cloth, rather than from a single loom piece; Canepa (2009) 32 n.149, 189–90, 201f. For non-Persian examples of cultural exchange and influence in dress between Roman and other societies, see e.g. Dode (2012); Rothe (2012a), (2012b), (2013); Kaczamarek (2014).
96 Canepa (2009) 155, 188, 206, 209f. Cf. the discussion of expensive textiles to churches by the wealthy laity in Chapter 4.
97 See discussion above regarding Rufinus' dress and legal prohibitions against 'barbarian' clothing.
98 Cormack (1992) 230, 236; Canepa (2009) 8, 22, 30. During the Sasanian period elite hostages were not held for any period of time significant enough to provide them with an influential instruction in Roman culture and the complex semiotics of clothing as had happened in the earlier period (Lee (1991) 369ff., 374 n.49). In addition, the Romans gave as well as received (temporary) hostages in their dealings with Persia.
99 Faustus Buzandats'i, *History of the Armenians*, 3.21 (Dodgeon and Lieu (1994) 309).
100 It is not clear from the text whether this blindness had occurred naturally or as a result of Persian violence while Tiran was a prisoner, but there was a tradition of the Persians disqualifying potential candidates for the throne by mutilation. My thanks to Professor Doug Lee for bringing this to my attention.
101 The 'Greek Emperor/King' is commonly identified as the Caesar Constantius, later Constantius II, but cf. Dodgeon and Lieu (1994) 307 n.3 for problems with this identification. The episode is strikingly similar to one that is told of Galerius, Diocletian's Caesar, who captured the royal harem of the Persian king Narses, after defeating his forces in 298 (Dodgeon and Lieu (1994) 125–31).
102 Faustus Buzandats'i, *History of the Armenians*, 3.21 (Dodgeon and Lieu (1994) 309).
103 Cf. Agathangelos, *History of the Armenians* 1.18–37; 46–47; 123 (Dodgeon and Lieu (1994) 313, cf. 321); Faustus Buzandats'i, *History of the Armenians*, 3.8–9, 20–21 pp.110–116 (Dodgeon and Lieu (1994) 308–9; Sebeos, *The Armenian History*, 24 (96), 27 (99), 28 (101), 49 (109). See also Ross (2008) 14 for the practice in the Inca empire of limiting the wearing of the highest-status clothing as a reward to those who were loyal.
104 Tiberius II Constantius: Joh. Eph. *HE* 6.29 (Nechaeva (2014) 179)); Maurice: Sebeos, *The Armenian History*, 12 (80).
105 Eunap. *VS* 6.5.1–10.
106 Likewise, the gifts of clothing given to the Persian ambassadors during their journey to Constantinople should be seen as practical gifts to make their journey more comfortable, rather than formal presents, and moreover were not destined for the Persian king (Šāhnāma, 281 cited in Canepa (2009) 131).
107 *pace* Nechaeva (2014) 179, I see this as a deliberate policy on the part of the empire, not a lack of interest on the part of the sources.
108 E.g. Canepa's statement that silk was a staple of diplomatic gift exchange between the two empires ((2009) 157) is not supported by the examples he provides (164–5). These

Weaving a tranquil work of peace? Clothing gifts in late antique diplomacy   87

cannot conclusively be proved to be part of diplomatic exchange and so are not evidence of Roman silk gifts to Persia. On this topic see below.
109 Canepa (2009) 32, 186, 190.
110 Cormack (1992) 230; Canepa (2009) 204, 225.
111 Procop. *Pers.* 1.20.
112 *De cer.* 1.89; Gillett (2003) 226; Canepa (2009) 30–31, 135, 154f., 187. Cf. Cassiod. *Var.* 5.1 who shows Theodoric experiencing similar feelings of anxiety in the west.
113 Particularly via gold items, possibly because a law of Valens seems to have prohibited the export of this metal and objects made from it (Cutler (2005a) 15), which would naturally make it more valuable to the Persians. Cf. Ps.-Josh. Styl. *Chron.* 81; Procop. *Pers* 1.15.26; Socr. 7.18.1–7 (363.2–365.24) (where the Persians and Romans go to war in 421 because the Persians are unwilling to hand back Roman gold-diggers working at a mine which may have been in Armenia (in Greatrex and Lieu (2002) 38, 257, n.37, see also Greatrex (1998) 190 n.53 for a similar dispute in 530)). See Cutler (2005a).
114 Ὡς γε καὶ κατὰ τὸ πλέον τῶν ἄλλων ἀνθρώπων χρωμένους (Men. *fr.* 10.1.50–51). This could also be a comment on contemporary concerns with *luxuria*.
115 Men. *fr.* 10.1.20–26; 10.1.33–47; Blockley (1985) 262 n. 115.
116 Ethiopians: Procop. *Pers.* 1.20; Canepa (2009) 190 n.7; Turks: Men. *fr.* 10.1–5; Canepa (2009) 27 n.114. See also Blockley (1985) 262–3 n.117.
117 Pacatus, *Pan. Lat.* 2 (12) 22.4–5 (Greatrex and Lieu (2002) 16–17); Cutler (2005a) 11. The Persians also use this type of language, e.g. their envoys claim to the Turkish Khagan that the Romans are their tributaries (Joh. Eph. *V. SS. Or.* 6.23; Whitby (2008) 138–9).
118 Blockley (1985) 29; Lee (1991) 374; Kazhdan (1992) 14; Tinnefield (1993) 208; Allen (2006) 141 (although not in reference to Persia); Whitby (2008) 125–9 (who highlights the complexities surrounding this fraternal language); Canepa (2009) 32–3.
119 Canepa (2009) 191. On the gifting of an 'emperor's old clothes' between Byzantine and Muslim rulers and its relationship to the transmission of power, see Cutler (2005b).
120 HA *Aurel.* 29.2–3.
121 Agathangelos, *History of the Armenians* 1.18–37; 46–47; 123 (Dodgeon and Lieu (1994) 313, cf. 321); Faustus Buzandats'i, *History of the Armenians*, 3.8–9, 20–21 pp.110–116 (Dodgeon and Lieu (1994) 308–9; Sebeos, *The Armenian History*, 12 (80), 24 (96), 27 (99), 28 (101), 49 (109); Whitby (2008) 136 (although he does not discuss the clothing aspect of this episode).
122 *Khuzistan Chronicle*, 20–21 (in Greatrex and Lieu (2002) 232).
123 See Braund (1994) 262–7, and, especially, Chapter 9 'War in Lazica' for a discussion of the Lazi and Lazica.
124 Braund (1994) 274, 276.
125 Braund (1994) 280
126 For a discussion of this passage see Braund (1994) 276–81; Canepa (2009) 32–3; Woodfin (2012) 159, 161; Nechaeva (2014) 207–20.
127 Καὶ δεχθεὶς παρὰ τοῦ βασιλέως ἐφωτίσθη, καὶ χριστιανὸς γενόμενος ἠγάγετο γυναῖκα Ῥωμαίαν, ὀνόματι Οὐαλεριανήν. καὶ ἔλαβεν αὐτὴν μεθ' ἑαυτοῦ εἰς τὴν ἰδίαν αὐτοῦ χώραν, στεφθεὶς παρὰ Ἰουστίνου, βασιλέως Ῥωμαίων, καὶ φορέσας στεφάνιον Ῥωμαϊκὸν βασιλικὸν καὶ χλαμύδα ἄσπρον ὁλοσήρικον, ἔχον ἀντὶ πορφυροῦ ταβλίου χρυσοῦν βασιλικὸν ταβλίον, ἐν ᾧ ὑπῆρχεν ἐν μέσῳ στηθάριον ἀληθινόν, ἔχοντα τὸν χαρακτῆρα τοῦ αὐτοῦ βασιλέως Ἰουστίνου, καὶ στιχάριον δὲ ἄσπρον παραγαύδιον, καὶ αὐτὸ ἔχον χρυσᾶ πλουμία βασιλικά, ὡσαύτως ἔχοντα τὸν χαρακτῆρα τοῦ αὐτοῦ βασιλέως. Tr. Jeffreys *et al.* with Woodfin (2012) 159.
128 Joh. Mal. 11. (267); cf. 17.16 (421); Sid. Apoll. *Carm.* 15.154–157; Delbrueck (1929) 38–40; MacCormack (1981) 250–52; Braund (1994) 280; Canepa (2009) 192.
129 This is also the case in 'domestic' investitures, i.e. the attiring of potential heirs to the Roman imperial throne by the current emperor indicates their close relationship and is a way to secure the position of both parties: Amm. Marc. 27.6.11–12 (the investiture

of the eight-year-old Gratian to Augustus by his father Valentinian I after the latter suffered a dangerous illness); Amm. Marc. 23.3.2, 26.6.2; Philost. *HE* 9.5; Zos. 4.4.2–3 (Julian supposedly handed over his imperial cloak to Procopius before he embarked on his Persian campaign (cf. 4.8.4) (discussed in Chapter 3).

130 Military service: Canepa (2009) 192, n.2; general's cloak: Liddell and Scott s.v. 'χλαμύς' especially A.3. Cleland *et al.* (2007) 34 s.v. 'chlamys;' Rothe (2012a) 164–5.

131 Braund (1984) 27–9, 55, 66–7, 82; Kazhdan (1992) 14 – 'The Greek authors . . . considered [the borderland rulers] as military commanders appointed in Constantinople'. Cf. Veyne (1990) 103 who suggests (in reference to the Hellenistic period) that 'a foreigner's gifts might be symbols of dependence'.

132 Braund (1984) 91, 95 for a discussion of the roles of these kingdoms as buffer zones for the empire (cf. Kazhdan (1992) 13).

133 χλαμύδα ἄσπρον ὁλοσήρικον, ἔχον ἀντὶ πορφυροῦ ταβλίου χρυσοῦν βασιλικὸν ταβλίον – Joh. Mal. 17.9 (412–413). Usually prohibited unless granted specially: *Cod. Theod.* 10.21.1–3; *Cod. Just.* 11.9.2.382 (in Nechaeva (2014) 212).

134 Heather and Matthews (1991) 23–4, for gifts in general functioning in this way.

135 Woodfin (2012) 159–61, who adds that the practice of giving silks adorned with the imperial image continued into the Middle Byzantine period (161). The portrait weavings on his *paragaudes* were part of a long tradition which saw clothing borders as sites of symbolic importance (e.g. the *toga praetexta*) as the wide variety of Greek and Latin terminology which distinguishes between patterns, positionings and widths implies (see further Cleland *et al* (2007) 21–2 s.v. 'borders', 138 s.v. 'paragauda/is').

136 Cf. Amm. Marc. 27.12.4.; Braund (1994) 280; Woodfin (2013).

137 Ando (2000) 228–53 some of whose arguments I follow in this section; Swift (2009) 20.

138 Woodfin (2012) 161; Nechaeva (2014) 213.

139 R.P.H. Green (1991) 548; Elsner (1998) 56–8; Ando (2000) 232; Delmaire (2003) 96–7; Olovsdotter (2005) 212; Parani (2007) 501, n.11. This will be revisited throughout Chapter 3.

140 Scott (1992) 162; Braund (1994) 281. For a modern parallel cf. Ross (2008) 87 who states that 'it is clear that in many of the Pacific island societies the acceptance of Christianity was associated with the assumption of a variety of European dress', and 'It was accepted that a change of religion entailed a change of dress' (89). A similar instance occurs in the non-Christian Roman context of Tac. *Ann.* 2.56–58, where the original king of Armenia appointed by the Romans is offensive to the Parthians, partly because, as a hostage brought up in Rome, his identity is too foreign (i.e. Roman) for their liking. This almost leads to war until Zeno, a son of the king of Pontus, is installed there instead, another hostage, but one who instead lived in Armenia and had taken on the culture, including their dress. The result was a treaty offered by the Parthians to Germanicus after Zeno's coronation (Allen (2006) 230–31 for discussion).

141 Allen (2006) 29, 141; Woodfin (2012) 61.

142 Malalas 17.9 (412–413). Nechaeva (2014) 218. Of course, it may be that he kept his own shoes at the permission of the emperor.

143 Tzath's own decision to switch his allegiance from the Persians to the Romans shows that the rulers of the Lazi had some measure of autonomy. This made them both valuable and problematic allies because they could be persuaded to change sides (see Braund (1994) Chapter 9).

144 Joh. Mal. 17.9 (412–413).

145 Cf. Webster (2001) 217–18 referring to creolised objects.

146 Blockley (1992).

147 Woodfin (2012) 159, 161.

3 Portable portraits

Consular *trabeae* and figural decorations in Late Antiquity

For late antique authors, the diplomatic practice explored in the previous chapter provided a 'real' lens through which their own use of clothing gifts could be viewed by their audiences. Furthermore, descriptions of these events drew upon earlier literary traditions and accounts in order to cast foreign rulers in familiar and understandable roles of authority; late antique diplomatic clothing gifts set new neighbours in traditional roles. At the same time, these practices could be, and were, adapted to contemporary experiences; for Justin I and Tzath, King of the Lazi, the late antique interest in lavish decoration provided emperors, wearers and authors with the means to adjust the messages of clothing gifts to suit their own interests and clearly demonstrate connections between the giver and receiver. This was also the case for those who operated within the empire's borders, where the inclination towards highly decorated clothing in the later Roman period enabled presentations of these types of garments to become meaningful spaces of communication for some members of society. As a result, this style of clothing will be the focus of this chapter, which will explore the implications for the visual landscape of a clothing gift functioning within the empire. In particular, it will investigate the instances of decorating consular *trabeae* with historical portraits – sometimes imperial, sometimes ancestral – as a medium for the new consul to broadcast his position in society or ties to the emperor's authority. Some of these examples appear in literature, specifically in *Carmina* 15 of Sidonius (an *Epithalamium* written c. 468) and Claudian's *De Consulatu Stilichonis* (produced for the consulship of Stilicho in 400). Other evidence for this chapter comes from consular diptychs: the fifth-century Halberstadt diptych (Figure 3.1) which possibly depicts Flavius Constantius (western consul 417), the diptychs of Anicius Faustus Albinus Basilius (western consul 541; Figure 3.2) and Areobindus (eastern consul 506), and the engraving of the lost diptych of Anthemius (eastern consul 515).[1] These cannot, as some scholars have concluded, be assumed to be gifts,[2] but their importance here lies in their ability to provide the visual backdrop to the one *trabea* which both features in a text and was certainly a gift – the consular *trabea* decorated with the image of Constantius II, given by the emperor Gratian to Ausonius of Bordeaux upon his consulship in 379. Like Martial before him, Ausonius used a literary offering – the *Gratiarum Actio*, produced in thanks for his consulship – to advertise the clothing gift he had received from the emperor, and the pains the author took to ensure his audience understood the providence of this item underscores its significance as a 'case study' here. This gift certainly reflected well on Ausonius, linking him to the main figure of imperial authority and thus confirming the close proximity of this provincial rhetorician to official power. However, as will be seen, the two items – the speech and the gift – were also working together in service of the self-representation of the imperial donor, creating a positive image of Gratian, and were thus functioning in a similar way to those garment presents encountered in the previous chapters.

3.1 Figural decoration on non-consular clothing

Late Antiquity saw an increase in decoration on clothing, which could be added in the form of patches or *segmenta*, pieces of tapestry or tablet weave, which were made separately and attached to the main fabric of the garment after it was complete.[3] Such pieces would have been an economical way to make an item of clothing more attractive and last longer, rather than paying for a completely new decorated garment, and they probably had the practical application of covering holes in older clothes as noted in the Introduction.[4] More commonly, however, decoration was woven in during the manufacture of the garment as a whole, using, for example, differing shades of threads or weaving techniques which created patterns through contrast that would stand out when hit by light at the right angle.[5] It is usually only these decorative pieces that survive in the archaeological evidence.[6] The round *orbiculi*, square *tabulae* and *clavi* of tunics, the locus of late antique clothing's decorative elements in the majority of extant examples, were often cut from their original housing in the process of excavation or later in order to present museums and private collectors with ancient treasures more easily accommodated than a full garment.[7] The context and material of these finds (often wool or linen) make it unlikely that they were part of the consul's garment which is the focus of this chapter, as it is usually presumed this would be made from costlier materials such as silk.[8] The intricate woven patterns of the surviving textiles show, however, that those depicted on diptychs (see Figures 3.1 and 3.2, discussed further below) and the portrait of Caesar Gallus as consul from the Codex-calendar of 354,[9] or those described by authors such as Ausonius, Sidonius and Claudian, were certainly not beyond the skill of weavers. The material evidence of the extant textiles, of which the late antique period is well-represented, suggests that decorative elements containing figures and portrait busts seen in the diptychs and texts could be and were produced in real life on contemporary looms, perhaps by using 'cartoons' like those found from the fourth century onwards.[10]

In the archaeological evidence, the subject of many of the woven figures on non-consular clothing appears to have been mythical or, in the later period, Biblical, although these latter are not as numerous in the surviving pieces.[11] Henry Maguire has shown that common figures such as a horseman riding down a wild animal or human enemy were thought to help protect the wearer from evil, or were to attract good luck, wealth or prosperity, as the woven personification of *Gē*, or Mother Earth, was also meant to do. Christian figural decorations had similar functions, particularly those of Christ, the Virgin Mary, scenes from the Bible or nimbed soldier saints, whose images were to shield the wearers of the clothes they adorned from negative external influences.[12] This was perhaps because, as will be discussed in more detail below, such images were felt to connect the wearer directly to the power held by the original of the image.[13] The Adoration of the Magi is another theme on surviving tunics, for they were seen as the protectors of travellers and pilgrims. The appearance of the Magi on the robe of Theodora in the mosaic of San Vitale, Ravenna,[14] is particularly fitting for the context of her actions within the mosaic. Offering a jewelled chalice or ritual cup, her pose is reflected by the Magi on her garment who are bringing gifts to Christ;[15] like them, she is a pilgrim come to worship the son of God.

For Christian writers, such items were additionally seen as deliberately designed to attract God's favour for their wearers, as Asterius, the fourth-century bishop of Amaseia in northern Anatolia, makes clear:

> . . . [wealthy laymen] devise for themselves, their wives and their children gay-coloured dresses decorated with thousands of figures (ὕλαι καὶ πέτραι, καὶ ἄνδρες θηροκτόνοι καὶ πᾶσα ἡ τῆς γραφικῆς ἐπιτήδευσις μιμουμένη τὴν φύσιν). When they come out in public dressed in this fashion, they appear like painted walls to those they meet (Ἔδει γὰρ μὴ τοὺς τοίχους αὐτῶν μόνον, ὡς ἔοικεν, καὶ τὰς οἰκίας κοσμεῖσθαι). . . . The more religious among rich men and women, having picked out the story of the Gospels, have handed it over to the weavers (ἀναλεξάμενοι τὴν εὐαγγελικὴν ἱστορίαν τοῖς ὑφανταῖς παρέδωκαν) – I mean our Christ together with all His disciples. . . . You may see . . . the woman with an issue of blood seizing the hem of [Christ's] hem, the sinful woman falling at the feet of Jesus, Lazarus coming back to life from his tomb. In doing this they consider themselves to be religious and to be wearing garments that are pleasing to God (καὶ ταῦτα ποιοῦντες εὐσεβεῖν νομίζουσι καὶ ἱμάτια κεχαρισμένα τῷ Θεῷ ἀμφιέννυσθαι). (*Homilia* 1.3–4)[16]

Although Maguire does not make this point, Asterius' comments show that these scenes were also viewed as a way for wearers to broadcast publicly in no uncertain terms their personally chosen loyalties (in this case to their religion) as if they were 'painted walls'. The use to which gifts of clothing were put by Christian writers will be examined in more detail in the next chapter. Yet the implications of Asterius' observations are also relevant in a secular context to the figural decorations on consular robes, particularly on those of Ausonius discussed in the case study below. While mythological figures or those from the Bible continued to be incorporated into the design elements of a garment, portraits of individuals from the historical past or important persons from the present began to appear on clothing from the fourth century onwards. For instance, in the sixth century,

Justinian's funeral dress described by Corippus incorporates Justinian's achievements and a figure of the emperor himself, and the judge in the mosaic of Christ before Pilate in Sant'Apollinare, Ravenna, possibly has an imperial image on his right sleeve.[17] Although an anachronistic decoration on bureaucratic clothing during the period when Christ was thought to live, it would mark Pilate as a man who held high office to the late antique viewer of the mosaic.

Indeed, for the sixth-century audience and the mosaic artist this was probably one of the ways they would have expected authority to be dressed, as it corresponds to the presence of imperial portraiture on the clothes of government officials, mentioned by some Christian writers. Worn by these men while executing their duties, the garments adorned with the emperor's portrait meant their wearers were not only representatives of his authority, but also came under the protection of his sacrosanct power:

> Men who undertake public service ... often wear the mark of imperial images on their robes ... These men would never do anything unworthy of the robe which bears the imperial insignia; even if they ever attempt to do so, they have many to prevent them. And if there are some who would wish to treat these men ill, the robe they wear is a sufficient guarantee that they will suffer no indignity. (John Chrysostom, *Ad illuminandos catecheses*, 4.17)[18]

It is difficult to determine which holders of office John is referring to here, but for this chapter as a whole as well as for Tzath's clothing in Chapter 2, what is significant is that imperial figural decorations adorned the dress of those who worked in the imperial bureaucracy, and marked them as representatives of 'official' imperial power.[19]

The decoration seems to be have seen by John Chrysostom as acting and being treated by viewers in a similar way to imperial statues – these were felt to have the same status in law as the emperor himself and could provide protection to those who were in their presence.[20] Although some Christian writers tried to erode this belief, it is clear that images were felt to contain or have a connection to the power contained in the original; as Basil of Caesarea explained: '[t]he image of the emperor is also called the emperor, yet there are not two emperors. Power is not divided, nor glory separated ... for the honour given to the image is transferred to the prototype'.[21] Wearing items adorned with imperial effigies had a similar protective function as that of the mythological or Biblical figures discussed above, therefore, but in this case created a connection between the viewer, the wearer, and the emperor, as well as a strong, protective, and personal bond between the wearer and the emperor. This could also apply to those empresses who were depicted wearing imperial effigies on their dress:[22] they secured their own status and power by visually associating themselves with the source of that power, their connection to the emperor. As has been seen with Tzath's clothing, being wrapped up in the imperial image reinforced the wearer's connection with the power of the emperor, emphasising and increasing the authority of the former by reminding the viewer that they were acting in the emperor's name and were protected by their relationship to him.[23] It is significant, therefore, that figural decoration on consular clothing seems to have been primarily of imperial *imagines* (see discussion below); these connotations would have been all the more potent if adorning the *trabea*, the special garment of the consul who occupied one of the most prestigious offices in the empire.[24]

3.2 The *trabea*

As with much ancient clothing terminology, the question of what the *trabea* actually was is difficult to answer. The problem of identifying Roman clothing with specific material examples is a notoriously vexed one because, as noted in the Introduction, insufficient description by the Latin authors (who knew what the clothes they name looked like) often confuses the issue. Added to this is the strong probability that similar, or indeed the same, garments may have been called by different names depending on region – hardly surprising when the multi-ethnicity of the Roman Empire is taken into account.[25] It appears, however, that the *trabea* was the main component of the consul's official dress in this period; a number of ancient authors use this term in conjunction with the consulship,[26] and it seems that some authors use it to refer to a garment that had some sort of decoration.[27] This combination of circumstance and ornamentation has led some modern scholars to suggest that in the Later Empire the *trabea* was equivalent to the *tunica palmata* or *toga picta* of earlier periods, which seem to have been part of the garments worn by a general in his triumph and were absorbed into the dress of the imperial office. Unfortunately, however, this identification invites more questions than it answers, for these items of clothing are also difficult to define accurately.[28] While there may be some reason to accept the *trabea* as corresponding to or a development or replacement of the *toga picta* (on this see further below), a lack of consistency in the literary sources means it is too much to state that *trabeae* were always decorated consular garments which an analogy with this toga would suggest. For Claudian, at least, the *trabea* appears to be synonymous with consulship, and not all *trabeae* are described as decorated within his works.[29]

In addition, matters become further complicated when ancient authors use terminology for what seem to be separate and different clothing items to a modern understanding, but are clearly applying these terms interchangeably to just one garment. Calling the clothing gift he receives to celebrate his consulship *palmata*, *palmata vestis*, *toga*, and *picta vestis* (*Grat. Act.* 11), Ausonius presents a challenge to the modern reader's understanding of what it is he wears. Indeed, this varied vocabulary has led Michael Dewar to suggest that '[b]y the fourth century, then, the terms *trabea* and *toga picta* or *palmata* had become if not wholly interchangeable, then almost so, and in particular if an author is talking, as Ausonius is, of a consular robe'.[30] Despite the qualifier this seems an oversimplification; a closer look at the text shows that Ausonius uses specific terms in order to create certain juxtapositions. For instance, in *Gratiarum actio* 11 Ausonius draws on Cicero's famous aphorism *cedant arma togae* and its associated ideas,[31] changing his *trabea* into a toga in order to contrast his own, more peaceful situation with Gratian who was currently out on campaign: 'Armour-clad you manage the concerns of my toga' (*Loricatus de toga mea tractas*...). This idea is carried over in the choice of *palmata vestis* following, where Ausonius' garment is again contrasted with the emperor's preparations for the great battle that is close at hand.[32] It is then transformed into a 'happy and auspicious' omen of Gratian's victory (*feliciter et bono omine*); the *palmata vestis* was part of the triumphal costume of a general, a point Ausonius explicitly brings out in the next line: 'For, just as in peacetime that is the attire of the consul, so in victory it is the dress of the one who triumphs'.[33] Calling the garment *picta*,[34] as Ausonius does later in the passage, can also be explained by context rather than needing to equate it with the *toga picta*. It comes immediately after the author has informed his audience that the garment is decorated with a woven figure of Constantius II, and so is used to highlight this important element. Furthermore, that he does not use *toga* after *picta* here (preferring *vestis*) is suggests it should be seen in this way, especially as he does call the garment a toga earlier on in the passage, as noted above. It is clear then that rather than believing that 'the terms *trabea* and *toga picta* or *palmata* had become if not wholly interchangeable, then almost so', the decision to employ different clothing terminology should instead be seen as a deliberate rhetorical choice on the part of at least some authors in this period.

While Ausonius' use of differing terminology for what appears to be one item of clothing is more nuanced than Dewar suggests, the fact that Ausonius could use a number of terms and still expect his audience to comprehend what he was referring to implies that there was scope for some overlap in definition. Accurate terminology could be and was sacrificed for diversity of vocabulary in order to give speeches and poems potency and demonstrate the erudition of the author (as well as the recipient of the speech), while still accommodating an ancient audience's understanding of what the garment looked like and how it functioned within the social space. For a modern audience, however, a lack of knowledge and surviving textiles that can be securely identified as consular vestments limits a full comprehension of such nuances and visualisation of the *trabea*.[35] The ivory diptychs from the fourth and fifth centuries sent out by the consul himself to announce his ascension to that office[36] (discussed further below, Figures 3.1 and 3.2) can perhaps provide some aid in this area. Although none of the diptychs explicitly label any part of the consul's clothing a *trabea*, the diptychs themselves were disseminated as a celebration of the consul's inauguration, so it is to be expected that the consul would want to be portrayed in the signifiers of his office. The fact that the diptychs depict the consuls in garments very similar in style to one another implies that this must represent his official costume.[37] Thus, when this is coupled with the evidence given by the literature, which frequently uses *trabea* in the context of consuls and the consulship, it seems likely that at least some part of the official dress seen on the diptychs is called by this term by the fourth century.

Figure 3.1 The Halberstadt diptych of Flavius Constantius (consul 417) (left panel). Halberstadt, Domschatz, inv. 45 (photograph: Juraj Lipták)

Figure 3.2 The diptych of Basilius (consul 541) (left panel), Florence, Museo Nazionale del Bargello, inv. 8

A comparison of diptychs that feature garments with figural decoration, with descriptions of *trabeae* woven with figures in literary sources, may help us determine which part of the outfit was the *trabea*. In the former, it can be seen that such decorations usually appear on the outer garment of the consul's attire. The decoration occurs here either on the perpendicular front fold of this layer (as on the Areobindus diptych), on the right shoulder 'bridge' fold (as on the Basilius diptych, Figure 3.2), or on the *sinus* fold which went from behind the right hip to rest across the left forearm (the Halberstadt diptych, Figure 3.1).[38] The eighteenth-century engraving of Anthemius' lost diptych and the later reproduction of the Caesar Gallus as Consul of the Year from the lost Codex-calendar of 354 also show, however, that the decoration could occur at any number of places on the outer layer, and in fact could be the garment's main decorative pattern.[39] The evidence of the diptychs seems to correspond with literary descriptions of Sidonius, Claudian, and Ausonius encountered throughout this chapter, which make it clear that the decorative elements of the garments they are describing are highly visible. This suggests they adorn an outer garment of the consul's costume.

Anthemius' diptych and image of Caesar Gallus as Consul from the Codex-calendar of 354 additionally show, however, that figural imagery could occur on the second layer of the consul's clothing. In both cases, this garment – a long, wide sleeveless tunic perhaps called the *colobium* – seems to display figures in a similar fashion to the judge in the mosaic of Christ before Pilate in Sant'Apollinare, Ravenna, noted earlier.[40] This raises the possibility that the *trabea* might actually have been synonymous with this item, instead, but again a comparison with the literary evidence from the aforementioned authors is of help here and makes this seem unlikely; among the (admittedly confusing) terminology they use, all seem to call it a toga at some point. It has already been noted earlier that this is partly in order to construct a rhetorical comparison in the case of Ausonius (a literary device Claudian also employs), but Ausonius' use of the term as well as the omission of *tunica* with *palmata* in his speech is suggestive that the *trabea* should probably be understood as an outer layer instead. Furthermore, both the diptych and image show their consuls dressed in an outer garment decorated with figures, which means that they cannot provide firm proof that the *trabea* should be identified with this tunic. In light of this, it is difficult, therefore, to support the occasional modern interpretation of the *trabea* as equivalent to the *tunica palmata*.

By comparing the literary sources that discuss figural decoration and the ivory diptychs that depict the phenomenon, therefore, it appears that the *trabea* can be identified as the extreme outer layer of clothing, which wraps around the consuls in a manner similar to the toga but is different from another 'official' garment, the *chlamys*. Although it had obviously undergone some alterations in style – it was elaborately decorated, folded in a more complex, 'concertina-like' manner at some places and apparently narrower in size – it was perhaps a descendent (and replacement?) of the toga.[41] It is this layer that is usually decorated in the diptychs and seems to correspond to the literary descriptions of ornamented *trabea* – descriptions that identify this garment (patterned or plain) as an integral and fully visible part of the consular costume. Taken together with the evidence in previous sections, there may even be a case for stating that the *trabea* (or at least a certain type of *trabea*) was reserved only for the consul in late antique society, as other officials appear to have been dressed in the *chlamys* instead. At the very least, it is likely that the consular *trabeae* discussed by the literary sources in this chapter are visually represented by the decorated outer layer of the consul's costume in the diptychs.

3.3 A *trabea* store? Obtaining consular vestments

Attempts to understand what the *trabea* was lead to the question of where consuls obtained the garments that were to mark them as the holders of that office. Sidonius' evidence (discussed in more detail below) suggests that this could be through a talented member of the family; using her great-grandfather Agricola's garment as a guide, he presents Araneola as making the *trabea* herself.[42] The political turmoil during the year of her father Magnus' consulship in 460 may have required him to have his robes specially produced, as it would have prevented him from returning to Rome from Gaul where there may have been a special treasury of consular robes (on this, see below). However, while it may have been the case that some consuls' daughters could double as the family tailor,[43] it is unlikely that this was the regular method of acquiring such items.

As noted previously, some scholars have suggested that it was the emperor who always provided the new consul's clothing, and consuls who partnered an emperor in office, as well as ones who had a connection with the emperor, would perhaps be likely candidates for receiving such an item.[44] Ausonius' words would appear at first to support this idea, for Gratian is represented in the *Gratiarum Actio* as personally overseeing the process until it is ready to be sent to the new consul:

> For in your letter which had been given to me . . . you also condescended, so that you were asking what kind of *trabea* should be sent to me. You have worn out all the officers of the largess in your solicitude . . . it is not enough if you are asking what kind of *trabea* is being sent to me: you order it to be brought before your eyes. Nor do you have satisfaction from that, so that the officers of the largess might continue to perform their duties: you yourself choose one from the many and, when you have chosen, follow up your gift with honourable words. (*Gratiarum Actio*, 11)[45]

From Ausonius' statements it appears that he was at least given the opportunity to choose what sort of *trabea* should be sent to him, demonstrating that the new consul had some measure of control over the selection process. This also implies there were different types of *trabea* from which a consul could choose, perhaps suggesting he could ask for a patterned or plain garment.[46]

However, as will be discussed in more detail in the case study below, the relationship between Gratian and Ausonius as pupil and tutor may mean that Ausonius was unique in his experience of receiving his consular garment from the emperor personally. Rather, Ausonius' comments suggest how and by whom the process was usually handled. The emperor's intervention stops the *ministri largitionum* ('officers of the largess') from carrying out their customary duties (*nec satis habes, ut largitionum ministri ex more fungantur*). It also noteworthy to Ausonius that Gratian requires the garment to be shown to him (*te coram promi iubes*), and while it will be argued that this was because the garment was to play a role in Gratian's imperial self-representation, it also suggests that it was not usual for an emperor to become this involved in his consul's wardrobe choices. Therefore, if the mode of provision of Ausonius' *trabea* was a one-off occurrence, Ausonius' words here support the supposition that it was the *ministri largitionum* who normally had the responsibility for choosing and sending the *trabeae* to the new consuls.[47] This is not to say that Gratian did not use the mechanisms of the *ministri largitionum* to choose Ausonius' *trabea*, of course; Ausonius clearly thinks that he did: *omne largitionum tuarum ministerium sollicitudine fatigasti*.[48] Roland Delmaire provides a discussion of the role of these officials and 'les ateliers fiscaux' which had an essential part in the production of luxury goods destined to be employed by the emperor to show his generosity during the fourth century and beyond.[49] He suggests that the officers of the largess centralised the production of garments destined for use by the emperor and the court and that there was a central store, the *vestiarium*, which housed these objects.[50] This hypothesis may possibly be supported by statements in the *Historia Augusta*, which claims that the consul's costume (here the *tunica palmata* and *toga picta*) were kept either on the Capitoline or Palatine hills in Rome.[51] This work may not be the most reliable of sources[52] but, taken with Ausonius, it seems to lend weight to Delmaire's theory of the existence of a store of garments where the officials of the largess could retrieve a suitable attire for the new consul. If this is true, it is unlikely, however, that this is where such garments were stored by the fourth century, because emperors spent so little time in Rome. The *Historia Augusta* comments that the phrase 'the Capitoline *palmata* waits for you' (*te manet Capitolina palmata*), written in a letter from the current emperor Tacitus, was not in fact an omen of the new consul Probus' future imperial power, but was instead an expression which 'always used to be written to every consul' (*sed in hanc sententiam omnibus semper consulibus scribebatur*).[53] This seems to suggest that by the fourth century the consul no longer obtained his 'official' outfit from a possible *vestiarium* on the Capitoline (if indeed he ever did), although its supposed origins were obviously still remembered. Instead, it is reasonable to assume that had it existed, it would have resided in one of the cities used as imperial bases in Late Antiquity, where it would have been easy to commission and buy or manufacture replacements.[54]

The above-quoted passage of Ausonius certainly implies that there was a selection of 'ready-made' garments from which one was chosen for the consular inauguration, perhaps to ensure the emperor's representative was appropriately clad.[55] The later practice of storing silks for many years, often until they were needed as a diplomatic offering,[56] may be reflected in Ausonius' comments, although it is not clear of what material Ausonius' garment was made. Delmaire's assertion that it had been woven some 20 years before, placing it within the final years of Constantius' reign, could be close to the truth, and would account for the decoration.[57] This is supported by the evidence within the speech, for Ausonius says that the decoration Gratian personally chooses (*ornamenta disponis*) is interwoven *(Constantius intextus est)*, which would suggest the *trabea* was already made; decorative elements were usually incorporated during the weaving process which produced the final garment. He also suggests that there was an intense selection procedure for the right garment (*omne largitionum tuarum ministerium sollicitudine fatigasti; te coram promi iubes*), and that the emperor chose this one garment out of many shown to him (*eligis ipse de multis*), again implying the garment had existed prior to this activity. It is surely incorrect, however, to assume that Ausonius' new *trabea* once belonged to Constantius himself.[58] Ausonius would hardly have failed to make a point of mentioning this previous illustrious owner if it had been, primarily because it would show how highly he was regarded by Gratian.

In normal circumstances, then, the consul may have written to the *comes sacrarum largitionum* or one of his officials requesting the garment, or, more likely, they were sent a *trabea* (or perhaps the raw material for one) as soon as the names of the new consuls were known. Ausonius' remarks imply that these officials were the usual means of providing the consul's *trabea* and by not having to pay for his own dress, the consul (like Martial before him) could attribute this acquisition to the emperor's generosity. Sidonius includes the detail in the *Carmina* 15 that the consular garment of Araneola's great-grandfather was still available to copy. Perhaps reflecting a culturally universal practice of keeping clothing to be passed down as a family heirloom, the possibility of retaining the valuable consular *trabea* after office turns this item into an article of imperial largess. Rather than simply being a uniform to be worn during the consulship and then returned to the *vestiarium*, therefore, it becomes an imperial gift to the new consul, although of course it is not as immediately personal as that of Ausonius. But, while these items might have been seen as an indirect present from the emperor, in reality it is not possible to know whether the consular *trabeae* depicted in the diptychs were given personally by him, acquired through an official, or even commissioned by the wearer himself. This is unfortunate, as such knowledge would provide a better idea of how an observer was supposed to view the decorations and understand their message; a *trabea* received by a consul from the emperor himself (rather than his officials) and bearing an imperial portrait, has a different meaning to one obtained by the consul through other means. If the consul elected to have his own *trabea* design, perhaps because the *ministri largitionum* provided him with money or raw materials rather than the completed garment, then there was conceivably little to stop a consul (or his daughter) from 'customising' his *trabea* by adding family images.[59] Unless he had obtained imperial permission to have a bespoke decoration, this may have been a risky move, as the messages the consul decided to promulgate through his choice of decoration would reflect only on himself and his own status, rather than only honouring the emperor from whom he had received his consulship. This may account for the rarity of examples of *trabeae* with figural decorations which seem to have no imperial portraits at all. If the consul chose to ornament himself in portraits of the imperial family, however, the consul is shown to be an extension of the emperor, protected by the imperial power (which also guarded the empire as a whole), while also projecting and closely partaking in the emperor's authority. The proportionally small number of literary accounts or extant diptychs showing *trabeae* specifically with imperial decorations may suggest that only a few consuls were connected closely enough to the imperial family or considered sufficiently worthy of this high honour.

3.4 Figural decoration on the consular *trabea* i: Consular diptychs

Although small in number, these diptychs, extant or depicted in engravings, combine with the poetry of Sidonius and Claudian and the thanksgiving speech of Ausonius to provide important evidence for the practice of interweaving the *trabeae* of consuls with portraits of historical personages in Late Antiquity.[60] The significance of having an image of a historical person woven into clothing, and that it was especially symbolic when this person was or had been an emperor, has been noted above. There appear to be only four extant diptychs which show consuls in *trabeae* decorated with potential imperial *imagines*: the fifth-century Halberstadt diptych (Figure 3.1) which possibly depicts Flavius Constantius (western consul 417), and the diptychs of Anicius Faustus Albinus Basilius (western consul 541; Figure 3.2), Areobindus (eastern consul 506) and Anthemius (eastern consul 515). But these four diptychs are important for visualising the literary garments of these authors, particularly that of Ausonius in the case study.[61] Identifying the persons portrayed in the figural decorations on the diptychs' consular robes is problematic in the extreme, because the *imagines* are sometimes damaged and very small. However, it is clear that if such decorations were meant to depict the emperor or a member of the imperial family, this would have been read by the viewer of both the diptych and the *trabea* as a gesture of loyalty to the emperor and as a way to show the consul's ties to the imperial family. This would not only strengthen their authority, but would also provide social capital to reinforce further the consul's superior position in society. The engraving of Anthemius' diptych, for example, appears to depict a portrait of the current eastern emperor Anastasius I (491–518), among others.[62] Through this decoration Anthemius was clearly showing loyalty to the emperor who, after Anthemius had failed with his brother Marcianus to overthrow the previous emperor Zeno and been forced to flee the city in 479, had welcomed him back to Constantinople, protected him, and eventually awarded him the consulship.[63] Anthemius, however, also incorporates a portrait of his father and namesake, emperor in the west between 467–472. His clothing therefore directly connects him to two imperial families,[64] emphasising his close ties to each, cementing and displaying an elevated position upon his return to Constantinople. Indeed it appears that, if the honorand of the Halberstadt diptych is Flavius Constantius (consul 417),[65] Basilius is the only consul whose diptych *trabea* is decorated with figures that cannot be securely tied to imperial identification, and is significantly the only consul without close imperial connections.[66] If this was the case then the figurally decorated robes of Anthemius, Flavius Constantius, and Aerobindus should be seen as part of a desire to publicise their links to a past or present ruling family, perhaps to show loyalty, but also as a way to increase or strengthen their authority and broadcast their social standing.

The figural decorations, therefore, may have had personal meaning, but they also reflected the consul's relationship to the emperor, and this could be further reinforced in the pose of the figure in the decoration. An interesting feature of the other surviving diptychs with this clothing style (the Halberstadt (Figure 3.1), the Basilius (Figure 3.2), and the Areobindus) is that the figures in the decorations are commonly portrayed with consular attributes. They are often depicted with the *mappa* (which signalled the beginning of the chariot races in the consular games) in one hand and the *scipio eburneus* (a sceptre, sometimes tipped with a bust or eagle) in the other, or even in a *currus bigalus*, a two-horse chariot driven by the consul at the opening of the *pompa circensis*.[67] In addition, the dress, pose or arm gestures often reflect that of the consul honoured by the diptych, perhaps encouraging the viewer to see in that consul the achievements or attributes of the figure within the decoration (if it was identifiable) – the smaller figures are a mirror, up to which he could be held. If the figure in the garment decoration was an emperor, and reflected the honorand's pose, the viewer was being asked to see a connection between the two. This connection would have been perceived in different ways, such as those that will be encountered in Ausonius' case, where a previous emperor was held up as a model for the current one through the consul's *trabea*, and helped to legitimate him.

If the *imago* is of the current emperor – not unlikely, but difficult to confirm – then the consul would have been seen as an extension of the emperor's power through their reflecting poses, and the emperor's strong connection to the office through the common practice of repeated imperial consulships. The implication would be that the emperor was the consul's support, the source of the consul's power and authority, which was also, by inference, conditional upon the consul's ability to reflect imperial ambitions and policies, and maintaining his relationship with the emperor.[68] The consul was literally the emperor's representative (complete with imperial *imagines*) when the latter could not be present himself, and this will be returned to in more detail with reference to Ausonius' *trabea* later in the chapter. The potency of these images has already been discussed, but taken with the above they showed that the consul was something more than a man. Despite the office's loss of formal power, the continued limitation of number to two per year and use of the consuls' names as a dating formula for the year meant the consulship continued to be a sought-after and prestigious role.[69] Furthermore, the consulship was an office of weighty antiquity; predating the emperors, it was intimately connected with the idea of *Roma Aeterna* and the continued triumph of the Roman state, a status also embodied by the emperor.[70] A consul dressed in his robes of office woven with images of the emperor was therefore doubly invested with authority.

Yet the difficulties presented by the small size and sometimes damaged nature of the figural decoration on the diptychs means that often scholars assert the identities of such figures on the basis of intelligent guesswork only. This is most prominent in Cecilia Olovsdotter's descriptions of the Halberstadt and Areobindus diptychs, where she claims the figural decorations on the consular robes are examples of imperial portraits or figures.[71] This stems from her assumption that this style of clothing was always a gift from the emperor, and it leads her to conclude that '[i]t may be seriously doubted that the emperor would ever have presented a consul with a toga adorned with figural insets representing other than himself . . .'; as will be seen of the decoration on Ausonius' *trabea*, however, this was clearly not always the case.[72] It seems, therefore, that the identification of these portraits as imperial can be open to doubt. Coupled with the evidence from Sidonius and Claudian (discussed further below) who describe such garments covered in wedding scenes or family portraits, this uncertainty and variation suggests that the woven portraits represented on the diptychs could also be images of illustrious relatives and ancestors, members of the current or a previous imperial family, or a mixture of the two. This leads to a different interpretation entirely of such decorations, for instead of highlighting the consul's loyalty to the current emperor, portraits of the consul's own, different, imperial ancestors or illustrious relatives could have been seen as exalting an eminent family name in the face of an emperor who has none. Thus, while some members of the aristocracy were of course related to members of the current imperial family, others were descended from previous rulers or a long line of consuls, and the decorations appear to have been used to highlight these relationships. And, in fact, Olovsdotter does allow that the sole figure on Basilius' *trabea* could perhaps be designated as a consular (and not imperial) ancestor.[73] If it is the case that the figures on the *trabeae* of the other consular diptychs could be identified as private citizens and consular ancestors as well as the imperial family, then it can be seen that the consul is emphasising his ancestral status.

In flaunting the prestige of an aristocratic heritage, perhaps in the presence of emperors who had no family pedigree, the consul was thus elevating his claim to the consulship above his rivals.[74] Ancestral portraits on clothing were clearly important in negotiating status external to the consulship during the fourth century, as can be seen in the description of a man of dubious descent choosing to depict Mars, Romulus, and Remus on his robe in a bid to claim a (or rather *the*) superior ancestry.[75] Within the context of the consulship, this could include portraits of relatives who had been consuls themselves, as is perhaps the case in Basilius' diptych. This would be doubly potent if they were also previous emperors, as on Anthemius' *trabea*: Anastasius I had himself held the consulship three times before (in 492, 497, and 507) and Anthemius' imperial father had been eastern consul in 455. Such *imagines* would suggest that the consul was born to his office, for they promulgated the idea that he was from a family that had been producing such officials for generations.[76] This would have meant much to some, particularly at a time when the candidate pool could consist of 'barbarian' generals and even rhetoricians like Ausonius. That the latter was aware that some traded on their ancestry to win prominence at court is hinted at in his thanksgiving speech,[77] and so weaving illustrious family members into the consular garment would have emphasised that their own consulship was a natural and inevitable conclusion.

3.5 Figural decoration on the consular *trabea* ii: Poetry

This is also the case for the figural decorations, which can be 'seen' not only in the material evidence, but through late antique poetry. These items must be treated with caution, of course, for, depicted by Claudian and Sidonius, these *trabeae* are caught in a poetic world between myth and history. In several ways the consular robe of Stilicho, described by Claudian as a gift from Roma herself, in the *De Consulatu Stilichonis* composed in honour of the general's consulship in 400, combines many of the different messages which the figural decorations found in the consular diptychs and Ausonius' speech convey.[78] Claudian's *ekphrasis* of the garment incorporates both imperial and dynastic imagery in the form of Stilicho's children and grandchildren, who are depicted as the wives, mothers, fathers, sisters, and brothers of future emperors. It thus negotiates his position and authority within the political sphere, as well as his relationship with Roman society and the imperial family:

> 'Here I have prefigured your pledges, your children who have been promised and hoped for by the world. Soon you will admit me a true prophet and our warp threads will give coming fate confidence'. [Rome] spoke and brought forth from her breast the rigid gift, *trabea* heavy with gold. The sign of office breathes Minerva's labour ... [Here] Stilicho, older of age, hands over lessons of war to his grandson, future emperor ... Here Venus ... joins the third marriage with imperial ties, and winged Loves crowd around the daughter-in-law to be, child of emperors and sister of emperors ... This house now seeks the diadem with either sex, it gives birth to queens and to the husbands of queens. (Claudian, *De Consulatu Stilichonis*, 2.336–361)[79]

Through this *trabea* Claudian shows Stilicho's dynastic hopes, and as it is this decoration, not rich jewels, which are the focus of his description, the importance of family or, more dangerously, dynastic ambition is emphasised.[80] It will be seen in the case study that, in some ways, this is a similar device to Gratian's gift to Ausonius depicting Gratian's father-in-law Constantius II. Stilicho's garment looks forward, rather than back, however, in order to highlight his suitability to wield power – the expected attainment of high positions by Stilicho's descendants legitimates his influence now, just as his marriage to Constantius' daughter will be seen to help legitimate Gratian's current right to rule. Gratian's desire to emphasise his family connections will be discussed further below. It appears his motivation was not unique; but such a message must have been much more potent if the wearer of the garment was the head of the family it depicted, as Stilicho was. In addition, just as the ancestral portraits on the consular diptychs remind the viewer of the wearer's heritage through his illustrious ancestors, or perhaps his connection to the emperor via the latter's portrait, Claudian enables Stilicho's clothing gift to do both. Stilicho does not have illustrious ancestors, but his suitability for the consulship is cemented by his genetic or marital connection to emperors present and future; and in looking forward rather than back Claudian creates a clever inversion of the expected forms of glorifying oneself.

In general, having ancestors and emperors on the consular robe – a robe that would have been seen by many at the inaugural ceremonies and perhaps even at games and dinners[81] – would have placed him within an established tradition of exemplary men. It would have implied the new consul's authority, whilst reminding him of the expectations he had to live up to. In an empire populated with representations of human (and divine) *exempla*, as well as the coins and statues promulgating the imperial image, images provided the viewer with a frame of reference. It is not unreasonable to propose that the audience would have recognised a previous emperor,[82] and the poses of the woven *imagines* may have helped elucidate this. Furthermore, these *exempla* can suggest another context in which consular *trabeae* woven with portraits can be viewed, therefore implying the significance that could be attributed to this kind of decoration. By clothing Stilicho through the benevolence of the goddess Rome and Minerva's skill, Claudian removes his protagonist out of the realm of reality and places him within the world of myth; he is Mars and Romulus returning in triumph to Rome:

> Then the shoulders expert for bearing arms, [Rome] now encircled with the clothing of Romulus; the dress of the Latins settles on his chest and the toga is fitting in place of the cuirass. Just like Mars Gradivus, returning victorious from Istria or from the Scythian region; having laid down his shield, he is dressed in a *trabea*, gentle, he enters the city with shining white horses. (*Cons. Stil.* 2.365–370)[83]

That the present is from the personification of Rome is, of course, potent symbolism. Claudian is using a gift of clothing to imply not only that Rome desires a connection between herself and Stilicho and is offering her protection, but also that she is at the same time providing him with the mantle of authority. With this gift, Claudian is suggesting that Stilicho will reciprocate by bringing dignity back to the office of the consulship which had lately been 'destroyed' by the appointment in 399 of the eunuch Eutropius as consul in the east.[84] The poet is thus using the messages inherent in both clothing and gifts to emphasise fully that Rome (and the empire) supports Stilicho's rise to power and his ambitions for his dynasty.

Through this scenario, the poet also encourages the audience to think of the beneficiary in the light of great heroes like Achilles and Aeneas, particularly as Claudian's description of the cloak, as an *ekphrasis*, echoes Homer and Virgil's depictions of the fabulous works of craft their own heroes received from divine patrons. While in reality Stilicho's *trabea* was of course not a god-given present, Claudian's depiction of it as embellished with figural decorations, like the garments awarded to the victor of the Trojan Games or the tapestry woven by Minerva in Ovid's *Metamorphoses* in an evocation of the shield of Achilles or of Aeneas,[85] places Stilicho in a heroic tradition. By claiming Stilicho's *trabea* is of divine craftsmanship, Claudian is clearly asking the audience to view his hero within this epic context. Stilicho, therefore, was to be understood as the heir of Aeneas, as well as of Mars and Romulus, sanctioned by Rome herself; and like these founders his descendants are destined to rule the world. Stilicho was himself a successful general, but in a period when the idea of Roman military might was increasingly challenged, appropriating and evoking heroic ideals through clothing that had strong associations with the costume worn by a general during his triumph must have been useful for reassuring the court of the continued supremacy of the Roman empire. This may have been particularly potent in light of the fact that, although active generals did sometimes hold the consulship, they were in the minority.[86] Thus, Claudian's use of the *trabea* gift not only allowed him to praise the subject of this poem, by showing him as an epic hero, but may have enabled his elite audience to interpret their own lavishly decorated clothing as part of this framework. It allowed those who had limited access to real power the ability to partake of the potent rhetoric of heroic myth. That this still had cultural value even in a nominally Christian empire, can be seen on the non-consular clothing described in Ausonius' *Epigram* 45, noted above. Although Ausonius ridicules the man for claiming ancestry to Mars Romulus and Remus through his clothing, his portrayal does show that it was felt to have social capital.[87] For the civilian consul, such clothing provided a different and highly visual route to heroism. This must have been particularly gratifying at a time when the office of the consulship itself involved far less power than it had done in earlier centuries. In this way Claudian's depiction therefore can be seen to provide his audience with the interpretative tools to cover up the disparity between reality and ideal.

Carmina 15, an *Epithalamium* of Sidonius, also places a consul and his family into a mythical tradition, for his description of the decoration woven by the consul's daughter onto his *trabea* appears too as an *ekphrasis*, and has similarities to those mentioned above. In the poem, Araneola makes a *trabea* for her father, who is soon to be a consul, and despite the solemn occasion for which the *trabea* is being prepared, she playfully weaves wedding scenes into her father's robe:

> Here therefore [Araneola] copies the stiff *trabea* of her grandfather, preparing herself a *palmata* for her father, a consul as well and by which route he might match his grandfather Agricola [consul 421] and teach his grandchildren to unite the consulships not only of their grandfather, but of their

grandfather's grandfather ... But yet on a raised section she had playfully woven those famous early knot-tying stories into the *trabea*. (150–153, 158–169)[88]

Although these were real people, with its spidery overtones Araneola's name may have suggested to Sidonius the opportunity to present her weaving skills as better than those of the average consul's daughter. Furthermore, the embellishment seems to contain more subject matter than might be thought possible on one clothing item.[89] The decoration, therefore, becomes instead a space on which the poet can weave his (and his conception of Araneola's) own concerns, celebrating not only her family's long connection to the consulship – suggesting, like Claudian, that this predestines more prestige to come – but also, through the woven mythological nuptials, Araneola's marriage to Polemius. The circumstances of her activity, which takes place in Minerva's weaving workshop ('*textrino ... Minervae*' (126)), and the scenes she creates, place Araneola into the mythical sphere. Araneola can therefore also participate in the heroic rhetoric that located Stilicho above, but in a form that is appropriate to her gender – she is a Penelope, Helen, or Andromache rather than an Achilles or Aeneas. Furthermore, casting her in this light allows her father and her future husband a share in this through reflected glory, their connection to her places them within this world by proxy. Thus, the perhaps fictional clothing gift woven by Araneola becomes in Sidonius' hands a space to exalt the family, turning it into a real gift to her, her father, and her future husband in the form of a poem.

While the poetic version of Araneola may have been able to weave what she liked onto her father's *trabea*, once the decorative decision-making process was taken out of a consul's hands because he had been given an already embellished *trabea* as a gift, he was no longer wrapped up in his own messages but those of the donor. When the benefactor was not a family member but the emperor himself, this became all the more important and it is this that makes Ausonius' *trabea* significant. Carefully selected by the emperor Gratian, it is the only *trabea* that can be securely attributed to direct and personal imperial generosity in this period, and as a result it will be the focus of the rest of this chapter. The following discussion will suggest that Ausonius' special connection to the 19-year-old emperor Gratian, and that emperor's own uncertain authority and relationship to his imperial colleagues, made the gifting of a figurally decorated consular *trabea* a particularly significant action. It is thus a highly informative instance of an emperor's methods of self-representation.

3.6 Case study – wearing the emperor: Ausonius' consular *trabea*

In 379 a rhetorician from Bordeaux was inaugurated into what was still the highest dignity a private citizen could achieve in Roman society (bar the imperial purple), namely the consulship.[90] Ausonius received this honour, to which was added the distinction of being named consul *prior*,[91] because of his close relationship with the young emperor Gratian, to whom he had been a mentor and tutor during his early years (from 367).[92] Gratian's generosity did not stop there, however. As has been seen, he also sent Ausonius a *trabea*, which, significantly, the emperor chose himself, decorated with an imperial figure, though, somewhat surprisingly, not of Gratian but of his father-in law Constantius II:

> You say, 'I have sent you a *palmata* in which the divine Constantius, my parent, has been woven'.... This plainly, this is a *picta vestis*, as it was called, not greater with its own gold than with your words. But there is more in its many decorations, which, since being instructed by you, I understand. For the names of twin *Augusti* shine from one attire. Constantius has been woven into the garment in fact, but Gratian is felt in the honour of the gift. (Ausonius, *Gratiarum Actio*, 11)[93]

In both these choices (the decoration and the appointment of Ausonius to consul), however, Gratian was not merely gratifying his former tutor's vanity. This final section will explore why Gratian, young and inexperienced in military and administrative matters, felt that the image of Constantius, rather than his own father Valentinian I, was the better choice to demonstrate his legitimacy as emperor. It will become clear that decoration could work both with the consul and independently from him in order to promote Gratian's ideas and ambitions for his reign and his imperial authority. It will also be clear that Ausonius is a willing participant in this; he reciprocates Gratian's generosity by making sure the emperor's messages are understood.

By looking in detail at Gratian's possible reasons for choosing a *trabea* adorned with Constantius' figure, it will be seen that dress could be used to publicise military success and an individual's dynastic links, which would have been connected by viewers to Gratian, not to Ausonius – to the benefactor, not the wearer. This would have been all the more forceful if the receiver had been dressed in the garment whilst making a speech of thanks for the gift in front of the emperor himself,[94] and so a brief discussion of this subject will be considered before turning to the decoration itself.

While it is difficult to know for certain whether Ausonius was wearing the garment at the time of the speech, it is highly probable that this was the case. He is certainly likely to have worn it for the inaugural celebrations, as the garment appears to be an integral part of such events, and Ausonius' *trabea* was sent in celebration of his elevation. Ausonius, Claudian, and Sidonius all seem to imply that it was given to the consul to be worn at his inauguration; and the consular diptychs, which have common costume traits, portray the honorand in what must be his official dress, thus further corroborating that it was worn on official business.[95] It is likely that it was worn at the *processus consularis* and the *pompa circensis*,[96] the inaugural ceremonies for the consulship, for the above authors place their descriptions of the *trabea* before their subjects actually become consuls. Furthermore, Claudian implies that Stilicho enters the city in his *trabea* in a procession that appears to have all the trappings of a triumph, but is accompanied by the insignia of the consulship.[97] In the Republic and Early Empire it seems that some triumphators wore their ceremonial robes outside of official duties, for instance to dinners or to the circus games. Particularly with regards to emperors, accounts of this behaviour were used to convey the inappropriateness of attiring oneself in such dress within these situations, and thus the questionable character of the wearer. Suetonius and Dio Cassius, for example, feel the emperor Caligula's triumphal costume is just better than his being dressed as a divinity, while Claudius' restraint at only wearing triumphal dress while sacrificing, as opposed throughout the whole celebration, is almost praiseworthy to the latter author.[98] Yet these examples do also show that in certain circumstances high status men were voted the privilege of, or felt they could get away with, wearing their ceremonial costumes outside of the usual situation, in order to show their new honour.[99] Ausonius, then, may have worn his *trabea* not only at his inauguration, but also on important occasions, which would allow more people to view the garment's decoration. Furthermore, it is almost certain he would have been dressed in this item to attend the arrival of the imperial donor of the gift, and, coupled with the speech, this would make the connection between the wearer, the donor, and the decoration plain.

This arrival, however, was not at the investiture itself, for it appears that the emperor was absent due to the more pressing need for his presence in Sirmium.[100] In this period, the emperor was often not able personally to oversee consular inaugurations, due to regular fighting on the frontiers of the empire which needed the imperial presence. It became common, therefore, for the new consul to be inaugurated in the most convenient city for the official; Ausonius' inauguration in Trier, without Gratian, may have been such an occasion.[101] However, providing a garment with an emperor's figure woven into it ensured an imperial attendee, symbolic if not physical:[102] as noted in the beginning sections of the chapter, later authors talk of clothing worn by imperial officials woven with a portrait of the emperor, which were felt to contain an intimate connection with their imperial original. That there was a continuing belief that an image was 'actually real, [and] that it was related to, and could not always be entirely distinguished from, the prototype it represented',[103] is reflected in the opinions of Basil of Caesarea and John Chrysostom discussed previously. Imperial *imagines*, therefore, could perhaps have been seen as standing in for the emperor in certain situations when his appearance would have been expected, but he could not attend; in this circumstance he was still the consul's colleague even when he had given that privilege to someone else.[104] It would have marked Ausonius out as the emperor's representative, therefore, even if the emperor depicted, as in the case of Ausonius' *trabea*, was long dead; his portrait would remind viewers of the current emperor by association.

This would have been important if the speech was not delivered in front of the emperor when he arrived in Trier later in the year, but at the consul's inauguration ceremony usually held in its initial months.[105] While the internal evidence from the speech does point towards composition and delivery at a later date, the surprising absence of Theodosius in the speech is suggestive.[106]

The persuasive arguments of Neil McLynn have proposed that Theodosius was not formally elevated as Augustus until mid-January 379, after being proclaimed so by his troops on 19 January.[107] If McLynn's proposed dating is correct, then Theodosius' absence from the speech both suggests and may be explained by an earlier dating: Ausonius composed it for delivery at his own inauguration on 1 January, before Theodosius had come to power. The assertions of Gratian's presence in the circumstances and decoration of the *trabea* are therefore revealing for considering when Ausonius gave this speech. They suggest there is a possibility that the thanksgiving was given during Ausonius' consular inauguration ceremony, without the physical attendance of the addressee.[108] The decoration on the consul's garment would have been important in this circumstance, then, as it allows Gratian to be in two places at once; Gratian is felt to be present in Trier through the gift of the *trabea*: *Gratianus in muneris honore sentitur*. Ausonius' words would have been even more powerful if the opinion that this kind of image was actually a visual manifestation of the emperor himself was felt by the audience at large,[109] and Ausonius himself draws on the idea of an emperor being present through his portrait: *Constantius in argumento vestis intexitur*. The implication that Constantius was symbolically present would be aided by the weaving of the decoration itself and the play of light (*radiat*) on the golden threads (*auro suo*) of the *trabea*.[110] Combined with Ausonius' own movements while he gave his speech, this would animate the decoration, suggesting the figure had physicality and lending weight to Ausonius' assertion that both Gratian and Constantius were manifest in the decoration (*Geminum quippe in uno habitu radiat nomen Augusti*).[111] The gift of the clothing reinforces these literary notions emphatically, and both text and fabric draw attention to the imperial duality held in the decorated image. While it is likely that Gratian would have seen Ausonius in his *trabea* gift when he eventually arrived, the concern to assert that he is present in the present perhaps suggests Gratian's absence for the initial performance of the speech.

Whatever the circumstance of the delivery of the speech, Ausonius' reference to Gratian's metaphorical presence in the gift was important in other, more significant, ways. It ensured that the emperor was continually in the minds of the audience whenever they looked at the *trabea* – whether Gratian was physically in attendance during the investiture, his imperial manifestation would always remain implicit in the garment on every occasion Ausonius wore it. Ausonius aids this further by making no secret of the fact that the decoration is not of his own choosing (*cum maxime dimicaturus palmatae vestis meae ornamenta disponis*). He repeatedly emphasises Gratian's personal role in the decision making process, making it appear that the emperor is taking an interest in a job that customarily fell to an official, as noted above (*nec satis habes, ut largitionum ministri ex more fungantur*). While this could simply be a matter of Ausonius demonstrating the care and respect Gratian has for him as his friend and advisor in order to enhance his own prestige and status, an alternative interpretation can be proposed. In repeatedly highlighting Gratian's role, Ausonius lessens his own connection with the *trabea* and its decoration, and thus ensures that the audience of his *Gratiarum Actio* connect it primarily with Gratian; any messages the embellishment conveys will be associated with the giver rather than the wearer. In behaving in this way, Ausonius is acting as Martial had in his character as the perfect *cliens*, and ensures that Gratian is set in the role of the noble patron, generous and willing to repay anyone who has aided him.

The sense that Gratian is the primary focus is reinforced by the reference to Constantius, for Gratian had a much stronger link to Constantius than Ausonius did. It is doubtful that Ausonius ever met the former emperor, even though his maternal uncle was friendly with the half-brothers of Constantine I, and was a tutor to a Caesar in Constantinople, possibly either Constans or Constantine II.[112] Gratian, on the other hand, was linked to Constantius through his marriage to the latter's daughter Constantia.[113] Therefore, it is possible that Gratian's use of Constantius' image was not related to Ausonius at all, but was rather a bid by Gratian to emphasis his own connections to the previous ruling dynasty and strengthen his authority.[114] Indeed, Ausonius' remarks seem to suggest that the decoration needs to be 'read' in more detail, and that Gratian himself has instructed him in how this was to be done (*sed multo plura sunt in eius ornatu, quae per te instructus intellego*). The garment is valuable already due to its golden thread, but it is the meaning behind the decoration which enriches the *trabea* even more (*non magis auro suo quam tuis verbis*) – a reference to Gratian's generosity and kindness, of course, but also that the figure of Constantius should be understood at a deeper level.

From Ausonius' description of his garment it becomes clear that Valentinian I is absent, despite being Gratian's father. This seems odd, particularly if it is considered that, as his son, Gratian's legitimacy to rule stemmed primarily from his father – the immediately preceding emperor – rather than through an emperor to whom he was only related by his marriage to Constantius II's daughter. It may be that as Gratian's connection to Valentinian would have been obvious to the audience of Ausonius' speech, the emperor decided that choosing a garment bearing his image would have been dynastic 'overkill'. However, Valentinian I's claim to legitimacy was tenuous as he was unrelated to any of the previous rulers and had been the third choice during the council held at Nicaea to determine the new emperor.[115] Gratian's decision to gift a *trabea* with the image of his father-in-law Constantius, therefore, could have been viewed as reinforcing his authority by providing him with a strong claim to imperial power, through an established and revered dynasty.[116] By introducing the figure of Constantius into the consular proceedings, Gratian is emphasising the continuity of his reign with that of Constantius and his ancestors, who, upon the death of Julian, had ruled the empire for the second longest period of time of any dynasty. Ausonius encourages his audience to make this association by saying that Gratian calls Constantius *parens noster* in his letter accompanying the consular garment in *Gratiarum Action* 11, suggesting that Gratian is directly descended from Constantius,[117] and thus enabling the Constantinian dynasty to continue.

That Constantius was a useful figure to appropriate as a forbear can be seen in the revolt of Procopius in 365 during the reign of Valentinian I and Valens.[118]

Related to Julian but not to Constantius, Procopius and his supporters claimed that he had been named as Julian's successor, and that this had been expressed through the gifting of Julian's own imperial, purple cloak (*paludamentum purpureum*) to Procopius just before his death.[119] Although both Ammianus and Philostorgius dismiss this story as mere rumour, it demonstrates that the transference of authority could be symbolised potently through the gifting of special types of clothing in the late antique world. In addition, Procopius stressed his (false) relationship to Constantius by not only parading Constantius' widow, but also by carrying around the emperor's daughter Constantia (Gratian's future wife) and so won over the divisions of infantry and cavalry that were passing through Thrace at that time.[120] Indeed, it was so successful that Procopius repeated this strategy in Asia in a more dramatic fashion by taking the child 'not only on the march but even into the line of battle'.[121] Ammianus' observations on this shrewdness in cunning plans (*has calliditatis argutias*) show just how potent a tactic it could be, for 'it inflamed the anger of [Procopius'] soldiers so they would fight more courageously for the imperial offspring, to which he was adding by connecting himself as well' (*ut pro imperiali germine, cui se quoque iunctum addebat, pugnarent audentius, iras militum accenderat*). Indeed, it could only be countered by one of Constantius' generals, who was induced to come out of retirement for the sole purpose of condemning Procopius' actions.[122] If, therefore, merely carrying the child of Constantius (or even just the words of one of his generals) was sufficient to win the loyalty of military units, Gratian's claims through marrying Constantia must have been perceived as that much stronger.[123] Contenders for the imperial purple, legitimate or otherwise, needed to do all they could to prove they were better than their nearest rival, and that Constantius was felt to be of use for legitimating a claim is demonstrated by Procopius' bid for power.[124]

For some elements of the Roman empire, then, a link to the previous ruling family and the 'cherished memory'[125] of a previous emperor could elevate a citizen above even the current ruler(s), who were often themselves successful in claiming imperial power without any previous qualifications of nobility or family. This demonstrates the power that dynastic associations could still exercise, and has been seen already on the *trabeae* of other consuls in the diptychs examined earlier in the chapter. However, rather than being able to demonstrate his own illustrious ancestry, Ausonius is displaying Gratian's. By joining two imperial families, the young emperor was bolstering his right to rule which was primarily derived from Valentinian I's weaker claim with the much stronger one of the dynasty of Constantine. Doing so enabled him to emphasise his legitimacy above any potential pretenders; he was entitled to the imperial title twice over, and reinforced this combined and therefore superior claim through Ausonius' *trabea*. By incorporating the figural image of Constantius into Ausonius' robe, then, Gratian could demonstrate his imperial authority through visual suggestion via a potent combination of differing dynastic legacies to an audience that had been habituated to seeing the sons of emperors rule for over six decades.[126] For an emperor like Gratian, who still had much to prove in exercising imperial power,[127] this was an effective weapon in demonstrating his greater suitability to rule. It elevated him over his imperial colleagues and those who might seek to depose him who did not have such a strong claim to imperial continuity.

At 19, as a young but maturing emperor, Gratian needed to consolidate imperial power in his own right, particularly as he had already been made to share this authority with his younger brother Valentinian II, who was elevated without Gratian's consent in 375.[128] The image on the gift implicitly excludes from the consular proceedings not only his father but also this half-brother in an attempt to ensure that the people of Trier, and beyond, maintained their loyalty to him alone. Choosing to give a *trabea* with the figure of Constantius to Ausonius may have seemed like Gratian was emphasising his weaker claim to power because Constantius was his father-in-law, but it was in fact a connection with the previous ruling family that only he could make. It marked him out as being legitimate not only through his status as the son of Valentinian I, but also, through his marriage to Constantius' daughter, the heir to that family's power and prestige, and thus strengthened his imperial authority with a double dynastic claim.

Ausonius' *trabea* interwoven with Constantius should be read, therefore, within the context of a wider pattern of attempts by Gratian to distance himself from his family to strengthen his own imperial position and personal authority. Choosing this emperor to adorn his consul's *trabea*, rather than Valentinian, demonstrated particular political intelligence with regard to the aristocracy, for the last years of Valentinian I's reign were viewed as oppressive, especially by those at Rome, due to a spate of prosecutions aimed at the senatorial elite, and it is unlikely Valentinian would have been remembered by them fondly.[129] Constantius, on the other hand, appears to have had good relations with the senate, who reacted negatively to an attack on Constantius' reputation by Julian in a letter sent to them during his usurpation.[130] Of course, the immediate audience for Ausonius' thanksgiving speech was unlikely to be from the Roman senate, but the author had close ties with its members, corresponding frequently with Symmachus who recommended his friends for assistance by Ausonius in the political sphere.[131] It is not improbable, therefore, that Ausonius may have sent this speech to some of his acquaintances at Rome, or perhaps mentioned the generous gift of the emperor in a letter to his correspondents there, thus enabling the *trabea* gift and its decoration to be 'seen' by a wider audience.

That Gratian was clearly taking measures to distance himself from the actions of his father and heal the hurts of the recent years can be seen in his elimination of Valentinian's former associates and elevation of prominent senators to the consulship such as Ausonius' colleague, Olybrius. Ausonius was certainly part of these reforms, placing his own relatives and friends in positions of power once occupied by Valentinian's officials.[132] By replacing them with Ausonius' associates, no doubt under his guidance, Gratian was widening his support to influential members of the aristocracy, and was thus simultaneously consolidating his power and authority by demonstrating he was a different emperor from

Valentinian, while removing the temptation some of those men may have felt to support a challenge to his position.[133] Ausonius was, therefore, a crucial link between the young emperor and the Roman Senate because he was well liked by some of its influential members and could promulgate the positive aspects of Gratian's reign.[134] Knowing about the ties between Ausonius and the senate, Gratian's action of gifting him with a *trabea* decorated with an emperor other than Valentinian may have been a further attempt to show that he was making positive changes in imperial attitudes towards the senate. By erasing Valentinian from the family equation in both the thanksgiving speech and gift, and highlighting the image of Constantius on Ausonius' *trabea*, the author and the emperor are working together to help the young ruler's efforts in this direction.[135] This would in turn contribute to bolstering his claim to imperial authority among some of the most important men in the empire, by demonstrating his willingness to distance himself from the imperial father who had displeased them so much.

This could also be achieved by suggesting a different influence and education of the young emperor other than his father. By providing Ausonius with a garment chosen personally by him, Gratian emphasises this departure by highlighting a strong relationship with his tutor. This would have been encouraging for the Roman elite, and it furthermore served the additional purpose of demonstrating that Gratian was an erudite man. This continued to be a desirable quality in those men who held high office, for to be a man of culture implied possession of authority and encouraged respect; more importantly, as Alan Cameron succinctly explains, '*paideia* bred leadership'.[136] Clearly, this was a valuable attribute for Gratian as an emperor to have, but also for him to display to members of the elite, who felt that having shared cultural bonds with the emperor, created by this type of education, would make him more amenable to their viewpoint.[137] As a result, they may have initially felt unsure of the son of Valentinian, for that emperor appears to have been viewed in the sources as only moderately well educated; moreover he came from Pannonia, an area populated in ancient literature with boorish people. If Ammianus is to be believed, Valentinian lived up to this stereotype and expressed a hatred of the educated; such an attitude, therefore, would have hardly endeared him to the Roman senatorial elite.[138] In contrast, Constantius was considered an emperor of some learning and rhetorical skill, who promoted many men accomplished in literary studies to various offices in the empire.[139] Gratian's elevation of Ausonius echoes Constantius' positive conduct towards such men. Constantius' image on the garment of Gratian's tutor may, therefore, be a further effort on Gratian's part to distance himself from his 'under-educated' father, while simultaneously implying his own higher learning in order to appeal to the senate, and show his suitability to rule.[140]

That Valentinian was himself aware of the disadvantages of being an undereducated ruler is shown in his employment of Ausonius as his son's tutor from a young age. Furthermore, the success of this venture, and the importance that was attached to having a well-educated emperor at the helm, can be seen in the admiration for Gratian's learning which is repeated in a number of sources.[141] Ausonius' thanksgiving speech is one of these; it praises Gratian's education highly, and can be seen as working to ensure that the audience understands that the emperor is a man of education, particularly when it is paired with the *trabea* gift, which had rewarded Gratian's own tutor. Ausonius applauds the 'excellences of [Gratian's] mind' (*bona animi*) in *Gratiarum actio* 4 and returns to this subject again in sections 14 and 15. He further emphasises this quality through the description of the garment. As noted earlier, he uses various terms (*palmata vestis*, *toga*, and *vestis* or *toga picta*) as synonymous with his *trabea* in order to create clever contrasts between his own peaceful situation and Gratian who was out on campaign, which also show Gratian as the ideal emperor, successful in war, but desirous of peace. Ausonius is here acting in a similar way to Martial, who sent his patrons poems full of obscure references to publicise their (and, of course, his own) superiority in understanding. By emphasising this continued close relationship between tutor and pupil, as well as Gratian's connection to Constantius through a mutual love of learning, both the *trabea* and the speech reflected well on the young emperor's suitability for authority and his ability to wield power rationally; in the Roman world knowledge was (a basis for) power.

Gratian may have been strengthening his claim to imperial authority by making shrewd manoeuvers in the political sphere and demonstrating his intelligence, but this had the potential to be undermined by his young age and inexperience in the military arena where he had yet to prove himself as an able commander. That is not to say Gratian did not have some successful campaigns (Ammianus even calls Gratian *bellicosus*),[142] but he was still relatively untested in war, and the speech and the figural decoration should be viewed as also performing together in an attempt to ease anxieties about the emperor in this sphere. In the *Gratiarum Actio* itself Ausonius appears to do this by appropriating military successes and titles not in fact won by Gratian. For instance, while Ausonius lists titles (*Alamannicus*, *Germanicus*) attested in an inscription from 370 as having been won by Gratian,[143] they were in fact due to Valentinian I, whose military reputation made this safer ground for association.

He also calls the emperor *Sarmaticus* in *Gratiarum actio* 2, saying he might name Gratian thus because he conquered and forgave the Sarmatians (*vocarem . . . vincendo et ignoscendo Sarmaticum*). However, this title is not substantiated by inscriptions, and it appears to be a fiction created by Ausonius.[144] Neil McLynn has explained away the author's inclusion of this title as a translation of Gratian's clash in the summer of 378 with the Alans into 'classically acceptable victory material',[145] but the title of *Sarmaticus* should perhaps rather be viewed in relation to the figure of Constantius on Ausonius' *trabea*. This is because the title *Sarmaticus* was won by Constantius II twice.[146] Gratian, therefore, could be shown to be connected to Constantius, not only through his (Gratian's) wife and their mutual erudition, but also through military titles which proclaimed 'victories' for Gratian against the same enemy as Constantius himself had faced. The fact that Gratian had not won the titles himself was not particularly important; there were precedents for such a requisition. Gratian himself had already

116 *Portable portraits*

won the title *Gothicus* with his father and uncle merely on the strength of being the co-Augustus of Valens who had actually fought them in the late 360s,[147] and it has been seen already that Ausonius calls Gratian by his father's titles *Alamannicus* and *Germanicus*. Similarly, Constantius II was said to have taken the credit for Julian's Alamannic victories in Gaul.[148] Moreover, honouring Gratian by titles won by an inferior, as previous emperors had been before, meant Ausonius was providing the young emperor with a future added bonus coming at Theodosius' expense, as it was the latter who had won a victory against the Sarmatians in 374 in his capacity as *dux* of Moesia.[149] By appropriating from an inferior a title previously won by Constantius, it is possible that Ausonius was attempting to make his audience understand the connection between Gratian and the figure on his *trabea*, in order to show Gratian as Constantius' heir, not only through marriage but also through his military 'achievements'. It has been seen above how both a familial and military relationship to Constantius had been put to good use by Procopius and his opponents in order to bolster their own claims or undermine those of a potential rival. Thus, by both mentioning the title *Sarmaticus* in his speech and drawing attention to the figure of Constantius on the *trabea*, Ausonius' oration is working with the decoration on his gifted *trabea* by emphasising Gratian's suitability for imperial power and authority. This he does through allusions to Gratian's martial and familial 'ancestry' and 'victories' in war via the application of Constantius' own military titles.

Ausonius' possible appropriation of Constantius' title and the interwoven figure of the emperor should also, however, be placed back into the context of triumphal and military messages inherent in consular dress, as this would also help the viewer to understand how to read the correlation between a previous emperor's past successes and the current emperor's ability in war. Ausonius ensures that his audience are fully aware of this by calling his garment gift a *palmata vestis*, and then immediately reminding them of its connection to military triumph, as has been noted above. The incorporation of such an image into the decoration on a *palmata*, which certainly formed some part of the *vestis triumphalis*, could visually remind the viewer of past achievements in war, while the decoration simultaneously hinted at a continued glorious future.[150] The triumphal connotations inherent in some elements of the consul's outfit, the very name (*palmata*) implying the palms awarded to victorious generals, and the decoration (which can be seen on the *trabea* of Basilius in his diptych, Figure 3.2) that made this explicit, also contributed to the idea of perennial triumph. It encouraged the viewer to associate the emperor (or the private citizen) depicted with military success, whether they were able war leaders or not.[151] The figurally decorated *chlamys* and tunic worn by Stilicho in his consular diptych from Monza sets this type of embellishment squarely within a military context, for although a consul he is depicted instead as a *magister militum* complete with weaponry. The Halberstadt diptych (Figure 3.1) also visualises this notion through its consular *trabea* containing two figures, one with the emperor[152] holding an attribute of the consulship, the *mappa*, and the other containing a helmeted male bust, complete with shield. The figure is here expressly connected with military success, and so the decoration on this type of clothing celebrates the emperor's achievements while perhaps at the same time reminding the viewer of the consul's own success in war.[153]

Even if this was not the reality, the associations between imperial power and triumph could be appropriated through triumphal dress, as parts of the costume became increasingly associated with the emperor. The status and glory of triumph could be transferred to the wearer,[154] and, in the case of Ausonius, beyond him to the donor of the costume. Evidence from the diptychs suggests that Constantius' portrait may have been portrayed as a bust, which would be displayed on one of the folds of the *trabea*, that is, on an extremely prominent and highly visible part of the garment. Ausonius has already represented Gratian as personally choosing the decoration of the *trabea* within the speech. Wherever it was placed, therefore, its position on a garment that formed the outermost layer of the consul's dress meant that Gratian wanted the viewer to understand the importance of the figure in relation to himself and its connection to victory. In drawing attention to the figure on his *trabea* and calling the garment by a name that directly associates it with military triumph, Ausonius' thanksgiving speech and his clothing can be seen as working together. The result creates a fiction of the young and inexperienced Gratian as a great and successful war leader – a message of particular importance in disturbing times that had seen an emperor (Gratian's uncle Valens) recently killed in battle, and in which usurpers were not an uncommon occurrence.

3.7 Conclusions

Ausonius' description of the circumstances and process of selecting his gift presents Gratian as fighting for the security of the empire on the one hand, while overseeing the inauguration of its officials and distributing largess on the other. In doing so, he combines the dual (and ideal) roles of the emperor as successful war leader and beneficent ruler, covering over Gratian's inefficiencies particularly in the military sphere. He does more than this, however; for in helping his audience to identify the figure on his garment, Ausonius emphasises its importance by making them understand that they should see a connection not only between the provider of the *trabea* and its receiver, but also between Constantius and Gratian. By these means, he is reciprocating Gratian's gift, working with the decoration on the garment to promulgate Gratian's ambitions for his reign, creating a narrative of dynastic legitimacy, *paideia*, and military prowess in order to strengthen the young emperor's own authority. Although the gift and the speech allow Ausonius to demonstrate his close ties to the reigning emperor and simultaneously flaunt and partake in imperially appointed consular power, the author's prime concern is in fact predominantly not to negotiate his own relationship with society at large or even to enhance his own authority. While he is shown to be high in Gratian's favour because of the gift given to him, through his literary description of his clothing the consul is reciprocating the emperor's generosity by allowing himself to be the 'painted wall'[155] on which his protégé can project his claims to power and consolidate his authority with a unique reference to the previous ruling dynasty.

In a period where clothes were often embellished with intricate decorations in order to protect the wearer, attract good fortune, or demonstrate their loyalty or religious allegiance, it should not come as a surprise that some *trabeae*, which clothed one of the most prestigious officials in the Roman empire, would be woven with complex designs. Other dress items decorated similarly, such as the *chlamys*, were already in the social consciousness, due to the diplomatic presents seen in Chapter 2 and the adornment of other officials with portraits of the emperor; they marked their wearers clearly as belonging to him, allowing them to partake of his authority whilst at the same continuing to be subject to it. While all *trabeae* functioned in this way, it is noteworthy that only a small selection of the evidence for these important consular vestments, ascertained from diptychs and literary sources, are decorated with imperial images, perhaps because only these consuls had such a strong link to the imperial family. Furthermore, there is very little to show how they were made, where they could be obtained, and when it was appropriate to wear such a showy costume. Ausonius' brief digression on his new *trabea* provides the modern reader with a valuable insight into the interaction between an emperor and his officials, and the process by which a consul would usually (and unusually) obtain the official dress for his inauguration. The evidence provided by Sidonius indicates another avenue by which a consul could acquire his *trabea*, but Ausonius' comments imply that the customary method was through the officials of the largess, which, relieving the consul of the burden of paying for it, turned the item into an indirect gift of imperial benevolence.

The evidence from all three writers, as well as from the diptychs, suggests that although there may have been 'ready-made' *trabeae* available to the consuls, a select few holders of the office were perhaps allowed some measure of control over its decoration (unless, of course, the emperor intervened). If this was the case, the consul could choose to promulgate his own messages through his clothing, such as his superior ancestry or loyalty to the emperor, while at the same time being indebted and tied to the ruling authority whose distant generosity had provided him with the clothing. Claudian provides the viewer with a potential framework within which to understand the decoration, placing the consul into a heroic tradition and elevating him beyond his own mortal limitations, a narrative Sidonius also reflects. When the emperor took this choice away, however, he also took away the consul's voice and replaced it with his own. If the consul took the further step of highlighting his disassociation from the clothing he wore in a public speech as an act of reciprocity for a gifted *trabea*, this facilitated the 'reading' of the garment through the lens of imperial self-representation. In these circumstances, the figurally decorated *trabeae* become something more than garments to mark out those with consular powers. They become literary devices as well as real spaces upon which an emperor can project his own ambitions for his reign. Furthermore, they enabled an audience to read his attempts to reinforce insecure imperial authority on the body of his personally chosen consul. By attaching a particular set of meanings to the garment through the act of writing and talking, Ausonius (and Gratian) limit alternative understandings, over-writing them so that the literary becomes the authoritative interpretation. As will be seen in the next chapter, this was also a concept that could be mapped onto the saintly bodies of Christian holy men, this time for the purposes of strengthening orthodox religious authority.

Notes

1 These are reproduced and discussed by Delbrueck (1929), Volbach (1976) and Olovsdotter (2005): the Halberstadt diptych (Delbrueck (1929) N 2, discussion 87–93; Volbach (1976) Taf. 19, nr. 35; Olovsdotter (2005) plate 2; see 99–100 for a discussion, with bibliography, of the problems in identifying the honorand)); the diptych of Anicius Faustus Albinus Basilius (Delbrueck (1929) N 6, discussion 100–103; Volbach (1976) Taf. 3, nr 5 (who identifies it with Caecina Decius Maximus Basilius western consul 480, following Graeven (1892) 210, 216–17, but see Cameron and Schauer (1982) for the identification of this diptych with the consul of 541); Olovsdotter (2005) plate 8); the diptych of Areobindus (Delbrueck (1929) N 11, discussion 107–10, 112–13; Volbach (1976) Taf. 5, nr. 10; Olovsdotter (2005) plate 9.3a); the eighteenth-century engraving of the lost diptych of Anthemius (Delbrueck (1929) N 17, discussion 121–2; Olovsdotter (2005) 73; plate 15). Cf. the diptych of Stilicho (consul 400) from Monza, which presents the consul dressed in a figurally decorated *chlamys* and tunic, but as *magister militum* rather than consul (Delbrueck (1929) N 63, discussion 242–8; Volbach (1976) Taf. 35, nr. 63; see von Rummel (2007) 206–13; Cameron (1970) 47–9, 303; Woodfin (2013).
2 For instance Olovsdotter (2005) 72, 73. Her claim is based on the evidence of consular diptychs, which however cannot provide firm verification on the matter.
3 Lewis and Short s.v. *segmentum* I; II.B; cf. MacMullen (1990) 95, 99; *DarSag* 1172 col.2 s.v. *segmentum* makes this point while noting the differences between *segmentum* and *clavus*: 'La racine du mot (*seco*) indique, de prime abord, la différence entre le *segmentum*, pris strictement, et le clavus, dont on ne l'a pas toujours distingué: c'est un morceau coupé dans une étoffe et appliqué sur une autre'. Cf. Pritchard (2006) 19, 49, 60; Granger-Taylor (1983) 148 who notes evidence of tapestry ornaments 'sewn to . . . silk ready-made' and believes they are applicable to the decoration of Stilicho's *chlamys* on his diptych (see further below). This also seems to be behind Cecilia Olovsdotter's use of *segmenta* throughout her 2005 volume to discuss *trabea* with figural decorations. The evidence of Ausonius and the other authors discussed throughout this chapter suggests, however, that it is likely that the decoration on these specific garments would have been introduced as part of the weaving process of the *trabea*, rather than sewn on separately, see discussion throughout. *Segmentum* can also be translated as 'section', and this may be more applicable here, as in the case of Sid. *Carm.* 15 examined below.
4 Cf. Bogensperger (2014). It may also suggest that Ausonius' *trabea* with its decoration woven in (*intextus est* (*Grat. act.* 11)) was expensive not merely because of its golden threads, but also because of its incorporated design. Cf. Granger-Taylor (1983) 138.
5 Granger-Taylor (1983) 142, 144, *passim*; Pritchard (2006) 32, 45, 49, 63–4. For intricate patterns on textiles see, for example those displayed in Maguire (1990) figs 1, 6–9, 12–14, 17, 19–22, 24–26, 29, 31–36; Elsner (1998) fig. 73, detail of fig. 73 facing page 1; Kalavrezou (2003) catalogue nos. 80–82, 89–96; 164 fig. 15. For discussions of textile manufacture and patterns, see e.g. Wilson (1938); Jones (1960); Wild (1970); Granger-Taylor (1983); Cleland *et al.* (2007) 70–71 s.v. 'Figured textiles', 139–42 s.v. 'Patterned textiles', 'Pattern weaving;' Bender Jørgensen (2008); Ciszuk (2004); Woodfin (2012) 88, 92–3; Verhecken-Lammens (2013).

120 Portable portraits

6 These come mainly from Egypt (see e.g. Pritchard (2006)). Examples can be seen in the *Byzantium Women and Their World* exhibition catalogue (Kalavrezou (2003)), nos. 80–82 and 89–96; 164 fig. 15. While these are presented as belonging to women, their context is mostly unknown and so there is no reason to not to believe that some may have in fact belonged to men.
7 Pritchard (2006) 1, 13, 15–17, 49. *Orbiculi* and *tabulae* were usually placed symmetrically at the shoulders and knees, close to the *clavi* in the late antique period (Pritchard (2006) 49).
8 See Granger-Taylor (1983) for a discussion of two late antique silk clothing items that have survived.
9 See Stern (1953) planche XV, especially 166–7 for Gallus' clothing (which he refers to as a toga) and Salzman (1990) fig. 14. Its companion piece, depicting Constantius II in consular dress (Stern (1953) planche XIV), will not be discussed, despite being a portrait of an emperor who will feature often in this chapter. This is because he is depicted wearing garments that appear to be adorned with jewels rather than woven figures, and as such his dress is not relevant to the discussion.
10 Granger-Taylor (1983) 138. For a discussion of Roman looms see e.g. Granger-Taylor (1983) 149–51 (late antique looms, silk weaving); Ciszuk and Hammarlund (2008). For the term 'cartoon' in this context and a general discussion of this topic, see Stauffer (1996) and (2008); Pritchard (2006) 61–2. Despite the prevalence of 'embroidery' in translations of ancient authors and some surviving evidence of this technique (Pritchard (2006) 31–2; Letellier-Willemin (2103); Mérat (2013)), it was rare and was unlikely to have been used for decorative elements such those as discussed in this chapter, see e.g. Granger-Taylor (1982) and (1983) 133; Droß-Krüpe and Paetz gen. Schieck (2014).
11 More problematically they could also be a combination of both, cf. Krawiec (2014) 71–3.
12 Maguire (1990). Cf. Pritchard (2006) 60–61; Davis (2005); Lechitskaya (2013); Müller (2013); Oscharina (2013); Taylor (2014).
13 Just as the clothing relics of a saint were thought to do, see Chapter 4.
14 Not mentioned by Maguire. For the mosaic see MacCormack (1981) plate 62 with 260; Deliyannis (2010) plate 8b with 240–243.
15 Alchermes (2005) 374.
16 Tr. Maguire (1990) 220; cf. Theod. *Or.* 10.4 (*De providentia*): textiles decorated with 'figures of men, be they hunting or praying' (cited by Mango (1972) 50 n.146) and *In natali SS. Nazari et Celsi martyrum*, 6 (attributed to Ambrose or Maximus of Turin) which compares those who have received baptism with those that have 'received a garment of pure silk upon which a figure of a divine image is interwoven' (*holosericam, in qua sigillum divinae imaginis acceperamus impressum*) (cited by Delmaire (2003) 97).
17 Justinian's funeral dress: Coripp. *Iust. Aug.* 272–293; Sant'Apollinare mosaic: Deichmann (1958) Taf. 200; Delmaire (2003) 96–7.
18 Εἰ γὰρ ἄνθρωποι τὰς βιωτικὰς λειτουργίας ἀναδεχόμενοι καὶ ἐπὶ τῆς ἐσθῆτος πολλάκις ἣν περίκεινται τὸν τύπον τῶν βασιλικῶν εἰκόνων ἐπιφερόμενοι ... οὐδὲν ἀνάσχοιντο ἄν ποτε πρᾶξαι τοιοῦτον ὃ τῆς ἐσθῆτος ἐκείνης τῆς τοὺς τύπους ἐχούσης τοὺς βασιλικοὺς ἀνάξιον ἂν γένοιτο, ἀλλὰ κἂν αὐτοί ποτε ἐπιχειρήσωσι, πολλοὺς ἔχουσι τοὺς διακωλύοντας, κἂν ἕτεροί τινες αὐτοὺς κακῶς διαθεῖναι βούλοιντο, ἱκανὴν ἔχουσιν ἀσφάλειαν τοῦ μηδὲν ἀηδὲς παθεῖν τῆς ἐσθῆτος τὴν περιβολήν ... Tr. P. Harkins.
19 Wenger (1970) 191–2 n.1; cf. Woodfin (2012) 161 for this practice in the later Byzantine era. The men mentioned by John Chrysostom could be consuls; the generalised language when referring to both the wearers of these images and their clothing make it seem unlikely, however.
20 Ando (2000) 228–53 some of whose arguments I follow in this section; Swift (2009) 20.
21 Ὅτι βασιλεὺς λέγεται καὶ ἡ τοῦ βασιλέως εἰκών, καὶ οὐ δύο βασιλεῖς. Οὔτε γὰρ τὸ κράτος σχίζεται, οὔτε ἡ δόξα διαμερίζεται ... διότι ἡ τῆς εἰκόνος τιμὴ ἐπὶ τὸ πρωτότυπον διαβαίνει.

Portable portraits 121

(Basil of Caesarea, *De spiritu sancto*, 18.45; tr. Elsner (1998) 57)). Swift (2009) 21; cf. Hales (2005) esp. 133; Squire (2011) 154–201, esp. 159–60, 187–9.
22 Cf. Cameron (1976) fig. 6b (and possibly 6c) (see also Volbach (1976) Taf. 27, nr. 51 and 52 for the same diptych, probably of Ariadne (c.450–515) wife of emperors Zeno and Anastasius I. He identifies the image on the empress's garment in nr. 52 as Constantinople or Rome, but it is so worn that it is difficult to make out any details which could identify it as anything more than simply a portrait – indeed, Woodfin suggests it may be a portrait of either of her husbands, a more likely conclusion in light of evidence presented in this chapter: Woodfin (2012) 159, fig. 4.9).
23 R.P.H. Green (1991) 548; Elsner (1998) 56–8; Ando (2000) 232; Delmaire (2003) 96–7; Olovsdotter (2005) 212; Parani (2007) 501, n.11. For a discussion of imperial images on clothing (but not on Ausonius' *trabea*) see Woodfin (2013).
24 For the continuing prestige of the consulship, despite a decline in the power the office wielded see Bagnall *et al.* (1987) 1, 3, 4, 6.
25 For an attempt to identify and reconcile some clothing items see e.g. Rothe (2012a), not all of whose arguments are convincing, however, because the often-fragmentary nature of evidence used does not always seem to fully support her conclusions.
26 E.g. *Pan. Lat.* 3.9: *trabeatos*; Amm. Marc. 23.1.1; Claud. *Stil.* 2. 367–370 (where Stilicho is portrayed as Mars); Auson. *Grat. act.* 11, *Epist.* 22.92–93, *Carm.* 3.44; Sid. Apoll. *Carm.* 15.150–153; the consular diptychs reproduced by Olovsdotter (2005) also show the consul in what must be his *trabea*; McCormick (1986) 21; Beard (2007) 278.
27 E.g. Ausonius (*Grat. act.* 11), Claudian (*Stil.* 2. 340, 407), and Sidonius (*Carm.* 15.158), discussed further below, and of particular importance in the context of this chapter.
28 Anderson (1936) 236 n.2, for this suggestion; see also Wilson (1924) 85; Delbrueck (1929) 50–54 (esp. 53–4), 59–61; Gabelmann (1977) (the *trabea* in the Republic and Early Empire); Olovsdotter (2005) 3 (with bibliography), 71–4 for representations of the *vestis triumphalis* in the consular diptychs; Beard (2007) 228–9.
29 Cf. e.g. *in Ruf.* 1. 249; *Eutr.* 1. 9–10; *III Cons. Hon.* 5; *IV Cons. Hon.* 641–642; see Dewar (2008) for a fuller discussion of the meaning of the *trabea* in Claudian. Cf. MacMullen (1990) 97 *toga picta* equated with consulship. In the *Gratiarum Actio*, Ausonius' supposed recitation of Gratian's words that he is sending a *palmata* may imply that the more general *trabea* became a *palmata* if decorated (*Grat. act.* 11). This appears to be supported by Sidonius' *Epithalamium* (*Carm.* 15) where the consular *trabea* is also referred to as a *palmata*, perhaps because it will be decorated (15.150–151, 158–159). However, this is unlikely as Sidonius continues to call the garment a *trabea* when he discusses the decoration (15.158–159) and Claudian also uses *trabea* for a consular robe even after its fabulous adornment is described (*Cons. Stil.* 339–341, 367–370). Furthermore, as will be seen, Ausonius' discussion of his clothing gift deliberately choses certain clothing terms to create contrasts between himself and Gratian to enhance both, and this seems to be the case for Sidonius and Claudian as well. Therefore, while it is attractive to conjecture that the *palmata* is a decorated form of the *trabea* the evidence is not conclusive enough to support this suggestion.
30 Dewar (2008) 220.
31 Fr. 12 Courtney (Dewar (2008) 218). Claudian also employs the toga in this way: *Cons. Stil.* 2.365–370
32 *in procinctu et cum maxime dimicaturus palmatae vestis meae ornamenta disponis:* See also the phrase immediately before this: *in Illyrico arma quatiuntur: tu mea causa per Gallias civilium decorum indumenta dispensas.*
33 *Namque iste habitus, ut in pace consulis est, sic in victoria triumphantis.*
34 *haec plane, haec est picta, ut dicitur, vestis, non magis auro suo quam tuis verbis.* 'Ornamented', 'decorated', 'of different colours': Lewis and Short s.v. *pictus* B.2; cf. Festus p.228 l.18–21; however the fact that *pictus* can also mean 'painted' (s.v. *pictus* II. Trop.) suggests the interesting possibility that the decorations could perhaps have been painted on – either

on the original *togae pictae* or for their later developments. cf. Cleland *et al.* (2007) 2 s.v. 'agu pingere', 57 'pictus;' Droß-Krüpe and Paetz gen. Schieck (2014). Painting elaborate scenes on items of clothing turning them into luxury goods is practised in many cultures e.g. silk painting in China/Vietnam (although obviously silk is already a luxury item); cloth painting in some African cultures.

35 Cameron (1970) 303.
36 Bagnall *et al.* (1987) 87; Olovsdotter (2005) 1.
37 Delbrueck (1929) 59–61; Bagnall *et al.* (1987) 87; Olovsdotter (2005) 1.
38 Olovsdotter (2005), 3.
39 Anthemius: Olovsdotter (2005) plate 15; Gallus: Salzman (1990) fig. 14.
40 For this item, see e.g. Wild (1994) 9–36; Olovsdotter (2005) 20; Pritchard (2006) 46; Rothe (2012a) 145–50 (where it is also called *tunica manicata* or *tunica dalmatica*). Gallus seems to have a portrait bust on his left arm while Anthemius has one on his right, and there is possibly another towards the lower hem on the right side.
41 For other interpretations of the *trabea*, not necessarily dissimilar from my own, see, e.g. Wilson (1924) 112, 115; Delbrueck (1929) who lists the 'Trabeakostüm' under 'Grade des Togakostüms' (51–4); Bonfante (1976) 49–50, 129; Granger-Taylor (1982) 24 n.48 (a misinterpretation of Bonfante's definition); Cleland *et al* (2007) 197 s.v. 'trabea'.
42 *Carm.* 15.150–153.
43 Cf. Sid. Apoll. *Carm.* 15.154–157 where Araneola has apparently also made her father the *chlamydes* he wore as *magister* in Spain and upon his prefecture.
44 E.g. Olovsdotter (2005) 73, 74. Fl. Constantius, the suggested honorand of the Halberstadt diptych (Fig. 3.2), who shared the consulship with the emperor Honorius in 417 (Bagnall *et al* (1987) 369), and wears a *trabea* with figural decorations could be one of these likely candidates.
45 . . . *enim litterarum ad me datarum . . . eo quoque descendisti, ut quaereres, qualis ad me trabea mitteretur. Omne largitionum tuarum ministerium sollicitudine fatigasti . . . parum est, si, qualis ad me trabea mittatur, interroges: te coram promi iubes. nec satis habes, ut largitionum ministri ex more fungantur: eligis ipse de multis et, cum elegeris, munera tua verborum honore prosequeris.*
46 Whether these may have been referred to by different terminology is difficult to know for certain, see above fn.29 regarding the use of *palmata*.
47 Delmaire (1989) 468. It appears that the consul did not have control over the type of garment he was sent (Ausonius is asked what kind of *trabea* he would like, not what sort of *vestis*), further supporting the idea that the *trabea* was the usual dress of a consul.
48 *Grat. act.* 11; Delmaire (1989) 468.
49 Delmaire (1989) 443 – 'celles-ci jouent un rôle essential dans l'artisanat des produits de luxe . . . et permettant au prince de montrer sa richesse et sa générosité'.
50 Delmaire (1989) 469–70.
51 E.g. *Gord.* 4.4 – where *Palatium*, could also possibly be the palace; *Alex. Sev.* 40.8; *Probus*, 7.2, 4–5. Cf. Beard (2007) 229–31 for a discussion of the Temple of Jupiter on the Capitoline Hill and triumphal vestments.
52 Cf. Cameron (1968a).
53 *Probus*, 7.2, 4–5.
54 Delmaire (1989) 447 cites the locations of 'les ateliers fiscaux' listed in the *Notitia Dignitatum* (west) which are explained by local wool production or operating as a base for the imperial court – Trier and Sirmium (locations relevant to the case study below) are two of these. In the tenth century precious clothing stores did seem to travel with the emperor on campaigns, although these were not to give to their officials, but to distinguished refugees and powerful foreigners (a gift-giving practice similar to that examined in Chapter 2) (Cutler (2001) 262–3).
55 Cf. Pritchard (2006) 29.
56 Muthesius (1992) 237, 240.
57 Delmaire (2003) 97; cf. (1989) 468: Ausonius' *trabea* had been in the imperial *vestiarium* 'déjà longtemps'.

58 As Green does (1991) 548.
59 Except perhaps that, as an example of imperial largess, the consul was still bound to the emperor through the ties of gift-giving; his autonomy in decoration may have been tempered by his indebtedness to imperial generosity.
60 There appear to be no references to consular robes with figural decorations before the fourth century. This raises the question of whether these only came into use from Diocletian onwards, as part of the elaboration of court ceremonial.
61 See fn.1 for references. The diptych of Anthemius is lost and survives only in images of an eighteenth-century engraving. Of course, other surviving diptychs that appear to present the consular outfits without figural decoration may have had this detail painted on instead, but the trouble taken to engrave this feature into the diptychs presented in the chapter seems to suggest otherwise. Cf. Olovsdotter (2005) 73.
62 See Olovsdotter (2005) 73 for discussion of the identities.
63 *PLRE* 2 Procopius Anthemius 9. Cf. Lee (2013) 159–77.
64 Olovsdotter (2005) 73.
65 Olovsdotter (2005) 115; cf. Delbrueck (1929) 40, 87, 91f; Engemann (1999) 164–7.
66 Fl. Constantius was married to Galla Placidia, Honorius' half-sister, Aerobindus was married to the daughter of the emperor Olybrius, and Anthemius was the son of the emperor of the same name (467–472) (Olovsdotter (2005) 74, n.106). If Claudian's evidence from *Stil.* (2.341–361; discussed further below) is taken as reflecting, as opposed to accurately describing, the garment depicted in Stilicho's diptych, it is decorated with the members of his family (it should be noted Claudian calls it a *trabea* whereas the diptych seems to dress Stilicho in a *chlamys*). It shows instead, therefore, those whom he hopes one day will also be members of the imperial household, and of course he was closely tied by marriage to the imperial house himself, see further below.
67 Delbrueck (1929) 59–66; Olovsdotter (2005) 69, 71, 72, see also 20 (discussion of Halberstadt diptych), 35 (Basilius), 41 (Areobindus).
68 Olovsdotter (2005) 212. This is also the case for items decorated with the imperial image given to foreign allies, see Chapter 2 case study.
69 Bagnall *et al.* (1987) 1, 3, 4, 6.
70 Olovsdotter (2005) 212, 216.
71 Olovsdotter (2005) 73–4.
72 Olovsdotter (2005) 74, a seeming contradiction of her earlier assertion that one of the figures on Anthemius' robe is 'his brother Macrianus, twice consul' (73).
73 Olovsdotter (2005) 73–4. However, because she is uncomfortable with non-imperial portraits she is forced to conclude that 'all representations of *segmenta* are not "true" in the sense that they present faithful depictions of the consul's real costume, but that they were images within images . . .' (74). This is an interesting point but, again, Ausonius' speech, as well as the evidence discussed at the beginning of this chapter, Chapter 2 and the archaeological evidence of clothing decorated with figures, would suggest otherwise. Indeed, there is no reason why they can't function on multiple levels as both 'real' and 'image'.
74 Cf. Cameron and Schauer (1982) 140–42, who highlight that prominent consuls, particularly those who were also successful generals and encouraged their own popularity with generous donations of money and games during their consulship, could be viewed as potential rivals by emperors.
75 Auson. *Epig.* 45. During a period when 'senatorial status ceased . . . to designate a body of men marked out by particular biological descent', ancestral claims must have been that much more valuable in the competition for social capital, particularly in Rome where 'this element never entirely disappeared' (Heather (1998) 189).
76 Cf. Sid. Apoll. *Carm.* 15.150–153, discussed below.
77 *Grat. act.* 3–4.
78 2.330–376. Whether this robe was an actual garment or purely an imaginative exercise on Claudian's part has been discussed by modern authors: see Dewar (2008) 230 for a

124 *Portable portraits*

brief summary. As Dewar comments, this amount of detail does not seem to be beyond the medium of the garment, as archaeological evidence from the period also attests. Claudian's portrayal may not be an accurate sketch of this diptych, where Stilicho is dressed in a *chlamys* and tunic rather than a *trabea*, possibly as a *magister militum* (see Granger-Taylor (1983) 143 for a discussion of the *chlamys* decoration, which she suggests could be achieved by a damask weave; see also von Rummel (2007) 206–13 for a discussion of the costume worn by the male figure, but not the decoration. Neither mentions the possible connection to Claudian's description, despite von Rummel's referencing of the latter (213)). However, it is not unreasonable to suggest (as Cameron (1970) 47–9, 303 and Woodfin (2013) do) that the poem and the diptych are related, for, like his clothing in Claudian's lyrical description, Stilicho's garments in the diptych are also adorned with many portraits, and it may be that one inspired the other.

79 *veram mox ipse probabis/me vatem nostraeque fidem venientia telae/fata dabunt/dixit gremioque rigentia profert/dona, graves auro trabeas insigne Minervam/spirat opus . . . /Stilicho maturior aevi/Martia recturo tradit praecepta nepoti . . . /Venus hic . . . tertia regali iungit conubia nexu, pennatique nurum circumstipantur Amores progenitam Augustis Augustorumque sororem . . . /iam domus haec utroque petit diademata sexu/ reginasque parit reginarumque maritos.*

80 Dewar (2008), 229–30.

81 For where a consul may have worn his robes outside of his inauguration, see discussion below.

82 Ando (2000) 228–52.

83 *Tunc habiles armis umeros iam vestibus ambit/Romuleis; Latii sederunt pectore cultus/loricaeque locum decuit toga. talis ab Histro/vel Scythico victor rediens Gradivus ab axe/deposito mitis clipeo candentibus urbem/ingreditur trabeatus equis.* . . .

84 *Stil.* 2.291–329, especially 318–319: *consul succurre gravatis/consulibus, quicumque fuit, quicumque futurus.* . . .

85 Verg. *Aen.* 5. 252ff.; Ov. *Met.* 6. 577ff.; cf. Catull. 64. 50, 265. Roberts (1989) 114; Dewar (2008) 230; Faber (2008) 205–7. On Claudian's use of the epic tradition particularly with regards to Stilicho, see Ware (2012) *passim.*

86 See Cameron and Schauer (1982) 138 for a breakdown of the figures.

87 The garments decorated with religious scenes, discussed at the beginning of this chapter, work in a similar way, albeit in a different context. For clothing that places the wearer in a Christian heroic tradition, see Chapter 4.

88 *hic igitur proavi trabeas imitata rigentes/ palmatam parat ipsa patri, qua consul et idem/ Agricolam contingat avum doceatque nepotes/ non abavi solum sed avi quoque iungere fasces . . . /attamen in trabea segmento luserat alto/quod priscis inlustre toris.* It is unlikely that the *segmentum* mentioned here is a separate piece to be added later to the *trabea*. It is clear she is weaving the (very elaborate) stories of mythological marriages into the garment while she is making it. The high section '*segmento . . . alto*' might instead refer to a type of weaving technique where some areas are raised, see e.g. Bender Jørgensen (2008).

89 Dewar (2008) 231.

90 Bagnall *et al.* (1987) 1.

91 An additional distinction because the *consul prior* had his name entered first in the fasti. As this implies, Ausonius was a *consul ordinarius*, rather than *suffectus*, which further enhanced the honour involved (Bagnall *et al.* (1987) 20–22).

92 For a study of Ausonius' life, see Sivan (1993). For the reign of Gratian, see McEvoy (2013) 48–70.

93 '*palmatam*', *inquis*, '*tibi misi, in qua divus Constantius parens noster intextus est*' . . . *haec plane, haec est picta, ut dicitur, vestis, non magis auro suo quam tuis verbis. Sed multo plura sunt in eius ornatu, quae per te intructus intellego. Geminum quippe in uno habitu radiat nomen Augusti. Constantius in argumento vestis intexitur, Gratianus in muneris honore sentitur.* For a brief discussion of this gift in the wider context of late antique gift-giving practices see Wood (2000) 309.

94 At the least because it would suggest to the audience ideas of wider imperial benefaction, which was more materially obvious in the largess often given by the emperor when he was a consul himself: cf. the portrait of Constantius II himself as a consul distributing largess in the Codex-calendar of 354: Stern (1953); Salzman (1990) fig. 13; MacCormack (1981) 7.

95 E.g. Auson. *Grat. act.* 11, *Epist.* 22.92–93, *Carm.* 3.44; Claud. *Stil.* 2.367–370 (where Stilicho is wearing his *trabea* during his procession), *Cons. Manlius* 256–260; Sid. Apoll. *Carm.* 15.150–153; McCormick (1986) 21; Beard (2007) 278.

96 Beard (2007) 277; Olovsdotter (2005) 180; The consular procession in late antiquity no longer ended at the Capitoline in Rome (when it could be held in Rome – absent consuls were common at this period often due to their military duties cf. Bagnall *et al.* (1987) 21), but at the Atrium Libertatis in the Forum Traiani, and in Constantinople possibly at the Hippodrome (Olovsdotter (2005) 1, 180). Presumably, when the new consul was inaugurated in another city, as Ausonius was in Trier (Bagnall *et al.* (1987) 21), a correspondingly public setting was chosen. The new consul also presided over the *pompa circensis*, the games for which the consul paid from his own pocket (Olovsdotter (2005) 35; Cameron and Schauer (1982) 139; cf. Beard (2007) 280–84).

97 Claud. *Stil.* 362ff., cf. Beard (2007) 278, 280 for triumphal associations with the consulship. Auson. *Grat. act.* 11 forms part of Gratian's letter informing Ausonius that he has been made a consul; Sid. Apoll. *Carm.* 15.150ff. Araneola is looking forward to her father holding this office.

98 Caligula: Suet. *Cal.* 52; Dio Cass. 59.26.10; Claudius: Dio Cass. 60.6.9. In addition, Domitian wore it whenever he was in the senate house (Dio Cass. 67.4.3). Republic examples: Aemilius Paullus in 167 BCE was allowed to wear his triumphal costume at circus games 'by the people and by the senate', as was Pompey (Aemilius Paullus: Suet. *Vir. Ill.* 56.5; Pompey: Vell. Pat. 2.40.4; Dio Cass. 37.21.4). Marius, still dressed in this costume, called the senate into session in 104 BCE (Plut. *Mar.* 12.5). Metellus Pius, after defeating Sertorius, wore it to dinners (Val. Max. 9.1.5; Plut. *Sert.* 22.2; Sall. *Hist.* 2.59). References from Beard (2007) 273–4, 275–7; see also, McCormick (1986) 21.

99 This also has implications as to the ownership and keeping of such items as discussed above in the previous section.

100 *Grat. act.* 18: *quia interesse primordiis dignitatis per locorum intervalla non poterat*; Bagnall *et al.* (1987) 20; Barnes (1999) 166–7.

101 Bagnall *et al.* (1987) 21.

102 Cf. *Grat. act.* 1 *ades enim locis omnibus*. . . . For a discussion of the 'metaphysical' presence of an absent emperor in speeches of panegyric, see Rees (2002) 12–17, esp. 14–15, 17 (although he does not refer to Ausonius' *Gratiarum Actio* here).

103 Swift (2009) 20.

104 Cf. Claud. *Cons. Man.* 256–260.

105 This dating is contrary to most scholars' opinion, who propose September or perhaps at the end of the year, when Gratian returned to Trier, seemingly because it is assumed that Ausonius would have only delivered the speech in the emperor's presence: e.g., Matthews (1975) 72, 98 n.2; Bagnall *et al.* (1987), 20; McLynn (2005) 94, n.64; and Dewar (2008), 217. Barnes (1999) 166–7 helpfully provides a table of Gratian's movements at this time. Hagith Sivan states that the speech was given 'to Gratian in front of a Treveran court audience', (Sivan (1993) 49), but then goes on to contradict herself by claiming August/September 379 as a possible date, saying it was 'before Gratian returned to Trier' (Sivan (1993) 119).

106 Internal evidence: e.g. *Grat. act.* 18. The only possible reference to Theodosius has been detected at *Grat. act.* 2 in the phrase *tali principe oriens ordinatur* (McLynn (2005) 94, n.64), but it relies on the emendation of *principe* to *participe*, without compelling reasons: see Sivan (1996) 205 n.52. It was certainly not due to a lack of personal knowledge of Theodosius by the author, as it appears that Ausonius was previously acquainted with the new Augustus (Auson. *Epist. Theodosii Aug.* (Matthews (1975) 54)). Furthermore,

as Sivan ((1996) 205) has pointed out, it would be the perfect place to praise Gratian's qualities in putting concern for state over dynasty, with the appointment of a successful general to the imperial office, had he been instrumental in Theodosius' elevation as is usually held.
107 McLynn (2005).
108 The internal contradictions in the text may be grounds to suggest that the speech was actually given on two separate occasions. The first was Ausonius' inauguration, from which Gratian's was absent, and where the author's audience would consist of the inhabitants of Trier and possibly members of the court. Then, once Gratian had arrived in the city in September, the speech was repeated in the emperor's presence. This would have allowed Ausonius to comment on Gratian's surprise return to Trier and to demonstrate his gratitude to the emperor in person; it may have been a smaller affair with a mostly courtly presence. Although not strictly a *gratiarum actio*, there was a precedent for the repetition of a speech praising the emperor: Themistius gave his *Oratio* 5 in celebration of the Emperor Jovian's consulship at Ancyra on 1 Jan 364, and then again later in Constantinople (Socr. 3.26.3; Errington (2006) 174). There could, of course, be another possibility for Ausonius' speech – that it was perhaps given at Ausonius' consular investiture and then sent to Gratian by Ausonius in written form, and therefore was never performed in front of the emperor at all.
109 Elsner (1998), 56–8 with references; Ando (2000) 228–53; Swift (2009) 3–4.
110 Gold in textiles see e.g. Chioffi (2004); Gleba (2008). This may also suggest Ausonius' *trabea* was a damask weave (cf. Amm. Marc. 14.6.9 with Granger-Taylor (1983) 148). For this technique and others which would also create a contrast in light and perhaps animate the image see e.g. Granger-Taylor (1983) 142, 148 (silk damask); Bender Jørgensen (2008); Ciszuk (2004).
111 Cf. Woodfin (2012) 86, 88, 92–3 regarding holy images on Byzantine clothing.
112 Auson. *Prof. Burd.* 16.9–12, 15: *illic dives opum doctoque ibi Caesare honorus*; Hopkins (1961) 242; cf. Sivan (1993) 123 'Ausonius, it seems, never left Gaul. . .'.
113 Amm. 21.15.6; Evelyn White (1967) 248 n.1; R.P.H. Green (1991), 548.
114 This is the interpretation of Dewar (and others): (2008) 219 'This is the age of explicit dynastic propaganda, in the context of the most ostensibly republican of institutions. . .'. However, this is as far as the curious incident of having a previous emperor's figure on a consular robe is explored and explained.
115 Amm. Marc. 26.1–2.
116 Cf. Lenski (2002) 89: 'In any period, dynastic claims rendered an emperor's position more secure by providing a guarantee of inherited authority'.
117 Lewis and Short s.v. *parens*; Lenski (2002) 98, 103.
118 For a discussion of this revolt, see Lenski (2002) 68–115.
119 Amm. Marc. 23.3.2, 26.6.2 (cf. 26.6.15 where no *paludamentum* can be found, thus casting suspicion on Procopius' claims. As a result he is elevated whilst half-dressed as a court official instead – as is common in Latin literature, his inappropriate clothes signify his unworthiness to rule); Philost. 9.5; Zos. 4.4.2–3. See Lenski (2002) 69, who says while 'there is no doubt that Procopius was kin to Julian, it seems likely that he had no connection to the agnatic family of the emperor'. Cf. Zos. 4.8.4, where Procopius acts in a similar way, handing his own *paludamentum purpureum* to his relative Marcellus to indicate his place as Procopius' successor (Lenski (2002) 69–70).
120 Amm. Marc. 26.7.10.
121 *in agminibus et cum prope in acie starent* (Amm. Marc. 26.9.3).
122 26.9.3–6.
123 Cf. Lenski (2002) 79, 101–3.
124 Cameron (1993) 101; Lenski (2002) 98–9.
125 *cuius recordatio colebatur* (Amm. Marc. 26.7.10). Tr W. Hamilton.
126 Lenski (2002) 89.

127 Sivan (1993) 125.
128 Amm. Marc. 30.10.
129 Amm. Marc. 28.1.1–56; see Matthews (1975) 55, 63, 65–6; Heather (1998) 199; Lenski (2002) 218–23. In addition, Constantius would have been a wise choice of decoration to aim at the senatorial elite because he had in fact dismissed Valentinian I from his service in the army in 357 (Amm. Marc. 16.11.6f.; Matthews (1975) 34, n.2). If the incident was remembered, it is possible that they thought favourably of Constantius in light of his actions in dismissing someone they disliked.
130 Amm. Marc. 21.10.7; cf. Constantius' visit to Rome in 357 (16.10).
131 Matthews (1975) 12, 53, 70.
132 Matthews (1975) 54–5. For the changing nature of the aristocracy and the senates of Rome and Constantinople in the fourth century, see Heather (1998).
133 Cf. Heather (1998) 198: 'Established senators from old families did not tend to put themselves forward as candidates for the throne in the fourth century – most emperors and imperial candidates . . . were drawn from the upper reaches of the military or the bureaucracy – but many senators . . . were deeply implicated in different regimes'.
134 This is not to say, however, that Ausonius was the obvious choice for the consulship, and Ausonius himself notes that many were surprised by Gratian's decision, particularly in his choice to make him *consul prior* (*Grat. act.* 3–4, 8, 12, 18). It was especially flattering to Ausonius, because Olybrius, as a member of the Roman senate and of a very powerful family should have had this privilege in the name of political expediency. The frequency with which Ausonius returns to this subject implies that he may have felt the honour too much, but it also suggests that he felt the need to justify Gratian's decision and that it was not welcomed by all. By naming Ausonius *consul prior* and (apparently) providing him alone with a special clothing gift, Gratian was therefore reinforcing both of their positions in the face of potential opposition – associating himself with Ausonius, while simultaneously enhancing Ausonius' connection with imperial authority (which the *trabea* further aided), and thus justifying their places of seniority.
135 Indeed, it is perhaps telling that Valentinian is mentioned only once in the *Gratiarum Actio* at 16. While Ausonius does explicitly say that Gratian is his son and praises Valentinian's goodness, generosity, and ability to control his severity, it is notable for its unique appearance and its location, coming as it does after the description of Constantius as *parens noster*.
136 'The ideal that men of culture should be running the empire continued into Late Antiquity' (Cameron (2004) 344); cf. Heather (1998) 193; Lenski (2002) 93: 'In a world where "learning" in the broadest sense provided those in authority not just with the proper refinement but with a veritable code of conduct, an uneducated emperor was both unseemly and threatening'. Constantius himself made the connection between correct conduct and education (*Or. Const.* 20b–c (in Henck (2001) 179)).
137 Brown (2002) 85.
138 Amm. Marc. 30.8.10; Lenski (2002) 86–7, 93–4.
139 See Zon. 13.11; *Cod. Theod.* 14.1.1 (a. 360); Them. *Or.* 3.45b, especially 20d. Rhetorical skill: Jul. *Or.* 1.32a, 3.75b–d; Them. *Or.* 2.29a, 34b, 37a – b, 3.45c, 4.54a; Aur. Vict. *Caes.* 42.1–4, 23; Lib. *Or.* 59.97; cf. Amm. Marc 21.16.4; Epit. 42.18 (references: Lenski (2002) 92, n 151); Henck (2001). Literary men: most notably Themistius (Henck (2001) 180–81).
140 The usurper Procopius, who was seen earlier employing his relationship to Constantius as part of his propaganda, also uses the weapon of education in order to contrast himself with the un(der)-educated Valens and Valentinian (see Lenski (2002) 96). Henck notes that under Constantius' rule the consular *fasti* are littered with the literati, in comparison to Valentinian's reign, where many of the consuls 'were uneducated military men often of barbarian origin' ((2001) 182).

141 Symm. *Or.* 3.7; *Ep.* 1.20.2, 10.2.5; Them. *Or.* 9.125c; Auson. *Prec. var.* 1; Amm. Marc. 27.6.9, 31.10.18 (cited in Lenski (2002) 95). For praise of education as forming part of the section on *anatropē* (nurture) in panegyrics influenced by Menander Rhetor's *Basilikos Logos* treatise, see Buckland (2010) 71. Ausonius' *Gratiarum Actio* is considered by Rees as one of the 16 surviving Latin panegyrics (Rees (2002) 6, 17 n.66).
142 Amm. Marc. 31.10.18.
143 McLynn (2005) 92, n.57.
144 Rösch (1978) does not list *Sarmaticus* among Gratian's victory titles.
145 McLynn (2005) 92, n.57.
146 Amm. Marc. 19.30.
147 Rösch (1978).
148 Amm. Marc. 16.12.69–70.
149 Evelyn White (1967), 244 n.1; Errington (1996) 449; McLynn (2005) 92; 92, n.57. It is a 'future' bonus here, because it is unlikely that the speech would be deliberately attempting to appropriate or suppress Theodosius' name in order to enhance Gratian's military reputation if it was composed for recital on 1 January 379, as proposed above. If the later date in the year of 379 given by most scholars (i.e. when Theodosius was a fully-fledged Augustus) is correct, however, this would give added significance to the omission of any explicit reference to Theodosius and an appropriation of his titles. It has been noted above that McLynn (2005) has argued persuasively for Theodosius' acclamation being in all probability engineered without Gratian's consent, just as Gratian's younger brother's accession had been only four years before (Amm. Marc. 30.10; Matthews (1975) 64). Theodosius, a former successful *dux* with heirs, was a different proposition to an infant brother, and while there is no hint of opposition to Theodosius from Gratian, it appears that he did not go out of his way to help Theodosius secure his claim. This was particularly the case in the military sphere, leading to a series of embarrassing defeats for the new emperor (McLynn (2005) 94; cf. Sivan (1996) 202). Gratian's attitude would be understandable if McLynn and Sivan's suggestions that Theodosius may effectively have been a usurper are correct (Sivan (1996); McLynn (2005); cf. Errington (1996)), and these circumstances would have made it unnecessary and perhaps imprudent for Ausonius to include any comment or praise of this new imperial colleague. It is unlikely an earlier rendition of the speech would have such a motive, however. As noted, Ausonius' use of *Sarmaticus* here can be explained by Constantius and is therefore not conclusive support for either date.
150 Cf. Beard (2007) 273.
151 Beard (2007) 273; Olovsdotter (2005) 189, 208.
152 This identification is open to interpretation, however.
153 Olovsdotter (2005) 187.
154 Beard (2007) 273, 275, 277.
155 Asterius, *Hom.* 1.3, see beginning of chapter.

4 Holy habits

Clothing gifts in late antique Christian contexts

Within political life and diplomacy during Late Antiquity, clothing gifts functioned as part of a wider framework of political and social representation, providing mutual benefit for the receiver and donor. Special items that had strong associations with offices of authority allowed those who may have operated outside or at the margins of the empire, both in a geographical and social sense, to strengthen their position and partake in power, while enabling the donors of the items to broadcast their own resources and dominance. In the empire, the carefully chosen decoration on a consul's *trabea* could act in a similar way, highlighting the right to social and political prominence through the ancestral and imperial connections of the wearer. When the item was given as an imperial gift, however, these ideas could be reflected back on the donor (especially if the wearer was a prominent author willing to provide his audience with the tools necessary to read the garment correctly), and the receiver then became a 'wall'[1] upon which an emperor could paint, or rather weave, his political designs.

As this chapter will show, gifts of clothing operated in a similar way for Christian authors, perhaps influenced by imperial practices, but also from drawing on Biblical episodes such as Elisha receiving the cloak and authority of Elijah, and personal experiences as recipients of clothes from lay benefactors and fellow clerics. As a result, it will be suggested that late antique Christian writers used clothing gifts as tools of personal promotion, and as devices to engage with anxieties that emerged in the Church during this period, providing interesting parallels to the material discussed in the previous chapters. At a time when it was not always clear who was or should be heir to the spiritual authority of Christ and his disciples – the institution of the Church or the charismatic monk? – or indeed how this authority was to be recognised, clothing became an important part of this dialogue. After an initial discussion of clothing presents amongst the laity, churches, and clergy, which manifested themselves as charitable donations and presentations of relics, this chapter will investigate how ideas about the close connection between the body and clothing enabled some Christian authors to discuss their concerns. These concerns manifested around the inheritance and legacy of spiritual authority from famous holy men, which was perceived as being transferred through the gifting of clothing; and authors sometimes even questioned their own suitability for the role of heir. It will be argued further, however, that clothing gifts represented more than this in the hands of Christian authors who were often high in the Church hierarchy. The ideological association of the *pallium* and the *melōte* with the offices of bishop and monk respectively provided those writers with the means to envelop, literally and figuratively, the holy man in the mantle of orthodoxy, co-opting his charismatic powers for the benefit of the Church.[2] Finally, the ideas explored within this chapter, as well as many of those presented in the ones preceding, will be brought together in the concluding 'case study' which considers how the same garment of Antony is gifted in different ways in the *Vita Antonii* of Athanasius, Bishop of Alexandria, and the *Vita Pauli primi eremitae*, written by Jerome.

4.1 (A)dressing Christian charity: The benefits of clothing

Although, as will be seen in later sections, it is not always easy to discover whether the depictions of a presentation of clothing by a holy man to his successor were based on a real event, their air of authenticity derives from the fact that garments were certainly given as gifts within the context of late antique Christianity. As the following sections will discuss, this happened within the framework of charity, a Christian concept that built on, competed with, and was enacted alongside traditional ideas of euergetism.[3] However, the relationship between these ideas meant that when well-off lay members of the congregation came to donate clothing to churches for the use of the clergy and the poor (which included those at the very margins of society), it is likely that they would continue to see themselves within their role as civic patron. They were benefitting the Christian community of their city through almsgiving, as well as continuing to provide building works and other activities that had characterised earlier euergetism. In assisting the church, its leaders, and their fellow men and women in this way, then, the elite laity continued to display the qualities expected in a pre-Christian patron, such as *liberalitas*, *philanthropia*, and *humanitas* that had been lauded by Martial. They were thus benefitting from the social capital of these traditional roles, while the Christian context provided them with a spiritual capital that was advantageous in both this world and the next. This was despite the notion that the religious ideology behind Christian charity was one in which donors should not expect their gift to be repaid with an increase in earthly influence;[4] this concept could be difficult to embrace for those who were used to a position of dominance. Unsurprisingly, there was sometimes an expectation on the part of such socially prominent donors that the clergy should acquiesce to their demands as to how their donations of clothing were used, and also to their requests for pieces of saintly attire which would bring spiritual benefits and status.

As in the other spheres of society that have been encountered in the previous chapters, the giving of clothing was a common, and perhaps even necessary, part of a Christian's life in Late Antiquity. To their congregations, the clergy expounded upon Christ's lesson in Matthew 25.40, that whatever was done to the least of His brothers was done also to Him. This meant that within the religious context, the most important gifts a lay Christian could give were those that came from the practice of charity, and the provision of clothing to the poor was a significant aspect of this.[5] Imitating Biblical precepts enabled a charitable Christian to demonstrate that he (or she) was leading a righteous life.[6] Church leaders encouraged these givers to think of themselves in this way, while at the same time urging others to do likewise, through the use of such paradigms within their sermons and religious texts. The Biblical story of Tabitha, who was resurrected because she gave garments to widows, was exploited, for instance, by Cyprian to encourage charitable giving while Basil, in *The Long Rules*, claimed that clothing the naked was 'the greatest commandment and the one especially conducive to salvation'.[7] Jerome, in his typically blunt fashion, put these expectations succinctly when discussing the best way a member of the elite could use their wealth upon dedicating themselves to Christianity: building and adorning churches was all very well, but 'there [was] another possibility: clothe Christ in the person of the poor . . .'.[8]

The examples provided by saints in hagiographical texts further emphasised not only that those who had a special place in Christianity gave charitably and were thus worth imitating,[9] but also that they were worth imitating because those who gave charity could also partake in the special respect accorded to such saintly figures. After all, as St Martin had discovered, Christ was always on the lookout for those who did good deeds:[10]

> Therefore, in the following night, when Martin had given himself over to sleep, he saw Christ clothed in the part of his own *chlamys*, with which he had covered the beggar. He contemplated the Lord most carefully and he was commanded to recognise the clothing which he had given . . . The Lord remembering well his own words (which he had foretold before: 'As long as you did this to one of the least, you did this to me'), declared that he himself had been clothed in the beggar; and in order to confirm his witness to such a good deed, he condescended to show himself in the same clothing that the beggar had received. (Sulpicius Severus, *Vita Martini*, 3.3–4)[11]

Martin is thus recognisable as a saint (to Christ and the audience) because he clothes the poor – his innate holiness is identifiable through his actions. Emulating such figures proved that the donor was serious about the teachings of Christ, and, in dressing the poverty-stricken donors were not simply giving their clothing to their fellow men and women, but were able to demonstrate their relationship to Christ by caring for him in the form of the poor.[12] Their actions mirrored those who were praised highly in Christianity, and allowed lay Christians who were unwilling to give up all of their wealth and live in the desert a share in the holy capital of those who did – a share their biographers were only too keen to emphasise.[13]

Indeed, these episodes formed part of a wider concern to present the subjects of hagiographical texts as humble patrons of the needy who were happy to interact personally with the lowest levels of society, in order to show them as superior lay Christians because they faithfully followed Christ's precepts.[14] The emperor Constantine, for example, provided 'even for the beggars in the forum, miserable and shiftless ... not ... money only, or necessary food, but also decent clothing', and his mother behaved in a similar manner on her journey through the East.[15] However, clothing the poor did not always, or necessarily, result from such direct gift-giving, and while Eusebius and others may be keen to show the distributions of clothing by their protagonists as being done directly and in person, it is likely that for the majority of the wealthy gifts of clothing were given via an intermediary.[16] This could be through agents paid to allocate revenues or handouts in a more official capacity for the imperial or wealthy family, or by personal servants when an individual was accosted in the street.[17] In the latter instance, however, it is doubtful that the items given out to impromptu beggars would have been spare clothing the person just happened to have on them – money and perhaps food were more to be expected. Furthermore, it appears that unless on a deliberate gift-giving spree in the city streets, churches and their officials, particularly bishops, more commonly acted as the main liaison point between those who gave and those who received. It was felt that as stewards of the religious community bishops could be trusted to distribute donations appropriately, and it allowed the elite to avoid direct contact with the poor.[18]

Although urban gift-giving would have its audience, the offerings of the faithful were 'a major ceremony performed each Sunday' within the church.[19] Such a venue allowed for a more concentrated performance in front of peers (and others) who witnessed the donation against a religious backdrop. The timing ensured their actions were seen as a significant part of the celebrations carried out on the holiest day of the week, while also allowing them to continue to partake in the drama and prestige that had surrounded traditional euergetism.[20] This of course benefitted the giver as much as (if not more than) the church – a benefit reflected (and spread further) in the writings of Christian authors who showed these donors as blessed patrons of the Church and the poor and justified the respect that they were accorded.[21] The actions of both the authors and the givers of clothing had the potential to bestow superior spiritual standing in the community upon the donor by visibly connecting them with exemplary Christian behaviour and involving them in part of the sacred administrations of the church.[22] At the same time, however, they also provided social profit by placing the actors in the traditional role of the noble patron already encountered in Martial's epigrams from Chapter 1.

The gifts of clothing given to churches could take different forms. Some clothing was given to the clergy for their own use.[23] As bishops and some of the clergy expected to be supported by donations, their clothing would come either from the direct giving of such items or by purchasing them with church funds, although, as will be seen below, they could also receive garments from their fellow clerics.[24] Items for the lay poor in the wider community, however, would have been given by those of middling means or even clergy from other churches, as well as from wealthy patrons. These pieces would have been suitable for immediate distribution as they were or stored in the church and handed out when required.²⁵ The inventory of 303 from a church in the African town of Cirta held a quantity of clothing that does not appear to be for liturgical purposes. In this case, the '82 women's tunics, 38 capes, 16 men's tunics, 13 pairs of men's shoes, 47 pairs of women's shoes' are more likely to have been a store for the needy,²⁶ and the list suggests the type of garments that were thought to be appropriate for their use. The story told by Basil of thieves apprehended stealing 'cheap clothing belonging to the destitute' (ἱμάτια εὐτελῆ πτωχῶν ἀνθρώπων) from a church in Caesarea suggests that such garments were of low quality; perhaps a high level of manufacture was not deemed necessary for the destitute who may have been appreciative of anything that protected them from the elements.²⁷ Although Basil dismisses their value by calling them cheap (εὐτελής), they had great worth for those who needed them, and, as his story shows, were of sufficient economic value to make them worth stealing, either for their resale price or for their ability to clothe the thieves themselves.²⁸

The relatively cheap nature of some clothing items, however, also meant that a greater quantity could be obtained with church funds, and one of the ways these funds could be attained was through the sale of any luxury clothing gifts donated by wealthy patrons.²⁹ The gifting of clothing (and other items) by the wealthy after their conversion to the ascetic life was a familiar trope in hagiographical texts, but they also provide evidence that such pieces had immense material value in themselves.³⁰ As such, these were of course to be distinguished from the lower-quality apparel given for direct distribution to the poor. These more elaborate pieces of attire seem to be fairly rare in church inventories compared to cheaper clothing items or gifts of textiles.³¹ The latter could still be an expensive donation, however, as many of them were made of silk; and next to precious metals, these were in fact the items most highly valued as gifts by the Church in this period.³² These textiles were used extensively in churches, as, for example, decorative hangings, curtains, and altar cloths,³³ and they served to increase the wealth of the church to which they belonged. They also made it a beautiful space, imitating the shining radiance indicative of divinity through their brilliant colours, metal thread, and precious jewels.³⁴

These pieces did not always come as textiles fit for purpose, but rather as luxurious clothing gifts that could be converted into veils and μανδήλη due to their size:³⁵

> And when all her husband's clothes had been cut up, [Sosiana] went on to bring her own fine clothes in no small number . . . And, while we were again thinking, 'Perhaps it would have pleased God more that they should be sold and given to the poor', and we were saying so to her and she on her part was insisting on cutting them up . . . [but eventually] we ceased advising the woman so and standing in the way of her wish. (John of Ephesus, *Vitae Sanctorem Orientalium*, 55)³⁶

The refashioning of worldly goods into sacred items mirrored the process of transformation the wealthy donor was attempting to achieve through this gift.³⁷

John of Ephesus' internal thoughts on Sosiana's conversion of her clothing and that of her husband's (the *cubicularius* of Caesaria, a patrician possibly related to the imperial family),[38] also implies a more practical transformation, however. The expensive clothing could (and was perhaps expected to) be liquidated by the church to obtain immediate resources, which would then be used to benefit the poor. Thus, while, like other textiles, expensive clothes were given to increase the portable wealth of the church, and, in a similar way to diplomatic gifts, could be stored for years, their less frequent appearance on church inventories (as opposed to general textiles and cheaper clothing) may suggest that they were more often used as John had wished.[39]

Gifts of clothing to the church from the laity, and from wealthy patrons in particular, therefore, aided all parties and established a relationship of lasting and continuous mutual benefit and reciprocity. For the poor it meant they received clothing directly or were provided with other necessities via the church sale of clothing, while for the church itself, such items were used to increase its wealth or beauty, and helped them cater to both the clergy's own needs and those who depended on them. Finally, the donors themselves, when public in their giving, both received spiritual capital through the gift and proved themselves to be living according to the teachings of Christ, while at the same time placing themselves into the traditional role of patron and public benefactor.

4.2 Clothing relics

The episode between Sosiana and John of Ephesus, however, also demonstrates a different side to the patronage of churches by the wealthy laity during this period and implies the shift in power that a donation of immense wealth created in the clergy–elite relationship and the constraints such a donation placed upon a cleric who wanted to retain the donor's favour.[40] Thus, while the clergyman may be her spiritual superior, Sosiana's wealth (and sheer pig-headedness) means that the gift created an obligation which John felt he had to repay by following her instructions – despite his misgivings about the wisdom of them.[41] The necessity of maintaining good standing with the wealthy laity or imperial benefactors in order to ensure the continued financial health of a church created problems for the clergy particularly when such people requested the saintly relics which helped bring money in.[42] Although body parts were naturally the most sacred and desired items, pieces of clothing and the textiles in which the relics were wrapped were highly regarded.[43] This was because they were felt to have soaked up some of the saintly power believed to emanate from the holy figure and were thus, like the imperial images on clothing discussed in the previous chapters, still connected to the power of the prototype.

The Late Antiquity notion that the body of a saint exuded sanctity was drawn from Biblical precedents, particularly Mark 5.25–34 (with Luke 8.43–48) where touching the ἱμάτιον of Jesus healed the woman who had had 'a discharge of blood for twelve years' and Acts 19.11–12 where the σουδάρια ἢ σιμικίνθια of Paul were 'carried away from his body to the sick' to effect cures.[44]

The simple dress of Christ and His Apostles in the New Testament suggested that a special ceremonial priestly costume was now no longer necessary for mediating with God, and therefore allowed for the idea that it was not ritual clothing that consecrated the body and made it into a vessel for receiving the divine, but rather the sacred body itself, which sanctified whatever it touched.[45] For Christian figures like Jesus, Paul, and Peter,[46] then, their bodies were holy things that emitted divine power: 'Immediately Jesus, perceiving in himself that the power had gone out from him, turned around in the crowd, and asked, "Who touched my clothes?"'[47] Consequently, their clothing was consecrated through its proximity to the body, enabling these items to act as conduits for the holy figure's miraculous healing skills, just as much as their touch would do. This could also be applied to their later followers, whose close imitation of the lifestyle of Christ and His Apostles situated them as heirs to this tradition and gave them powers similar to those associated with these Biblical figures. As a consequence, their dress also behaved in the same way: 'Even the skin of this man [Peter the Galatian], acting through his clothes, had a similar power [to heal], as in the case of the most godly Paul'.[48] Indeed these pieces of clothing could be accepted as an equally potent substitute for body parts: Gregory of Tours claimed that the *pallium* that covered the remains of the bishop Nicetius was felt to be 'better still' at effecting a cure than the possession of a relic of his.[49]

That they could be given as a substitute for the saint and were seen to be just as efficacious in producing 'powerful effects', even when separate from the body, appears to have been understood as arising from their initial close proximity to the saint's body. Although such things were perhaps suggested by 'everyday' experiences which showed that cloth itself not only absorbed dye, but also the sweat and smell of an ordinary person,[50] it was a perception that was also expressed in the Bible: clothing was easily 'stained by corrupted flesh' (Jude 23). Garments were therefore clearly believed to be capable of taking in (and displaying) their owner's internal state. This enabled them to imbibe and 'remember' the holy power emanating from the body of a sacred individual in both life and death, as well as their spiritual authority (discussed in the final sections of this chapter), enabling them to live on through their clothing:[51]

> Moreover, let my most tranquil lady [Constantina, wife of emperor Maurice] know that it is not the custom of the Romans, when they give relics of saints, to presume to touch any part of the body; but only a *brandeum* [a linen or silk covering] is put into a casket, and placed near the most sacred bodies of the saints. When it is taken up it is deposited with due reverence in the church that is to be dedicated, and such power happens through them in that very place, it is as if their bodies were in that special place. (Gregory the Great, *Epistularum Registrum*, 4.30)[52]

Here, it is simply proximity to the holy body which leads to the cloth's connection with the saint, manifested by its resultant powers, and Gregory reinforces this with a following story about Pope Leo I cutting a piece of cloth which had been placed in a box near the body of Peter. His action produced the same result as cutting into a body: blood flowed from the incision.[53] The story demonstrates that the connection forged between the body and the cloth was considered very powerful. Even the smallest threads could work wonders.[54] Such items were particularly agreeable gifts to give, as Gregory's letter as a whole makes clear. They allowed the original possessor of the relic to keep the sacred body intact, while donating something that could still be considered to be part of the saint whether it originally belonged to them or not.

The benefit of owning such items stemmed not only from their curative powers or 'the power which [happened] through them' however. The stories encountered previously along with others concerning the more general translation of saintly relics between churches, or of some saintly bodies which had to be protected by armed guards 'in order to strike fear into those who tried to relieve the body of its clothing or to loosen bits from it', demonstrate the intense desire in Late Antiquity to own, touch, and associate with holiness.[55] That this was applicable to every level of society, can be seen in further sections of Gregory's letter from which the above is taken: while the empress Constantina feels she can demand the head of Paul or another part of his body (*caput eiusdem sancti Pauli, aut aliud quid de corpore ipsius, suis ad se iussionibus a me praecepit debere transmitti*) for the church she is building to the saint, others could obtain a little part of holiness through filings scraped from the chains of Peter by a priest whose duty this was (*quia dum frequenter ex catenis eisdem multi venientes benedictionem petunt, ut parvum quid ex limatura accipiant, assistit sacerdos cum lima . . .*). Constantina may have been unsuccessful in this instance, having to make do likewise with part of Peter's chains, but tangible holiness was a certainly seen as a commodity that could increase the spiritual and social standing of the owner, more so than donating clothing gifts to churches could achieve.[56] In protecting and caring for such items there was an expectation that the saint would reciprocate, rewarding this good deed, and by acting in their role as an intermediary close to God (a proximity which grew even closer once they had died), the saint could intercede on the possessor's behalf.[57] Clothing relics thus functioned in a similar way to the images of the emperor on the clothing of his officials discussed the previous chapters, for they were closely linked to the power of the 'prototype' and both encouraged good behaviour and protected those who could touch or possess such items.

4.3 Fitting clothing

It was not only the laity who desired such items. As will be seen in the final parts of the chapter (particularly in reference to the garments of the monk Antony), the ability of the possessor to care for clothing which once belonged to holy men became an increasingly important indicator of a cleric's ability to fulfil his role as the protector and inheritor of their memory and authority. This was because, as seen above, there was a feeling that the important qualities of the holy man were imbibed by his clothing, and this included not just his abilities to heal, but also his spiritual authority.[58] When another monk or member of the clergy was given such an item as a gift and then wore it, there was a sense that they were enveloping themselves in the original owner and his authority.[59] This was accordingly transferred to the new possessor, transforming them into a person of greater power. Such items, then, had to be given and used very carefully.

The idea of 'putting on' a persona as if it were a garment was a well-known trope in classical literature, where it often signified the taking up of the characteristics of a person's political or social role and the subsequent transference of these qualities to the wearer.[60] In a Christian context the receivers of these personal gifts would have understood themselves as being placed in a similar position, due to the Pauline notion that the baptised 'put on Christ' (Χριστὸν ἐνδύειν/*induere Christum*).[61] It was a phrase that both explained the conduct expected of the newly baptised and the ritual itself as an act of character transformation; having stripped off their old attire which represented their worldly and sinful life for immersion in water, the participants were then provided with white linen garments to symbolise their spiritual reclothing during the actual ceremony.[62] It is not clear from the ancient authors who describe the ritual in this period whether the new clothing received by the baptised should be seen as a gift. Yet, the performance of receiving new attire, which was an important feature of the ritual, enabled John Chrysostom to employ an elaborate and sustained literary conceit in his late fourth-century work *Ad illuminandos catecheses* (c. late 380s to 390s).[63] Playing on the fact that there was a real garment involved in the baptism ritual, he presented the baptised's new Christian life as a shining garment received as a gift from God.[64] Thus, while it may not have been a gift in 'reality', the acceptance of new clothing by the baptised, suggested to John Chrysostom at least that the meanings behind the ceremony could be understood and explained through a literary gifting of clothing.

The garment that the recently baptised put on was 'this new and shining cloak, this royal robe'.[65] In its brilliant colour and unstained nature the baptised's attire symbolised the Christian's inner self, clothed anew by the power of the rite and now no longer sullied by sin.[66] For the poorer members of society, then, this imagery allowed them to metaphorically possess the luxury garments owned (and sometimes donated to the Church) by the wealthy, to which their financial circumstances and social standing normally prevented access; all were one in Christ. Like real expensive garments, however, maintenance was costly – particularly if worn at all times – it was liable to be dirtied, frayed and torn unless kept with great care by the wearer.[67] It was thus the possessor's constant responsibility to keep the 'royal robe shining even more brightly than it now does, by … godly conduct and … strict discipline'.[68] Stains were easily acquired by neglectful treatment, of course, but if they do their 'fair share [of work in guarding the spiritual robe], the garment of virtue will not become soiled nor feel the onslaught of age, but as time passes, so much more does it reveal the fresh sheen of its beauty and its radiant light'.[69]

This duty was particularly important because this new Christian clothing was a gift from God: 'I exhort you who have just deserved the divine gift to keep careful watch and to guard the spiritual garment bestowed on you, keeping it clean and spotless' (5.24).[70] It was also irreplaceable: 'Guard, then the garment you have received: if you ruin it, you will not be able to buy or borrow another. There is no place where this kind of garment is for sale'.[71] Exploiting the newly baptised 'real-world' experience of caring for clothing, an essential but sometimes costly necessity, John suggests the Christian's duty to live a careful life which avoided the taint of sinful and inappropriate behaviour – they had to be worthy of the robe entrusted to them.[72] As his clothing metaphor suggests, this attire was an 'investment piece' and not an easy charge, and it is in this way that he highlights the importance of continual devotion. The clothing of the soul, which was easily damaged yet extremely valuable, indicates that, for this author at least, Christianity was a complete and life-altering decision, which required constant vigilance to maintain the correct standards of behaviour.[73] The garment and its role as a divine gift becomes a way therefore for John Chrysostom to explore and explain baptism to the neophytes. Through providing metaphorical access to a luxury good normally beyond the means of many of them, John explores the relationship between a Christian and his God, forged during this rite with the receipt of this gift.

Their new clothing, then, symbolised their new identity and responsibilities, but the nature of dress, and the phrase 'to put on Christ' also suggested to other authors besides John Chrysostom, that 'Christians . . . [had to] grow into [and become like] the Christ they wear', imitating His deeds and becoming like Him.[74] This echoed attitudes toward the dress of actors in the theatre, which were also considered to have the power to transform a person's character, changing ordinary people into the gods, monsters, and heroes of myth and history before the very eyes of an audience.[75] That this was a sentiment held in Late Antiquity is clear from the fact that Libanius found it necessary to negate such claims:

> For if the style of one's clothing had such power and one's way of life was transformed by it (εἰ γὰρ τοσοῦτον ἴσχυε τὰ τῆς ἀμπεχόνης εἴδη καὶ τὰς μεταβολὰς ὁ τρόπος ἐκεῖθεν ἐλάμβανεν), it would be a chance for the men in the brothels to dress up like Heracles (ἐνσκευάσασθαι κατὰ τὸν Ἡρακλέα) and change their life-style (μεταστῆσαι τὸν βίον) with the lion-skin and the club. But it is not possible (ἀλλ' οὐκ ἔστιν) . . . (Libanius, Oratio, 64.53)[76]

Libanius may deny that costume had the potential to change the nature of the actor. Yet, by engaging with and answering the second-century philosopher Aelius Aristides' claims about clothing, he demonstrates that for some in Late Antiquity clothes continued to have transformative power in and of themselves.

This is perhaps due to their ability to conceal and disguise; like cosmetics for women, the potential for clothing to act in this way upon the wearer was powerful and problematic precisely because, as noted in the Introduction, the sartorial world of the ancients was built on the notion that a person's clothing should reveal who they were.[77] The actor-martyr story of Philemon demonstrates this concept working in an earlier Christian context.[78] Here, during the Diocletianic persecutions in Egypt, Philemon, a former mime, is asked to dress up in a deacon's clothes in order to take the latter's place in performing a sacrifice and thus help the deacon avoid imprisonment and martyrdom. Philemon, agreeing to the ruse, dresses in the deacon's clothes, and he is consequently recognised as a Christian. He is required to offer the sacrifice, but before he can begin he is visited by the Holy Spirit, leading to a public declaration of his new-found Christianity. This is unlike other conversion-martyr stories of those in the same profession, where clothing visually confirms and finalises the genuine conversion of the actor who was participating in a mock baptism.[79] Instead, here it is only the deacon's clothing that acts as the conduit for transforming Philemon the mime into a Christian.[80] Philemon's change of dress, although initially a disguise, instead allows the real nature of the actor to be revealed.[81] Philemon's clothing, however, not only unveils his Christianity, but also shows him as better suited to being a leader of the church than the deacon whose garments he is wearing. His decision to confront the fate the donor of his attire strove so hard to avoid makes him appear more worthy than the deacon of the clothes he is now wearing. Philemon uses the clothing as it was intended – to demonstrate his adherence to Christianity – while the author turns Philemon into a *de facto* deacon, complete with a cleric's ability to convert likely candidates through the example of his story. The clothes are thus a much better fit for Philemon than their original owner.

4.4 Fake couture and fashion disasters

In the period after Constantine, when the orthodox Church no longer suffered official persecution and could now enjoy the benefits that accompanied imperial favour and promotion,[82] the relative safety of being a Christian brought with it new concerns. One of these was how (and by what criteria) to assess spiritual authority, when anyone could claim they were a holy man with little danger of having to prove this through martyrdom like Philemon.[83] As will be explored in more detail below with regard to Antony, the gifting of clothing by a famous holy man (and the correct use of the garment by the recipient) was one way of identifying those who were felt to be genuine. This was not only because it highlighted the relationship between the two men and demonstrated the established holy man's approval of one who would partake and inherit his charismatic authority, but also because the gifting of specific items such as the *pallium* and the *melōte* literally marked out the wearer's position of authority. This is also seen in the *Vita Martini* (discussed earlier in the chapter). The *chlamys*, cut in half and gifted by Martin to the beggar-Christ, was not only standard military attire during this period, but was also (as has been observed in Chapter 2) the item worn to mark those who held office in the imperial bureaucracy and the emperor himself. It was therefore a fitting garment to be given to and worn by the king of heaven.[84]

But though Martin correctly attires a disguised Christ in a mantle of authority that reveals his true nature, the same text also provides an example of the deceitfulness of clothing and its ability to conceal, which was viewed with anxiety in antiquity. In the following anecdote about a false monk, Anatolis, who came to live among Martin's disciples and declared that he received a garment from God as a gift,[85] this quality was used by Sulpicius Severus to discuss the questions surrounding identifying 'real' religious authority, during a period that seems, from the sources, to have been rife with religious con men:

> Finally it went up to the point with [Anatolis] . . . that he was now wanting to be considered as one of the prophets. Clarus, however, could by no means be forced to believe . . . At last [Anatolis] was said to have burst forth with these words: 'Look! Tonight the Lord will give me a white garment from heaven, and having put this on I will transform in your midst: and that will be your sign, that I am the power of God, who has been presented with the garment of God'. (Sulpicius Severus, *Vita Martini*, 23)[86]

As Jacques Fontaine has argued, the receipt of a white garment as a sacred object gifted from God is designed to reinforce Anatolis' assertion that he is a prophet. This is because 'le "vêtement blanc" est l'accessoire par excellence du vestiaire apocalyptique', echoes the clothing worn by those in both the Old and New Testaments, and is also the colour of non-Christian religious clothing in antiquity.[87] Listed last in Anatolis' catalogues of assertions calculated to show his superiority in the community (and his status above Clarus, Martin's favoured disciple, in particular),[88] its placing reinforces the importance of the garment in providing proof of Anatolis' claim.

It is soon clear from Sulpicius' language, however, that the garment is not all it seems; the identification of the item by the general term, *vestis*, during the sections narrated in the authorial voice are juxtaposed with its classification as the more specific (and evocative) *tunica* when it appears that Anatolis is narrating.[89] This is surely a deliberate choice by Sulpicius to alert his audience that this vestment will not be tailored to Anatolis' needs. While the latter may view his garment as the item that adorns monks and (of particular significance for this context) Martin,[90] for Sulpicius, Anatolis' generic *vestis*, shows him to be inappropriately attired for someone claiming to be something special. The language of the text at this point, therefore, underlines the idea that this man is a fraud who would not be worthy of such a gift (had it been given), which would have cemented and identified his superior authority as one approved by God; his clothing reflects his inner mundanity. Indeed the garment then becomes a metaphor for Anatolis' waning credibility within the community. At its initial appearance, because it was 'of the utmost softness, of marvellous brightness, and of glittering purple' (*summa mollitie, candore eximio, micanti purpura*) and appeared to be made of an undiscoverable material, the item dazzles some of the viewers into belief, just as Anatolis claims it would do and had done himself. However, 'when it was more minutely examined by the eyes or fingers, it seemed nothing other than a garment (*Curiosius tamen oculis aut digitis attrectata, non aliud quam vestis videbatur)*', just as Anatolis was no more than a man. Furthermore, neither the man nor the garment can stand up to being examined by one who had real religious authority and had actually clothed Christ himself. Any last thread of credibility vanishes with the garment, which disappears at the threat of Martin's powers, the insight of Clarus, and his deference to Martin's authority: 'And when they compelled him [to go to Martin] against his will, the garment vanished from among the hands of those who were conducting him' (*cumque invitum ire compellerent, inter trahentium manus vestis evanuit*).[91]

Sulpicius' account demonstrates the general concern felt during this period about who was considered worthy of the gift of spiritual authority, and his use of a clothing gift to highlight this is reflected in other writers. In 'real life' clothing was certainly bequeathed by famous holy men to their heirs in wills,[92] and the ideas suggested by the proximity of clothing to the body, examined previously, meant that a garment could imbibe the essence of its original owner. As in the diplomatic and political contexts of Chapters 2 and 3, it could also confer power and status. As a result, gifts of clothing provided an understandable tool for late antique authors to discuss the transference of authority between a holy man and his successor, which drew on contemporary practices and beliefs. In particular, it was useful for underscoring both the author's mistrust of those who appeared undeserving of the burden of a holy man's legacy, and, as will be seen in the last part of the chapter with regard to Athanasius and his use of Antony's cloak, for reinforcing the position of those who laid claim to it.

In the case of authorial misgivings, it was the subsequent treatment of the clothing gift that was valuable for demonstrating not only what was expected from those who were entrusted with authority, but also what would happen when these expectations were contravened. The story told by Gregory of Tours about the Bishop Priscus, a 'stong opponent' of Nicetius (whose *pallium* was seen previously to be more effective at curing sickness than his bodily relics), and his deacon illustrates this well. Priscus gave to his deacon 'the *casula* [a cape-like item] which Nicetius had worn' (*diacono cuidam huius casulam tribuit*). The deacon wore it everywhere, '. . . never thinking that its fringes, if his faith had been firm enough, could have brought health to the sick' (*de cuius fimbriis, si credulitas certa fuisset, reddi potuit salus infirmis*). Despite an admonition that he does not know the power of God, because if he did he should use the garment with more care (*cautius te cum eo vivere oportebat*), the deacon replied:

> '. . . I wear this cape to cover my back – and as the hood is too big for me, I shall make socks out of it (*et de capsa eius parte prolixiore decisa tegumen pedum aptabo*)!' The wretched man [doing this] . . . fell immediately to the vengeance of divine judgement. Indeed, as soon as he had cut the hood, made the socks and put them on his feet, the devil seized him . . . and his feet were stretched towards the hearth; the fire devoured his feet, and the socks as well (*verum ubi deciso cucullo aptatis pedulis pedes operuit, extemplo arreptus a daemone ruit in pavimento . . . extensis ad focum pedibus, pedes cum pedulibus ignis pariter devoravit*). (Gregory of Tours, *de vita Patrum*, 8.5)[93]

142 *Holy habits*

Here, it can be seen that neither the original receiver of the gift nor its final owner recognised the significance of this present, and they are shown to be incapable of using authority correctly. Little is known about this Priscus – he is the successor to Nicetius as bishop of Lyon – but the fact that he is initially identified as an adversary of Nicetius already marks him out as dubious in Gregory's text and lays the groundwork for the reader to understand his subsequent actions. Priscus is further shown to be completely unworthy as Nicetius' successor, however, through his inappropriate gifting of the mantle – the only story which Gregory narrates of him. Thus, rather than carefully keeping Nicetius' *casula/cappa* (a symbol of the transference of the saint's authority and presumably entrusted to him as Nicetius' successor), Priscus, the initial recipient, instead carelessly gifts it to a deacon. It is an action that implies he does not understand how to use the authority with which he has been entrusted, because he immediately delegates its power to someone of a lower rank, resulting in Nicetius' holy (and clerical) authority being wielded by one who is clearly not up to the task. The deacon, similarly ignorant of how this power (symbolised by the cloak) should be used, employs the item not to bring health to the sick, but for his own selfish benefit. This is demonstrated by the deacon's conversion of the hood of the cloak into socks, which ensures that the item which it was felt could aid many, can now only be employed by one.

Similar stories of deadly garments can be found in both religious and non-religious contexts, and have their traditions in Classical Greek tragedies (see Chapter 1 for some examples). Their recurrence in various sources suggests that authors saw clothing gifts as a powerful way to present a cautionary tale about the misuse of authority, while, as has also been seen with regard to Attila in Chapter 2, the way these items were utilised functioned as an implicit statement on the employer's character as well. For example, Theodoret relates a similar story told originally by Acacius, bishop of Caesarea (340–366), against Cyril bishop of Jerusalem (early to mid-300s–361).[94] Cyril sells to a stage dancer a 'holy robe . . . all fashioned with golden threads' (τὴν . . . ἱερὰν στολήν . . . ἐκ χρυσῶν δὲ αὕτη κατεσκεύαστο νημάτων) given by Constantine to the bishop of Jerusalem to be worn during the baptismal rites.[95] 'Dancing about when he was wearing it, [the stage dancer] fell down and perished' (καὶ ταύτην τινὰ τῶν ἐπὶ τῆς θυμέλης λυγιζομένων πριάμενον περιβαλέσθαι μέν, ὀρχούμενον δὲ πεσεῖν καὶ συντριβῆναι καὶ θανάτῳ παραδοθῆναι). Although the focus of Theodoret's authorial disapproval is centred upon the figure of Acacius, who was an Arian bishop, Acacius' use of the story in order to undermine Cyril in the eyes of the emperor Constantius II, suggests that this device was a successful and recognisable way of damaging a religious (and political) opponent.[96]

This tool could also be aimed at low-level authority abusers, as Theodoret's tale about his mother's cook demonstrates.[97] The cook had usurped holy power to which he was not entitled whilst play-acting with the servant girls, by putting on a goat hair cloak (σισύρα). Unknown to their distracted mistress, who was caring for her ill husband at the time, the cook 'exorcised them like a monk' (αὐτὸν δὲ ἐκεῖνον τὸν οἰκέτην σισύραν περιβαλλόμενον μοναχικῶς ἐξορκίζειν ἐκείνας). This had piqued the curiosity of a demon who 'intruded [himself] into the man, wanting to find out how [he] would be driven out by the monks' (Τούτου εἵνεκα τὰς παιδίσκας καταλιπὼν εἰς τοῦτον ἐμαυτὸν εἰσέφρησα, μαθεῖν ἐθελήσας ὅπως ὑπὸ τῶν μοναχῶν ἐξελαύνωμαι). Primarily, this story is designed as part of the wider narrative to honour Peter the Galatian, a hermit Theodoret knew as a child,[98] by demonstrating his power in exorcism. Yet it also suggests the dangers of unsupervised, idle servants misappropriating charismatic authority, which is here signified by a goat hair mantle.[99] The gruesome outcome for the inappropriate possessor of the clothing gift in such tales was designed to resolve any anxiety that the audience and author may feel about those who are unworthy to be given such power, implying the dire consequences such people would justifiably suffer. For religious authors like Gregory of Tours and Theodoret, this would come in the form of punishment from God or possession by a demon, and it was intended to ruin any attempt by the undeserving to build a secure footing to power through the use of saintly clothing.

4.5 Threads of tension

Most garment gifts were not quite so dangerous, however, and it was through the literary device of successful presentations that such items allowed for the positive resolution of tensions that were felt during the period. For those whose authority derived from the Church as a religious institution, this anxiety was centred around hermits and monks, whose remote locations, large following, and God-granted (but not necessarily Church-granted) authority were viewed as having the potential to undermine the Church's position as the only authority and interpreter of God's will on earth.[100] These competing ideals of authority are sometimes seen as a conflict between the differing traditions from which the eastern and western churches sprang, but it was also a conflict about where spiritual authority came from and how it was to be visualised and expressed – through an austere ascetic lifestyle which imitated Christ and his Apostles and resulted in miracle working abilities, or by a position in God's own Church which maintained and administered his faithful.[101] The conflict was more nuanced than this suggests,[102] of course, but one of the ways it came to be articulated was through clothing, as Lynda Coon, particularly in her chapters on 'Gender, hagiography, and the Bible' and the 'Rhetorical uses of clothing in the lives of sacred males' in *Sacred Fictions* (1997), has shown.[103] The next section utilises Coon's research on male religious apparel, and will discuss how a marked difference in the dress of a cleric and a monk allowed the wearer to display their different claims to divinely derived superiority.[104] It will then build on this to propose that, in the Christian literature of the period, the use of specific garments as gifts (which were symbolic attempts at controlling and repositioning the receiver under Church authority) were employed as devices to express these tensions.[105]

The general dress of a monk or hermit imitated the plain clothes of Christ and the Apostles, and in doing so it implied not only that their spiritual pre-eminence was drawn from their close imitation of the latter's lives, but that, like them, the ascetics' authority was obtained through inner sanctity, not special clothing.[106] The addition of a goatskin or hairy mantle, the μηλωτή (melōte), served to strengthen this Biblical tie even further, for it was an important part of the identity of Old and New Testament prophets such as Elijah and Elisha (who owned the same cloak), as well as John the Baptist.[107] Whether conscious or not, dressing in similar items, therefore, had the potential to place the wearer within this tradition. It could doubly mark them as a monk, for it was not only part of the outfit they received on entering the vocation, but also the identifying attire of the calling's Biblical founders.[108] It suggested therefore, that the wearer drew his charismatic authority not from a position within the Church hierarchy, but rather from his association with these powerful figures who had been ordained by God.[109] Furthermore, if the person whom a cloak adorned was a saintly monk or hermit who was felt to have prophetic powers, the clothing worked with the individual to strengthen this position.[110] Their clothing therefore functioned both with their own lifestyle and with their special powers, to connect them with the prophets of old and to legitimate and strengthen their charismatic authority.

For members of the Church hierarchy, their clothing had also originated in that of Christ and his disciples, but had become increasingly elaborate from the fourth and fifth centuries in order to deal with the practicalities of managing an expanding Church – visually separating them from the laity and delineating the different levels of authority.[111] While other clothing items, such as the *stolē*, demonstrated status, it was the *pallium* that would come to mark out high clerical authority.[112] This cloak had originally been equated with the Greek ἱμάτιον (*himation*), and as a result it had taken on the latter's stereotypical identification as the costume of philosophers and intellectuals; wearing such an item therefore allowed Christian wearers to display their *paideia*.[113] However, it was also the dress of Jesus himself in the Bible, and this was reflected in late antique art, where Christ, his Apostles, and even Moses, are depicted wearing the *himation/pallium*.[114] As the garment worn by Jesus and his Apostles, this originally unassuming item was made special by its holy wearers; it 'receives honour from the honour given to him who wears it'.[115] It also meant that those clerics who wore the garment could partake in their holy authority through the imitation of their dress. This was also felt to be the case when the *pallium* became instead the term for a narrow white scarf-like garment which encircled the neck (comparable to the eastern *omophorion*) by the sixth century; for Gregory the Great, for example, it 'mystically linked' the wearer to the apostle Peter.[116] Additionally, it connected them to the papacy itself as an institution, through Peter and his heirs, and this was solidified by the sixth century when it was worn only by patriarchs and those bishops granted metropolitan status; indeed access was so restricted that those in the west who wanted the privilege of wearing it needed papal authority to do so from this period.[117] Although this association was not as clearly defined in earlier periods, the *pallium* was becoming increasingly associated with the bishops, while also retaining its strongly religious origins as the dress of the head of the Church and the Apostle from whom papal power was felt to be inherited, Christ and Peter themselves. This perhaps implied the superiority of the clergy in religious authority over monks, for while the latter may have colonised the *melōte* and its associations with the charismatic power of the Old and New Testament prophets, the clergy were distinguished by the garment favoured by Christ and Peter.[118] Thus, as will be discussed in more detail below, its emerging role as an identifier of those in official religious power in Late Antiquity enabled Christian authors to use this garment as an extremely effective symbol within their texts.

These associations may have only been understood by a select few viewers of this item, but even for those who did not appreciate the subtleties of its meaning, the garment would likely have been paired with the clergy of the Church by virtue of being worn by its members.[119] In this case, the *pallium* would have been read in a non-religious way as an indicator of authority as well, particularly as it was initially a mantle item like the *chlamys* and the *trabea* of the previous chapters, which were worn by those who operated at the top tiers of the imperial bureaucracy. Thus, this type of item would still allow those unfamiliar with the symbolic association of religious dress items to read this clothing correctly as a display of the wearer's authority within his own sphere. Dress thus appears to have worked with the physical environment of the wearer to demonstrate his relationship with the Church. The *pallia* of the urban clergy have associations with official (church and non-religious) authority, while for those monks who lived in the desert their *melōte* and location positioned them with the prophets and made their charismatic and spiritual power clear. Thus (and perhaps because of this) the mantles of religious figures appear as part of the wider visualisation of the formal authority within late antique society through outer garments, and (like diplomatic clothing in the non-religious sphere) both demonstrate and help to identify to the uninitiated their wearers' special position within the religious landscape.

Religious clothing also echoed the diplomatic and political garments examined previously in the notion that these types of attire could transfer the authority they visualised to the wearer.[120] The gifting of dress items in these circumstances indicated a transmission of political power to the wearer, whilst also demonstrating both the origin of that authority and that the receiver had permission to partake in it with the confidence of the donor. Christian authors may have found some inspiration in these connotations, enabling the gifting of garments to work in a similar way, although the religious context of relics that absorbed saintly powers and Biblical imagery provided another apposite background against which this was to be understood. The main episode that furnished the religious framework for this symbolic gift-giving was 1 Kings 19.19–21 and 2 Kings 2.8–15, in which Elijah identifies Elisha as his successor by casting over Elisha his powerful cloak, which had the ability to part the water of the Jordan and was symbolic of his prophetic authority.[121] Furthermore, it was the only thing left of Elijah when he is taken up by a whirlwind to heaven, and, when picked up by Elisha was put to use immediately, parting the waters

146 *Holy habits*

in the same way as Elijah had done. This prompted onlookers to view Elisha as the heir of Elijah's spiritual and holy authority; their conclusion that 'the spirit of Elijah rests on Elisha' (Ἐπαναπέπαυται τὸ πνεῦμα Ηλιου ἐπὶ Ελισαιε) is closely related to his acquisition and use of the cloak, which will also 'rest on' Elisha.[122] Although the garment is not a direct gift to Elisha, the cloak appears to be left as a symbol of the transference of his authority to the new owner.[123] The ability of Elisha to continue to use the cloak in the same way as its original owner, moreover, suggests through the imagery of clothing that Elisha is not only approved as one able to care for this legacy, but that he is also allowed to share in the divine power which Elijah had channelled.

That this episode could be considered as a formal presentation of clothing from Elijah to Elisha is displayed by a wall hanging from late antique Egypt,[124] which introduces a radical change to the story and, in doing so, appears to reflect the symbolism of garment gifts within Christian literature. Instead of Elisha simply picking up Elijah's fallen mantle from the ground, the textile shows him receiving clothing from Elijah himself (cover illustration, Figure 4.1).[125] Maguire has suggested that this reflects real, though general, gifting practice, which, as has been seen throughout the previous chapters, the texts of the period also imply;[126] after all, for symbolism to work an audience must be able to recognise it, and this could only be achieved if they were familiar with the imagery because of real life experience. What it also shows, however, is that the Biblical transference of authority and power from Elijah to Elisha was understood in Late Antiquity through the performance of gifting clothing. As will be seen, literary texts also reflect the woven interpretation of this tapestry, so that by receiving the mantle of a saint, who in his ascetic lifestyle and prophetic powers could be viewed as Elijah, the new owner became another Elisha, the heir to his spiritual authority and charismatic power.[127] In the religious environment of this period, therefore, the presentation of garments was viewed as involving the transmission of power and authority, just as it was in the political and diplomatic spheres.

4.6 Under the mantle of orthodoxy

Christian writers, therefore, drew on their Biblical heritage and fused it with their own cultural context and understanding of the symbols of non-religious authorities when they included the giving of specific items of clothing, like the *pallium*, within their texts. As a result, such episodes have to be viewed through these underlying notions, in order to understand the function of clothing gifts as narrative devices used to discuss ideas of the correct transference of authority and to reposition powerful ascetics under the banner of the Church. Although this will be examined further in the case study of Antony below, the *Life of Euthymius* by Cyril of Scythopolis (c. 525–558)[128] is useful as an initial illustration of how this combination of ideas worked.

In the narrative, Cyril describes the appearance of the deceased saint Euthymius, who founded several monasteries in the Egyptian desert, in a

Holy habits   147

Figure 4.1 Detail of late antique wall hanging of Elijah and Elisha (fourth century), Egypt; Abegg-Stiftung, CH-3132 Riggisberg, inv. no. 2439 © Abegg-Stiftung, CH-3132 Riggisberg, 2003 (photograph: Christoph von Viràg)

vision to his deacon Fidus, after the latter has called on his aid when he was shipwrecked and left clinging to a plank in the middle of the sea.[129] Agreeing to rescue him, Euthymius then commands Fidus to 'depart to my laura and build a coenobium in the place where you built my burial vault . . .' (αὐτὸς δὲ ἄπελθε εἰς τὴν ἐμὴν λαύραν καὶ κοινόβιον οἰκοδόμησον ἐν ὧι τόπωι τὸ ἐμὸν ᾠκοδόμησας). After promising to follow the saint's orders, Fidus is given a garment by Euthymius and transported to safety:

> But the great Euthymius, veiling him with his *pallium* (σκεπάσας αὐτὸν τῶι ἑαυτοῦ παλλίωι), dismissed him in peace, at which Fidus, snatched up and becoming airborne, in the manner, I suppose, of Habakkuk [Dan. 14.36], found himself in a twinkling of an eye on the shore and then in the holy city, without any consciousness of things human. Going into his own house, he took off the *pallium* given by God with which he was clad and put on his own clothes, at which the *pallium* disappeared (τὸ θεόσδοτον ἐκεῖνο παλλίον ἀποθέμενος, ὅπερ ἦν περιβεβλημένος, καὶ τὰ ἴδια ἱμάτια ἐνδυσάμενος, τὸ μὲν παλλίον ἄφαντον γέγονεν). (Cyril, *Vita Euthymii*, 64–64.7)[130]

The *pallium* is here functioning like the garments from the previous chapters, providing protection for Fidus while he is being rescued, and symbolising the transference of authority from the saint to his deacon, which will allow the latter to make radical changes to Euthymius' monastery. It symbolises the authority granted to the wearer, but also (as a gift) highlights where that authority comes from; and in its protective function it resembles the symbolism of the mantles adorned with the imperial portrait which have been discussed previously.[131]

As has been noted above, however, the Christian context adds further meanings to the gift and the circumstances of its giving, for Fidus is to a certain extent the Elisha to Euthymius' Elijah. Moreover, it appears that Cyril has chosen his vocabulary deliberately so that its full contemporary religious meaning could be understood. Thus he labels Euthymius' garment by rendering the Latin term *pallium* into Greek, so that the saint is clothed in an item that, as has been discussed above, was by this period (the sixth century) particularly associated with the highest echelons of 'official' – i.e. Church – religious authority, the bishops.[132] As Euthymius is a holy member of the monastic profession, it would be more appropriate for his mantle to be the *melōte* – the distinctive attire that symbolised the charismatic authority of saintly monks. Furthermore, as a monk himself it would appear natural if, in light of the tensions noted previously, the author Cyril was to present this monastic hero in an item so associated with their special brand of religious power. Cyril was also a priest, however, and was thus part of the Church hierarchy. More importantly, he was also concerned to present Euthymius, the founder of the monastery in which he lived, as orthodox. This was because Cyril had been part of the group of monks that had expelled the Origenists from the New Laura and 'reclaimed [it] for orthodoxy'.[133] In deliberately choosing to clothe Euthymius in the *pallium*, therefore, Cyril is bringing the holy man under the mantle of orthodoxy – an important repositioning in light of these events – by presenting him in the attire of a member of the upper ranks of Church authority.

As will be seen in more detail in the case study, this device was employed by other earlier writers, who drafted in famous holy figures to the cause of the

Church through the rewriting of their *Lives* to suit their (and the author's) own agenda. By operating outside of the boundaries of the official church authority, monks were to some extent a problematic but also extremely influential part of the Christian landscape.[134] Indeed, as hagiographies frequently show, these figures gathered a large, often unsolicited, following, which resulted in them retreating further and further into the desert to maintain their solitary life.[135] Despite the annoyance supposedly felt by the holy men that they hardly had a moment of peace, this illustrates that monks and hermits had the potential to influence many outside the more official spaces in which the Church operated, and moreover that people wanted them to do so.[136] Co-opting such liminal figures and associating them with the authority of the Church, therefore, meant it could benefit from their special, charismatic authority, allowing the Church to partake in their holiness and strengthening the position of orthodoxy as the doctrine of the saints.[137]

4.7 Case study – fashioning and refashioning Antony's vestment

That certain clothing gifts could be refashioned to suit the literary agendas of authors can be seen particularly in the different lives of the *himation/pallium* of Antony (c. 251–356), the Egyptian ascetic considered as the pioneer of anchoritic or eremitic asceticism.[138] A single (and possibly, but not necessarily, factual)[139] garment, the mantle nonetheless has two conflicting stories about its transmission in authors who are contemporaneous. Its curiously different biographies make it an interesting case study and of particular relevance to this chapter, as it brings together many of the threads of discussion concerning gifts of clothing in religious situations. It will therefore be the focus of this final section.

The *himation/pallium* of Antony appears in two hagiographical texts, the *Vita Antonii* written soon after Antony's death around 365 by Athanasius, Bishop of Alexandria (328–373),[140] and the *Vita Pauli primi eremitae*, written in the late 370s by Jerome.[141] As a renowned figure in late antique Christianity, Antony needs little introduction; the significance of his garment and its relationship to Athanasius has been the subject of discussion by scholars such as David Brakke, Michael Williams (who also comments on its importance in the *Vita Pauli primi eremitae*), and Brian Brennan, and their arguments provide a foundation for this section. Paul of Thebes, on the other hand, is less famous: information about him stems entirely from Jerome's *Vita* and there is good reason to believe he may have been completely fictional.[142] In the text, he is presented as the first hermit, a 'much better' man than Antony (*multo se meliorem*).[143] Although 'a wealthy heir . . . and highly educated in both Greek and Egyptian letters' (*in haereditate locupleti . . . litteris tam Graecis quam Aegyptiacis apprime eruditus*), he retreated into the desert due to the persecutions and the betrayal of his brother-in-law, eventually dwelling in solitude in an abandoned mint until he was found by Antony.[144] Older in age and a hermit for longer than Antony, Paul is presented by Jerome as the originator of anchoritic asceticism and the author is keen to rob Antony of some (although not all) of his borrowed feathers as the pioneer of this practice. As will be examined more fully in the final part of the case study, this is of significance to the reading of the differing lives of Antony's *himation/pallium* – an item that, as others have observed, is noteworthy because it is employed by the authors to further their own religious, political and literary agendas. It will be argued, however, that the importance of the garment goes beyond this, and lies in its ability to demonstrate the function of clothing gifts in understanding and resolving an underlying anxiety for the Church in this period. This was namely the problematic position of saints whose charismatic power operated outside of the Church, but whose competing authority had the potential to undermine episcopal authority, and who therefore needed to be confined and controlled within these boundaries.[145]

In both texts the garment has the same initial biography, appearing as a gift given by Athanasius to Antony:

> ... the *himation* on which I lie [Athanasius] gave it me new, and it has grown old alongside me ... (Athanasius, *Vita Antonii*, 91.8)[146]

> [And Paul said:] 'Therefore go, I beg ... and entrust to me the *pallium* which bishop Athanasius gave to you, to wrap my poor body in'. ... Antony was astonished that Paul had heard of Athanasius and his *pallium*. (Jerome, *Vita Pauli primi eremitae*, 12)[147]

The correspondence between the two texts here is significant because it implies that at this early stage both authors are working towards the same literary goal with regards to Antony. As others have suggested, Athanasius' agenda in the *Vita Antonii* is to bring the saint under the banner of orthodoxy, as part of his wider concern to unite ascetics and the episcopacy under his leadership;[148] the gift of the *pallium* of a bishop contributes to this reimagining.[149] In this he is followed by Jerome, who reflects Athanasius' treatment because of their common religious viewpoint, and who also has a further interest in presenting Antony in this way because it has important consequences for how the audience is meant to view Paul of Thebes.

It has been seen throughout the previous chapters that the gifting of clothes displays the existence or establishment of a relationship between the giver and receiver, and in both lives the garment also functions in this way. There may be a possibility that it was a real gift; the surviving letters of Church Fathers demonstrate that parcels of clothing were making their way fairly regularly across the empire to benefit those brothers (and sometimes sisters) who were in need.[150] In addition, they were part of the notion of charitable giving seen at the beginning of this chapter, which was expected to be exercised by all good Christians. While perhaps not as expensive as other clothing gifts examined in these chapters, such items were of great practical benefit to the receiver, whose lack of wealth or more isolated situation may have made the acquisition of such items problematic. They also helped to maintain or initiate relationships between people whose geographical situation or religiously induced poverty would make regular face-to-face contact difficult to achieve.[151] However, it is significant that, while mantles do make an occasional appearance, the most common garment presents appear to be tunics in 'real world' religious communication. Thus, the frequent occurrence in hagiographical texts of items such as the *himation/pallium* and *melōte* as gifts, demonstrates a discrepancy that implies they are employed in these works because they have greater symbolic capital, and this appears to stem from their associations with spiritual authority. As will be explored throughout this section, this is certainly how Antony's apparel works in Athanasius' *Vita Antonii*. Although the problems Athanasius encountered on a number of occasions during his time in Alexandria required him to flee into the countryside of Egypt, it is not certain how often he actually met Antony.[152] This suggests there may be reasons to doubt that the garment was a real gift, given that Athanasius may have actually had minimal contact with the monk. For the purposes of the discussion, the reality of the gift is less important than the 'reality' created by Athanasius in which Antony receives this gift, for the symbolism of the item works regardless. Along with other allusions in the *Life* that function in a similar way, the textual presentation of his own *himation/pallium* to Antony means that Athanasius (and Jerome) are in fact strengthening the potentially fictional bond between the two men by creating a 'reality' where instead a long-established and close relationship exists.[153]

The garment has more levels of symbolism than this, however, because, as will be seen, its association with Athanasius literally envelops Antony in the mantle of Church authority. This is because, while the *himation/pallium* given to Antony by Athanasius does not have the stronger connotations with episcopal authority that the later *pallium* was to have, the fact that it is donated by a bishop combines with the previously encountered concepts surrounding the gifting of clothing. As a result, it functions to show Antony as firmly entrenched in the Church as a cleric high in the hierarchy. It has been seen throughout that clothing was felt to have the potential to transform its wearers, allowing them to take on characteristics signified by or imbibed in the garment. By receiving and putting on the apparel of Athanasius, therefore, Antony is symbolically assuming the orthodoxy for which Athanasius stands as a leader of the Church, and is disguised by this literary device as part of the hierarchy both within the text and (if this was a real gift) without. Of course, Antony's isolation in the desert would have meant that few people would have the opportunity actually to witness him in this guise. By (over)writing the mantle into the *Life*, however, Athanasius, like Martial, Malalas, and Ausonius, ensures that Antony is 'seen' with this *himation/pallium* by a much wider audience.[154] The gift had the potential, therefore, to transform Antony visually into a cleric of the Church, despite the fact that he was not ordained, especially because, in ancient texts and reality, clothes made the man. Although written soon after the original by bishop Evagrius of Antioch in the fourth century, the Latin translation of the *Life* would have perpetuated this visual and literary fiction when read or heard by later audiences by calling the cloak a *pallium*; while in the earlier period it was a common parallel for the *himation*, by the sixth century this would have gained further significance as *the* item which marked out a bishop.[155]

In addition, through the associations that accepting a gift had with submission, reciprocity, and clothing's ability to transform the wearer, the gift of the *himation/pallium* further repositioned Antony under the banner of the Church and implied a yielding of his charismatic power to its influence.[156] For Athanasius, manoeuvring Antony towards orthodoxy was essential because he was claiming to be the heir to Antony's charismatic power, and it would therefore reflect rather poorly on him if his mentor appeared to be an adherent (and even teacher) of heretical beliefs.[157] It claimed Antony's power for the Church alone, thus potentially preventing him from becoming a figurehead for a heretical sect. Athanasius' *Life* was an extremely popular and influential text, and his Antony became the definitive version that allowed little room for a different interpretation that could exist in isolation from his text.[158] In the gift of his own *himation/pallium*, therefore, Athanasius permanently redefines the saint's relationship to the Church and suggests the symbolic submission and binding of Antony's charismatic authority for the Church's (and Athanasius' own) benefit; in this authoritative text, he is over-written as a paradigm and supporter of Christian orthodoxy.[159]

Composing later, Jerome capitalises on this reimagining of Antony, but uses it instead to imply certain ideas about Paul. He certainly knew Athanasius' text, probably through the Latin translation of Evagrius, as he notes it in his *Lives of Illustrious Men*.[160] His own hagiographical text was produced only a few years after this had appeared, and by writing the *Life* of a Latin saint he was filling a gap in western Christian literature.[161] This was despite Jerome's assertions that Paul was from Thebes; his authorship of the *Life* along with the widely held view that Paul's real origin was in Jerome's imagination meant the saint was firmly rooted in the west. In some ways his text is a companion piece to Athanasius' *Vita Antonii*, as it focuses on Antony, and it is through his actions, rather than Paul's, that the narrative moves forward.[162] As Jerome himself seems to suggest in *Vita Pauli* 1, a knowledge of Athanasius' text is a prerequisite for reading this *Life* and for understanding how clothing, or rather gifts of clothing, function within it.

In Jerome's narrative, he agrees that Athanasius is the original giver of Antony's *pallium*;[163] however, while this works on one level in the same way as in Athanasius' *Life* (considered above), Jerome is also colluding in the repositioning of Antony within orthodoxy for his own ends. Thus, when Antony gives his *pallium* as a burial garment to Paul, it is as a piece of clothing that the audience should (and are told that they do) recognise from the *Vita Antonii*. This episode of intertextuality is important for Paul: he is wrapped in an item that carries over its connotations from Athanasius' text, enveloping Paul in the mantle of the Church just as it had covered Antony. Although not a bishop, like Athanasius Jerome was a believer in the orthodoxy of the Church interested in co-opting and subsuming the charismatic authority of desert fathers for its benefit;[164] he therefore had a vested interest in presenting his own creations as fellow followers.

After this initial continuity, however, Jerome's version of events surrounding the *pallium* of Antony diverges significantly from those related in the *Vita Antonii*, and it is in this divergence that the literary use of clothing gifts for conveying ideas of authority can most clearly be seen.

Indeed, Jerome's biography of Antony's *pallium* differs so widely from Athanasius' that Jerome completely erases Athanasius from the rest of Antony's story, which furthermore lends weight to the theory that the text was written in the late 370s – after Athanasius' death in 373. At first this discrepancy may be seen as an attempt by the author to undermine Athanasius' credit as an accurate chronicler. Jerome makes a point of mentioning that he has consulted other followers of Antony in compiling his narrative, some of whom also appear in Athanasius' story, but from which list Athanasius himself is significantly absent.[165] In citing these other sources, Jerome implies a desperation to prove the truthfulness of his account, and the importance to him of his audience's faith in the narrative is demonstrated by his complaints within the follow-up text that people did not believe his story or that Paul actually existed.[166]

Despite Jerome's claims of veracity, however, the discrepancies between Jerome and Athanasius' depictions of corresponding episodes in Antony's life do raise suspicions in the reader, and the most obvious of these inconsistencies appears in the story of the afterlife of the *pallium*. To take Athanasius' text first, as it is against this that Jerome's narrative must be read, in his *Life* the *himation/ pallium* is returned to him in the form of a legacy in Antony's verbal will:

> 'Distribute my clothing: to Athanasius the bishop, give one of my *melōte* and the *himation* on which I lie – he gave it to me new, and it has grown old alongside me; and to Serapion the bishop, give the other *melōte*, and you keep the hair garment . . .' Each of those who received a *melōte* from the blessed Antony, and the *himation* used by him, looks after them as items of great value. For looking at them is like seeing Antony, and wearing them like contemplating his reproofs with joy . . . (91.8–9; 92.3)[167]

In both the religious and non-religious worlds, clothing could be left as an inheritance,[168] and for the ascetics in particular, their way of life meant that the few possessions they owned and could pass on necessarily (and sometimes only) included the clothes off their back. Antony's bequest has a basis in real practices, therefore, but the symbolic function of gifts of clothing that have been seen throughout these chapters means that it should be understood when occurring in literature as having something more to say.

Serapion and Athanasius both receive the symbolic garment of desert ascetics, the *melōte*, from Antony and thus appear to be equal heirs to his charismatic legacy.[169] However, it is Athanasius alone who receives a *himation/pallium*, and the significance of this does not seem to have been fully understood in modern scholarship. The exception is Brian Brennan,[170] whose arguments are followed here; but Brennan does not give enough weight to this episode as a two-sided exchange, because he fails to recognise the importance of *pallium* as a symbol of Athanasius' clerical authority within this text.[171] It is understandable that the gift Athanasius gave would have been restored to him, but, as has been seen, when it comes to the literary appearance of these types of presents, it returns with further meanings attached. Because in the language of clothing the *melōte* and the *himation/pallium* are symbols of authority, and have the power to absorb the qualities of its owners and transfer them, what Athanasius actually receives is not simply his own gift returned, but a transference and acceptance of Antony's charismatic power fused with his own episcopal authority. Athanasius and Serapion may be Antony's legal and charismatic heirs equally, but just as Elisha with Elijah, Athanasius alone is the sole inheritor of both the saint's spiritual and earthly authority, placing him above Serapion, and this is signified by the gifting and re-gifting of the *himation/pallium*.[172] Furthermore, although it has no miraculous powers, when read in a similar way as the clothing that could enact cures (such as that from relics considered earlier), the inheritance of Antony's garment shows that Athanasius alone has been approved of and proven worthy to maintain this burden – he is the favoured heir. Athanasius knows the value of this legacy that keeps Antony alive; he 'looks after them as items of great value. For looking at them is like seeing Antony …'.[173] It is clear through his careful and correct use of the inheritance entrusted to him, Athanasius' feet will be safe from the fire which had been so disastrous for Priscus' deacon.

Positioning himself in such a way was of great importance because Athanasius, acting in a comparable manner to Gratian in Chapter 3, was using an established and well-loved figure of authority in order to shore up his own power. During the multiple exiles of Athanasius (which had the potential to damage his reputation and required him to fight for his arch-episcopal see throughout the years 356–362), Antony was a useful figure for gathering support to Athanasius from both the clergy and the monks. Yet the assertion within the *Life* that this important historical and religious figure had effectively appointed Athanasius as his heir, was also part of the bishop's wider 'campaign of self-justification' designed to reclaim his position within the fold of the Church.[174] The re-gifting of this mantle (with a *melōte*, no less), therefore allows an urban bishop to acquire and partake in all the authority of a holy desert hermit, and by combining both Church and charismatic power in these clothes, he lays claim to both types of influence, places himself on a higher level than his peers and strengthens his position.[175] Only he is allowed to partake completely in the holy capital attached to being a saint's heir and in writing his *Life*. Presenting their relationship in this way, Athanasius ensures Antony's authority cannot be used to enhance others without referring first to himself (as is evidenced by Jerome's narrative). The gifting and re-gifting of this one item of attire throughout the *Life* thus reflects the agenda of the text as a whole. It functions not only to reposition Antony as a champion of Church orthodoxy and eulogise his life, but also to extol the author Athanasius himself, by showing him as the chosen and only heir to Antony's impressive holy legacy of authority.[176]

Within Jerome's text, however, the gifting of the garment to Paul occurs while Antony is still alive and is presented (perhaps deliberately) in a way that makes it completely impossible for Antony to later bequeath it to Athanasius. Why Jerome should want to change this aspect of the item's biography is initially puzzling, particularly as he needs Athanasius' initial gift story to be thought of as reliable, in order to build the foundation of his own *pallium* narrative. There seems, then, to be some other reason that Athanasius is disinherited (and disrobed). That this has more to do with Antony than with the bishop is demonstrated by the employment of Antony in the account as a literary device rather than a historical figure. By reading Antony within the text in this way, the saint's main *raison d'être* becomes clear: he is functioning to legitimate Jerome's claim that Paul was the founder of eremitical monasticism. Indeed, Antony is in fact of vital importance to this claim, which would not work at all without his presence. He was considered by the wider world outside the narrative as the first hermit himself; however as Jerome's aim is to claim this title for Paul instead, Antony must appear within the text in such a way as symbolically to pass on this title to Paul, while seeming to receive it from him, to legitimate this transferral of authority:[177]

> However others, in whose opinion all the common people share, claim Antony the leader of this way of life, which is true in part: for it is not so much that he came before everyone else, than the zeal of all was inspired by him ... the disciples of Antony ... assert even now, that a certain Paul of Thebes was the founder of such practice, although not of the name; an opinion I also am satisfied with. (*Vita Pauli primi eremitae*, 1)[178]

Thus Jerome announces his rewriting of Antony's myth from the very beginning of the *Vita Pauli*, and the *pallium* becomes a visual symbol of this attempt to appropriate Antony's fame for a western saint.

Understanding Antony's central role in Paul's *Vita* in this way, furthermore, presents the solution to the differences between the stories concerning the *pallium*. It has already been noted that, in giving Athanasius' garment to Paul via Antony, Jerome is enveloping Paul in the orthodox and clerical authority of the original owner in order to bring his charismatic power into the Church. However, by wrapping Paul in this mantle for his burial garments, which negates the chance of removal, Jerome is signalling that Antony is also passing over his title of first hermit to Paul permanently: 'Antony therefore wrapped Paul's body up and brought it outside, singing hymns and psalms according to the Christian tradition ... '.[179] As observed earlier, by providing a western saint with a *Life*, Jerome's text fills a gap in a hagiographical market dominated by eastern holy figures. In giving Antony's garment to Paul, Jerome is therefore using the *himation/pallium* to signify an attempt to 'overwrite' eastern ascetical prestige and transfer it onto a western 'saint'. Clothing imbibes the qualities of its owners, particularly if those owners are influential figures, and within a literary context clothing also appears to absorb specific characteristics (like apostolic healing abilities) which are important to the character or to the wider narrative agenda of the story. Thus, by burying Paul in his cloak, Antony passes onto him his legacy, which in this context is his place as the first hermit and the authority which comes with such a position. The 'reality' of Athanasius' inheritance, therefore, no longer has a place in the 'reality' of Jerome's Antony, for it would detract from his own authorial agenda regarding Paul.[180] Jerome therefore has to exorcise and excise Athanasius completely from the story at this point in order for the clothes to fit properly in their new context and say the right things about Paul and his relationship to Antony's place as a pioneer. The original bequest cannot be accommodated here and so Jerome has to rob Athanasius to clothe Paul.

Jerome then moves further away from Athanasius' 'reality' by adding an extra clothing gift not found in the *Vita Antonii* in order to remedy his reallocation of the symbolic and spiritual capital of being the first hermit from Antony to Paul. This is in the form of Paul's handmade palm tunic which Antony takes up from the floor, a scene which indicates that Jerome is keen to retain Antony as an influential (although not the initial) figure in the history of eremitical monasticism:

> But when the next day dawned, in case this dutiful heir [Antony] should possess none of the goods of the intestate man [Paul], he took the tunic that Paul had woven for himself out of palm leaves like a wicker basket. He then returned to the monastery ... and on the feast days of Easter and Pentecost he always wore Paul's tunic. (*Vita Pauli primi eremitae*, 16)[181]

In picking up the tunic cast off by Paul, Antony mimics the action from 2 Kings 2.8.15 discussed earlier. Thus, Jerome positions Antony in the role of Elisha to Paul's Elijah[182] (a role already suggested by Antony's claim to his own disciples in *Vita Pauli* 13 that he has seen Elijah on his return from visiting Paul). In receiving this item (and in the narrative as a whole), Antony is therefore shown to be the successor to Paul's place as the founder of the eremitic life. By this action Jerome takes the reader back to his opening discussion of who was the initiator of the practice – while Paul may be the original anchorite, it is Antony who will spread the word and inspire everyone with devotion to this way of life; Athanasius has no part to play here. Once again, therefore, clothing gifts symbolise the concerns of the author – in this case, reassigning the title of first hermit to Paul from one who been given it 'erroneously' because he had made it popular, whilst still enabling Antony to continue to be honoured in a different way.

4.8 Conclusions

By exploring the varying fates that befell Antony's *himation/pallium* in the *Vita Antonii* and the *Vita Pauli primi eremitae*, it can be seen that clothing gifts had a special place for Christian authors in the exploration and justification of the transference of authority. It was a literary device that allowed influential, but potentially problematic, holy figures to be co-opted for the benefit of the

Church, by covering them in the cloak of official Church authority in order to domesticate their charismatic power and help promote the orthodox cause. Like those seen in Chapters 2 and 3, these gifts of garments did not exist only in the literary realm, however; they reflected (and directed) real practices. In the dressing of a fellow ascetic, these narratives functioned alongside the more explicit exhortations to charity that would be aimed particularly at the wealthy in a congregation, encouraging them to imitate these figures in holiness by clothing the poor and needy. Donations of garments and textiles (or even garments that could become textiles) allowed the one giving to gain a share in the spiritual capital of holiness and demonstrated superiority to their fellow Christians by their ability to live according to Christ's teachings. This holy capital could be better acquired, however, through the possession of relics, which could be items of clothing worn by the saint, particularly when these relics had been given as a gift. This superior present demonstrated the worthiness of the receiver to possess such items, and reflected the symbolism behind clothing gifts between figures such as Antony, Athanasius, and Paul, or Euthymius and Fidus.

These latter garments, particularly when they were the *pallium* or *melōte*, however, also had significance as indicators of authority and, when given between a monk and a leader the orthodox Church, became an opportunity to highlight and even resolve tensions. This was perhaps suggested by the harmonious nature of cloth itself, as has been seen in other contexts throughout this study. Although not always successful, the gifting of these specific items was important because of their associations with the different authoritative groups within Christianity at the time and their origins in Biblical examples of authority. Within the religious landscape of Late Antiquity, then, gifts of clothing, whether 'real' or created by a writer's imagination, worked in similar ways to that seen in the political and diplomatic examples of previous chapters: promulgating authority, worthiness, social standing, and relationships. In their Christian context, however, they also served to engage with and debate wider concerns within the Church, particularly how to unite and bind the charismatic influence of holy men with episcopal power and place them all under one mantle of Church authority.

Notes

1 Cf. Asterius, *Hom.* 1.3, see Chapter 3.
2 As noted in the Introduction, although its religious connotations are relevant for the examples presented in this chapter, 'orthodoxy' is also used to suggest ideas of 'institutional' or 'official' authority.
3 The interaction between euergetism and charity is a subject beyond the scope of this study. For general discussions of charity and almsgiving in the Greco-Roman world see e.g. Hands (1968); Parkin (2006); in a Christian context see e.g. Marshall (1987); Wood (2000); Caner (2006); Finn (2006a) and (2006b). For classical euergetism which had focused on public benefactions, and its relationship to Christianity, see Veyne (1990); Brown (2002). For Christian wealth in Late Antiquity, see Brown (2012).
4 But they could expect an increase in heavenly influence: there was an 'exchange of material for spiritual goods in each act of almsgiving' (Finn (2006a) 181).

158 *Holy habits*

5 Caner (2006) 331. Although this phrase is used for convenience, 'the poor' were not a distinct social group in Greco-Roman society, as levels of poverty varied (Finn (2006a) 19). Within the context of Christian charity, however, 'the poor' were no longer only members of the community who had fallen on hard times who had previously benefitted by traditional euergetism, but also those on or outside the margins of society (but not slaves) (Brown (2002) 5, 61). It is interesting to note that these levels of poverty could be classified with reference to clothing, e.g. some lacked 'food not clothes' or 'lacked not clothing but shelter' (Salvian, *Four Books of Timothy to the Church*, 4.21 (in Finn (2006a) 18–19)). For discussions of poverty in the Roman world see Brown (2002); Atkins and Osborne (2006).
6 Jer. *Ep.* 4.1 (cf. Brown (2002); Caner (2006) 330; Finn (2006b) 141).
7 Tabitha: Acts 9.36–42; Cyprian, *de Opere et Eleemosynis* (*Treastise* 8) 5; Basil, *Regulae fusius tractatae* 7.
8 *sed tibi aliud propositum est: Christum vestire in pauperibus* . . . *Ep.* 130.14.
9 Finn (2006a) 135.
10 For the notion that 'Christ was . . . hidden in the ranks of the poor' see Brown (2002) 73, 92, 94. For the use of clothing in the *Vita Martini*, see Labarre (2003); and for the function of the cloak in particular in the *Vita* see Coon (1997) 67.
11 *Nocte igitur insecuta, cum se sopori dedisset, vidit Christum chlamydis suae, qua pauperem texerat, parte vestitum. Intueri diligentissime Dominum, vestemque quam dederat, iubetur agnoscere . . . Vere memor Dominus dictorum suorum (qui ante praedixerat: Quamdiu fecistis uni ex minime istis, mihi fecistis) se in paupere professus est fuisse vestitum; et ad confirmandum tam boni operis testimonium, in eodem se habitu quem pauper acceperat, est dignatus ostendere.* Cf. 2.8 (Finn (2006a) 135). The use of beggar's clothing to disguise a divinity or hero was well known literary device in the non-Christian Greco-Roman world, and was particularly associated with the return of Odysseus to his home (see Chapter 1; Brown (2002) 94).
12 Brown (2002) 92; Veyne (1990) 32. For another way the wealthy could advertise their 'devotion' to Christ, see Chapter 3, where their own clothes were decorated with scenes from the Bible, in order to gain social and spiritual capital.
13 Cf. Veyne (1990) 32.
14 Brown (2002) 1, 7 (although the emperor was still 'a towering exemplum of old-fashioned euergetism'.)
15 Τοῖς μὲν ἐπ' ἀγορᾶς μεταιτοῦσιν οἰκτροῖς τισι καὶ ἀπερριμμένοις οὐ χρημάτων μόνον οὐδέ γε τῆς ἀναγκαίας τροφῆς ἀλλὰ καὶ σκέπης εὐσχήμονος τοῦ σώματος προὐνόει (Euseb. *V. Const.* 1.43; Helena: 3.44); cf. Finn (2006a) 57, 109.
16 Finn (2006a) 57, 100, 101, 108; Parkin (2006) 69 (with reference to non-Christian alms-giving). Cf. Jer. *Ep.*, 66.4–5 where Paula's silks are now being used to clothe the poor after her death (although perhaps not literally!) and Gerontius *V. Mel.* 11–13 where Melania's attempt to give gifts of *vestes pretiosas et sericas* to the *ministris, eunuchis vel cubiculariis* when she visits the court of Serena in late 407 or early 408, is refused by Serena who also orders her palace personnel to act likewise. This, Gerontius reports, was because she judged 'the man taking any of [Melania's] possessions, except for the saints and the poor, to be sacrilegious'.
17 E.g. Euseb. *V. Const.* 4.44; Finn (2006a) 108.
18 Finn (2006a) 36, 77–8, 88, 90–101; cf. Sozom. 7.2.7; *Acts of Paul and Thecla*, 41 – a rich widow gives clothing to Thecla to be distributed by Paul for the care of the destitute (cf. *Acts of Peter* 17) (Finn (2006a) 36, 130–31); Joh. Chrys. *Hom. act.* 45.4, who felt that individual Christian charity had become slack because of the increase of poor relief through the churches (Brown (2002) 65–6). Constantine's 'care and forethought in fully providing the naked and destitute with clothing' (ἤδη δὲ σὺν πολλῇ φροντίδι καὶ περιβλημάτων πλείστων ὅσων γυμνοῖς καὶ ἀνείμοσι προὐνόει) is listed as part of a chapter on Church endowments, and therefore may have been distributed by the churches rather than the emperor himself (Euseb. *V. Const.*, 4.28; cf. Finn (2006a) 57, 130). See also Caner (2006).
19 Brown (2002) 26 citing Euseb. *HE* 6.43.18.

Holy habits 159

20 Brown (2002) 28, 77; Finn (2006a) 2–3, 101.
21 Finn (2006a) 36–7, 79–182, 196, 203, 214, 260.
22 Finn (2006a) 101.
23 These worked in a similar way as the other charitable garment gifts discussed in this section.
24 Brown (2002) 19, 24. Cf. Jer. *Ep.* 130.14 referring to 'the servants of God' (such as virgins and monks rather than the urban poor) who '[i]f they have food and clothing, . . . rejoice as if these were riches, and desire nothing more . . .' Jerome also presents himself as being content if he has only 'food and clothing' (*Ep.* 52.5) and his letters in general provide numerous examples of clothing gifts received by him from his worthies; Greg. Tur. *V. Pat.* 1.5: Chilperic I, king of the Burgundians (460s and 470s), gives '100 gold solidi for clothing the brothers'. Caner (2006); Finn (2006a) 81.
25 The bishop of Rome, Pelagius I, wrote to the bishop of Arles in 557 requesting the supplies of cheap clothing he had set aside for the poor, because there was a shortage in his own city (Pelag. *Ep.* 14 (Brown (2002) 56)); Paulinus of Nola purchased and distributed to the poor clothing worth 40 gold *solidii* (Uranius, *De obitu Paulini*, 3); Hypatius rebuked a monk attempting to store clothing which should have been distributed immediately as alms (Callin. *V. Hypatii* 34.4–6 (both cited by Finn (2006a) 35, 210–11)); Brown (2002) 55–6; Finn (2006a) 81. For the location and practice of the storage of liturgical vestments, see Michel (2007) 594. Cf. Pritchard (2006) 60.
26 Opt. *Adversus donatistas*, *App.* 1 (in Edwards (1997) tr. 154); M.M. Mango (1986) 264 (cf. 263) and Finn (2006a) 81 for a translation and discussion of this inventory. Cf. *P.Wisc.* 2.64 (Oxyrhynchos, 27 Jan 480) where Peter the steward of the church of St Kosmas is told by 'the holy church' to provide 'one cloak only' to a widow Sophia 'from the cloaks which you have which are fit for use' (in Rowlandson (1998) 80, no. 63).
27 Basil of Caesarea, *Ep.* 286.1 (Finn (2006a) 81 for translation and brief discussion). Basil, however, also claims that the provision of clothing could pose a problem for beggars, as it made them appear too well dressed to need the alms they begged for (*Hom.* 6 (Finn (2006a) 21)).
28 The theft of clothing appears to have been a common crime in the Roman world affecting all levels of society and showing the worth of garments – from Martial's peers who frequented the bathhouses to those whose economic and social standing was little removed from that of thieves themselves (Finn (2006a) 25; cf. Treggiari (1975) 53: slave in charge of clothes at bath, presumably to prevent their theft; *P.Heid.* 3.237 (Theadelphia, third century): a husband claims his wife has absconded with various household items including clothing to which she was not entitled (in Rowlandson (1998) 182–3 no. 137)). Theft of clothing is also mentioned frequently in the Bath curse tablets (Tomlin (1988) 59–277; Gager (1992) 121).
29 E.g. Joh. Eph. *V. SS. Or.* 55; *Acts of Paul and Thecla*, 41 (Finn (2006a) 130); as a non-clothing example, John, patriarch of Alexandria (609–619) calculated that selling on an expensive bed-cover, given to him by a rich man and costing 36 gold pieces, could clothe 144 of the poor (Leont., *V.S. Joannis Eleemosynarii*, 21 (in Brown (2002) 12–13)).
30 The examples are too numerous to list, but see, e.g., Paulinus of Nola (Uranius, *De obitu Paulini*, 6 in Finn (2006a) 34–5); Melania the Younger (Gerontius, *V. Mel.* 19); Publius (Theod. *HR* 5.1).
31 For example, in the list of gifts given by emperors in the *Lib. Pont.* (up to 715) there are a number of entries which include textiles, but none which appear to list clothing.
32 Guillou (1979) 17–21; M.M. Mango (1986) 262, (1992) 124. For examples of church inventories with discussion see e.g. Caseau (2007b) 563–7, (564–5 silk tunic in a seventh- or eighth-century Egyptian church inventory).
33 For gifts of textiles see e.g. *The Cornutian Deed* (in Lee (2000) 230–32); Greg. Tur. *V. Pat.* 8.11; Gerontius, *V. Mel.* 60; Paul. Nol. *Carm.* 18.29–37 (in Grig (2006) 151); *Lib. Pont.* 54.10; 55.7; 58.2; 62.3; 78.2; 66.4; 83.2; 86.11, 15; 87.3 (the first four of these include *pallia*, but while the garment *pallium* was highly valued in the Church, as shall be seen

160   *Holy habits*

below, the context suggests that these items listed here should be considered as altar cloths rather than garments (Davis (2010) 121). Mango (1992) 262–3; Caseau (2007b) 562–7; Michel (2007) 588 for some further examples.
34 Grig (2006) 149–50, 152; Caseau (2007b) 567. In the Byzantine period wall mosaics and the polished and finely cut stone which decorated churches were often equated with textiles in the literature: Nicholas Mesarites (writing between 1198 and 1203) felt that the walls of the Church of the Holy Apostles seemed to be 'covered with many-coloured woven cloths' (37) because of its stonework, and the act of decorating the same church with marble and metal by Isidore or Anthemius is seen as 'clothing it' (640–644) by the tenth-century poet Constantine Rhodios (both cited in James (1996) 114).
35 These seem to have been cloths for hands or tablecloths (Latin: *mantele*), but may be altar cloths in this context. Mango (1992) 263.
36 Tr. E.W. Brooks.
37 Cf. Grig (2006) 160: '. . . beautiful ecclesiastical buildings could stand as a model for interior transformation'.
38 Sosiana's husband: Harvey (1990) 129 (discussion of background to Sosian's decision to give the clothes away (129–30); Caesaria: *PLRE* 2 Caesaria 3.
39 Diplomatic silk storage: Muthesius (1992) 240, 242 (however, cf. the eleventh-century compilation the *Book of Rarities and Gifts* (*Kitāb al-Haddāyā wa al-Tuhaf*) which relates the story of the opening of the treasury of the vizier Abū Ja'far Muhammad bin al-Qāsim al-Kharki. It held 40-year-old sacks of silk which disintegrated upon opening due to their age (190, 243)). See also the different attitude towards immovable property in Justinian, *Novel*, 120.1, 10 (544 Constantinople) which forbids 'those who administer the affairs of the [Hagia Sophia and its associated charitable institutions] . . . to sell, or give, or exchange, or give as a reciprocal gift, or alienate in any way whatsoever, immovable property . . .' (in Lee (2000) 238).
40 Cf. Caner (2006) 356.
41 Cf. the story of Isidore, the *economus* of Theophilus of Alexandria, who refused to hand over to Theophilus money donated by a noblewoman in order to buy clothes for the poor, because Isidore knew that the bishop would use it for building works instead (Pall. *Dial.* 6 (Brown (1980) 20)).
42 E.g. Greg. M. *Ep.* 4.30, discussed below, where Gregory deftly refuses the order of Empress Constantina for the head (or another body part) and the handkerchief of Paul to be sent for the benefit of her own church to the saint, by offering part of Peter's chains instead. Gregory's refusal is also partly due to his great reluctance to touch the holy body (cf. Theoph. 86 (Finn (2006a) 109) – Theodosius II receives (non-clothing) relics of the protomartyr Stephen in 427/8 after sending large quantities of gold to the patriarch of Jerusalem). For the cult of saints see Brown (1981); Howard-Johnston and Hayward (1999); Grig (2004); Price (2008) with bibliography; for relics in general see e.g. Caseau (2007a).
43 Jer. *Adversus Vigilantium* 4–5, for the practice of wrapping relics in pieces of cloth. For a brief examination of this type of textile relic, see Metzger (2004).
44 Cf. Brown (2002) 105. The σουδάρια ἢ σιμικίνθια may have been handkerchiefs and an apron or semi-girdle (Latin: *sudarium* and *semicinctium*). For the significance accorded to the ἱμάτιον/*himation* (equated with the Latin *pallium*) in later Christian literature, see below.
45 For a discussion of this topic see Coon (1997) 12, 55, 56, 59–60; Ferguson (2009) 332 n.9. For the relationship between dress and the body in Christian literature, see e.g. Neri (2004).
46 Peter's remains are the subject of Gregory the Great's comments in *Epistularum Registrum*, 4.30 discussed below.
47 Καὶ εὐθὺς ὁ Ἰησοῦς ἐπιγνοὺς ἐν ἑαυτῷ τὴν ἐξ αὐτοῦ δύναμιν ἐξελθοῦσαν ἐπιστραφεὶς ἐν τῷ ὄχλῳ ἔλεγεν, Τίς μου ἥψατο τῶν ἱματίων . . . Mark 5.30.
48 Theodoret, *Historia Religiosa*, 9.15.

49 *Aut certe si pallium, quo sancti artus teguntur mererer attingere, fierem sanus.* (*V. Patr.* 8.12). To give just a few more examples: Ambrose, *Ep.* 22.9 (cited by Granger-Taylor (1983) 135); *Apophthegmata* Arsenius 19, Abba Daniel says of the late Arsenius, 'He left me his leather tunic, his white hair-shirt and his palm-leaf sandals. Although unworthy, I wear them, in order to gain his blessing'. (Vivian and Athahassakis (2003) 257 n.516); 'the incalculable numbers ... all trying to touch [Symeon the Stylite] and gain some blessing from his clothing of skins ...' (Ἐπειδὴ τοίνυν ἀριθμοῦ κρείττους οἱ ἀφικνούμενοι προσψαύειν δὲ ἅπαντες ἐπεχείρουν καί τινα εὐλογίαν ἀπὸ τῶν δερματίνων ἐκείνων ἱματίων τρυγᾶν) (Theod. *HR* 26.12); for Theodoret himself, the 'old cloak of great James [of Cyrrhestica]' which lay under his head 'had been stronger than any defences of steel' (*HR* 21.16). Theodosius II puts on the filthy robe of an ascetic 'so that he might be blessed thereby' (*The Chronography of Gregory Abū'l Faraj*, 1 (cited by Cutler (2005b) 198)). An abbess sends part of the garment of Shenoute (348–465), head of the White Monastery in Egypt, to another monastery as a curative item (Maguire (2009) 11 n.55); the mantle of Euthymius in the Georgian translation of Cyril of Scythopolis, *Vita Cyriaci* (Binns and Price (1991) 260, n.5); Julian (Saba)'s mantle which healed a beggar (Theod. *HR* 2.19); Coon (1997) 55, 69. Belts could also heal: e.g. Gerontius, *V. Mel.* 61; Theod. *HR*.15, and could even grant military victories: the Bohairic *Life of Shenoute* 106–108. This may be because they had a similar association with authority as cloaks did in Late Antiquity. On the significance of the *pallium* see below.

50 Cf. Theod. *HR* 31.2: 'For it is not, as some suppose, tunics, coats, and cloaks that supply heat to the body ... Instead, they preserve the warmth of the body ...'.

51 For the continuing emanation of power from a dead saint see Paul. Nol. *Carm.* 18.154–160; Coon (1997) 12, 55; Metzger (2004) 184. Cf. Athan. *V.Ant.* 92.3: looking at Antony's clothes is 'like seeing Antony' (Καὶ γὰρ καὶ βλέπων αὐτά, ὡς Ἀντώνιόν ἐστι θεωρῶν) (for Antony's clothing, see the case study below)); Theod. *HR* 9.2: those who love someone reap delight from seeing not only the person but also 'gaze in great joy at his home and clothing and footwear' (... ἀλλὰ καὶ τὴν οἰκίαν καὶ ἐσθήματα καὶ ὑποδήματα μετὰ πάσης θεωρεῖν εὐφροσύνης).

52 *Cognoscat autem tranquillissima domina, quia Romanis consuetudo non est, quando sanctorum reliquias dant, ut quidquam tangere praesumant de corpore, sed tantummodo in pyxide brandeum mittitur, atque ad sacratissima corpora sanctorum ponitur. Quod levatum in ecclesia, quae est dedicanda debita cum veneratione reconditur, et tantae per hoc ibidem virtutes fiunt, ac si illuc specialiter eorum.* Translation adapted from J. Barmby; Metzger (2004) 184, 186.

53 Greg. M. *Ep.* 4.30; cf. Greg. Tur. *V. Pat.*, 2.3 where a woollen string, hanging down from the relics whilst he held them over a fire to dry them out, caught fire but did not burn because the connection with the holy remains protected it.

54 E.g. Hilary of Arles, *Sermo de vita sancti Honorati*, 35 (Coon (1997) 62); Sulp. Sev. *V. Mart.* 13, 18; Greg. Tur. *V. Pat.* 8.6.

55 Ῥαβδοφόροι δὲ πολλοὶ τῇ κλίνῃ παρείποντο τοὺς γυμνοῦν τὸ σῶμα τῆς ἐσθῆτος πειρωμένους καὶ ῥάκια λαμβάνειν ἐκεῖθεν ἐφιεμένους ὡς παίσοντες δεδιττόμενοι (Theod. *HR* 17.10); cf. Greg. Tur. *V. Pat.* 13.2; Granger-Taylor (1983) 135, *passim* regarding history of the 'two dalmatics of Ambrose;' Squire (2011) 172.

56 Particularly as touching the relics themselves was not encouraged (see Gregory the Great's statements above) and close proximity to the shrine itself was restricted (Caseau (2007b) 643); however, see Theod. *HR* 21.19–20, 24.2. For the desire to be permanently associated with the saints, and the belief that the saints would benefit those whom they approved of, see, for example, the epitaph of Foedula from Vienne, which ends by saying: 'Now that the martyrs have provided her with this fitting resting-place/ .../By her faith she has gained deserved rest in this tomb/ She who lies associated with the saints has borne witness'. (*RICG* 15.39 – translation and discussion Lee (2000) 129–30).

57 Cf. Athan. *V.Ant.* 92.3. See Brakke (1995) 209–11; Brown (1981). This could even be on behalf of an entire city – the cloth from St Remigius' tomb was thought to have

162 *Holy habits*

protected Rheims from the bubonic plague (Greg. Tur. *De gloria confessorum*, 77 in Brown (1997) 72, 74).
58 Cutler (2005b) 200; cf. Brennan (1985) 223, discussing the sheepskins of Antony (see further below in the case study). This was also reflected in other clothing that signified authority, Christian and non-Christian, religious or political – 'Purple cloth by itself is a simple thing, and so is silk, and a cloak is woven from both. But if a king should put it on, the cloak receives honour from the honour given to him who wears it' (John of Damascus, *First Treatise on Divine Images*, rephrasing Athanasius (in James (1996) 123)).
59 In a similar way to the items of clothing associated with political authority given to the foreign kings and consuls of the previous chapters, in this religious context specific cloaks would also mark the wearer out as holding spiritual authority and thus were doubly potent. This will be seen in the final sections.
60 See e.g. Cic. *Off.* 3.43: 'But an upright man will never for a friend's sake do anything in violation of his country's interests or his oath or his sacred honour, not even if he sits as judge in a friend's case; for he lays aside the role of friend when he assumes (*induit*) that of judge;' Tac. *Ann.* 1.69: 'A woman of heroic spirit, [Agrippina] assumed (*induit*) during those days the duties of a general, and distributed clothes or medicine among the soldiers, as they were destitute or wounded'. For more examples, see e.g. Liddell and Scott s.v. ἐνδύω; Lewis and Short v.s. *induere*; Farrell (1974).
61 Gal. 3.27; Rom. 13.24; cf. Eph. 4.24; Col. 3.10. Like much else in Christian literature, the meanings and origins of this phrase have provoked a wealth of discussion and form a topic too large to be dealt with here in any detail. For discussions of this phrase see e.g. Burnish (1985) (with a specific focus on the fourth century); Harrill (2002); Johnson (2008) with bibliography; Ferguson (2009); and especially Farrell (1974); Brock (1992) 15–18, 23–4, 25–6 for Syriac interpretations of this phrase with references.
62 Farrell (1974); Harrill (2002); Ferguson (2009). Cf. e.g. Cyril, *Cat. Myst.* 2; Joh. Chrys. *Ad illum. catec.* 4.12; 11.28; Amb. *De mysteriis*, 7; Basil, *De baptismo*; Theodore of Mopsuestia, *Catechetical Homilies*, 2.3, 4 (Whitaker (1970) 49: the baptised emerges wearing a 'garment that is wholly radiant . . . a white garment that shines . . .'). The meaning of baptism and the garments involved has been the subject of much discussion, both ancient and modern, see e.g. Quasten (1942) 207, *passim*; Burnish (1985); Brock (1992) for Syriac interpretations of these garments; Ferguson (2009) 332 n.39, 450, 543, 575, 649–50, 706–7; Coon (1997) 40, 56 for the significance of linen. There is some debate over whether the baptised were completely naked, or retained some type of clothing, due to the difficulties posed by the terms *nudus*/γυμνός – see Guy (2003), Webb (2008) 101. For the relationship between baptismal clothing and the *toga virilis*, see Harrill (2002). For baptism in Later Empire, see e.g. Farrell (1974); Burnish (1985) (with a specific focus on the fourth century); Harrill (2002); Johnson (2008) with bibliography; Ferguson (2009).
63 Harkins (1963) 3, 15–18 for the date.
64 Cf. Ferguson (2009) 540–41, 543–4, 561–2 for a discussion of clothing in Chrysostom's *Baptismal Instructions*. See Krawiec (2014) for clothing and social memory in monastic practice.
65 Joh. Chrys. *Ad illum catec.* 4.12. Tr. P. Harkins throughout this section.
66 Joh. Chrys. *Ad illum catec.* 6.23 (cf. 4.31, 10.30). For the 'garment of the soul' see Kehl (1978) 945–1025 (Christian context: 973–1023). Cf. Serfass (2014) 88, 92: for Gregory the Great the splendour and colour of the *pallium* attests to the spiritual worthiness and holiness of the wearer.
67 Joh. Chrys. *Ad illum catec.* 4.31–32; 5.26, 28; 6.23.
68 Οὕτω καὶ εἰς τὸ διηνεκές . . . δυνήσεσθε τὴν φαιδρότητα τοῦ ἐνδύματος τοῦ βασιλικοῦ διατηροῦντες, ἀκριβέστερον ἢ νῦν διὰ τῆς κατὰ Θεὸν πολιτείας . . . Joh. Chrys. *Ad illum catec.* 4.18 (see also 7.24–27). Greg. Tur. *V. Patr.* 1. pref. also sees baptism as a 'white and shining robe' that could be 'soiled by shameful acts' (*neque post baptismi sacramentum niveam illam pollentemque regenerationis stolam impudicis actibus polluerunt*). See also Farrell (1974) 131.

69 Τὸ μέντοι τῆς ἀρετῆς ἔνδυμα, ἐὰν τὰ παρ' ἑαυτῶν εἰσφέρειν σπουδάζωμεν, οὔτε ῥύπον ποτὲ δέξεται οὔτε παλαιότητος πεῖραν λήψεται, ἀλλ' ὅσῳ ἂν ὁ χρόνος παρατρέχῃ τοσούτῳ μᾶλλον φαιδρότερον καὶ ἀκμαιότερον τὸ κάλλος καὶ τοῦ φωτὸς τὴν αὐγὴν ἐπιδείκνυσιν. Joh. Chrys. *Ad illum. catec.* 7.24. Cf. Farrell (1974) 147.

70 Διὸ παρακαλῶ, οἵ τε πρόσφατον ἀξιωθέντες τῆς θείας δωρεᾶς πολλὴν τὴν φυλακὴν ἐπιδείξασθε καὶ τὸ παρασχεθὲν ὑμῖν ἔνδυμα πνευματικὸν καθαρὸν καὶ ἀκηλίδωτον διαφυλάττετε. (cf. Joh. Chrys. *Ad illum. catec.* 4.27; 7.24; 12.19).

71 Τήρει τοίνυν ὅπερ ἔλαβες ἱμάτιον· ἂν γὰρ ἀπολέσῃς, χρήσασθαι οὐ δυνήσῃ λοιπόν, οὐδὲ πρίασθαι· οὐδαμοῦ γὰρ πωλεῖται τοιοῦτον ἱμάτιον. Joh. Chrys. *Ad illum. catec.* 12.20. The use of *himation* here may reflect that this was the clothing of Christ and the Apostles in the Bible (see below), and so makes it an even more important garment to preserve and protect.

72 See, for example, Joh. Chrys. *Ad illum. catec.* 4.12, 23; 5.18.

73 Farrell (1974) 144–5; Guy (2003) 133.

74 Quotation: Farrell (1974) 13; Ferguson (2009) 148.

75 Molloy (1996) 45, 222; Malineau (2003) 154, 155; Webb (2008) 151–63 (costume: 156–7).

76 Cf. Choricius, *Apologia Mimorum*, 77: 'The soul is not altered along with the costume ... even if I take off my orator's costume and put on military kit I will not become a soldier'. οὐ γὰρ συναλλοιοῦνται τοῖς ἐσθήμασιν ἡ ψυχή ... κἂν ἐγὼ τὸ σχῆμα τοῦτο τῆς ἀγωνιστικῆς ἀποθέμενος ἀναλάβω στρατιώτου σκευήν, οὐ γενήσομαί τις πολεμικός (both are cited, translated, and discussed by Webb (2008) 151–2; cf. Molloy (1996) 223).

77 Malineau (2003) 154, 155; Baratte (2004); Swift (2009) 6 (referring to decoration). Martial's poems also highlight this tension between concealment and revelation. See Chapter 1 and Introduction.

78 *ASS* 7, pp.751–753 (summarised and discussed in Webb (2008) 7–8, 157 whose arguments are built upon here).

79 E.g. Gelasinus (Joh. Mal. 12.50; see Webb (2008) with further references 228, nn.11–12; 7–8, 124–8). These stories were used by Augustine to demonstrate not only the efficacy of the ritual, but also solve the problem of whether baptism by heretics was legitimate (Aug. *de bapt. c. Don.* 7.53 (Webb (2008) 19)); for plays about Christianity in Late Antiquity see Malineau (2003) 167.

80 The *Historia Monachorum in Aegypto* tells a similar story about Philemon and the deacon, but with some differences, namely that it is the deacon, Apollonius, not his clothes, who brings about the conversion of Philemon. In fact, the clothes play no part in the narrative, which ends with both Philemon and Apollonius being thrown into the sea on the orders of the prefect (*Historia Monachorum in Aegypto*, 19).

81 Webb (2008) 157.

82 Harvey (2008) 608. Those persecutions which were enacted during Julian's short reign were not officially sanctioned.

83 This led to a redefinition of the language of martyrdom, particularly that asceticism was the new way to experience martyrdom (cf. Rousseau (1999) 123–4; Lee (2000) 189; Kuefler (2001)).

84 Fontaine (1968) 492.

85 For a discussion of chap. 23 of the *Vita Martini*, see Fontaine (1969) 994–5 (Anatolis), 988–1014, and especially 997–1014 for the role of clothing.

86 *Postremo eo usque processit ... iamque se unum ex prophetis haberi volebat. Clarus tamen nequaquam ad credendum cogi poterat ... Postremo in hanc vocem erupisse fertur: Ecce hac nocte vestem mihi candidam Dominus de coelo dabit, qua indutus in medio vestrum diversabor: idque vobis signum erit, me Dei esse virtutem, qui Dei veste donatus sim.*

87 Fontaine (1969) 999–1000, 1005.

88 Rousseau (1971) 414.

164 Holy habits

89 Particularly in 23.7. For the sections identified as narrated in Anatolis' voice, see Fontaine (1969) 998–1001, 1004. He does not however connect the change in terminology for the clothing with the change in narrative voice or see it as a deliberate choice on Sulpicius' part to show Anatolis as a fraud.
90 Fontaine (1969) 1003.
91 *Pace* Rousseau (1971) 414 who says that 'Martin quite literally saw through the falsity of this man's claim'. While the last sentence may imply this (*unde quis dubitet hanc etiam Martini fuisse virtutem, ut phantasiam suam diabolus, cum erat Martini oculis ingerenda, dissimulare diutius aut tegere non posset?*), the episode as a whole does not this bear out, for the garment vanishes *before* they even get to the holy man. That Martin's powers were so great that simply the threat of them vanquishes falsehoods instead seems to be an effort to temper Clarus' part in the story, which is in danger of overshadowing Martin; after all, it is Clarus who recognises Anatolis for what he is. Cf. Fontaine (1969) 1014 who sees this episode as a double panegyric of Martin and Clarus. Fontaine also suggests a more worldly solution to question of the disappearing garment: 'La tunique n'aurait-elle pas été mise en pieces au cours de la rixe?' ((1969) 1011).
92 E.g. Caesarius of Arles, *Testamentia*, 5: 'To my lord the holy bishop who worthily succeeds my unworthy self: . . . let all the paschal vestments that were given to me be of service to him, together with the better quality shaggy cloak, the better quality tunic, and the thick cloak, which I have left behind'. See also the will of Gregory of Nazianzus, which leaves to 'Evagrius the deacon . . . so that we not neglect the small tokens of friendship . . . one wool robe, one tunic, [and] two cloaks . . . Likewise . . . Theodulus [a deacon, is to] be given one wool robe, [and] two of the tunics of my native land . . . [and for] Elphaius . . . a versatile secretary . . . one wool robe, two tunics, three cloaks, [and] a plain garment . . .' (393b–393c) translated and discussed by Van Dam (1995) 118–48. For Antony's will, see case study below.
93 Tr. E. James. For a discussion of this passage see Coon (1997) 69 (although used there to demonstrate that audiences of hagiographies were taught that clothing possessed spiritual power).
94 Theod. *HE* 2.23.
95 cf. HA, *Car.* 19.3, 20.4 (Molloy (1996) 45).
96 In a non-religious context, the clothing the Armenian king Pap (c. 368–374) gives to Glak, his inspector of royal fortresses, eliminates a political enemy more directly. The disproportionately large size of the garments prevents him from defending himself against the axe-wielding assassins the king sends in response to reports that Glak had been intriguing against him with Shapur II of Persia (see Cutler (2005b) 208, n.48 for references). Those an author does not consider the best candidates for imperial office could also be victims of ill-fitting clothing, although this was not necessarily fatal: Jovian is so tall that for a while 'no royal robe could be found to fit him (*nullum indumentum regium ad mensuram eius aptum inveniretur*) (Amm. Marc. 25.10.14)), while in the same text the usurper Procopius (see Chapter 3) is dressed half as a court official, half as a page-boy, and he looks completely ridiculous for his short-lived imperial elevation (Amm. Marc. 26.6.15). These rulers get their dress sense from earlier emperors whose fashion faux pas were clear indicators of their bad (ruling) style; an example is Caligula, who tripped on his own toga in his anger, making him fall down the stairs (unfortunately he survived: Suet. *Calig.* 35.3). See Introduction and Chapter 1 for further examples.
97 Theod. *HR* 9.9.
98 Price (1991) 88 n.1.
99 Justinian's law (*Nov.* 123.44) against the wearing of clerical clothing by the laity could be a way to maintain social distinctions, but it also provides the earthly counterpart to the divine punishment the offender could expect to receive.
100 Brennan (1985) 210; Brakke (1995) 80–82, 109, 211, 213; Coon (1997) 30, 32; Lee (2000) 187.
101 Brakke (1995) 84, 109; Coon (1997) 63.

102 For instance, there were some who acted as bishop-monks (or vice versa): Theodoret presents his audience with one such called Abraham who 'after the monastic life ... brought distinction to the office of bishop ... [and who] when compelled to change his status, he did not alter is manner of living, but ... completed the course of life constrained by both the toils of the monastic life and the burdens of the episcopacy'. (Theod. *HR* 17.1; Lee (2000) 206–7). However, while this trend seems to have increased in Late Antiquity (Lee (2000) 206–7), that Theodoret felt his 'change in status' to be worth remarking upon suggests that he at least felt it was unusual. For attempts made by the episcopacy to ordain monks, see Brakke (1995) 82, 84, 99–110 and n.137 in this chapter. See also Rousseau (1971); (1999) 169–71; Coon (1997) 61: like ascetics, bishops also claimed prophetic and apostolic descent.
103 Coon (1997) 28–51, 52–70.
104 Coon (1997) 61: 'The distinction between monastic and hierarchical dress parallels the subordination of the cloister to episcopal power'.
105 In later times this was violently achieved by Constantine V (741–775) who attacked 'the authority of ascetics who remained outside its institutional hierarchy by stripping them of their unique dress, the monastic *schema* and by forcing them to put on wedding clothes as a symbol of their reintegration into the world' (Coon (1997) 63). For Athanasius' 'reconciliation' of ascetics with the church see Brakke (1995) – this was also the view in antiquity (Greg. Naz. *Or.* 21.19.20–22 (Brakke (1995) 80)).
106 Brakke (1995) 84; Martorelli (2004) 245; Parani (2008) 413; Maguire (2009) 15. See above regarding relics.
107 Cf. Theod. *HR* 21.20: 'I moved my eyes in that direction and surmised it was John the Baptist, for he wore his cloak ...' (Ἐμοῦ δὲ τὰς ὄψεις ἐκεῖσε μεταθέντος καὶ τὸν βαπτιστὴν Ἰωάννην ὑποτοπήσαντος – καὶ γὰρ τὴν αὐτοῦ στολὴν περιεβέβλητο); Coon (1997) 30, 31. For an older treatment of monastic clothing, see Oppenheim (1931) (*melōtē*: 199–234).
108 Cass. *Inst.* 1.1.2, 1.7 (Ramsey (2000) 29, with some references); Pachomius, *Praecepta*, 81 (cf. Jerome's preface to the *Rules*, 4) (Rousseau (1999) 82, 120); Coon (1997) 30, 32, 67; Williams (2008) 103; Maguire (2009) 11, 12; Krawiec (2014) 62, 64. It is perhaps significant that female monks were not supposed to wear the *melōtē* (Pall. *Hist. Laus.* 33.1), thus making this the province of male monks and ascetics only – the authority gender in antiquity.
109 Rousseau (1971) 384 (although not in reference to clothing); Coon (1997) 30, 53.
110 Cf. Symeon the Stylite's 'clothing of skins' and Julian (Saba)'s goat hair mantle which could heal (Theod. *HR* 26.12 (Symeon), 2.19 (Julian)); Antony's garment which was 'hairy on the inside and animal on the exterior' (Athan. *V.Ant.* 47.2). It appears that this should be distinguished from the cloak gifted by Athanasius and returned to him on Antony's death, as it is listed as a separate item (*V.Ant.* 91.8–9). See the case study below for a discussion of Antony's garments. Of course the associations of dressing in this way would suggest that the garment was once again implying sanctity, but the writers deal with this paradox by implying that this was not a conscious decision on the part of the saint, and thus the clothing has a passive rather than active role in marking out holiness.
111 Episcopal clothing: Mayo (1984); Coon (1997) 53, 59–62, 66; Lobrichon (2003); Martorelli (2004) *passim*, 243–6; Ristow (2004) 1268–74; Maier (2006) 34–60; Parani (2007) 497, (2008) 413, 416 fig. 7; Woodfin (2012) (although these latter two depict later developments).
112 *Stolē*: Theodore of Mopsuestia, *Commentary on Baptism*, 5 (84–85); Mayo (1984) 19–21. *Pallium*: e.g. Greg. M. *Ep.* 1.28, 5.16 (with Serfass (2014)); Mayo (1984) 12–13; Coon (1997) 62; Berthod (2001); Lobrichon (2003) 136; Martorelli (2004) 233, 245; Harlow (2004a) 62–3; Cleland *et al.* (2007) 92 s.v. 'himation', 137 s.v. 'pallium;' Rothe (2012a) 157; Serfass (2014) with bibliography. Some monks could also wear this item (as Oppenheim suggests ((1931) 104–19); however, see discussion below for a different interpretation of sources which dress monks in this item). For Tertullian in the second

166   *Holy habits*

century it was the *pallium* that was to be worn by the Christians of Carthage to distinguish them from the general populace (Tertullian, *De pallio*), see e.g. Daniel-Hughes (2011).
113 Coon (1997) 62; Urbano (2014).
114 Mark 5.25–34; Luke 8.43–48; Coon (1997) 62; Harlow (2004a) 63.
115 John of Damascus, *First Treatise on Divine Images* (rephrasing Athanasius (in James (1996) 123)), see above n.58. For a 'real-life' parallel, the crosses added to the lion-hunt dalmatic of Ambrose turned a secular garment into one suitable for a bishop (Granger-Taylor (1983) 148).
116 Serfass (2014) 85, 88–9, 92. Although attractive, his suggestion (86–7) that these *pallia* might have been stored near Peter's tomb during this period and could therefore be 'contact relics' (which also heightens their mystical link) cannot be substantiated by contemporary evidence, not least because it is unlikely Gregory the Great would have kept silent on this point when distributing them. In addition, despite his comments ((2014) 78 n.9) that the *himation/pallium* and the *pallium* in Gregory's letters should not be confused, the use of the same name for items which appear quite different does suggest some connection between the two *pallia*, particularly as they are discussed by similar sources in the same language and in close proximity to or even in the same geographical location. The *pallium*, then, appears to have undergone a change from the period of the fourth to the sixth centuries (as Coon surmises (1997) 62), or the term may have become attached to the *omophorion* in the west. It is tempting to suggest that this could be a result of Julian's ('the Apostate') adoption of the *himation/pallium*, which Urbano has claimed ((2014) 186–9) tarnished the garment's reputation somewhat for Christians; but the continuing prevalence of this garment for some time after Julian's death in both literature and art would make it appear otherwise.
117 The Council of Mâcon in 585 required that archbishops must wear the *pallium* when reciting Mass (Martorelli (2004) 245, cf. 233); *Lib. Pont.*, 35.2; Cyprianus, *Life of Caesarius of Arles*, 1.42: Pope Symmachus (498–514) 'being moved by the great worthiness of Caesarius' good deeds and by a great reverence of his sanctity, not only most properly honoured him as metropolitan, but also decorated him by the specially granted privilege of the *pallium*'. Woodfin (2012) 16 n.45; Serfass (2014) 85, 88–9, 92. Its symbolic connection with upper echelons of Church authority meant that stripping this garment from the wearer was both visually indicative of his deposition and the destruction of his political power and support. This can be seen in *Lib. Pont.* 60. 6.8–9 where Pope Silverius (536–537) is stripped of his *pallium* by Antonia and Belisarius nominally for being suspected of treason with the Goths. However, rather than turning into the naked *barbarus* that was the fate of foreign rulers in Chapter 2, he is dressed in monastic attire and, as a monk, is thus placed outside the hierarchy of the Church (see also Serfass (2014) 80, 91).
118 Rousseau (1971); Coon (1997) 61, 63: bishops define their superiority in the Church hierarchy by also claiming prophetic and apostolic descent usually associated with ascetics.
119 Serfass (2014) 82–3.
120 See Serfass (2014) for a survey of the (later) *pallium* working in this way in the letters of Gregory the Great. Although Serfass doesn't make this point explicitly, it is interesting in light of the suggestions made here that all the examples he provides are within the context of Gregory providing the *pallium* either to support someone whose authority is weak and who requires this (visual) support, or to increase Gregory's own authority.
121 For a discussion of this important item and its use in hagiography, see Coon (1997) 30–31. See also Serfass (2014) 80. On its place in Christian imagery during the Byzantine period see Cutler (2005b) 196–8 (although he states that 'conveyance of authority' was not the 'primary topic' of these pieces during this period (197)). For its place within the *Vita Antonii*, see Brennan (1985) 223 and the discussion below.
122 2 Kings 2.15.

123 This is explicitly stated in the gifting of clothing to Eliakim by God, who will hand over the sash and thus the authority of Shebna, the palace treasurer of Jerusalem (Isaiah 22:15, 20–21): 'This is what the Lord . . . says: 'In that day I will summon my servant, Eliakim son of Hilkiah. I will clothe him with your robe and bind your sash on him and commit your authority to his hand. He will be a father to the inhabitants of Jerusalem and to the house of Judah'.
124 Rutschowskaya (1990) 130–31 (discussed in Maguire (2009) 5–6).
125 Rutschowskaya (1990) 128. Maguire has posited the item presented is the *schema* (the leather apron and later the identifying feature of a monk's dress (see Coon (1997) 63)), but admits it is difficult to define. Rutschowskaya calls it a mantle, presumably based on the Biblical text, for the Vulgate calls this item a *pallium* (noted also by Serfass (2014) 80). It does not look like the larger *pallium*, but could be the narrower scarf-like item called this in the later period (although it was probably known as the *omophorion* at this date); it may even be a *melōte*.
126 Maguire (2009) 5–6.
127 In 530, when he was ill, Pope Felix IV handed over his *pallium* to Boniface to demonstrate that he had appointed the archdeacon as his successor. Significantly he was not allowed to keep it if Felix recovered to prevent confusion over who held authority (Serfass (2014) 80, for discussion and bibliography). For further examples see following sections.
128 Price (1991) xxxviii, xl.
129 63.5–64.23. For the connection between visions and authority see Rousseau (1971) 386.
130 Tr. Price (1991) 60.
131 This may be why the mantle then disappears – it has served its role in protecting Fidus and marking him as having the saint's approval, and it therefore is no longer needed. The mantle of Euthymius also appears performing more protective miracles in an extra paragraph added in the Georgian translation of Cyril's *Vita Cyriaci* (at 226.5 (Binns (1991) 260 n.5)).
132 This association was more powerful in the west than the east where Cyril is based, but, as will be seen, it is clear that Cyril is using this term to make a deliberate statement about Euthymius in his narrative, and this is bound up in an understanding of the *pallium* as a mark of a bishop. Although the ἱμάτιον makes an appearance as Fidus' attire, and it would be tempting to claim that Cyril is using it to imply Fidus' authority as well, the use of the plural by Cyril suggests that this should be considered as general clothing (as Price translates it) rather than the more symbolic *himation/pallium*.
133 Price (1991) xl.
134 Brakke (1995) 80–82; Coon (1997) 63.
135 Cf., for example, Maro (Joh. Eph., *V. SS. Or.*, 4) who, despite shutting his door in people's faces and 'violently and with anger driv[ing] away those who came to gaze at him . . .' still could not deter them (pp. 57, 65) (tr. E.W. Brooks in Lee (2000) 212); Hilarion had a similar problem (Jer. *V. Hil.*); Williams (2008) 129.
136 These people could also be very determined: cf., for example, the crowd of people who break down Antony's door after he has not been seen in 20 years, just so he can talk to and instruct them, in addition to those who lie outside of his door even after he has refused to let them in (Athan. *V.Ant.* 14.2–3, 48).
137 Rousseau (1971) 400–401. This was of particular importance during this period, when differing doctrinal interpretations were the major source of conflict within the Church. Cf. Coon (1997) 63. The importance of ordaining influential monks in order to control their authority and employ it for the promotion of orthodoxy (and the lengths the Church would go to in order to achieve this) can be seen in the tales of holy men who have been tricked into ordination (cf. (Bohairic) *Life of Pachomius*, 28 (tr. A Veilleux (1980)). Athanasius is particularly keen to do this: Brakke (1995) Chapter 2, 82, 83, 113–20)). While this may reflect an authorial concern to present the subject as humble

168   *Holy habits*

in his holiness, its repeated appearance suggests that there was a real anxiety to bring such people under Church authority and legitimate their external influence for its own advantage.
138 Harmless (2008) 494, 498–501; see also Brakke (1995) 208, chap. 4. *Himation/pallium* is here used to encompass both its Greek and Latin 'lives'.
139 See below.
140 It was written during the reign of Constantius II (Henck (2001) 185). For authorial controversy over the *Vita* see Williams (2008) 105 nn.10–11; 119 – Athanasius was established as the author within 20 years, as the heading of Evagrius' Latin translation (374) makes clear; for a detailed discussion of the *Vita* see Brennan (1985); Brakke (1995), especially chapter 4; Williams (2008) chapter 3.
141 For the dating (possibly 377) see Brakke (1995) 263; Rebenich (2002) 14. For discussions of the text in general see White (1998) 73–74; Rebenich (2000), (2002) 14, 25–27, 85; Williams (2008) chapter 3. Like Athanasius' text, Jerome's *Vita* was also very popular – it was quickly translated into Greek, Syriac, Coptic, and Ethiopic (Rebenich (2002) 167 nn.23, 25).
142 Jerome complains that some of his readers believed Paul was imaginary (*V. Hil.* 1), see final part of case study.
143 *V. Paul.* 7.
144 *V. Paul.* 4, 5–6, 9.
145 Cf. Brennan (1985) 210–11; Brakke (1995) 80–81.
146 ὃ ὑπεστρωννυόμην ἱμάτιον, ὅπερ αὐτὸς μέν μοι καινὸν δέδωκεν, παρ' ἐμοὶ δὲ πεπαλαίωται. Tr. in Lee (2000) 195.
147 *Quamobrem, quaeso, perge . . . et pallium quod tibi Athanasius episcopus dedit, ad obvolvendum corpusculum meum, defer . . . Stupefactus ergo Antonius, quod de Athanasio et pallio eius audierat . . .*
148 Brennan (1985); Brakke (1995) chapter 4, particularly 201–3; White (1998) 3–4.
149 This is not the *pallium* granted only to bishops by the sixth century, of course, but the earlier *himation/pallium*. However, it is still the *pallium* of *a* bishop – Athanasius – and so the connotations of the later item are appropriate here, as will be seen. Furthermore, it is likely that when read during later periods, the use of *pallium* in the Latin translation (see below) would have associated Antony with episcopal authority even more strongly in the audience's minds through this item.
150 E.g. Greg. M. *Ep.* 9.147 (vest to Secundus), 14.15 (asking Venatius of Perugia to send a tunic to Ecclesius of Chiusi) (in Wood (2000) 305); the letters of Jerome also provide ample evidence of this practice; Caner (2006) 350.
151 Caner (2006) 365.
152 Antony visited Alexandria only twice – in 311 and perhaps 338 (Brakke (1995) 205–6).
153 Cf. Brennan (1985) 222.
154 Furthermore, Antony's solitude ensures that there are few to contradict this if the gift is fictional.
155 *V. Ant.* 91 (55).
156 Cf. Williams (2008) 106–7; Serfass (2014) 92 regarding the *pallium* in Gregory the Great's letters.
157 See Brennan (1985) 217–19; Brakke (1995) 82, 204, 214, 246–7.
158 Its quick translation into Latin suggests demand (Williams (2008) 119). For a well-known example of its influence cf. Aug. *Conf.* 8.6.15. Brakke (1995) 203, 247.
159 Brennan (1985) 210, 220, 224; Brakke (1995) 80, 110, 247; Williams (2008) 107. Cf. Martin of Tours who gets a similar treatment from Sulpicius Severus (although without the *pallium*) (Coon (1997) 67) and whose decision to tear his *chlamys* (which symbolised both his military career and allegiance to the pagan emperor) in half to clothe a disguised Christ 'more than covers up or outweighs the embarrassment of a bishop who once bore arms' and was once considered too wild for episcopal office (Finn (2006a) 135–6; see also beginning of this chapter). Here, clothing is functioning in a similar way

160 *De vir. ill.* 87.125.
161 Williams (2008) 119, 127.
162 Brakke (1995) 85; Williams (2008) 119–25, 127, 263.
163 *V. Paul.* 12.
164 Cf. Brakke (1995) 80–81.
165 *V. Paul.* 1.
166 *V. Hil.* 1.
167 Διέλετε δέ μου τὰ ἐνδύματα· καὶ Ἀθανασίῳ μὲν τῷ ἐπισκόπῳ δότε τὴν μίαν μηλωτὴν καὶ ὃ ὑπεστρωννυόμην ἱμάτιον, ὅπερ αὐτὸς μέν μοι καινὸν δέδωκεν, παρ' ἐμοὶ δὲ πεπαλαίωται. Καὶ Σεραπίωνι δὲ τῷ ἐπισκόπῳ δότε τὴν ἑτέραν μηλωτήν· καὶ ὑμεῖς ἔχετε τὸ τρίχινον ἔνδυμα … Καὶ τῶν λαβόντων δὲ ἕκαστος τὴν μηλωτὴν τοῦ μακαρίου Ἀντωνίου καὶ τὸ τετριμμένον παρ' αὐτοῦ ἱμάτιον, ὡς μέγα χρῆμα φυλάττει. Καὶ γὰρ καὶ βλέπων αὐτά, ὡς Ἀντώνιόν ἐστι θεωρῶν· καὶ περιβαλλόμενος δὲ αὐτά, ὡς τὰς νουθεσίας αὐτοῦ βαστάζων ἐστὶ μετὰ χαρᾶς. Tr. in Lee (2000) 195.
168 See above, n.92 the wills of Caesarius of Arles and Gregory of Nazianzus. For non-religious examples, e.g. *P.Kron.* 50 (will of Kronion, Tebtynis, 13 June 138); *SB* 8.9642(1) (will of Tamystha, Tebtynis c. 112); *P.Diog.* 11–12 (will of Isidora, Ptolemais Euergetis, 213) (in Rowlandson (1998) 127 no. 101, 198–200 no.147, 200–201 no.148),
169 Brakke (1995) 207; Williams (2008) 106–7.
170 Brennan (1985) 210, 222–4. Cf. Brakke (1995) 246–7; Williams (2008) 107.
171 This is perhaps signified by his implied confusion about why Athanasius is being given a ἱμάτιον/*pallium* within an exchange that closely reflects that of Elijah and Elisha, rather than the expected *melōte* which is used of Elijah's mantle in the Septuagint (Brennan (1985) 227, n.39).
172 *pace* Williams (2008) 107, who suggests they are 'twin Elishas' to Antony's Elijah.
173 ὡς μέγα χρῆμα φυλάττει. Καὶ γὰρ καὶ βλέπων αὐτά, ὡς Ἀντώνιόν ἐστι θεωρῶν *V. Ant.* 92.3.
174 Brennan (1985) 209–10, 224–5, quotation 224.
175 Cf. Lee (2000) 189. It is interesting that the hair tunic makes no further appearance after being listed in Antony's verbal will, and the receiver ('you' – ὑμεῖς) remains cryptic, perhaps to devalue any claim to Antony's authority by the receiver, or even to suggest that Athanasius also receives this item too.
176 Brakke (1995) 246–7, Chapter 4.
177 Cf. Brakke (1995) 263; Rebenich (2002) 26, 27.
178 *Alii autem, in quam opinionem vulgus omne consentit, asserunt Antonium huius propositi caput, quod ex parte verum est: non enim tam ipse ante omnes fuit, quam ab eo omnium incitata sunt studia … discipuli Antonii … etiam nunc affirmant, Paulum quemdam Thebaeum principem istius rei fuisse, non nominis; quam opinionem nos quoque probamus.* In light of this discussion, it is interesting that *probo* also has the sense of 'to make a thing credible' as well as 'to be satisfied with'. (Lewis and Short s.v. *probo,-are*).
179 *Igitur obvoluto et prolato foras corpore, hymnos quoque et psalmos de Christiana traditione decantans … Antonius …* (*V.Paul.*16)
180 Cf. Williams (2008) 124 n.101.
181 *Postquam autem alia dies illuxit, ne quid pius haeres ex intestati bonis non possideret, tunicam eius sibi vindicavit, quam in sportarum modum de palmae [palmarum] foliis ipse sibi contexuerat. Ac sic ad monasterium reversus … diebusque solemnibus Paschae et Pentecostes semper Pauli tunica vestitus est.* Tr. C. White, with adaptations. Writing tablets from Roman Britain provide evidence of cloaks made from bark (*sagum corticum*) (Pritchard (2006) 117).
182 Ramsey (2000) 32: 'There is clearly … an allusion [to Elijah in the *himation/pallium*] in Athanasius, *V.S. Antonii* 91; Jerome, *V.S. Pauli* 12;' Williams (2008) 124.

5 Drawing the threads together
Conclusions

For those in antiquity clothing had power in and of itself. It was a highly visual signifier, which in one glance could imply a person's status, gender, wealth, age, and even religious or political allegiances. Furthermore, it was made by harmonising difference, a central tenet also of gift-giving, a practice that underpinned all aspects of society, establishing, maintaining, and reinforcing relationships. A gift of clothing, therefore, combined all these elements and made it the perfect metaphor for authors to demonstrate what the practice of gift-giving was trying to achieve. As historical gifts between a donor and receiver gifts of clothing worked on a fundamental level to establish a relationship between these two participants that was personal, not just because of the ideas which surround gift-giving practice, but because of the gift itself as an item of clothing, and this is an idea which lies at the heart of the examples considered here. In the ancient world, to give a gift was to create a bond between the giver and receiver, and this was a connection in which both had identifiable parts to play. Similarly, clothing created a promise between the wearer and the viewer because it seemed guaranteed to be a visual reflection of the character of the wearer; yet it was this very quality that created uncertainties that authors of every period in the ancient world exploited to varying degrees. The process of its manufacture, moreover, provided tools for vocalising ideas about social cohesion, for it was an item worn by all and made by the combination of disparate elements into a harmonious whole, an integration which was also achieved in the ancient world through the practice of gift-giving and reciprocity. For those in antiquity, therefore, gifts of clothing entailed a negotiation of identity and social concord in every transaction; and, as has been seen, these central ideas allowed participants and authors to explore further meanings when these items performed in specific contexts.

Thus, when gifts of clothing appear within texts, they should not only be read as simple items that were valuable merely for their material worth. It becomes clear that for those in Late Antiquity – a period when the perceived certainties of past centuries were increasingly challenged, whether by barbarian incomers or the impact of Christianity – this device was often employed to negate potential challenges to authority, and particularly in order to reinforce 'official' power within texts. When it was not always clear who held or could hold superior authority, or indeed how this was to be recognised, clothing gifts provided the audience with the means to unravel these knotted threads. Using the authoritative nature of the written word, authors attempted to eliminate uncertainty for their audience by over-writing reality through their interpretations of clothing items. Dressing up those whose status might be problematic in the mantle of official authority allowed the wearers to become paradigms of political or religious orthodoxy, strengthened the position of both the donor and recipient, and provided late antique authors with a symbol of an ideal relationship.

These ideas did not spring fully formed in the minds of the writers of this period, however, but drew on a tradition of clothing gifts performing in texts and society. This was a lengthy and weighty heritage, which could trace its roots to the beginning of classical literature and social practice. In a diplomatic context this was expressed through a continuance of various concepts found in earlier periods, not least that ambassadors were weavers of peace. Due to the manufacture of clothing from disparate threads (symbols of an 'uncivilised' landscape tamed), garment gifts visualised what an envoy was trying to achieve: the harmonious entwining of different elements. On a more pragmatic level, the gifting of clothing items, often of great value, was a late antique custom that Alexander and the inhabitants of the Roman Republic and Early Empire would have recognised to a greater or lesser extent. As in the later period, for them it was a way to secure and acknowledge the support of foreign allies: the donating of expensive garments created a bond between the donor power and the foreign potentate. This was a bond which was considered personal because of the connotations of gift-giving, and which the intimate nature of clothing visualised and reinforced arguably more so than any of the other objects that were given in this context. In any period, presenting gifts to those external to the empire demonstrated the approval of their rule from the donor, while also carrying within them the promise of support for that individual, should he (or she) need it. Clothing, however, literally and metaphorically wrapped the recipient in garments that displayed these concepts in a highly visual manner. Furthermore, because this was enacted through the performance of gift-giving, the items received created an obligation that the foreign ruler was expected to repay, usually in the form of military aid to the empire. The gifting of apparel that had specific connections with Roman offices helped illustrate this further – the *toga purpurea*, *palmata tunica*, and *toga praetexta* in the earlier periods gave way to the *chlamys* in the later – and placed the recipients into the heart of authority. By wearing clothing that attired those who administered and protected the empire, these garments demonstrated that the foreign ruler should be seen as having derived their authority from the empire and emperor, while the act of gift-giving further emphasised this transferral. The combination of both, however, showed approval from and participation in 'official' power.

Yet, while the ruler and those outside the borders may have understood the meaning behind a gift of these particular clothes or could have relied on ambassadors to elucidate their significance within Roman society, their unmistakeable

Roman style requires consideration of the question of at whom were these gifts actually aimed. That this clothing was also to be found on the bodies of imperial officials within the empire provided a recognisable visual framework in which to recognise as persons of power 'other' authoritative figures like foreign rulers, and defined their role in relation to the empire. As a result, these items created the expectation that the foreign ruler would behave in the same way as those who were clothed in similar attire within the empire – that is, to protect it; and that this was understood has been seen in the actions of the Avars and the queen of the Sabir Huns. Yet, while some in Late Antiquity would have been able to observe the foreign ruler in his (or her) new clothes at their investiture, it was their inclusion in texts that allowed for further 'viewing' (and understanding), an action that continued long after the wearer of such items was deceased. Furthermore, the presence of these real rulers in written contexts, acting or dressing in expected Roman ways, creates them anew as literary constructs and allows the reality of their 'otherness' to be overwritten by the familiar: Attila's use of clothing gifts is understandable because it mirrors Roman practice, and makes him all the more intimidating as a result. This was not always a complete cover-up, however, and authors appear to have included incongruent elements to remind their audience that the wearer of these Roman clothes was anything but local. In Malalas' composition, an indication of the ruler's status externally to the empire was implied by calling the garment gifts 'royal' or noting that the gold *tablion*, which normally appeared on the imperial *chlamys*, also adorned that of Tzath; but more obviously non-Roman elements were also employed in this way. Tzath's shoes merit attention in the text because the history of the Lazican relationship to Persia, their previous provider of authority, is detailed in their Persian-style decorative elements. This foreign footwear is a wrinkle in Tzath's otherwise Roman outfit; his *chlamys* may dress him up in the clothes of a late antique imperial official and integrate him into the fabric of Roman society in some ways, but his shoes, gold *tablion*, and geographical location suggest that he should be considered predominantly as a decorative border at its edge.

Such dress elements also allowed authors to suggest the continued independence of some foreign rulers, despite the implication of submission that accepting and wearing gifted garments firmly tied to Roman authority inferred. Additionally, they indicate wider anxieties about the influence of the empire in the late antique world that do not necessarily appear in earlier texts that discuss diplomatic situations. This reflects the changed circumstances in which the empire found itself in Late Antiquity, where defensive diplomacy replaced the relatively stronger military positions of the Roman Republic and Early Empire. Indeed, the importance of showing the empire, in literature and real life, as the superior partner in diplomatic exchanges increased during this period, and gifts of clothing became an important part of this narrative. This was partly because of their role in as real diplomatic gifts – as expensive and beautiful objects they principally demonstrated the value of the foreign ruler's worth to the empire. Yet the qualities that made this clothing precious, such as the materials they were made from or the dyes used, also enabled the empire to suggest the consequences of continued positive interaction with it as an avenue to luxury goods. Sartorial gifts could additionally be a form of costly intimidation, however, hinting at a vast reserve of resources that the empire could mobilise for its own use. This position of superiority in the possession of luxury goods could be undermined when the empire interacted with Sassanid Persia, however, which was why silk clothing in particular was omitted from the gifts given to the latter by the Romans (metalware worked better here); this is seen in the desire to cast the Persian king as a tributary when he gave beautiful silk apparel to the emperor from his own wardrobe. That the empire's hegemony was seen as a growing fiction more generally is demonstrated further by the number of sartorial gifts that appear to have more than a hint of bribery about them, particularly when given to those who were clearly threats during this period. Although other objects were utilised in this way, presentations of garments were particularly useful in these circumstances. They enabled both the emperor and authors to cloak obvious bribery in the idea that such items were taking Roman culture and influence into the heart of foreign territory, or that they were facilitating the submission of a foreign potentate to Roman power. Clothing gifts thus helped create a narrative of superiority when interacting with external force, which the empire's authors fully aided and abetted. They dressed up the weakened empire in the robes of continuing military power, vital trade-partner and awesome wealth to justify and reinforce its increasingly precarious claim to dominance.

Validating and strengthening insecure authority was not only important to the welfare of the empire as a whole, but also to some of its emperors. Those who were young and yet to prove themselves, such as Gratian, were particularly vulnerable. But a link to a well-considered previous imperial ruler was one way to allay anxieties. Gratian's decision to dress his tutor, Ausonius of Bordeaux, in a consular *trabea* with the figure of Constantius II should be seen within this context of insecurity. It further emphasised and strengthened the emperor's marital ties to the second-longest ruling dynasty in Roman imperial history, of which Constantia was the last legitimate descendant. As the son-in-law and elder son of emperors he was doubly legitimated to rule, a claim which placed him above his brother Valentinian II, who had been elevated without his consent due to concerns which had already appeared about Gratian's ability to rule the empire alone. The figure of Constantius allowed Gratian to say something further than this, however, particularly with regard to his own character and ambitions for his reign. It linked him to an emperor whose *paideia* had been noted by contemporaries and who was considered militarily successful – two problem areas for Gratian due to his father on the one hand, and youth on the other. That the figure of Constantius on the gifted *trabea* should be read as reflecting on Gratian rather than its recipient and wearer is made clear from Ausonius' speech giving thanks for his consulship (as well as his garment). Although the *trabea* gift and the office gave this rhetorician the honour of imperial sanction and participation in the highest authority, Ausonius worked hard to deflect any messages the garment contained back onto its donor. Thus, the text functions to encourage viewers to take a deeper look at the meaning of the *trabea* and its decoration, as Gratian had instructed Ausonius himself to do. Rather than writing the wearer into a position of secure authority, as is the case with diplomatic clothing gifts (although it serves to do that as well), it is the donor who is re-dressed. Ausonius' determination to demonstrate the connection of the garment's decoration to Gratian works with the thanksgiving speech as a whole to present an authoritative image of Gratian as a doubly legitimate emperor, secure in knowledge, familial connections, and military achievements. The *trabea* itself lends further aid to Ausonius' interpretation: he connects it to the *toga picta* of the triumphing general of earlier years, in order to show Gratian as able in war. Additionally, however, the contemporary poetry of Late Antiquity gave the wearers of the *trabea* a further role to play, which allowed them, and by proxy the imperial donors of the garment, to place themselves in the long tradition of heroic acceptance of divinely gifted clothing.

By personally providing Ausonius with his *trabea*, Gratian could have been located in this divine role by the author's audience due to their previous exposure to this literary trope. Even if he was not, however, his gift still places him in another long-standing tradition – that of the good *patronus* – as was also the case in other imperial reigns when consuls acquired their *trabea* through the *ministri largitionum* instead, in a more indirect performance of imperial largess. The gifting of clothing had a history in expressing the relationship between the *patronus* and *cliens*, including in circumstances of diplomacy; foreign potentates could also be the clients of the emperor, particularly from the time when he took over as the focus of this social practice from other Roman notables. As with these gifts, which symbolised the desired outcome of an embassy, so presents of garments in the context of patronage signified the concordant whole of the fabric of society to which this relationship was supposed to contribute. As a result, for Martial in the Early Empire – who presents the largest distinct body of evidence for clothing gifts in any context – the presentation of a garment from one of his patrons, and especially of a toga, was a particular symbol of a successful *cliens–patronus* relationship, and not only because it was the item which allowed a client to 'be' a client. His poems suggest he is a recipient of clothing very rarely, however, and instead the missing apparel allows him to emphasise the gulf between reality and ideal by juxtaposing the image of a completed, whole garment with the incomplete and ruptured patron–client relationship. This leads the poet (as he exists as a persona in the poems) to expose vice rather than extol virtue (one of the usual duties of a *cliens*), while the real poet Martial creates these patrons anew as the paradigms of bad social practice. In contrast, those who do provide the poet-persona with clothing gifts receive their expected due – in interacting correctly together (symbolised by the successful presentation of a garment) Martial can become the ideal *cliens*, recording his patron's largess for eternity and praising their high qualities in a way which was echoed in Ausonius' treatment of Gratian.

Although not necessarily deliberately, it was also mirrored by the flattering descriptions of the charitable actions of the wealthy laity in late antique Christian texts, a performance of which allowed these men and women to continue to partake in the traditional concepts of euergetism. Despite the notion that this new religious setting should have theoretically negated the expectation of reciprocal benefit, it is clear that charitable giving allowed the laity a share of the praise that usually covered and was reserved for men and women of exceptional holiness. This praise was voiced not just in reality, but in contemporary texts as well, and it gave these wealthy (and not so wealthy) givers religious, and therefore also social, capital. They could add to this through the possession, and more importantly the diligent care, of holy clothing relics, which were felt to have imbibed the power of the saint due to the widespread belief that its proximity to the body meant clothing absorbed the characteristics of its wearer-owner, including holy authority. Moreover, these qualities could be transferred to a new wearer, especially if that garment had been bequeathed to them by the original owner. This meant that when they dressed in this special clothing they were also dressed up in the authority of the original, whilst simultaneously being able to display their approval from and relationship with its source. In this context the saint continued, then, to be present in the gifted clothes, connecting the wearer to the power of the prototype. That this was a general belief in Late Antiquity is determined not only by the many examples in Christian texts which provide descriptions of clothing still emitting saintly powers after their original possessor has died, but also in the response to imperial portraiture on *chlamydes* and *trabeae*, owned by men such as Tzath and Ausonius, in other contemporary literature.

This attitude may have sat uneasily with some Christian authors, but they also took advantage of it to employ clothing gifts to discuss their anxieties about who was worthy to inherit a holy man's authority after he was gone, and moreover how this worthiness was to be recognised. In a period when it was not always easy to identify or indeed define who should be responsible to continue that legacy, clothing gifts provided a way to explore these concerns. When those who succeeded the saintly figure were met with approval by an author, they were to be found caring for his sartorial presence correctly, treating his garments with proper reverence, and employing them in much the same manner as the saint had done originally. Drawing on the classical literature of their education alongside Biblical precepts like the transmission of clothing between Elijah and Elisha, and in their similar use of clothing gifts found in contemporary diplomatic and political practices, authors suggested that these garments demonstrated that their new possessor had received a transfer of saintly authority. Their ability to tap into the power of these items and use them correctly showed they were 'officially' approved to partake in, benefit from, and use the saints legacy to continue his holy work, while their careful custody justified the original transference of authority. Thus, as in many of the examples considered throughout, albeit in different settings, the effective performance of their responsibility not only provided the inheritor with the sanctified authority to carry out their duties as an exalted member of Christianity, but continually renewed it every time the garment was brought out and worn. In contrast, those who were felt to be unworthy of such special and powerful clothing gifts were not quite so lucky, and they found themselves instead in the dire circumstances with which those who received deadly clothing gifts in classical Greek tragedy would empathise. While authors of these texts also used dangerous dress to explore problematic usurpations of authority (here, female appropriation of male power, individual authority over collective), the late antique versions delivered a satisfactorily permanent conclusion to this issue. They offered a morality tale to warn of the extreme risks run by those who managed to get their hands on authority to which they were unsuited and thus unentitled.

For Christian writers, then, clothing gifts provided a means to show their support of those who they felt were worthy to put on the mantle of a saint's holy authority or to undermine those who they deemed inadequate for this task. If the author was also the inheritor of such an item, however, a garment gifted by a holy man became instrumental in promoting his own merits and authority. This was certainly the case for the bishop Athanasius, who utilised a clothing exchange between himself and Antony as part of the more general policy of strengthening of his own personal 'brand' to garner support which can be found in the wider context of the *Vita Antonii*. As with many of the examples presented here, the historicity of this exchange is secondary to its importance as a literary device within the narrative, for the clothing gift acts to recreate Athanasius as the primary heir to Antony's remarkable holy legacy. He receives not only the symbol of charismatic monasticism (the *melōte*), as others do, but also Antony's *himation/pallium*. That this is actually Athanasius' own garment returned, which he gave to the saint previously, is of great importance to the narrative as a whole. The item that has been used to clothe both a bishop and a holy man is thus infused with the authority of both and allows its final possessor Athanasius to be covered in episcopal and charismatic power combined – that is until Jerome decides to strip him of it to dress his own saint in Antony's legacy instead.

Writing oneself as possessing the authority of both bishop and saint was powerful rhetoric in Late Antiquity, when it was not always clear which held superior religious authority, due to the competing dialogues between the Church and charismatic holy men. The gifting of special clothing within texts therefore allowed Church authors to present potentially problematic figures as being under the mantle of Church authority, by dressing them in the clothing of the clergy. Just as it did for foreign rulers in diplomatic settings, disguising these figures as officers of the Church overwrote their reality and located them in an authoritative manner through an official position within the ecclesiastical hierarchy. While this went some way to negating their 'otherness' it was not in the interests of those writers who more strongly identified with the institution of the Church to erase this quality fully: a holy man's charismatic powers were influential and thus better used for a Church which could benefit from this authority, while being able to control and limit it within its own boundaries.

The use of clothing gifts by authors to settle conflicts had a pedigree that reached back to the Homeric poems, and it was a device used extensively in Late Antiquity. As before, many of these tensions centred on individuals, and were particularly concerned with how best to place that individual in society, yet now they had to be positioned in a society in a state of transition but reluctant to let go of the long-standing traditions that had once served it so well. Like the figure of Odysseus, many of the individuals who make a guest appearance in late antique texts are transformed by their clothes so that they can fit into the right, or rather, the expected, social context. Yet these situations were no longer as secure and unproblematic as they were perceived to have been in earlier periods, and this was particularly the case with regards to authority. The advent of Christianity as the predominant religion of the empire, the arrival of soldier-emperors from lowly backgrounds, the prominence of 'barbarians' at the imperial court, and the circumstances that led to areas which had long been part of empire finding themselves now under foreign rule, meant that earlier traits of authority, such as birth, education, and wealth, were no longer its exclusive markers. For late antique authors, therefore, the ability to create new realities within their texts presented them with an opportunity to eliminate these uncertainties surrounding authority, even if this could not change the reality of the world they lived in. Gifts of clothing that had special associations with offices of high power, in particular, were an invaluable means to make the presence of authority both clear-cut and convincing. In late antique texts, unlike reality, any anxieties surrounding a weak empire, emperor, or Church could be easily fixed through a wardrobe change; clothing gifts offered authors the means to cover up and reinforce any suggestion of insecure authority, by dressing those vulnerable to such an interpretation in the mantle of official authority and superior prestige.

When clothing gifts functioned in late antique texts to provide meditations on the transference of authority, they could do so in a meaningful way because such items already carried symbolic connotations in the cultural consciousness of the educated elite at whom such messages were primarily aimed. On their appearance in the literature of earlier periods, these items helped established the relationship and strengthened the relative positions of the donor and recipient and surrounded these participants in ideas of submission, protection, identity, and reciprocity, while also presenting a visual symbol of an ideal, harmonious social bond, all through their combined performance as both gift and garment. Yet, while many of these earlier concepts were preserved and built upon in late antique clothing gifts, their later context saw them being employed for different ends; Martial's sartorial presents, which broadcast the disparity between the ideal and real, are no longer effective in the later Roman period. This was also true of Epictetus' metaphorical garment, encountered in the Introduction, which communicated the unbearably restrictive nature of a society that lives under tyranny, where everyone must remain uniform and confined in a rigid pattern to avoid standing out. In Late Antiquity, however, clothing gifts were used to convey precisely the opposite sentiments; instead it was a literary device which was put to work covering over tears and which reinforced weak links to avoid unravelling the concordant whole. These were spaces where each thread in the fabric of society not only knew its place, but was content to be locked into a familiar and firm position; they suggested stability at a time when everything appeared to be coming apart at the seams.

Bibliography

Biblical references are taken from *The English Standard Version* (Wheaton, IL 2001); A. Rahlfs (ed.) *Septuaginta*, 9th edition, Vol. 1 (Stuttgart 1935); and K. Aland, M. Black, C.M. Martini, B.M. Metzger, and A. Wikgren (eds) *The Greek New Testament*, 2nd edition (Stuttgart 1968).

Ancient Sources

Agathias, *The Histories*, trans. J.D. Frendo (Berlin 1975).
Agathangelos, *History of the Armenians*, trans. with commentary R.W. Thomson (Albany, NY 1976).
Ambrose, *On the Mysteries*, trans. T. Thompson (London 1950).
Ammianus Marcellinus, ed. and trans. J.C. Rolfe, *Ammianus Marcellinus*, Loeb Classical Library (Cambridge, MA 1952).
——— *The Later Roman Empire (A.D. 354–378)*, trans. W. Hamilton (Harmmondsworth 1986).
Aristophanes, *Birds*, ed. and trans. J. Henderson, Loeb Classical Library (Cambridge, MA 2000).
——— *Lysistrata*, trans. A.H. Sommerstein, *Lysistrata and other plays* (London 2002).
Arrian, *Anabasis*, trans. M. Austin, *The Hellenistic World from Alexander to the Roman Conquest: A Selection of Ancient Sources in Translation*, 2nd edition (Cambridge 2006).
——— *The Discourses of Epictetus*, trans. G. Long, *The Discourses of Epictetus with the Encheridion and Fragments* (London 1890).
——— *Epicteti dissertationes ab Arriano digestae*, ed. H. Schenkl (Leipzig 1916).
Asterius, *Homilia*, ed. J.-P. Migne, *PG*. 40.167–168 (Paris 1858).
——— *Homilia*, trans. C. Mango (Toronto 1986).
——— *Homilia*, trans. H. Maguire, *DOP* 44 (1990).
Athanasius, *Life of Antony*, trans. A.D. Lee (London 2000).
——— *The Life of Antony*, trans. T. Vivian and A.N. Athanassakis (Kalamazoo, MI 2003).
——— *Vita Antonii*, ed. G.J.M. Bartelink, *Athanase d'Alexandrie, Vie d'Antoine*, Sources Chrétiennes 400 (Paris 2004).
Augustine, *Confessions*, trans. A.D. Lee (London 2000).
——— *Rules*, trans. R. Canning (London 1984).
Ausonius, *Decimi Magni Ausonii Opera*, ed. R.P.H. Green (Oxford 1999).
——— *Opuscula*, ed. and trans. H.G. Evelyn White, Loeb Classical Library (Cambridge, MA 1967).

——— *The Works of Ausonius*, ed. R.P.H. Green (Oxford 1991).
Basil of Caesarea, *Ascetical Works*, trans. M.M. Wagner (Washington, DC 1950).
——— *De Baptismo*, ed. J.-P. Migne, *PG* 31.1513–1628 (Paris 1885).
——— *De spiritu sancto*, ed. B. Pruche, *Basile de Césarée, Sur le Saint-Esprit*, 2nd edition, Sources Chrétiennes 17 (Paris 1968).
——— *De spiritu sancto*, trans. J. Elsner (Oxford 1998).
——— *The Long Rules*, trans. M. Wagner in *Ascetical Works* (Washington, DC 1950).
——— *Regulae Fusius Tractatae*, ed. J.-P. Migne, *PG* 31.901–1052 (Paris 1857–66).
——— *Select Works and Letters*, trans. Rev. B. Jackson (Grand Rapids, MI 1894).
Benedict, *The Rules of Saint Benedict*, trans. T. Fry (New York 1998).
Caesarius of Arles, *Caesarius of Arles: Life, Testament, Letters*, trans. W.E. Klingshirn, Translated Texts for Historians 19 (Liverpool 1994).
Canons of the Council in Trullo (692 C.E.), trans. J.C. Skedros in R. Valantasis (ed.) *Religions of Late Antiquity in Practice* (Princeton 2000): 289–300.
Cassian, John, *De Coenobiorum Institutis*, ed. J.-P. Migne, *PL* 49.53–476 (Paris 1849).
——— *The Institutes*, trans. B. Ramsey, Ancient Christian Writers 58 (New York 2000).
Cassiodorus, *Variae*, trans. S.J.B. Barnish, Translated Texts for Historians 12 (Liverpool 1992).
Cassius Dio, *Roman History*, ed. and trans. E. Cary, Loeb Classical Library (Cambridge, MA 1914–27).
Catullus, *The Complete Poems*, trans. G. Lee (Oxford 1990).
Chronicon Paschale, trans. M. Whitby and M. Whitby, Translated Texts for Historians 7 (Liverpool 1989).
Chrysostom, John, *Ad illuminandos catecheses*, ed. J.-P. Migne, *PG* 49.223–240 (Paris 1857–66).
——— *Baptismal Instructions*, trans. P.W. Harkins (New York 1963).
——— *Homilies on Acts of the Apostles*, trans. Rev. J. Walker, Rev. J. Sheppard, and Rev. H. Browne, *NPNF* 1.11 (Grand Rapids, MI 1975).
——— *Huit Catéchèses Baptismales*, ed. and trans. A. Wegner, 2nd edition, Sources Chrétiennes (Paris 1970).
Cicero, *De Officiis*, ed. and trans. W. Miller, Loeb Classical Library (Cambridge, MA 1913).
——— *Laelius de amicitia*, ed. and trans. W.A. Falconer, Loeb Classical Library (Cambridge, MA 1923).
——— *Second Philippic Oration*, trans. W.K. Lacey (Warminster 1986).
Claudian, *Works*, ed. and trans. M. Platnauer, Loeb Classical Library (Cambridge, MA 1922).
Codex Theodosius, ed. J. Harries and I. Wood (Ithaca, NY 1993).
——— *The Theodosian Code and Novels and Sirmondian Constitutions*, trans. C. Pharr, T. Sherrer Davidson, and M. Brown Pharr (Princeton 1952).
Constantine Porphyrogenitus, *De Ceremoniis*, trans. Greatrex and Lieu (2002): 124–8.
Corippus, *In laudem Iustini Augusti minoris libri IV*, trans. Averil Cameron (London 1976).
Cyprian of Carthage, *Liber de Opere et Eleemosynis*, ed. J.-P. Migne *PL* 4.601–622 (Paris 1844).
——— *On Works and Alms*, trans. Rev. E. Wallis, in A. Roberts and J. Donaldson *ANF* 5 (Grand Rapids, MI 1885).
Cyprianus, *Life of Caesarius of Arles*, trans. W. Klingshirn, *Caesarius of Arles: Life, Testament, Letters* (Liverpool 1994).
Cyril of Jerusalem, *The Catechetical Lectures*, trans. E.H. Gifford, *NPNF* 2.7 (Grand Rapids, MI 1893).
Cyril of Scythopolis, *The Lives of the Monks of Palestine*, trans. R.M. Price (Kalamazoo, MI 1991).
Dexippus, *Fragments*, trans. J. McInerney, in I. Worthington (ed.) *Brill's New Jacoby* [online]: http://referenceworks.brillonline.com/entries/brill-s-new-jacoby/dexippos-100-a100#BNJTEXT100_F_7 [accessed April 2013].

Diodorus Siculus, *Library of History*, ed. and trans. C.H. Oldfather, Loeb Classical Library (Cambridge, MA 1935).
Dionysius, *Roman Antiquities*, ed. and trans. E. Cary, Loeb Classical Library (Cambridge, MA 1937).
Eunapius, *Fragments*, ed. and trans. R.C. Blockley (Liverpool 1983).
——— *Vitae Sophistarum*, ed. and trans. W.C. Wright, Loeb Classical Library (Cambridge, MA 1921).
Euripides, *Medea*, ed. and trans. D. Kovacs, Loeb Classical Library (Cambridge, MA 1925).
Eusebius, *Ecclesiastical History*, trans. R.J. Deferrari (Washington, DC 1953).
——— *Historia Ecclesiastica*, ed. G. Bardy, *Eusèbe de Césarée: Histoire Ecclésiastique*, 3 vols, Sources Chrétiennes 31, 41, 55 (Paris 1952–58).
——— *Life of Constantine*, trans. Averil Cameron and S.G. Hall (Oxford 1999).
——— *Vita Constantini*, ed. F. Winkelmann, *Eusebius Werke*, Band 1.1: *Über das Leben des Kaisers Konstantin* (Berlin 1975).
Evagrius, *Life of Antony by Athanasius*, trans. C. White, in *Early Christian Lives* (London 1998).
——— *Vita Antonii*, ed. J.-P. Migne, *PL* 73.125–169 (Paris 1849).
Gerontius, *Life of Melania the Younger*, trans. E.A. Clark (New York 1984).
Gregory of Tours, *Glory of the Martyrs*, trans. R. Van Dam, Translated Texts for Historians 4 (Liverpool 2004).
——— *Life of the Fathers (Vitae Patrum)*, trans. E. James, 2nd edition (Liverpool 1991).
——— *Vitae Patrum*, ed. J.-P. Migne, *PL* 71.1011–1096 (Paris 1849).
Gregory the Great, *Registrum Epistularum*, trans. H. Wace and P. Schaff, *NPNF* 2.12 (Grand Rapids, MI 1956).
——— *Registrum Epistularum*, ed. J.-P. Migne, *PL* 77.441–1328 (Paris 1849).
Gregory Nazianzen, *Orations*, trans. C.G. Browne and J.E. Swallow, *NPNF* 2.7 (Grand Rapids, MI 1893).
——— *Testament*, trans. R. Van Dam, *JThS* (n.s.) 46.1 (1995).
Herodotus, *The Histories*, trans. R. Waterfield (Oxford 1998).
Historia Monachorum in Aegypto, trans. N. Russell, *The Lives of the Desert Fathers* (Kalamazoo, MI 1981).
Historia Augusta, ed. and trans. D. Magie, Loeb Classical Library (Cambridge, MA 1922–32).
——— *Lives of the Later Caesars*, trans. A. Birley (Harmondsworth 1976).
Homer, *The Iliad*, trans. R. Lattimore (Chicago 1951).
——— *The Odyssey*, trans. E.V. Rieu (Harmondsworth 1946).
Horace, *Epistles*, ed. and trans. H. Rushton Fairclough, Loeb Classical Library (Cambridge, MA 1926).
Horsiesios, *Regulations*, trans. A. Veilleux (Kalamazoo, MI 1981).
Jerome, *Against Vigilantius*, trans. W. Fremantle, *NPNF* 2.6 (Grand Rapids, MI 1954).
——— *Letters*, ed. and trans. F.A. Wright, Loeb Classical Library (Cambridge, MA 1933).
——— *Life of Hilarion*, trans. C. White (London 1998).
——— *Life of Paul of Thebes*, trans. C. White (London 1998).
——— *Lives of Illustrious Men*, trans. E.C. Richardson, *NPNF* 2.3 (Grand Rapids, MI 1892).
——— *Translatio Latina Regulae Sancti Pachomii*, trans. A. Veilleux (Kalamazoo, MI 1981).
——— *Vita S. Pauli Primi Eremitae*, ed. J.-P. Migne, *PL* 23.17–28 (Paris 1845).
John of Ephesus, *Lives of the Eastern Saints*, ed. and trans. E.W. Brooks (Paris 1926).
Justinian, *Novellae*, ed. R. Schoell, *Corpus Iuris Civilis*, Vol. 3 (Berlin 1928–29).
Juvenal, *The Sixteen Satires*, trans. P. Green (Harmondsworth 1998).
Libanius, *Orationes*, ed. R. Foerster, Libanii opera (Leipzig 1903–27)
——— *Oration 64*, trans. M. Molloy (Hildesheim 1996).
Liber Pontificalis, trans. R. Davis, revised. ed. (Liverpool 2010).

Bibliography

Life of Pachomius (Bohairic), trans. A. Veilleux, in A.D. Lee (London 2000).
Livy, *History of Rome*, ed. and trans. F. Gardener, Loeb Classical Library (Cambridge, MA 1943).
Malalas, *Chronicle*, trans. E. Jeffreys, M. Jeffreys, and R. Scott (Melbourne 1986).
——— *Chronologica*, ed. I. Thurn, *Ioannis Malalae Chronographia*, Corpus Fontium Historiae Byzantinae, Series Berolinensis 35 (Berlin 2000).
Malchus, *Fragments*, ed. and trans. R.C. Blockley (Liverpool 1983).
Martial, *Apophoreta*, ed. T.J. Leary (London 1996).
——— *Epigrams*, ed. and trans. D.R. Shackleton Bailey, Loeb Classical Library (Cambridge, MA 1993).
——— *Select Epigrams*, trans. L. Watson and P.A. Watson (Cambridge 2003).
Maximianus, *Elegia*, ed. E. Baehrens, *Poetae Latini Minores*, Vol. 5 (Leipzig 1879).
Menander, *Fragments*, trans. R.C. Blockley (Liverpool 1985).
Olympiodorus, *Fragments*, trans. R.C. Blockley (Liverpool 1983).
Optatus, *Against the Donatists*, Appendix 1, trans. M. Edwards (Liverpool 1997).
Ovid, *Heroides*, ed. and trans. G. Showerman, revised G.P. Goold, 2nd edition, Loeb Classical Library (Cambridge, MA 1977).
——— *Metamorphoses*, trans. A.D. Melville (Oxford 1986).
——— *Metamorphoses*, ed. and trans. F.J. Miller and G.P. Goold, Loeb Classical Library (Cambridge, MA 1977).
Pachomius, *Precepts*, trans. A. Veilleux in A.D. Lee (London 2000).
——— *Precepts*, trans. A. Veilleux (Kalamazoo, MI 1981).
Palladius, *Lausiac History*, trans. A. Veilleux (Kalamazoo, MI 1981).
Panegyrici Latini, ed. R.A.B. Mynors, trans. C.E.V. Nixon and B.S. Rodgers (Berkeley 1994).
Petronius, *Satyrica* ed. and trans. R. Bracht Branham and D. Kinney (London 1996).
Phlegon of Tralles, *Book of Marvels*, trans. with commentary W. Hansen (Exeter 1996).
Plautus, *Curculio* in *Plautus, Titus Maccius*, ed. and trans. W. de Melo (Cambridge, MA 2011).
Pliny, *Natural History*, ed. and trans. H. Rackham, Loeb Classical Library (Cambridge, MA 1952).
Plutarch, *Lives*, ed. and trans. B. Perrin, Loeb Classical Library (Cambridge, MA 1917).
——— *Roman Lives*, trans. R. Waterfield (Oxford 1999).
Polybius, *The Histories*, ed. and trans. W.R. Paton, Loeb Classical Library (Cambridge, MA 1922–27).
Priscus, *Fragments*, trans. R.C. Blockley (Liverpool 1983).
Procopius, *History of the Wars*, ed. and trans. H.B. Dewing, Loeb Classical Library (Cambridge, MA 1914–54).
Pseudo-Joshua the Stylite, *Chronicle*, trans. F.R. Trombley and J.W. Watt, Translated Texts for Historians 32 (Liverpool 2000).
Sebeos, *The Armenian History*, trans. R.W. Thomson and J. Howard-Johnston, Translated Texts for Historians 31 (Liverpool 1999)
Seneca, *De beneficiis*, ed. and trans. E. Hosius, Loeb Classical Library (Cambridge, MA 1914).
——— *Hercules Oetaeus*, ed. and trans. F. Justice Miller, *Seneca's Tragedies*, Loeb Classical Library (Cambridge, MA 1917).
——— *Moral Epistles*, ed. and trans. R.M. Gummere, Loeb Classical Library (Cambridge, MA 1925).
——— *Moral Essays*, ed. and trans. J.W. Basore, Loeb Classical Library (Cambridge, MA 1928).
Sidonius, *Poems and Letters*, ed. and trans. W.B. Anderson, Loeb Classical Library (Cambridge, MA 1965).

Silius Italicus, *Punica*, ed. and trans. J.D. Duff, Loeb Classical Library (Cambridge, MA 1934).
Socrates, *Ecclesiastical History*, trans. Rev. A.C. Zenos, *NPNF* 2.2 (Grand Rapids, MI 1886).
Sophocles, *Women of Trachis*, trans. D. Raeburn, *Electra and Other Plays* (London 2008).
Sozomen, *Church History*, trans. A.D. Lee (London 2000).
Suetonius, *The Twelve Caesars*, trans. R. Graves (Harmondsworth 1979).
——— *Lives of the Caesars*, trans. C. Edwards (Oxford 2000).
Sulpicius Severus, *Vita Martini*, ed. J.-P. Migne, *PL* 20.159–176 (Paris 1845).
——— *Life of Martin of Tours*, trans. C. White (London 1998).
——— *Life of Martin of Tours*, trans. Rev. Alexander Roberts, *NPNF* 2.11 (Grand Rapids, MI 1955).
Tacitus, *Annals*, trans. M. Grant, revised edition (Harmondsworth 1996).
Tertullian, *De Pallio*, trans. Rev. S. Thelwall, *ANF* 4 (Grand Rapids, MI 1885).
——— *The Cornutian Deed*, trans. A.D. Lee (London 2000).
Themistius, *Themistii Orationes quae supersunt*, ed. G. Downey and H. Schenkl (Leipzig 1965–74).
——— *Orations*, trans. P. Heather and J. Matthews (Liverpool 1991).
Theodore of Mopsuestia, *Commentary on Baptism*, trans. E.C. Whitaker (London 1960).
Theodoret of Cyrrhus, *A History of the Monks of Syria [Religious History]*, trans. R.M. Price (Kalamazoo, MI 1991).
Theophanes, *Chronographia*, trans. C. Mango, R. Scott, and G. Greatrex, *The Chronicle of Theophanes Confessor: Byzantine and Near Eastern history, AD 284–813* (Oxford 1997).
Theophylactus Simocatta, *The History of Theophylactus Simocatta*, trans. M. Whitby and M. Whitby (Oxford 1986).
Valerius Maximus, *Memorable Doings and Sayings*, ed. and trans. D.R. Shackleton Bailey, Loeb Classical Library (Cambridge, MA 2000).
Vellius Paterculus, *Compendium of Roman History, Res Gestae Divi Augusti*, ed. and trans. F.W. Shipley, Loeb Classical Library (Cambridge, MA 1924).
Virgil, *Aeneid*, trans. C. Day Lewis (Oxford 1986).
———Vol. 1: *Eclogues, Georgics, Aeneid*, ed. and trans. H. Rushton Fairclough and G.P. Goold, Loeb Classical Library (Cambridge, MA 1966).
Xenophon, *Symposium*, trans. and commentary A.J. Bowen (Warminster 1997).
Zosimus, *New History*, trans. W. Green and T. Chaplin (London 1814).
——— *Historia Nova*, ed. F. Paschoud, *Zosime, Histoire nouvelle* (Paris 1971–89).

Modern Sources

Alchermes, J.D. (2005) 'Art and Architecture in the Age of Justinian', in M. Maas (ed.) *The Cambridge Companion to the Age of Justinian* (Cambridge): 343–75.
Alfaro, C., J.P. Wild, and B. Costa (eds) (2004) *Purpureae Vestes I. Textiles y tintes del Mediterráneo en época romana* (Valencia).
Alfaro, C. and L. Karali (eds) (2008) *Purpureae Vestes II. Vestidos, textiles y tintes: Estudios sobre la producción de bienes de consumo en la Antigüedad* (Valencia).
Allen, J. (2006) *Hostages and Hostage Taking in the Roman Empire* (Cambridge).
Anderson, W.B. (1936) *Sidonius, Poems and Letters*, Vol. 1 (Cambridge, MA).
Ando, C. (2000) *Imperial Ideology and Provincial Loyalty in the Roman Empire* (London).
Arce, J. (2005) 'Dress Control in Late Antiquity: Codex Theodosianus 14.10.1–4', in A. Köb and P. Riedel (eds), *Kleidung und Repräsentation in Antike und Mittelalter*, Mittelalterstudien des Instituts zur Interdisziplinären Erforschung des Mittelalters und seines Nachwirkens, Paderborn 7 (Munich): 33–44.

Arthur, L.B. (1999) 'Dress and the Social Control of the body', in L.B. Arthur (ed.) *Religion, Dress and the Body* (Oxford): 1–8.
Atkins, M. and R. Osborne (eds) (2006) *Poverty in the Roman World* (Cambridge).
Bagnall, R.S., Alan Cameron, S.R. Schwartz, and K.A. Worp (1987) *Consuls of the Later Roman Empire* (Atlanta).
Baratte, F. (2004) 'Le vêtement dans l'antiquité tardive: rupture ou continuité?', *AnTard* 12: 121–35.
Barber, E.J.W. (1991) *Prehistoric Textiles: The Development of Cloth in the Neolithic and Bronze Ages with Special Reference to the Aegean* (Princeton).
Barnard, M (ed.) (2007) *Fashion Theory: A Reader* (London).
——— 'Introduction', Barnard (2007): 1–14.
Barnes, T.D. (1999) 'Ambrose and Gratian', *AnTard* 7: 165–74.
Barthes, R. (1967) *Système de la Mode* (Paris), trans. M. Ward and R. Howard (London, 1985).
Beard, M. (2007) *The Roman Triumph* (Cambridge, MA).
Bender Jørgensen, L. (2008) 'Self-Bands and other Subtle Patterns in Roman Textiles', in Alfaro and Karali (2008): 135–42.
Berg, R. (2002) 'Wearing Wealth: *Ornatus* and *Mundus Muliebris* as Status Markers for Women in Imperial Rome', in R. Berg, R. Hälikkä, P. Ratis, and V. Vuolanto (eds) *Women, Wealth and Power*, Acta Instituti Romani Finlandiae, Vol. 25 (Rome): 15–73.
Berthod, B. (2001) 'Le *pallium*, insigne des évêques d'Orient et d'Occident', *Bulletin de Liaison du CIETA* 78: 14–25.
Binns, J. and R.M. Price (1991) *Cyril of Scythopolis, The Lives of the Monks of Palestine* (Kalamazoo, MI).
Block, E. (1985) 'Clothing Makes the Man: a Pattern in the *Odyssey*', *TAPhA* 115: 1–11.
Blockley, R.C. (1981) *The Fragmentary Classicising Historians of the Later Roman Empire: I* (Liverpool).
——— (1983) *The Fragmentary Classicising Historians of the Later Roman Empire: II* (Liverpool).
——— (1985) *The History of Menander the Guardsman* (Liverpool).
——— (1992) *East Roman Foreign Policy: Formation and Conduct from Diocletian to Anastasius* (Leeds).
Blondell, R. (2005) 'From Fleece to Fabric: Weaving Culture in Plato's Statesman', *OSAPh* 28: 23–75.
Bogensperger, I. (2014) 'The Multiple Functions and Lives of a Textile: the Reuse of a Garment', in Harlow and Nosch (2014a): 335–44.
Bonfante, L. (1976) *Etruscan Dress* (Baltimore).
Bosworth, A.B. (1980) 'Alexander and the Iranians', *JHS* 100: 1–21.
——— (1988) *Conquest and Empire: The reign of Alexander the Great* (Cambridge).
——— (1993) 'Arrian and Rome: the Minor Works', *ANRW* 34: 226–75.
Bowditch, P.L. (2001) *Horace and the Gift Economy of Patronage* (Berkeley).
Bradley, M. (2002) 'It All Comes Out in the Wash: Looking Harder at the Roman *Fullonica*', *JRA* 15: 20–44.
——— (2009) *Colour and Meaning in Ancient Rome* (Cambridge).
Brakke, D. (1995) *Athanasius and Asceticism* (London).
Braund, D. (1984) *Rome and the Friendly King: The Character of the Client Kingship* (London).
——— (1994) *Georgia in Antiquity: A History of Colchis and Transcaucasian Iberia 550 BC–AD 562* (Oxford).
——— (1998) 'Herodotus on the Problematics of Reciprocity', in Gill, Postlethwaite, and Seaford (1998): 159–80.

Brennan, B. (1985) 'Athanasius' *Vita Antonii*: a Sociological Interpretation', *VChr* 39.3: 209–27.
Briscoe, J. (1973) *A Commentary on Livy, Books XXXI-XXXIII* (Oxford).
Brock, S. (1992) 'Clothing Metaphors as a Means of Theological Expression in Syriac Tradition', in S. Brock (ed.) *Studies in Syriac Christianity: History, Literature and Theology* (Hampshire): 11–38.
Brown, P. (1980) 'Art and Society in Late Antiquity', in K. Weitzmann (ed.) *Age of Spirituality: a Symposium* (New York): 17–27.
——— (1981) *The Cult of the Saints: Its Rise and Function in Latin Christianity* (Chicago).
——— (1988) *The Body and Society: Men, Women and Sexual Renunciation in Early Christianity* (New York).
——— (1997) *Authority and the Sacred: Aspects of the Christianisation of the Roman World* (Cambridge).
——— (2002) *Poverty and Leadership in the Later Roman Empire* (London).
——— (2012) *Through the Eye of a Needle: Wealth, the Fall of Rome, and the Making of Christianity in the West, 350–550 AD* (Princeton).
Brunt, P.A. (1988) *Fall of the Roman Republic and Relate Essays* (Oxford).
Buckland, C. (2010) *To Praise an Emperor: Late Imperial Panegyric and the Epideictic Tradition* (Saarbrücken).
Bundrick, S.D. (2008) 'The Fabric of the City: Imaging Textile Production in Classical Athens', *Hesperia* 77.2: 283–334.
Burnish, R. (1985) *The Meaning of Baptism: A Comparison of the Teaching and Practice of the Fourth Century with the Present Day* (London).
Cairns, D. (ed.) (2005) *Body Language in the Greek and Roman Worlds* (Swansea).
Calefato, P. (2004) *Dress, Body, Culture: The Clothed Body*, trans. L. Adams (Oxford).
Cameron, Alan (1968a) 'Three Notes on the *Historia Augusta*', *CR* (n.s.) 18.1: 17–20.
——— (1968b) 'Notes on Claudian's Invectives', *CQ* (n.s.) 18: 387–411.
——— (1970) *Claudian: Poetry and Propaganda at the Court of Honorius* (Oxford).
——— (2004) 'Poetry and Literary Culture in Late Antiquity', in S. Swain and M. Edwards (eds) *Approaching Late Antiquity: The Transformation from Early to Late Empire* (Oxford): 327–54.
——— and D. Schauer (1982) 'The Last Consul: Basilius and his Diptych', *JRS* 72: 126–45.
Cameron, Averil (1976) *Flavius Cresconius Corippus, In laudem Iustini Augusti minoris* (London).
——— (1993) *The Later Roman Empire* (London).
Campbell, B. (2001) 'Diplomacy in the Roman world (c. 500 B.C.–A.D. 235)', *Diplomacy and Statecraft* 12.1: 1–22.
Canepa, M.P. (2009) *The Two Eyes of the Earth: Art and Ritual of Kingship between Rome and Sasanian Iran* (Berkeley).
Caner, D. (2006) 'Towards a Miraculous Economy: Christian Gifts and Material "Blessings" in Late Antiquity', *JECS* 14.3: 329–77.
Caseau, B. (2007a) 'Objects in Churches: the Testimony of Inventories', in Lavan, Swift, and Putzeys (2007): 551–79.
——— (2007b) 'Ordinary Objects in Christian Healing Sanctuaries', in Lavan, Swift, and Putzeys (2007): 625–54.
Chapot, V. (1873–1919) 'Segmentum', in Daremberg and Saglio (1873–1919) 4.2: 1172–5.
Chausson, F. and H. Inglebert (eds) (2003) *Costume et société dans l'Antiquité et le haut Moyen Âge* (Paris).
Chioffi, L. (2004) '*Attilica* e altre *vestes* a Roma', in Alfaro, Wild, and Costa (2004): 89–95.

Chrysos, E. (1992) 'Byzantine Diplomacy, A.D. 300–800: Means and Ends', in Shepard and Franklin (1992): 25–39.
Ciszuk, M. (2004) 'Taqueté and Damask from Mons Claudianus: a Discussion of Roman Looms for Patterned Textiles', in Alfaro, Wild, and Costa (2004): 107–13.
——— and L. Hammarlund (2008) 'Roman Looms – a Study of Craftsmanship and Technology in the Mons Claudianus Textile Project', in Alfaro and Karali (2008): 119–34.
Clark, G. (1993) *Women in Late Antiquity: Pagan and Christian Life-Styles* (Oxford).
Cleland, L. (2005) *The Brauron Clothing Catalogues: Text, Analysis, Glossary and Translation* (Oxford).
Cleland, L., G. Davies, and L. Llewellyn-Jones (eds) (2007) *Greek and Roman Dress from A to Z* (London).
——— M. Harlow, and L. Llewellyn-Jones (eds) (2005) *The Clothed Body in the Ancient World* (Oxford).
Cloke, G. (1995) *This Female Man of God: Women and Spiritual Power in the Patristic Age, A.D. 350–450* (London).
Cloud, D. (1989) 'The Client–Patron Relationship: Emblem and Reality in Juvenal's First Book', in Wallace-Hadrill (1989c): 205–18.
Colburn, C.S. and M.K. Heyn (eds) (2008) *Reading a Dynamic Canvas: Adornment in the Ancient Mediterranean World* (Cambridge).
Coleman-Norton, P.R. (1948) 'Resemblances between Cicero's *Cato Maior* and *Laelius*' *The Classical Weekly*, 41.14 (Apr. 19): 210–16.
Collins, A.W. (2012) 'The Royal Costume and Insignia of Alexander the Great', *AJPh* 133 (3): 371–402.
Coon, L.L. (1997) *Sacred Fictions: Holy Women and Hagiography in Late Antiquity* (Philadelphia).
Cormack, R. (1992) 'But is it Art?', in Shepard and Franklin (1992): 219–36.
Corrigan, P. (2008) *The Dressed Society: Clothing, the Body and Some Meanings of the World* (London).
Courbaud, E. (1873–1919) 'Imago – Rome', in Daremberg and Saglio (1873–1919) 1.2: 402–15.
Courtney, E. (1980) *A Commentary on the Satires of Juvenal* (London).
Croom, A.T. (2002) *Roman Clothing and Fashion* (Stroud).
Cutler, A. (2001) 'Gifts and Gift Exchange as Aspects of the Byzantine, Arab, and Related Economies', *DOP 55* (Washington, DC): 247–78.
——— (2005a) 'Silver Across the Euphrates: Forms of Exchange Between Sasanian Persia and the Late Roman Empire', *Mitteilungen zur Spätantiken Archäologie und Byzantinischen Kunstgeschichte* 4: 9–37.
——— (2005b) 'The Emperor's Old Clothes: Actual and Virtual Vesting and the Transmission of Power in Byzantium and Islam', in M. Balard and J.-M. Spieser (eds) *Byzance et le monde extérieur: Contacts, relations, échanges*, Byzantina Sorboniensia 21 (Paris): 195–210.
Dam, H.-J., van (1984) *P. Papinius Satius Silvae Book II: A Commentary* (Leiden).
Damhorst, M.L. (2005) 'Introduction', in M.L. Damhorst, K.A. Miller-Spillman, and S.O. Michelman (eds) *The Meanings of Dress*, 2nd edition (New York): 1–12.
Damon, C. (1997) *The Mask of the Parasite: A Pathology of Roman Patronage* (Ann Arbor, MI).
Daniel-Hughes, C. (2011) *The Salvation of the Flesh in Tertullian of Carthage: Dressing for the Resurrection* (New York).
Daremberg, C. and E. Saglio (eds) (1873–1919) *Dictionnaire des antiquités grecques et romaines d'après les textes et les monuments* (Paris).

Davis, F. (1992a) *Fashion, Culture and Identity* (Chicago) (pp. 3–15, 168–86 reprinted as 'Do Clothes Speak? What Makes Them Fashion?', Barnard (2007): 148–58).

—— (1992b) *Fashion, Culture, and Identity* (Chicago).

Davis, R. (2010) *The Book of the Pontiffs (Liber Pontificalis)*, revised edition (Liverpool).

Davis, S. (2005) 'Fashioning a Divine Body: Coptic Christianity and Ritualized Dress', *Harvard Theological Review* 98: 335–62.

De Moor, A., C. Fluck, and P. Linscheid (eds) (2013) *Drawing the Threads Together: Textiles and Footwear of the 1st Millennium AD from Egypt* (Tielt).

Deichmann, F.W. (1958) *Ravenna, Hauptstadt des spätantiken Abendlande, Bd. 3: Frühchristliche Bauten und Mosaiken von Ravenna* (Wiesbaden).

Delbrueck, R. (1929) *Die Consulardiptychen und verwandte Denkmäler* (Berlin).

Deliyannis, D.M. (2010) *Ravenna in Late Antiquity* (Cambridge).

Delmaire, R. (1989) *Largesses Sacrées et Res Privata: l'aerarium impérial et son administration du IVe au VIe siècle* (Paris).

—— (2003) 'Le vêtement, symbole de richesse et de pouvoir, d'après les textes patristiques et hagiographiques du bas-empire', in Chausson and Inglebert (2003): 85–98.

Dewar, M. (2008) 'Spinning the *Trabea*: Consular Robes and Propaganda in the Panegyrics of Claudian', in Edmondson and Keith (2008): 217–37.

Dode, Z. (2012) 'Costume as Text', in Harlow (2012a): 7–16.

Dodgeon, M.H. and S.N.C. Lieu (1994 edition) *The Roman Eastern Frontier and the Persian Wars (AD 226–363): A Documentary History* (London).

Donlan, W. (1982) 'Reciprocities in Homer', *CW* 75.3: 137–75.

—— (1989) 'The Unequal Exchange between Glaucus and Diomedes in Light of the Homeric Gift-Economy', *Phoenix* 43.1: 1–15.

—— (1998) 'Political Reciprocity in Dark Age Greece: Odysseus and his *Hetairoi*', in Gill, Postlethwaite, and Seaford (1998): 51–72.

Droß-Krüpe, K. and A. Paetz gen. Schieck (2014) 'Unravelling the Tangled Threads of Ancient Embroidery: a Compilation of Written Sources and Archaeologically Preserved Textiles', in Harlow and Nosch (2014a): 207–35.

Dyck, A.R. (2001) 'Dressing to Kill: Attire as a Proof and Means of Characterization in Cicero's Speeches', *Arethusa* 34.1: 119–30.

Edmondson, J. (2008) 'Public Dress and Social Control in Late Republican and Early Imperial Rome', in Edmondson and Keith (2008): 21–46.

—— and A. Keith (eds) (2008) *Roman Dress and the Fabrics of Roman Culture* (Toronto).

Edwards, M. (1997) *Optatus, Against the Donatists* (Liverpool).

Elsner, J. (1998) *Imperial Rome and Christian Triumph: The Art of the Roman Empire AD 100–450* (Oxford).

Engemann, J. (1999) 'Das spätantike Consulardiptychon in Halberstadt: westlich oder östlich?', *JAC* 42: 158–68.

Errington, R.M. (1996) 'The Accession of Theodosius I', *Klio* 78.2: 438–53.

—— (2006) *Roman Imperial Policy from Julian to Theodosius* (Chapel Hill, NC).

Evelyn White, H.G. (1967) *Ausonius, Opuscula*, Vols I and II (Cambridge, MA).

Faber, R.A. (2008) 'The Woven Garment as Literary Metaphor: the *Peplos* in Ciris 9–41', in Edmondson and Keith (2008): 205–16.

Farrell, J.E. (1974) *The Garment of Immortality: A Concept and Symbol on Christian Baptism* (PhD thesis, Catholic University of America).

Ferguson, E. (2009) *Baptism in the Early Church: History, Theology and Liturgy in the First Five Centuries* (Cambridge).

Bibliography

Finley, M.I. (1999a) *The World of Odysseus*, 2nd edition (Harmondsworth).
——— (1999b) *The Ancient Economy*, 2nd edition (Berkeley).
Finn, R. (2006a) *Almsgiving in the Later Roman Empire: Christian Promotion and Practice (313–450)* (Oxford).
——— (2006b) 'Portraying the Poor: Descriptions of Poverty in Christian Texts from the Late Roman Empire', in Atkins and Osborne (2006): 130–44.
Fitzgerald, W. (2007) *Martial: The World of the Epigram* (Chicago).
Fontaine, J. (1968) *Sulpice Sévère: Vie de Saint Martin*, Tome II (Paris).
——— (1969) *Sulpice Sévère: Vie de Saint Martin*, Tome III (Paris).
Fredrick, D. (ed.) (2002) *The Roman Gaze: Vision, Power, and the Body* (London).
Fredricksmeyer, E.A. (1994) 'The Kausia: Macedonian or Indian?', in I. Worthington (ed.) *Ventures into Greek History* (Oxford): 135–58.
Gabelmann H. (1977) 'Die ritterliche trabea', *JDAI* 92: 322–74.
Gager, J.G. (ed.) (1992) *Curse Tablets and Binding Spells from the Ancient World* (Oxford).
Galán Vioque, G. (2002) *Martial, Book VII A Commentary*, trans. J.J. Zoltowski (Leiden).
Garnsey, P. and G. Woolf (1989) 'Patronage of the Rural Poor in the Roman World', in Wallace-Hadrill (1989c): 153–70.
George, M. (2008) 'The "Dark Side" of the Toga', in Edmondson and Keith (2008): 94–112.
Gernet, L. (1981) '"Value" in Greek Myth', in R.L. Gordon (ed.) *Myth, Religion and Society*, (Cambridge): 111–46, 251–4.
Gill, C., N. Postlethwaite, and R. Seaford (eds) (1998) *Reciprocity in Ancient Greece* (Oxford).
Gillett, A. (2003) *Envoys and Political Communication in the Late Antique West, 411–533* (Cambridge).
Gleba, M. (2008) '*Auratae Vestes*: Gold Textiles in the Ancient Mediterranean', in Alfaro and Karali (2008): 61–78.
Goldman, N. (1994) 'Reconstructing Roman clothing', in Sebesta and Bonfante (1994): 213–40.
Graeven, H. (1892) 'Entstellte Consulardiptychen', *RM* 7: 204–21.
Granger-Taylor, H. (1982) 'Weaving Clothes to Shape in the Ancient World: the Tunic and Toga of the Arringatore', *Textile History* 13.1: 3–25.
——— (1983) 'The Two Dalmatics of St Ambrose', *Bulletin de Liaison du CIETA* 57/58: 127–73.
Graser E.R. (1940) 'The Edict of Diocletian on Maximum Prices', in T. Frank (ed.) *An Economic Survey of Ancient Rome*, Vol. 5: *Rome and Italy of the Empire* (Baltimore): 305–422.
Grayling, A.C. (2013) *Friendship* (Yale).
Greatrex, G. (1998) *Rome and Persia at War, 502–532* (Leeds).
——— and S.N.C. Lieu (2002) *The Roman Eastern Frontier and the Persian Wars: Part II AD 363–630: A Narrative Sourcebook* (London).
Green, P. (1991) *Alexander of Macedon, 356–323 BC: A Historical Biography* (Berkeley).
Green, R.P.H. (1991) *The Works of Ausonius*, edited with an introduction and commentary (Oxford).
Grig, L. (2004) *Making Martyrs in Late Antiquity* (London).
——— (2006) 'Throwing Parties for the Poor: Poverty and Splendour in the late Antique Church', in Atkins and Osborne (2006): 145–61.
Guillou, A. (1979) 'Rome, centre transit des produits de luxe d'Orient au Haut. Moyen Age', *Zograf* 10: 17–21.
Guy, L. (2003) '"Naked" Baptism in the Early Church: the Rhetoric and the Reality', *JRH* 27.2: 133–42.

Haldon, J. (1992) '"Blood and Ink": Some Observations on Byzantine Attitudes towards Warfare and Diplomacy', in Shepard and Franklin (1992): 281–94.

Hales, S. (2005) 'Men are Mars, Women are Venus: Divine Costumes in Imperial Rome', in Cleland, Harlow, and Llewellyn-Jones (2005): 131–42.

Hammond, N.G.L. (1981) *Alexander the Great: King, Commander and Statesman* (London).

——— (2000) 'The Continuity of Macedonian Institutions and the Macedonian Kingdoms of the Hellenistic Era', *Historia* 49.2: 141–60.

Hands, A.R. (1968) *Charities and Social Aid in Greece and Rome* (London).

Harkins, P.W. (1963) *St. John Chrysostom: Baptismal Instructions* (London).

Harlow, M. (2004a) 'Clothes Maketh the Man: Power Dressing and Elite Masculinity in the Later Roman World', in L. Brubaker and J.M.H. Smith (eds) *Gender in the Early Medieval World: East and West 300–900* (Cambridge): 44–69.

——— (2004b) 'Female Dress, Third–Sixth Century: the Messages in the Media?', *AnTard* 12: 203–15.

——— (2005) 'Dress in Historical Narrative: the Case of the *Historia Augusta*', in Cleland, Harlow, and Llewellyn-Jones (2005): 143–53.

——— (2007) 'The Impossible Art of Dressing to Please: Jerome and the Rhetoric of Dress', in Lavan, Swift, and Putzeys (2007): 530–50.

——— (ed.) (2012a) *Dress and Identity*, BAR International Series 2356 (Oxford).

——— (2012b) 'Dress and Identity: an Introduction', in Harlow (2012a): 1–6.

——— and M-L. Nosch (eds) (2014a) *Greek and Roman Textiles and Dress: an Interdisciplinary Anthology*, Ancient Textiles Series Vol. 19 (Oxford).

——— and M-L. Nosch (2014b) 'Weaving the Threads: Methodologies in Textiles and Dress Research for the Greek and Roman world – the State of the Art and the Case for Cross-Disciplinarity', in Harlow and Nosch (2014a): 1–33.

Harmless, J.W. (2008) 'Monasticism', Harvey and Hunter (2008): 493–517.

Harries, B. (1993) '"Strange Meeting": Diomedes and Glaucus in Iliad 6', *G&R* 40.2: 133–46.

Harrill, J.A. (2002) 'Coming of Age and Putting on Christ: the *Toga Virilis* Ceremony, its Paraenesis, and Paul's Interpretation of Baptism in Galatians', *NT* 44.3: 252–77.

Harvey, S.A. (1990) *Asceticism and Society in Crisis: John of Ephesus and the Lives of the Eastern Saints* (Berkeley).

——— (2008) 'Martyr Passions and Hagiography', in Harvey and Hunter (2008): 603–27.

Harvey, S.A. and D.G. Hunter (eds) (2008) *The Oxford Handbook of Early Christian Studies* (Oxford).

Heather, P. (1998) 'Senators and senates', in Averil Cameron and P. Garnsey (eds) *Cambridge Ancient History*, Vol. 13: *The Late Empire, AD 337–425* (Cambridge): 184–210

——— (2006) *The Fall of the Roman Empire: a New History of Rome and the Barbarians* (Oxford).

——— and J. Matthews (eds) (1991) *The Goths in the Fourth Century* (Liverpool).

Heckel W. and L. Tritle (eds) (2009) *Alexander the Great. A New History* (Chichester).

Henck, N. (2001) 'Constantius' *Paideia*, Intellectual Milieu and Promotion of the Liberal Arts', *PCPS* 47: 172–87.

Herman, G. (1987) *Ritualised Friendship and the Greek City* (Cambridge).

——— (1998) 'Reciprocity, Altruism, and the Prisoner's Dilemma: the Special Case of Classical Athens', in Gill, Postlethwaite, and Seaford (1998): 199–226.

Heskel, J. (1994) 'Cicero as Evidence for Attitudes to Dress in the Later Republic', in Sebesta and Bonfante (1994): 133–45.

Hopkins, A. and M. Wyke (eds) (2005) *Roman Bodies: From Antiquity to the Eighteenth Century* (Rome).

Hopkins, M.K. (1961) 'Social mobility in the Later Roman Empire: the Evidence of Ausonius', *CQ* (n.s.) 11.2: 239–49.
Hopman, M. (2003) 'Satire in Green: Marked Clothing and the Technique of *Indignatio* at Juvenal 5.141–45', *AJPh* 124.4: 557–74.
Howard-Johnston, J. and P.A. Hayward (eds) (1999) *The Cult of Saints in Late Antiquity and the Middle Ages: Essays on the Contribution of Peter Brown* (Oxford).
Howell, P. (2009) *Martial* (London).
Hurlock, E.B. (1965) 'Sumptuary Law', in M.E. Roach and J.B. Eicher (eds) *Dress, Adornment and the Social Order* (New York): 295–301.
James, L. (1996) *Light and Colour in Byzantine Art* (Oxford).
Jeffreys, E. (2003) 'The Beginning of Byzantine Chronography: John Malalas', in G. Marasco (ed.) *Greek and Roman Historiography in Late Antiquity: Fourth to Sixth Century A.D.* (Leiden): 497–527.
———, B. Croke, and R.D. Scott (eds) (1990) *Studies in John Malalas*, Byzantina Australiensia 6, (Sydney).
Jenks, C. (2007) 'Series Editor's Preface', in Barnard (2007): xi–xii.
Johnson, M.E. (2008) 'Christian Initiation', in Harvey and Hunter (2008): 693–710.
Jones, A.H.M. (1960 [repr. 1974]) 'The Cloth Industry under the Roman Empire', *Economic History Review* 13: 183–92 repr. in P.A. Brunt (ed.) Jones, A.H.M. (1974) *The Roman Economy: Studies in Ancient Economic and Administrative History* (Oxford).
———, J.R. Martindale, and J. Morris (1971–1992) *The Prosopography of the Later Roman Empire*, 3 vols (Cambridge).
Jones, A.R. and P. Stallybrass (2000) 'Introduction', in *Renaissance Clothing and the Materials of Memory* (Cambridge) (reprinted as 'Renaissance Clothing and the Materials of Memory: Introduction', in Barnard (2007): 58–75).
Kaczmarek, Z. (2014) 'Roman Textiles and Barbarians: Some Observations on Textile Exchange Between the Roman Empire and *Barbaricum*', in Harlow and Nosch (2014a): 323–34.
Kalavrezou, I. (ed.) (2003) *Byzantine Women and Their World* (Cambridge, MA).
Kazhdan, A.P. (1992) 'The Notion of Byzantine Diplomacy', in Shepard and Franklin (1992): 3–21.
———, A-M. Talbot, A. Cutler, E. Gregory, and N.P. Ševčenko (eds) (1991) *The Oxford Dictionary of Byzantium* (New York).
Kehl, A. (1978) 'Gewand (der Seele)', *RAC* 10: 945–1025.
Kolb, F. (1973) 'Römische Mäntel: *paenula, lacerna,* μανύη', *RM* 80: 69–167.
Krawiec, R. (2014) '"The Holy Habit and the Teachings of the Elders": Clothing and Social Memory in Late Antique Monasticism', in Upson-Saia, Daniel-Hughes, and Batten (2014a): 55–73.
Kuefler, M. (2001) *The Manly Eunuch: Masculinity, Gender Ambiguity, and Christian Ideology in Late Antiquity* (Chicago).
Labarre, S. (2003) 'Le vêtement dans la *Vie de Saint Martin (IVe s.): signe social et valeur symbolique*', Chausson and Inglebert (2003): 143–51.
Lange, E. (1802–1878) 'Lacerna', *Paulys Real-Encyclopädie der classischen Altertumswissenschaft* (Berlin) 12: 327–9.
Lavan, L., E. Swift, and T. Putzeys (eds) (2007) *Objects in Context, Objects in Use: Material Spatiality in Late Antiquity* (Leiden).
Leary, T.J. (1996) *Martial Book XIV: The Apophoreta* (London).
Lechitskaya, O. (2013) 'Tabula with the Ascension of Alexander-Dionysus in The Pushkin State Museum of Fine Arts', in De Moor, Fluck. and Linscheid (2013): 176–93.

Lee, A.D. (1991) 'The role of hostages in Roman relations with Sasanian Persia', *Historia* 40.3: 366–74.
——— (2000) *Pagans and Christians in Late Antiquity: A Sourcebook* (London).
——— (2013) *From Rome to Byzantium AD 363 to 565: The Transformation of Ancient Rome* (Edinburgh).
Lee, M.M. (2004) '"Evil Wealth of Raiment:" Deadly πέπλοι in Greek tragedy', *CJ* 99.3: 253–79.
Lenski, N. (2002) *Failure of Empire: Valens and the Roman State in the Fourth Century A.D.* (Berkeley).
Letellier-Willemin, F. (2013) 'The Embroidered Tunic of Dush – A New Approach', in De Moor, Fluck, and Linscheid (2013): 22–33.
Lewis, C.T and Short, C. (1879) *A Latin Dictionary* (Oxford).
Lewis, N. and M. Reinhold (eds) (1990) *Roman Civilization: Selected Readings*. Vol. 3: *The Empire* (New York).
Liddell, H.G. and Scott, R. (1940) *A Greek-English Lexicon* (Oxford).
Liu, J. (2009) *Collegia Centonariorum: the Guilds of Textile Dealers in the Roman West* (Leiden).
Livingstone, N. and G. Nisbet (2010) *Epigram* (Cambridge).
Llewellyn-Jones, L. (ed) (2002) *Women's Dress in the Ancient Greek World* (Swansea).
Lobrichon, G. (2003) 'Le vêtement liturgique des évêques au IXe siècle', in Chausson and Inglebert (2003): 129–41.
Lovén, L. Larsson (2014) 'Roman Art: What Can it Tell Us About Dress and Textiles? A Discussion on the Use of Visual Evidence as Sources for Textile Research', in Harlow and Nosch (2014a): 260–78.
Lyons, D. (2003) 'Dangerous Gifts: Ideologies of Marriage and Exchange in Greek Myth and Tragedy', *CA* 22: 93–134.
MacCormack, S. (1981) *Art and Ceremony in Late Antiquity* (London).
McCormick, M. (1986) *Eternal Victory: Triumphal Rulership in Late Antiquity, Byzantium and the Early Medieval West* (Cambridge).
McEvoy, M.A. (2013) *Child Emperor Rule in the Late Roman West, AD 367–455* (Oxford).
McLynn, N (2005) '"*Genere Hispanus:*" Theodosius, Spain and Nicene Orthodoxy', in K. Bowes and M. Kulikowski (eds) *Hispania in Late Antiquity: Current Perspectives* (Boston): 77–120.
MacMullen, R. (1990) 'Some Pictures in Ammianus Marcellinus', in R. MacMullen (ed) *Changes in the Roman Empire: Essays in the Ordinary* (Princeton): 78–106 (originally published in *Art Bulletin* (1964)).
Maguire, E.D. (2009) 'Dressed for Eternity: a Prelude', in P. Sellew (ed.) *Living for Eternity: The White Monastery and its Neighbourhood. Proceedings of a Symposium at the University of Minnesota, Minneapolis, 2003* [online] available at: http://egypt.cla.umn.edu/eventsr.html [accessed March 2016].
Maguire, H. (1990) 'Garments Pleasing to God: the Significance of Domestic Textile Designs in the Early Byzantine Period', *DOP* 44: 215–24.
Maier, H.O. (2006) 'Kleidung II (Bedeutung)', *RAC* 21: 1–60.
Malineau, V. (2003) 'Les éléments du costume de théâtre dans l'antiquité tardive', in Chausson and Inglebert (2003): 153–68.
Mango, C. (1986) *The Art of the Byzantine Empire, 312–1453: Sources and Documents* (Englewood Cliffs, NJ).
Mango, M.M. (1986) *Silver from Early Byzantium: The Kaper Koraon and Related Treasures* (Baltimore, Maryland).
——— (1992) 'The Monetary Value of Silver Revetments and Objects Belonging to Churches, A.D. 300–700', in S.A. Boyd and M.M. Mango (eds) *Ecclesiastical Silver Plate in Sixth-Century Byzantium* (Washington, DC): 123–36.

Mannering, U. (2000a) 'Roman Garments from Mons Claudianus', in D. Cardon and M. Feugere (eds) *Archéologie des textiles des origins au Ve siècle. Actes du colloque de Lattes, octobre 1999* (Montagnac): 283–90.

——— (2000b) 'The Roman Tradition of Weaving and Sewing: a Guide to Function?' *Archaeological Textiles Newsletter* 30: 10–15.

Marotta, V. (1999) 'Liturgia del potere. Documenti di nomina e cerimonie di investitura fra principato e tardo impero Romano', *Ostraka* 8.1: 145–220.

Marquardt, J. (1873) 'Lacerna', *Römische Staatsverwaltung* (Leipzig): 568–9.

Marshall, P. (1987) *Enmity in Corinth: Social Conventions in Paul's Relations with the Corinthians* (Tübingen).

Martorelli, R. (2004) 'Influenze religiose sulla scelta dell'abito nei primi secoli cristiani', *AnTard* 12: 231–48.

Matthews, J. (1975) *Western Aristocracies and Imperial Court AD 364–425* (Oxford).

Mauss, M. (1923–24 [2002]) *The Gift: The Form and Reason for Exchange in Archaic Societies*, trans. W.D. Halls (London).

Mayo (1984) *A History of Ecclesiastical Dress* (New York).

Mérat, A. (2013) 'Étude technique et iconographique d'un ensemble de broderies égyptiennes antiques conservées au musée du Louvre', in De Moor, Fluck, and Linscheid (2013): 126–39.

Metzger, C. (2004) 'Tissus et culte des reliques', *AnTard* 12: 183–6.

Meyers, G.E. (2013) 'Women and the Production of Ceremonial Textiles: a Re-Evaluation of Ceramic Textile Tools in Etrusco-Italic Sanctuaries', *AJA* 117.2: 247–74.

Michel, V. (2007) 'Furniture, Fixtures, and Fittings in Churches: Archaeological Evidence from Palestine (4th–8th c.) and the Role of the *Diakonikon*', in Lavan, Swift, and Putzeys (2007): 581–606.

Millar, F. (1982) 'Emperors, Frontiers and Foreign Relations, 31 BC to AD 378', *Britannia* 13: 1–23.

Missiou, A. (1998) 'Reciprocal Generosity in the Foreign Affairs of Fifth-Century Athens and Sparta', in Gill, Postlethwaite, and Seaford (1998): 181–98.

Morgan, J.R. (1999) 'Review-Discussion: *Phlegon of Tralles' Book of Marvels*, translated with an introduction and commentary by William Hansen. University of Exeter Press, 1996 pp. xvi + 215', *Helios* 2: 302–7.

Mohler, S.L. (1928) 'Apophoreta', *CJ* 23.4: 248–57.

Molloy, M. (1996) *Libanius and the Dancers* (Hildesheim).

Morrell, K.S. (1997) 'The Fabric of Persuasion: Clytaemnestra, Agamemnon, and the Sea of Garments', *CJ* 92.2: 141–65.

Morris, I. (1986) 'Gift and Commodity in Archaic Greece', *Man* (n.s.) 21: 1–17.

Mouritsen, H. (2011) *The Freedman in the Roman World* (Cambridge).

Mueller, M. (2001) 'The Language of Reciprocity in Euripides' *Medea*', *AJPh* 122.4: 471–504.

——— (2010) 'Helen's Hands: Weaving for Kleos in the *Odyssey*', *Helios* 37.1 (Spring): 1–21.

Müller, M. (2013) 'Mythological Scenes, their Roman and Pharaonic Roots, and the Role of Symmetry on Byzantine Textiles', in De Moor, Fluck, and Linscheid (2013): 194–207.

Murnaghan, S. (1987) *Disguise and Recognition in the* Odyssey (Princeton).

Muthesius, A. (1992) 'Silken Diplomacy', in Shepard and Franklin (1992): 237–48.

Nagle, D.B. (1996) 'The Cultural Context of Alexander's Speech at Opis', *TAPhA* 126: 151–72.

Nechaeva, E. (2014) *Embassies – Negotiations – Gifts: Systems of East Roman Diplomacy in Late Antiquity*, Alte Geschichte, Geographica Historica, 30 (Stuttgart).

Neri, V. (2004) 'Vestito e corpo nel pensiero dei padri tardoantichi', *AnTard* 12: 223–30.

Olovsdotter, C. (2005) *The Consular Image: An Iconological Study of the Consular Diptychs* (Oxford).
Olson, K. (2008) *Dress and the Roman Woman: Self-presentation and Society* (London).
Oppenheim, P.P. (1931) *Das Mönchskleid im christlichen Altertum* (Freiburg).
Osharina, O. (2013) 'The Coptic Rider on Textiles from the Hermitage Collection', in De Moor, Fluck, and Linscheid (2013): 208–25.
Osteen, M. (2002a) 'Introduction', Osteen (2002b): 1–42.
——— (2002b) (ed.) *The Question of the Gift: Essays Across Disciplines* (London).
Pantelia, M.C. (1993) 'Spinning and Weaving: Ideas of Domestic Order in Homer', *AJPh* 114: 493–501.
Parani, M.G. (2007) 'Defining Personal Space: Dress and Accessories in Late Antiquity', in Lavan, Swift, and Putzeys (2007): 497–529.
——— (2008) 'Fabrics and Clothing', in E. Jeffreys, J. Haldon, and R. Cormack (eds) *The Oxford Handbook of Byzantine Studies* (Oxford): 407–20.
Parkin, A. (2006) '"You Do Him no Service:" an Exploration of Pagan Almsgiving', in Atkins and Osborne (2006): 60–82.
Perani, J. and N.H. Wolff (1999) *Cloth, Dress and Art Patronage in Africa* (Oxford).
Peterman, G.W. (1997) *Paul's Gift from Philippi: Conventions of Gift-Exchange and Christian Giving* (Cambridge).
Petersen, L.H. (2006) *The Freedman in Roman Art and Art History* (Cambridge).
Pitts, L.F. (1989) 'Relations Between Rome and the German "Kings" on the Middle Danube in the First to the Fourth Centuries A.D.', *JRS* 79: 45–58.
Porter, J. (ed.) (1999) *Constructions of the Classical Body* (Ann Arbor, MI).
Postlethwaite, N. (1998) 'Akhilleus and Agamemnon: Generalized Reciprocity', in Gill, Postlethwaite, and Seaford (1998): 93–104.
Price, R.M. (1991) *Theodoret of Cyrrhus: A History of the Monks of Syria* (Kalamazoo, MI).
——— (2008) 'Martyrdom and the Cult of the Saints', in Harvey and Hunter: 808–25.
Pritchard, F. (2006) *Clothing Culture: Dress in Egypt in the First Millennium AD* (Manchester).
Quasten, J. (1942) 'A Pythagorean Idea in Jerome', *AJP* 63.2: 207–15.
Rabinowitz, N.S. (1993) *Anxiety Veiled: Euripides and the Traffic in Women* (Ithaca).
Ramsey, B. (2000) *John Cassian: The Institutes* (New York).
Ramsey, J.T. (2003) *Cicero Philippics I-II* (Cambridge).
Rance, P. (2007) 'The Date of the Military Compendium of Syrianus Magister (Formerly the Sixth-Century *Anonymus Byzantinus*)', *BZ* 100: 701–37.
Rebenich, S. (2000) 'Der Kirchenvater Hieronymus als Hagiograph: Die *Vita s. Pauli primi eremitae*', in K. Elm (ed.) *Beiträge zur Geschichte des Paulinerordens* (Berlin): 23–40.
——— (2002) *Jerome* (London).
Reden, von, S. (1995) *Exchange in Ancient Greece* (London).
——— (1998) 'The commodification of symbols: reciprocity and its perversions in Menander', in Gill, Postlethwaite, and Seaford (1998): 255–78
Rees, R. (2002) *Layers of Loyalty in Latin Panegyric: AD 289–307* (Oxford).
——— (2004) *Diocletian and the Tetrarchy* (Edinburgh).
Reinhold, M. (1969) 'On Status Symbols in the Ancient World', *CJ* 64.7: 300–304.
——— (1970) *History of Purple as a Status Symbol in Antiquity* (Coll. Latomus 116) (Brussels).
——— (1971) 'Usurpation of Status and Status Symbols in the Roman Empire', *Historia: Zeitschrift für Alte Geschichte* 20.2/3 (second Qtr.): 275–302.
Rimell, V. (2008) *Martial's Rome: Empire and the Ideology of Epigram* (Cambridge).
Ristow, S. (2004) 'Kleidung I (Mode u. Tracht)', *RAC* 20 (Stuttgart): 1263–74.
Roberts, M. (1989) *The Jeweled Style: Poetry and Poetics in Late Antiquity* (London).

Rösch, G. (1978) *Onoma basileias: Studien zum offiziellen Gebrauch der Kaisertitel in spätantiker und frühbyzantinischer Zeit* (Vienna).

Ross, R. (2008) *Clothing: A Global History* (Cambridge).

Roth, P. (1993) 'The theme of corrupted xenia in Aeschylus' *Oresteia*', *Mnemosyne* 46.1: 1–17.

Rothe, U. (2012a) 'Clothing in the Middle Danube Provinces: the Garments, their Origins and their Distribution', *Jahreshefte des Österreichischen Archäologischen Instituts*, Vol. 81: 137–231.

——— (2012b) 'Dress and Cultural Identity in the Roman Empire', in Harlow (2012a): 59–68.

——— (2013) 'Whose Fashion? Men, Women and Roman Culture as Reflected in Dress in the Cities of the Roman North-West', in E. Hemelrijk and G. Woolf (eds) *Women and the Roman City in the Latin West* (Leiden): 243–68.

Rousseau, P. (1971) 'The Spiritual Authority of the "Monk-Bishop" Eastern Elements in Some Western Hagiography of the Fourth and Fifth Centuries', *JThS* 22.2: 380–419.

——— (1999) *Pachomius: The Making of a Community in Fourth-Century Egypt*, revised edition (London).

Rowlandson, J. (ed.) (1998) *Women and Society in Greek and Roman Egypt: a Sourcebook* (Cambridge).

Rummel, von P. (2007) *Habitus barbarus: Kleidung und Repräsentation spätantiker Eliten im 4. und 5. Jahrhundert* (Berlin)

Rutschowskaya, M.-H. (1990) *Coptic Fabrics* (Paris).

Sadashige, J. (2002) 'Catullus and the gift of sentiment in Republican Rome', in Osteen (2002b): 149–71

Saller, R.P. (1982) *Personal Patronage under the Early Empire* (Cambridge).

——— (1983) 'Martial on Patronage and Literature', *CQ* (n.s.) 33.I: 246–57.

——— (1989) 'Patronage and Friendship in Early Imperial Rome: Drawing the Distinction', in Wallace-Hadrill (1989c): 49–62.

Salomonson J.W. (1955) *Chair, Sceptre and Wreath: Historical Aspects of their Representation on Some Roman Sepulchral Monuments* (Amsterdam).

Salzman, M.R. (1990) *On Roman time: the Codex-Calendar of 354 and the Rhythms of Urban Life in Late Antiquity* (Oxford).

——— (2002) *The Making of a Christian Aristocracy: Social and Religious Change in the Western Roman Empire* (Cambridge, MA).

Sapir, E. (1931) 'Fashion', in *Encyclopaedia of the Social Sciences* (New York) (reprinted as 'Fashion', in Barnard (2007): 39–45).

Scheid, J. and Svenbro, J. (1996) *The Craft of Zeus: Myths of Weaving and Fabric*, trans. C. Volk (Cambridge, MA).

Scott, R. (1992) 'Diplomacy in the Sixth Century: the Evidence of John Malalas', in Shepard and Franklin (1992): 159–66.

Seaford, R. (1994) *Reciprocity and Ritual: Homer and Tragedy in the Developing City-State* (Oxford).

——— (1998) 'Introduction', in Gill, Postlethwaite, and Seaford (1998): 1–12.

Sebesta, J. and L. Bonfante (eds) (1994) *The World of Roman Costume* (Madison).

Serfass, A. (2014) 'Unravelling the *Pallium* Dispute Between Gregory the Great and John of Ravenna', in Upson-Saia, Daniel-Hughes, and Batten (2014a): 75–96.

Shackleton Bailey, D.R. (1993) *Martial Epigrams*, Vol. 3 (Cambridge, MA).

Shepard, J. and S. Franklin (eds) (1992) *Byzantine Diplomacy: Papers of the Twenty-Fourth Spring Symposium of Byzantine Studies, Cambridge, March 1990* (Aldershot).

Sivan, H. (1993) *Ausonius of Bordeaux: Genesis of a Gallic Aristocracy* (London).

―――― (1996) 'Was Theodosius I a usurper?', *Klio* 78: 198–211.
Smith, M.E. (2004) 'The Archaeology of Ancient State Economies', *Annual Review of Anthropology* 33: 73–102.
Squire, M. (2011) *The Art of the Body: Antiquity and its Legacy* (New York).
Stauffer, A. (1996) 'Cartoons for weavers from Greco-Roman Egypt', D.M. Bailey (ed) *Archeological Research in Roman Egypt: the proceedings of the Seventeenth Classical Colloquium of the Department of Greek and Roman Antiquities, British Museum held on 1–4 December, 1993* (Ann Arbor, MI): 224–30.
―――― (2008) 'A Closer Look to Cartoons for Weavers from Graeco-Roman Egypt', in Alfaro and Karali (2008): 159–63.
Stern, H. (1953) *Le Calendrier de 354: étude sur son texte et ses illustrations* (Paris).
Stewart, A. (1997) *Art, Desire, and the Body in Ancient Greece* (Cambridge).
Stone, S. (2001) 'The Toga: from National to Ceremonial Costume', in Sebesta and Bonfante (1994): 13–45.
Stoneman, R. (2004) *Alexander the Great*, 2nd edition (London).
Sullivan, J.P. (1991) *Martial: The Unexpected Classic – A Literary and Historical Study* (Cambridge).
Swift, E. (2009) *Style and Function in Roman Decoration: Living with Objects and Interiors* (Burlington, VT).
Tarlo, E. (1996) *Clothing Matters: Dress and Identity in India* (London).
Taylor, C.C. (2014) 'Burial Threads: a Late Antique Textile and the Iconography of the Virgin Annunciate Spinning', in Harlow and Nosch (2014): 399–414.
Taylor, L. (2002) *The Study of Dress History* (Manchester).
Thédenat, H. (1873–1919) 'Lacerna', Daremberg and Saglio (1873–1919): 901–2.
Thomson, R.W. and J. Howard-Johnston (1999) *The Armenian History Attributed to Sebeos*, Part I: *Translation and Notes, with Historical Commentary* (Liverpool).
Thompson, W. (1982) 'Weaving: a man's work,' *CW*, vol. 75.4: 217–22.
Tinnefeld, F. (1993) 'Ceremonies for Foreign Ambassadors at the Court of Byzantium and their Political Background', *ByzF* 19: 193–213.
Tomlin, R.S.O. (1988) 'The Curse Tablets', in B. Cunliffe (ed.) *The Temple of Sulis Minerva at Bath*, Vol. 2: *The Finds from the Sacred Spring* (Oxford): 59–277.
Treadgold, W. (2007) *The Early Byzantine Historians* (Basingstoke and New York).
Treggiari, S. (1975) 'Jobs in the Household of Livia', *PBSR* 43: 48–77.
Trinkl, E. (2014) 'The Wool Basket: Function, Depiction and Meaning of the *Kalathos*', in Harlow and Nosch (2014a): 190–206.
Upson-Saia, K. (2011) *Early Christian Dress: Gender, Virtue, and Authority* (Oxford)
――――, C. Daniel-Hughes and A.J. Batten (eds) (2014a) *Dressing Judeans and Christians in Antiquity* (Farnham)
―――― (2014b) 'Introduction: "What shall we wear?"', in Upson-Saia, Daniel-Hughes and Batten (2014a): 1–18
Urbano, A.P. (2014) 'Sizing Up the Philosopher's Cloak: Christian Verbal and Visual Representations of the *Tribōn*', in Upson-Saia, Daniel-Hughes, and Batten (2014a): 175–294.
Van Dam, R. (1995) 'Self-Representation in the Will of Gregory of Nazianus', *JThS* (n.s.) 46.1: 118–48.
Van Wees, H. (2005) 'Trailing Tunics and Sheepskin Coats: Dress and Status in Early Greece', in Cleland, Harlow, and Llewellyn-Jones (2005): 44–51.
Veilleux, A. (1980) *Pachomian Koinonia*, Vol. 1: *Life of Saint Pachomius and His Disciples* (Kalamazoo, MI).
―――― (1981) *Pachomian Koinonia*, Vol. 2: *Pachomian Chronicles and Rules* (Kalamazoo, MI).

Verboven, K. (2002) *The Economy of Friends: Economic Aspects of* Amicitia *and Patronage in the Late Republic* (Brussels).

Verhecken-Lammens, C. (2013) '"Flying Thread" Brocading – A Technical Approach', in De Moor, Fluck, and Linscheid (2013): 140–49.

Veyne, P. (1990) *Bread and Circuses: The Historical Sociology and Political Pluralism*, translated by B. Pearce, abridged edition (London).

Vivian, T. and A.N. Athahassakis (2003) *Athanasius The Life of Antony: The Coptic Life and The Greek Life* (Kalamazoo, MI).

Volbach, W.F. (1976) *Elfenbeinarbeiten der Spätantike und des frühen Mittelalters*, third edition (Mainz).

Vout, C. (1996) 'The Myth of the Toga: Understanding the history of Roman Dress', *G&R* 43.2: 204–20.

Wallace-Hadrill, A. (1989a) 'Introduction', in Wallace-Hadrill (1989c): 1–14.

⸻ (1989b) 'Patronage in Roman Society: from Republic to Empire', in Wallace-Hadrill (1989c): 63–88.

⸻ (1989c) *Patronage in Ancient Society* (London).

Ware, C. (2012) *Claudian and the Roman Epic Tradition* (Cambridge).

Webb, R. (2008) *Demons and Dancers: Performance in Late Antiquity* (London).

Weber, G. (2009) 'The Court of Alexander the Great as Social System', in W. Heckel and L. Tritle (eds) (2009): 83–98.

Webster, J. (2001) 'Creolizing the Roman Provinces', *AJA* 105.2: 209–25.

Wenger, A. (1970) *Jean Chrysostome: Huit Catéchèses Baptismales*, Sources Chrétiennes 2nd edition (Paris).

Whitaker, E.C. (ed.) (1970) *Documents of the Baptismal Liturgy* (London).

Whitby, M. (2008) 'Byzantine Diplomacy: Good Faith, Trust and Co-Operation in International Relations in Late Antiquity', in P. de Souza and J. France (eds) *War and Peace in Ancient and Medieval History* (Cambridge): 120–40.

White, C. (1998) *Early Christian Lives* (London).

White, P. (1975) 'The Friends of Martial, Statius, and Pliny, and the Dispersal of Patronage', *HSCP* 79: 265–300.

⸻ (1978) '*Amicitia* and the Profession of Poetry in Early Imperial Rome', *JRS* 68: 74–92.

Wild, J.P. (1970) *Textile Manufacture in the Northern Provinces* (Cambridge).

⸻ (1985) 'The Clothing of Britannia, Gallia Belgica, and Germania Inferior', *ANRW* II: 12.3: 364–422.

⸻ (1994) 'Tunic no. 4219: an Archaeological and Historical Perspective', *Riggisberger Berichte* 2: 9–36.

Williams, C.A. (2004) *Martial: Epigrams Book 2* (Oxford).

Williams, M.S. (2008) *Authorised Lives in Early Christian Biography* (Cambridge).

Wilson, E. (1985) 'Introduction', in E. Wilson *Adorned in Dreams: Fashion and Modernity* (London): 1–15 (reprinted as '*Adorned in Dreams:* Introduction', Barnard (2007): 393–7).

Wilson, L.M. (1924) *The Roman Toga* (Baltimore).

⸻ (1938) *The Clothing of the Ancient Romans* (Baltimore).

Wohl, V. (1998) *Intimate Commerce: Exchange, Gender, and Subjectivity in Greek Tragedy* (Austin).

Wolfram, H. (1987) *History of the Goths*, trans. T.J. Dunlap (Berkeley).

Wood, I. (2000) 'The Exchange of Gifts Among the Late Antique Aristocracy', in M. Almagro-Gorbea, J.M. Álvarez Martínez, J.M. Blázquez Martínez, and S. Rovira (eds) *El Disco de Teodosio*, Publicaciones del Gabinete de antigüedades de la Real academia de la historia: Estudios 5 (Madrid): 301–14.

Woodfin, W.T. (2012) *The Embodied Icon: Liturgical Vestments and Sacramental Power in Byzantium* (Oxford).
——— (2013) 'Repetition and Replication: Sacred and Secular Patterned Silks in Byzantium', in C. Nesbitt and M. Jackson (eds) *Experiencing Byzantium: Papers from the 44th Spring Symposium of Byzantine Studies* (Farnham): 35–55.
Wyke, M. (1998) *Parchments of Gender: Deciphering the Bodies of Antiquity* (Oxford).
Yamagata, N. (2005) 'Clothing and Identity in Homer: the Case of Penelope's Web', *Mnemosyne* 58 (4): 539–46.
Zanker, G. (1998) 'Beyond Reciprocity: The Akhilleus–Priam Scene in *Iliad* 24', in Gill, Postlethwaite, and Seaford (1998): 73–92.
Ziegler, K. (1949) 'Paradoxographoi', *RE* 18.3 1137–66.

Index

Achilles 23–4, 106–7
Aeneas 106–7
Agamemnon 24, 27
Agathangelos 68–9, 70
Agathias 62
Alexander the Great 29–32, 33, 171
ambassadors 55–6, 58, 59, 60, 61, 63, 69–70, 171
Ammianus Marcellinus 112, 114, 115
Andromache 107
Anthemius (consul 515) *see* diptychs, of Anthemius
Antony, saint 14, 17, 18, 130, 136, 139, 141, 146, 149–56; *see also* Athanasius, bishop of Alexandria
Areobindus *see* diptychs, of Areobindus
Arete 26
Armenia 57, 68–9, 70–3, 79; *see also* Agathangelos; Faustus Buzandats'i; Moses Khorenats'i
Arrian 8–9, 31–2
Asterius 91–2
Athanasius, bishop of Alexandria 14, 15, 17, 130, 141, 149–56, 157, 176
Athens 11, 27–9
Attila: appearance 66–7, 70, 142; embassies to 57–8, 59, 61, 69–70; gifts of clothing and 66, 69–70, 172
Ausonius 15, 18, 90, 91, 97, 104, 106, 117–18, 151, 175; gift of *trabea* 14, 17, 57, 78, 89–90, 93–4, 97, 98–100, 101, 102, 103, 107–17, 173–4; *Gratiarum Actio* (thanksgiving speech for consulship) 44, 89, 93–4, 97, 109–11, 174; tutor to Gratian 99, 107–8, 114–15, 173
authority 5, 7, 13–18, 22, 27, 29, 39, 48, 69, 70, 73; in diplomatic contexts 56–7, 60–9, 72, 74–5, 76–9, 80, 89, 171–2; imperial 46, 48, 90, 92, 101–3, 104, 107, 108, 111, 113–19, 173, 174; political 2, 9, 13–14, 16, 23, 29–33, 34, 92, 90, 92, 101–3, 104–5, 117–18, 129, 171–2; religious 2, 13–14, 16, 17, 23, 26, 129, 135, 136–7, 139–43, 143–6, 146–56, 157, 175–6; symbolised through clothing 2–3, 7, 13–18, 56–7, 65, 67–9, 72, 73, 76–9, 80, 112, 129, 135, 136–7, 139–43, 143–6, 146–56; uncertain or problematic 9, 14, 15, 17, 18, 27, 46, 66, 67–9, 79, 80, 107, 111, 118, 143–6, 146–56, 170–1, 173, 176–7
Avars 59, 62, 172

baptism 14, 78, 137–9, 142
Barthes, Roland 4–5, 14
Basilius, Anicius Faustus Albinus (consul 541) *see* diptychs, of Basilius
Basil of Caesarea 15, 92, 109, 131, 133
body, the 2, 3–4, 6–7, 15, 17, 28, 31, 39, 78, 79, 119, 129, 134–6, 141, 175; *see also* relics
bribery 10, 28, 62, 173

Caesar Gallus 90, 97
charity (euergetism) 10, 130–4, 175
chlamys 3, 13, 14, 68, 69, 116, 118, 131, 145; as costume of emperor and officials 14, 38, 69, 77–8, 97, 98, 139, 171; decoration 77–9, 172; Tzath's *chlamys* 1–3, 14, 76–9, 172; *see also* decorative clothing elements; imperial portraiture; purple
Christianity *see* clothing, in Christian literature
Chrysostom, John 92, 109, 137–8
Cicero 35, 44, 93–4
Claudian 63–4, 89, 90, 93, 97, 101, 103, 104–6, 107, 108, 118; *see also* Stilicho
clavi 90
clothing: ability to disguise/reveal 6–7, 25, 38–9, 138–9, 140; of bishops (*see pallium*); of Christ and Apostles 134–5, 139, 143–5;

in Christian literature (*see* Antony, saint; Athanasius, bishop of Alexandria; baptism; Gregory of Tours; Jerome; *melōte*; *pallium*; Paul of Thebes; relics; Sulpicius Severus); as a 'cultural symbol' 6–7, 11; deadly 26–8, 141–3, 142n96, 176; in diplomacy (*see* ambassadors; bribery; embassies; investiture; silk; tribute); economic value of 10–13, 24, 26, 38, 43, 59–60, 74, 133–4, 173; fashion *faux pas* 6, 139–41, 142n96; legislation 6–7, 63, 143n99; as a literary metaphor 8–9, 12, 26–8, 35, 44–5, 137–8 (*see also* baptism; clothing, fashion *faux pas*; Martial; weaving); manufacture of 8, 9–11, 22, 25, 42, 90, 99, 133, 170, 171 (*see also* weaving); monastic (*see melōte*); of officials (*see chlamys*; decorative clothing elements; insignia; investiture; toga; *trabea*); in patron-client relationship (*see* patronage; Martial); in philosophy 28; role in imperial succession 46, 112, 112n119, 142n96 (*see also chlamys*; clothing, fashion *faux pas*); as a status symbol (*see* status); terminology 4–5 (*see also trabea*); theft of 133; in tragedy 26–8; in wills 12, 141, 150, 153; and women 7, 26–8, 38, 43, 45, 57–8, 72, 91, 133–4; *see also chlamys*; decorative clothing elements; dress studies; gifts and gift-giving; gold; *himation*; imperial portraiture; investiture; Martial; *melōte*; memory; *pallium*; purple; relics; silk; *toga*; *trabea*; *tunica*; Tzath, ruler of the Lazi; *vestiarium*; weaving
Clytemnestra 27
Codex-Calendar of 354 *see* Caesar Gallus
colour 38–9; *see also* gold; purple; weaving
Constantia (daughter of Constantius II, wife of Gratian) 104, 111–13; *see also* Constantius II; Gratian
Constantine 46, 68–9, 111, 112, 132, 139, 142
Constantius, Flavius (consul) *see* diptychs, Halberstadt
Constantius II 68–9, 72, 117, 142; as decoration on Ausonius' *trabea* 17, 89, 94, 100, 104, 108, 110, 117, 173 (*see also* imperial portraiture); as Gratian's father in law 104, 108, 111–13 (*see also* Constantia); military titles 115–16; *paideia* 114–15; and the Roman senate 113–14; *see also* Gratian
consuls *see* Ausonius; diptychs; imperial portraiture; insignia; *trabea*

control (of resources) 1, 6–9, 18, 27, 32, 34, 40, 60–2, 64, 74, 76, 98, 118, 143, 150, 177; *see also* luxury; resources; silk; wealth
Coon, Lynda 143–5
Cyprian of Carthage 131
Cyril of Jerusalem 142
Cyril of Scythopolis 146–8

debt *see* obligation
decorative clothing elements 2, 11, 56, 89, 93, 100–1, 116–17, 118; embroidered (*see* weaving); figural 2, 11, 76–8, 90–3, 97, 100, 101–4, 104–7, 110 (*see also* diptychs; imperial portraiture; insignia; *trabea*, decoration of); religious 90–1; *see also chlamys*; *clavi*; clothing; gold; *orbiculi*; purple; *segmenta*; *tablion*; *tabulae*; *trabea*; weaving
Deianeira 27
Diodorus Siculus 31
diplomacy 61, 72, 80, 172; clothing in diplomacy 56, 59–63, 65–70, 70–5, 76–9, 174; gifts in diplomacy 10, 16–17, 59–63, 67; language of 75; weaving as symbol of 55–6, 58; *see also* ambassadors; bribery; embassies; investiture; Persia; silk; tribute
diptychs 14, 17, 89, 90, 94, 97–8, 100, 101–4, 105, 108, 112, 117, 118; of Anthemius 89, 97, 101–2, 103–4; of Areobindus 89, 102; of Basilius, Anicius Faustus Albinus *Figure 3.2*, 89, 101, 102, 103, 116; Halberstadt (Flavius Constantius) *Figure 3.1*, 89, 97, 101–2, 103, 116; of Stilicho (*see* Stilicho); *see also* imperial portraiture; *trabea*, decoration of
display 3, 6–7, 9, 12, 17, 43, 57, 71–5, 77–8, 102, 112, 114, 135, 143–6, 150, 171, 175; in museums 4; of wealth 9, 11, 26, 36, 61–2, 71–5 (*see also* luxury; wealth)
dress *see* clothing; dress studies
dress studies 3–7; *see also* clothing
dyes *see* colour; purple

Early Empire 7, 8–9, 22, 109; clothing gifts in 34–47, 171, 174 (*see also* Martial; patronage); diplomacy in 16, 61, 64, 66, 70, 77, 172
Elijah and Elisha *Figure 4.1* 14, 129, 144, 145–6, 148, 154, 156, 175
embassies 59, 61, 63; *see also* ambassadors
emperors *see* clothing, role in imperial succession; Constantius II; decorative

clothing elements; diptychs; Gratian; Justin I; Justinian; Maurice
epic (heroic) tradition 26–7, 30, 47, 103, 104–7, 118, 174; *see also* Claudian; clothing; Homer; Odysseus; Stilicho
Epictetus 8–9
Eumenes of Cardia 32–3
Eunapius 73
Eusebius 132
Euthymius 146–8

Faustus Buzandats'i 72

gifts and gift-giving 2, 14, 15, 16, 18, 23, 27, 30, 32, 36–7, 39–44; Christian 130–4, 136, 141–2, 145–6, 147–57 (*see also* charity); concepts surrounding 3, 9–10, 13, 22, 23, 29–30, 56, 65–80, 170 (*see also* memory; obligation; protection; submission); diplomatic 1–3, 10, 31, 33–4, 56, 58–62, 64–6, 68–80; from divinities 104–6, 137–8; to divinities 28, 34; domestic 15, 29, 39–42 (*see also* patronage); imperial 98–101 (*see also* largess; *ministri largitionum*); problematic nature of 10, 28, 30 (*see also* bribery; clothing, deadly; tribute); studies and theories of 9–10; value of 10, 29, 39–43, 56, 58–62, 74–5; *xenia* 23–6; *see also* bribery; clothing; diplomacy; Homer; obligation; Odysseus; patronage; reciprocity; tribute
gold 24, 36, 68; on clothing 1, 11, 47, 56, 60, 77–9, 104, 108, 110, 111, 142, 172; as diplomatic gift 10, 56, 59, 80; *see also* decorative clothing elements; insignia; Tzath, ruler of the Lazi
Goths 59, 67
Gratian 17, 42, 90, 98–119, 154, 173; and Ausonius 17, 57, 89, 90, 99, 108, 110, 117–18; and Constantius II 100, 104–5, 108, 111–19; education 114–15 (*see also paideia*); gift of *trabea* 17, 57, 89, 90, 98–100, 107–19, 173–5; marriage to Constantia 104–5, 111–13, 115; military abilities 94, 109, 115–17; and Theodosius 116; and Valentinian I 111–14, 115; *see also* Ausonius
Gregory of Tours 15, 135, 141–3
Gregory the Great 135–6, 144

Halberstadt diptych *see* diptychs, Halberstadt
Helen 107

Hellenistic period 29–33, 39, 42, 46, 47; *see also* Alexander the Great
Hercules 27
himation 144; of Antony 149–56, 176; *see also pallium*
Historia Augusta 46–7, 75, 99
Homer 2, 10, 23–6, 29, 30, 31, 41, 47–8, 57, 58, 106, 177
Homeric period *see* Homer
Horace 35–6, 40
Huns 58–9, 61, 66; *see also* Attila

identity 6, 13, 14, 22, 25–6, 36, 39, 41, 70, 138, 144, 170, 177; *see also* Odysseus
Iliad 23–5; *see also* Homer
imperial portraiture 90, 105; on clothing 1–3, 77–9, 89, 90–3, 100–1, 101–4, 105, 108–18, 148, 175; connected to the prototype 92, 109–10, 148, 175; *see also chlamys*; decorative clothing elements; *trabea*; Tzath, ruler of the Lazi
insignia 30, 33, 58, 68–9, 77–8, 108; *see also* investiture
investiture 31, 109–10, 172; foreign or diplomatic 1–3, 16, 33–4, 65, 68–9, 73, 76–9; when costume was worn 108–9; *see also* imperial portraiture; purple; Tzath, ruler of the Lazi

Jerome 6, 15, 17, 176; charity 131; *Vita Pauli primi eremetae* 130, 149–56
John of Ephesus 133–4
Julian 112, 113
Justin I 1–3, 16, 57, 76–9; *see also* Avars; Tzath, ruler of the Lazi
Justinian 62, 64, 74, 79, 92

lacerna 38–9, 42, 43, 44
largess (generosity) 31, 36, 42, 44, 46, 98, 99, 100, 108, 111, 118, 174–5; *see also ministri largitionum*
Lazica (the Lazi) 1–2, 56–7, 71, 75, 76, 79, 172; *see also* Tzath, ruler of the Lazi
Libanius 138
Livy 33–4
luxury 9–11, 17, 30, 32, 39–40, 60–1, 63, 74, 99, 133, 137, 138, 173

Malalas 1–3, 15, 64–5, 67, 76–9, 80, 151, 172; *see also* Justinian; queen of Sabir Huns; Tzath, ruler of the Lazi
Martial 6, 10, 16, 22, 36–46, 89, 100, 111, 130, 151, 174; clothing as a metaphor for

patron-client relationship in poems 43–6; and control of luxury resources 39–40; defines social status through clothing 38–9; gifts 37–8, 40–1; patron-client relationship 36–46; as perfect client 42, 44, 45; poetic persona 37
Martin, saint 131, 139–41; *see also* Sulpicius Severus
Maurice 73, 75–6, 135
Mauss, Marcel 9–10; *see also* gifts and gift-giving, studies and theories of
Medea 27
melōte 14, 130, 139, 144–5, 148, 151, 153–4, 157, 176
memory (remembrance) 10, 25, 31, 33, 36, 43–4, 61, 72, 74, 78, 79, 92, 105, 109, 112, 116, 117, 136, 172; *see also* Odysseus
Menander Protector 56, 59–60, 62, 74, 80
ministri largitionum 99–101, 118, 174
Moors 68–9
Moses Khorenats'i 68, 70

obligation (debt): clothing as a symbol of 3, 10, 32, 35, 42, 44, 47, 75, 118, 134, 171
Odysseus 23, 25–6, 34, 177
Odyssey see Homer; Odysseus
orbiculi 11, 90
Ovid 106

paideia (education) 13, 23, 94, 114–15, 117, 144, 173, 175, 177
pallium 3, 13, 14, 17, 38, 75, 130, 135, 139, 141, 144–5, 146, 148, 149–56, 157, 176
patronage 10, 16, 61, 106, 111, 115, 174–5; Christian 130–4; Republic and Early Empire 35–46, 48; *see also* Martial
Paul, Apostle 134–5, 136, 137; *see also* relics
Paul of Thebes 130, 149–56, 157; as a Latin saint 152, 153, 155; *see also* Jerome
Penelope 26, 107
Persia 1–3, 30, 64, 68, 70–9, 172; gifts of clothing and 29, 30–1, 47, 71–6; relations with Roman Empire 1–3, 16, 64–5, 70–6, 76–9, 173; and silk 74–5; *see also* bribery; gifts and gift-giving; gold; silk; tribute; Tzath, ruler of the Lazi
philosophy *see* clothing, in philosophy
Phlegon of Tralles 34
Plato 25, 27, 36
Plutarch 29, 31–3
Priam 23–4, 36
Priscus, author 15, 58, 59, 60, 61, 66–7, 69–70, 80

Priscus, bishop of Lyons 141–2, 154
Procopius, author 68–9, 70
Procopius, usurper 111–12, 116, 142n96
protection: clothing as a symbol of 2–3, 25, 27, 31, 36, 57, 65–6, 68–9, 72, 75, 78–80, 92, 105, 148, 177
purple 1, 9, 11, 12, 30–1, 32, 38, 68, 75, 77–8, 112, 140; *see also* Alexander the Great; decorative clothing elements; insignia; investiture; silk

queen of Sabir Huns 64–5, 76, 172

reciprocity 9–10, 22, 29, 76, 118, 134, 152, 172, 177; in Homeric poetry 9–10, 23–6; *see also* gifts and gift-giving; Homer; Odysseus
relics 129, 134–6, 141, 145, 157; clothing relics 17, 134–6, 154, 175
Republican Rome 7, 8, 16, 109, 171, 172; clothing gifts in 33–6; diplomacy in 56, 61, 64–6, 76, 77
resources 10–12, 36, 43, 46, 57, 60–3, 70–2, 74, 129, 134, 173
'Romanisation' 62–3
Rufinus 63–4

Saturnalia 36, 40, 46
Scheid, John and Jasper Svenbro 8–9, 14, 24, 34
segmenta 90
Seneca 36–7, 41
Sidonius Apollinaris 17, 89, 90, 97, 98, 100, 101, 103, 104, 106–7, 108, 118
silk 10, 11, 12, 39, 90, 133, 135; in diplomacy 56, 59–61, 66, 74, 77, 100; in relations with Persia 74–5, 173; *see also* gifts and gift-giving; investiture; Persia; purple
Sparta 29
sportula 41–2
status: clothing as a symbol of 2, 5–7, 9, 11–12, 22, 25, 29, 30–2, 34–6, 38–40, 42–5, 46, 56–7, 61, 63–5, 68–70, 73, 77–9, 92, 101–3, 109, 117, 130, 140, 141, 144, 170–2
Stilicho 89, 104–6, 107, 108, 116; *see also* Claudian; epic tradition
stripping: of the clergy 143n105, 144n117; of foreign rulers 67; *see also* investiture
submission: clothing as a symbol of 3, 16, 57, 61, 67, 70, 72, 75, 79, 80, 152, 172, 173, 177
Suetonius 36, 109
Sulpicius Severus 131, 139–41

tablion 77–9, 170, 172
tabulae 11, 90
Theodoret of Cyrrhus 142–3
Theodosius I 74, 109–10, 116; *see also* Gratian
Tiberius II Constantius 73
toga 9, 27, 33, 39, 41–2, 43, 44, 77, 97, 103, 105; *toga picta* 93, 94, 99, 115, 174; *toga praetexta* 33, 64, 171; *toga purpurea* 33, 171; *see also* insignia
trabea 3, 13, 93–8, 98–101, 173–4; Ausonius' *trabea* 14, 57, 89, 93–4, 98, 100, 107–17; as consular costume 14, 38, 57, 89, 93–8, 118; decoration of 97–8, 100–1, 101–4, 104–7, 118, 129; on diptychs 94, 97–8, 100, 101–4; in poetry 104–7; *see also* Ausonius; decorative clothing elements; diptychs; Gratian; imperial portraiture
tragedy *see* clothing, in tragedy
tribute 59, 62, 74–5; *see also* bribery; silk
tunic (*tunica*) 1, 9, 11, 12, 27, 35, 77, 90, 91, 97, 116, 133, 140, 151, 156; *tunica palmata* 33, 93, 97, 99, 171; *tunica purpurea* 33, 64; *see also* insignia

Tzath, ruler of the Lazi 1–3, 14, 18, 57, 72, 75, 76–9, 89, 92, 172, 175; discussion of clothing gift from Justin I 1–3, 76–9; shoes 79, 172; *see also chlamys*; imperial portraiture; investiture; Persia

usurpers *see* Procopius, usurper

Valentinian I 108, 111, 112, 113–14, 115; *see also* Gratian
Valentinian II 113, 173; *see also* Gratian
Vandals 69
vestiarium 98–101; *see also* largess; *ministri largitionum*
Virgil 106

wealth 5, 6, 11–13, 26, 28, 36, 38–9, 42–6, 61–3, 65–7, 71–5, 91, 131–4, 137, 150, 157, 170, 173, 175, 177; *see also* luxury; resources
weaving 11–12, 90, 100, 106–7, 110; as a literary metaphor 8, 26–7, 35, 44, 55, 57–8, 106–7

Xenophon 27